*The Dangers of Poetry*

# THE DANGERS OF POETRY

*Culture, Politics, and Revolution in Iraq*

KEVIN M. JONES

STANFORD UNIVERSITY PRESS
Stanford, California

Stanford University Press
Stanford, California

© 2020 by the Board of Trustees of the Leland Stanford
Junior University. All rights reserved.

No part of this book may be reproduced or transmitted in any form or by any means, electronic or mechanical, including photocopying and recording, or in any information storage or retrieval system without the prior written permission of Stanford University Press.

Printed in the United States of America on acid-free, archival-quality paper

Library of Congress Cataloging-in-Publication Data

Names: Jones, Kevin M. (Kevin Michael), 1983– author.
Title: The dangers of poetry : culture, politics, and revolution in Iraq / Kevin M. Jones.
Description: Stanford, California : Stanford University Press, 2020. | Includes bibliographical references and index.
Identifiers: LCCN 2020008440 (print) | LCCN 2020008441 (ebook) | ISBN 9781503613393 (cloth) | ISBN 9781503613874 (ebook)
Subjects: LCSH: Political poetry, Arabic—Iraq—History and criticism. | Arabic poetry—20th century—History and criticism. | Anti-imperialist movements—Iraq—History. | Nationalism—Iraq—History. | Iraq—Politics and government—20th century.
Classification: LCC PJ8040 .J66 2020 (print) | LCC PJ8040 (ebook) | DDC 892.7/16099567—dc23
LC record available at https://lccn.loc.gov/2020008440
LC ebook record available at https://lccn.loc.gov/2020008441

Cover design: Rob Ehle
Cover image: Jawad Salim, cover illustration to Buland al-Haydari, *Ji'tum ma' al-Fajr* (Baghdad: Matba'at al-Rabita, 1960). Background paper, iStock.

*For Kate and Zoey*

# CONTENTS

|   | | |
|---|---|---|
| | *Acknowledgments* | ix |
| | *Note on Transliteration and Translation* | xi |
| | Introduction: "The Spirit of the Rebel Poet" | 1 |
| 1 | Neoclassical Modernity: Poetry, History, and Authenticity, 1876–1914 | 21 |
| 2 | Rebel Poetry: Colonialism and the Poetry of Rebellion, 1914–1920 | 48 |
| 3 | Double-Edged Praise: Patronage, Power, and Panegyric, 1920–1932 | 75 |
| 4 | Patriots and Traitors: The Cultural Politics of Nationalism, 1932–1945 | 103 |
| 5 | Poetry of Public Spaces: Mass Politics and New Horizons, 1946–1958 | 130 |
| 6 | Cultural Hegemony: The Politics of Class, Gender, and Nation, 1958–1963 | 159 |
| | Conclusion: "We Are What Flows through Every Soul and Spirit" | 185 |
| | *Notes* | *199* |
| | *Bibliography* | *265* |
| | *Index* | *293* |

# ACKNOWLEDGMENTS

This book was made possible by institutional and financial support from the American Historical Association, the Eisenberg Institute for Historical Studies and Horace H. Rackham School of Graduate Studies at the University of Michigan, the George Washington University Institute for Middle East Studies, and the History Department and Willson Center for Humanities and Arts at the University of Georgia. I am particularly thankful to librarians and staff at these institutions for their endless support.

I am immensely grateful to Kate Wahl for believing in this project and overseeing the production of this book at Stanford University Press. I am also thankful for the thoughtful and professional advice provided by Tim Roberts and Bev Miller throughout the editorial process. The four anonymous readers of the manuscript offered detailed comments, thoughtful suggestions, and congenial encouragement, and this book is stronger because of their reflections and criticism.

I have benefited from the advice and criticism of numerous historians and scholars of the Middle East over the course of the past decade and a half. I owe a particular debt of gratitude to Juan Cole, Geoff Eley, Farina Mir, and Andrew Shryock, who helped me develop as a historian and scholar. I am also grateful to Pouya Alimagham, Qussay Al-Attabi, Ali Badr, Orit Bashkin, Elliott Colla, Emily Drumstra, Noah Gardiner, Dina Rizk Khoury,

Mark LeVine, Nancy Linthicum, Amir Moosavi, Suneela Mubayi, Pelle Olsen, Sara Pursley, Eric Schewe, Levi Thompson, and Josh White for comments, engagement, and encouragement over the years.

I am grateful to colleagues and students for their advice and inspiration over the years. Both faculty colleagues and graduate students at the George Washington University Institute for Middle East Studies provided particularly helpful comments on early drafts of several chapters. The Department of History at the University of Georgia has been immensely supportive of my work over the past six years, and I thank my faculty colleagues, graduate students, and undergraduate students for creating an environment conducive to good research and teaching practices and experiences.

Finally, I express my appreciation to the extended networks of friends and family who have encouraged and supported me in various ways as I worked on this project. I could never have made it through the intellectual and emotional journeys of the past two decades without the constant love, support, and encouragement of my mother, Mary Jones. The support of my siblings and their families has also been particularly meaningful me, and I thank Colin Jones, Kathy Jones, Owen Jones, Henry Jones, Kelly Goad, Jacob Goad, Jessica Woods, Charles Osborn, Christen Mucher, and Colleen Woods. Colleen, in particular, has been a sister, friend, colleague, collaborator, and mentor, and I cannot begin to calculate my debt to her. Jan Shanahan, Robert Woods, and Laura Walker have been immensely supportive of me and my family over many years. Britt Newman, Vince Messana, Brandon Bartholomew, Christopher Elder, Westin Galloway, Andrew Ice, Brian Smith, Sean Stevens, and Bradley Wharton have helped me to maintain my sanity during the process. Most important, I thank Kate Woods and Zoey Jones for their endless love and support, which has sustained me through good times and bad times. I dedicate this book to both of you, the loves of my life.

# NOTE ON TRANSLITERATION AND TRANSLATION

This book generally follows the transliteration guidelines of the *International Journal of Middle East Studies*, but diacritical and long vowel marks have been omitted. All translations in this book are my own unless otherwise indicated.

*The Dangers of Poetry*

INTRODUCTION

## "THE SPIRIT OF THE REBEL POET"

Muhammad Mahdi al-Jawahiri was thinking about the dangers of poetry when he went searching for a new suit on July 4, 1949. More than a decade earlier, he had boasted that his poems reflected "the spirit of the rebel poet against many of the customs of the society that surrounds him, who despairs of reforming them through patch and repair and instead calls for them to be created anew."[1] The fifty-year-old poet now explained to the tailor that he intended to put this "spirit of the rebel poet" into action that evening with a scathing poem of dissent. He had been invited to recite a panegyric for Hashim al-Witri, the dean of the College of Medicine in Baghdad, at a ceremony honoring Witri's acceptance of an honorary doctorate from the King's College School of Medicine in London. Jawahiri knew that most of the political and social elites of Baghdad would be there, and he wanted to look like he belonged among them. When the suit was ready, Jawahiri paid his bill and went home to bid farewell to his wife and children. He choked back tears as he handed his wife an envelope containing his life savings, a sum large enough to sustain the family for several years. He glanced with contempt at the ticket, gilded in gold as though it was a metaphor for state corruption, and left for the ceremony, wondering when he might see his family again.[2]

Jawahiri had good reason to fear arrest: he had already served one stint in prison for his dissident poems and avoided a second only through the intervention of the politician Sayyid Muhammad al-Sadr. He became one of the most daring voices of political dissent during the Wathba demonstrations of January 1948, when hundreds of thousands of Iraqis marched in the streets of Baghdad to protest the Portsmouth Treaty, widely seen as affirming British power and influence in the country and perpetuating the long-standing constraints on Iraqi independence. In the postcolonial era, Jawahiri's own brother was killed in the massacre on al-Ma'mun Bridge, inspiring the most memorable poetry performance in modern Iraqi history at the memorial ceremony, when Jawahiri climbed a ladder held upright by throngs of supporters in the middle of Rashid Street, held up a megaphone, and began to recite his emotional elegy, "My Brother Ja'far."[3] He had cited his own lingering grief over his brother's death when he declined the invitation to recite a poem for Hashim al-Witri several months earlier. The climate of repression only worsened as the government took advantage of the crisis in Palestine to manipulate new elections and arrest political dissidents. Jawahiri recalled how "terror reigned in the skies over the entire country and especially Baghdad, pervading streets, cafes, and even houses and whispered words" after the execution of communist leaders in February 1949.[4] He now intended to resist this culture of fear by showing up unannounced at the ceremony and reciting poetry that might once again inspire revolutionary action.

While guests chatted idly with one another, Jawahiri surreptitiously made his way to the platform, grabbed the microphone, and began reciting. He addressed his public absence over the preceding months in verses that inspired anxiety among politicians and anticipation among students: "I was informed that you have been inquiring / asking about my presence here and there / Wondering how such a dazzling star could / stay away from gilded gatherings of notables / But realization has come and overwhelmed you / like morning removes the dusk from your eyes / For I only ceased my sermons when I could not find / one who deserved to hear the echo of my complaint." Jawahiri denounced both the "rotten Thamesians" who dominated the state and their local collaborators "[who] liberally bestow our wealth on white men / while we brown men remain confined to the stables." In the most memorable line of the poem, he invoked classical *fakhr* (self-glorification) to articulate his revolutionary political message:

> They boast that a towering tyrannical wave
> has blocked the path to every outlet and escape
> But they lie, for my verses fill the mouth of time
> endlessly traversing from the east to the west
> Tearing them from their youth and dropping them
> to their fate, destroying their grand palace of lies
> For I am their death, bringing their houses upon them,
> inciting even doormen and babies to curse their name![5]

When he finished reciting the poem, Jawahiri flamboyantly tore his notes into shreds and walked away as they fluttered to the ground behind him.

Jawahiri returned home after this spectacular act of public dissidence, stunned that police had not impeded his exit, and waited to be arrested. Three days later, police arrived and demanded to see the text of the poem, but Jawahiri mischievously told them he had destroyed his only copy and could not recall the verses. Reluctant to pursue a legal case against the poet without evidence, the police grudgingly left. Unfortunately for Jawahiri, the Lebanese journalists Karim and Husayn Muruwwa had gathered the shredded notes and published the reconstructed poem in a Lebanese newspaper, and Jawahiri was arrested and imprisoned for one month.[6] His public stature saved him from the torture and mistreatment meted out to fellow communist poets like Muhammad Salih Bahr al-'Ulum in the aftermath of the Wathba. Jawahiri recalled the embarrassed guards apologizing for having to confine him, allowing him to choose his own cell, and asking him to recite some of his most popular poems.[7]

Jawahiri's willingness to suffer for the sake of poetry was characteristic of his enduring belief that "while [others] were poets of words, he was the poet of action."[8] He was convinced that the poet's platform should be a stage of revolutionary struggle and embraced the "poetry of public spaces," where new ideas about modernity, nationalism, and socialism were articulated and contested.[9] This vision was shared by poets like Bahr al-'Ulum, who articulated his own faith in rebel poetry in his defiant prison declaration: "I was a revolution from the moment of my birth / my revolution is the fire that burn the cities of tyrants!"[10] For more than three decades, Jawahiri and Bahr al-'Ulum led the struggle for national liberation in Iraq and defined the vision of anticolonial modernity that animated revolutionary politics in the country. From the platforms of public spaces and the shoulders of cheering crowds, they forged a new cultural politics of dissent that challenged the postcolonial state's claim to political hegemony.

This book narrates the history of rebel poetry in Iraq in the early twentieth century, but it does not confine poetry to the rarified landscape of intellectual and literary history. It emphasizes instead the social relevance of rebel poetry by showing how poetry was composed, recited, disseminated, criticized, and punished. The book engages a number of historical questions and concerns that have engaged cultural historians of Iraq and the Middle East in recent decades: How did Arabs reconcile tradition and modernity, and how did colonialism transform popular conceptions of modernity? How did states mobilize artists and intellectuals, and what forms of dissent were used to contest hegemonic narratives of state power and legitimacy? How did the cultural politics of anticolonialism facilitate new radical alliances and the rise of national front politics that linked communists, socialists, and bourgeois nationalists in the struggle against colonialism and imperialism, and why did these solidarities later collapse?[11] This book answers these questions by documenting the role of poets as national spokesmen in the long struggle for national liberation and locating their ideas and actions in the global currents of anticolonial modernity.

## The Cultural Politics of Anticolonialism

Rebel poetry was both the dominant cultural discourse and dangerous social practice of the long anticolonial struggle in Iraq. This pervasive struggle was defined less by resistance to colonial armies than by sustained opposition to political, social, and cultural structures of domination attributed to colonialism. The struggle against colonialism was not limited to the relatively brief period of colonial occupation but was instead shaped by the global currents that addressed anticolonial politics in the twentieth century. Even before the first British troops descended on Iraq in 1914, local poets struggled to reconcile their desires for cultural preservation and social regeneration in the language of anticolonial modernity. The anti-Western and pan-Islamic spirit that swept across Ottoman and Asian politics around the turn of the century shaped their response to imperial, intellectual, and cultural encroachments and allowed them to define modernity on their own terms.¹² While poets contested prevailing conceptions of modernity in more combative ways during the British occupation, they refused to accept that formal political independence marked the end of the anticolonial struggle. For poets and their publics, the "pastness of colonialism" remained a critical site of cultural contestation as long as the old structures of colonial power ensured the domination of particular individuals and communities over others.¹³ Collective memories of anticolonial "futures past" shaped their rejection of the new order and desire to return to the receding horizon of national liberation.¹⁴

Poets occupied a liminal position between scholars, public intellectuals, and political activists in the cultural landscape of modern Iraq. Eric Davis and Orit Bashkin have noted the important public role of poets in their studies of cultural and ideology in modern Iraq, and Maha Nassar makes similar observations about the Palestinian citizens of Israel.¹⁵ These histories show how poets could serve simultaneously as "traditional intellectuals" and "organic intellectuals," in Gramscian typology, representing and interacting with political elites while voicing the interests and concerns of popular classes.¹⁶ In the view of many cultural and intellectual historians, the emergence of the modern Iraqi intelligentsia represented the eclipse of the religious scholars (ʿulama) as representatives of the people in the age of secular nationalism.¹⁷ Poetry, however, remained a passion of both the traditional ʿulama and secular intellectuals, and modern poets were capable of linking the concerns of both classes in both substance and style, performing the role of "organic intellectuals" in didactic appeals to the masses and reproving lectures to political elites. As Yasmeen Hanoosh has argued, however, the constant tension and oscillation between hegemonic and counterhegemonic ideologies fueled an all-encompassing "rhetoric of contempt" that pit "state literature" against "street literature" in the contentious arena of Iraqi cultural politics.¹⁸

The intellectual genealogy of anticolonialism in Iraq begins in the late Ottoman period, in the first decade of the twentieth century, when the constitutional revolution fueled new engagement with Western ideas. The relaxation of press censorship drew a new generation of poets toward the modernist vision of cultural regeneration promoted in the seminal Egyptian and Syrian periodicals of the Arab *Nahda* (*al-nahda al-ʿarabiyya*), the intellectual, literary, and cultural renaissance of the late nineteenth and early twentieth centuries. They yearned to participate in these intellectual debates and experience these modernist landscapes, but their cosmopolitan desires were tempered by pride in their own cultural heritage and desire to preserve local and national traditions. New links between the poetry scenes of Najaf and Baghdad and new engagements between Iraqi poets and their Egyptian counterparts helped to construct a nascent national consciousness that eclipsed traditional religious and sectarian identities.[19] Neoclassical poetry enabled the reconciliation of these ambivalent impulses by allowing modern ideas to be articulated in classical style. The neoclassical concern for cultural authenticity made poets particularly cognizant of the political utility of anticolonialism, and their participation in the Ottoman jihad of World War I and the urban protests and tribal uprisings of 1920 became a symbol of nationalist legitimacy. New fault lines opened in the political debates on reform during the British Mandate, blurring the boundaries between political patronage and colonial collaboration and secularism and Westernization. The isolation of state poets stood in stark contrast to the popular resonance of nationalist poets, who proudly declared their resistance to colonialism as evidence of their cultural authenticity.

The cultural politics of anticolonialism were transformed by the formal transition from colonial rule to national independence. Poets celebrated the end of colonialism at independence banquets across the country, but their optimism for the future soon gave way to disillusionment. Britain carefully negotiated the transition to independence to protect imperial privileges, transferring power to an incumbent political class committed to protecting the Anglo-Iraqi alliance and preserving their own power and wealth.[20] For the next two and half decades, Iraqi politics was characterized by musical chairs political gamesmanship, as power rotated between the "old gang" of pro-British politicians.[21] Independence complicated popular understandings of colonial structures of power, revealing the manifold ways in which the political and social elite of the postcolonial state were invested in upholding unpopular regional alliances and exploitative class privileges. Anticolonial discourse became less superficial and provincial and more radical and global as vertical allegiances of national belonging were fused with new horizontal solidarities of class.[22]

Poets made critical contributions to the evolving politics of anticolonialism as both nationalist scribes and revolutionary activists. Early forms of resistance to British rule have often been attributed to tribal, sectarian, and provincial motives, evidence that Iraq possessed neither the requisite national unity nor the modern mentality necessary to sustain a viable national liberation struggle.[23] The popular poetry of these early struggles, however, shows the importance of the universal ideals of anticolonial modernity.[24] In the postcolonial period, poets became leading proponents of a succession of radical causes that gave a distinctly socialist character to the anticolonial struggle.[25] Leftist poets enthusiastically backed Bakr Sidqi's military coup d'état of October 1936 because they believed it would displace the old colonial elite and introduce radical social reforms. Five years later, nationalist poets supported the Rashid ʿAli movement because they saw authoritarian military rule as the only way to mobilize Arab resistance to colonial rule across the Middle East.[26] The failure of the two military coups chastened the poets who supported them and helped facilitate the reconciliation of leftists and nationalists in the new cultural politics of the anticolonial national front. These poets played key roles in promoting new visions of popular democracy and social justice in the radical political struggles of the late 1940s and 1950s, lending their verses, voices, and bodies to the popular demonstrations that constructed new horizons of anticolonial modernity.[27]

The social visions and cultural agendas articulated in protests were critical to the construction of postcolonial nationalism in Iraq. Sami Zubaida, Eric Davis, Peter Wien, Orit Bashkin, and other scholars have documented the contentious political struggle between proponents of competing conceptions of national community in Iraq, the ethnic nationalism (*qawmiyya*) of the pan-Arabists and the territorial nationalism (*wataniyya*) of the Iraqists.[28] As "organic intellectuals" of the anticolonial struggle, poets articulated and defended these divergent nationalist visions, and their poems became markers of political legitimacy and cultural authenticity.[29] Beyond the narrow framework of ideological debates, however, the question of national borders was less relevant than the cultural politics of class and gender to the poetry wars of the anticolonial struggle. The struggle between watani and qawmi nationalists for cultural hegemony made poetry the popular register of anticolonial nationalism, transforming abstract intellectual debates about the nation into bitter conflicts over social interests and cultural values.[30]

The resonance of poetry in the cultural politics of anticolonialism was unique in time and space, a product of the singular historical moment of the poetry of public spaces. The importance of poetry to the anticolonial struggle was shaped in part by language and the failures of colonial surveillance. Anticolonial poems regularly appeared on the front pages of newspapers and became the main appeal for many readers, who amplified the circulation of poems by reading them aloud in public cafés.[31] Gertrude Bell was the most proficient British Arabist in Iraq, but she confessed that she could not understand Arabic poetry, and the press summaries that she wrote for the colonial state reflected her superficial comprehension of anticolonial poems.[32] The colonial tendency to underestimate the dangers of poetry was not shared by the postcolonial state, but poets adapted their subversive intentions to new political contexts. Censorship and repression only encouraged rebel poets to transform their recitations of dissident poems into provocative acts of public protest.[33] The cadence and rhyme of neoclassical poetry carried mnemonic benefits that facilitated oral transmission, and the indelible links between poems and events enabled them to transcend the literary and intellectual restrictions of written texts. These singular dimensions of the poetry tradition in modern Iraq allowed poets to performatively enact their own visions of history and politics in a manner that blurred the boundaries between conventional categories of political activists and public intellectuals.

## Poetry, Politics, and History

This book challenges conventional distinctions between high culture and mass culture that consign poetry to literary and intellectual history. Cultural histories of preliterate societies and folk culture have long recognized the social relevance of poetry.[34] The insularity and subjectivity of modern lyric poetry, however, convinced many social historians that poetry was disconnected from collective experience.[35] Cultural historians and feminist scholars have challenged this tendency to dismiss poetry as apolitical, individualist, and reactionary, but neither the cultural turn nor the aesthetic turn has fully rehabilitated poets as historical agents.[36] My analysis challenges these views by affirming the relevance of poetry to popular culture. In his recent study of popular culture and language in modern Egypt, Ziad Fahmy rejected definitions of "popular culture" based on the nonelite character of artists and audiences in favor of a more expansive vision of cultural production targeting mass audiences.[37] Like other cultural historians of modern Egypt, Fahmy's conception of popular culture is primarily concerned with the boundaries between the cultural domains of different social classes.[38] Iraqi colloquial culture was always more marginal and more neglected than its Egyptian counterpart, but the robust participation of nonelite classes in the world of neoclassical party was a social phenomenon that has been noted only in passing.[39]

Historians of modern Iraq have largely treated poetry as a cultural expression of new political, social, and intellectual currents of thought. Following the example of Iraqi scholars like ʿAli al-Wardi, they use poetry to reveal attitudes and symbols that more conventional historical research might miss.[40] Popular poems are generally taken as representations of critical debates in the national press and public sphere, expressed in particularly pithy fashion.[41] Other scholars have explored the fraught cultural politics of poetry criticism as a way of deconstructing nationalist narratives and untangling the relationship of culture, history, and the state.[42] While these studies have acknowledged the relevance of poetry to political debates and the utility of poetry as a historical source, most treat individual poems as cultural ephemera and print culture rather than dynamic examples of social protest and oral culture.[43] The conception of poems as texts and ideas rather than events and actions has tended to reify artificial distinctions between elite and popular culture and intellectual and social history. This book echoes Ziad Fahmy's recuperation of popular culture in the production of Egyptian national identity, but it does so by emphasizing the popular resonance of elite culture rather than documenting elite participation in popular culture.

Historians and other critics interested in the relationship between poetry and politics beyond the Middle East have shown similar interest in the contributions of poets to intellectual history. Recent scholarship on poetry and revolutionary politics in France, Britain, and the United States has illustrated the role of amateur poetry in expanding the boundaries of the bourgeois public sphere.[44] Modernist poets created, constructed, and contested new cultural politics of nationalism, fascism, socialism, and communism in Europe, belying conceptions of poetic insularity and subjectivity with their defense of "proletarian art" and "collective civilization."[45] Even when poetry appeared individualistic or reactionary in the anti-Stalinist politics of Central Europe and the Soviet Union, the contributions of poets like Anna Akhmatova, Boris Pasternak, Osip Mandelstam, Marina Tsvetayeva, Aleksander Wat, and Czesław Miłosz, to these dangerous cultural politics reflected an enduring faith in the power of verse to move human history.[46] The new international brotherhood of communist poets contributed to the globalization of radical ideas that animated the anticolonial struggle for national liberation in Asia, Africa, and Latin America in the middle of the twentieth century.[47] Most assertions of the historical agency of poetry have used state persecution of radical poets as prima facie evidence of the "dangers of poetry." The shared fate of leftist poets like Federico García Lorca, Hans Beimler, Julian Bell, John Cornford, Christopher Caudwell, Calro Levi, Erich Mühsam, and Cesare Pavese in the struggle against fascism was a testament to the power of verse.[48] Beyond Europe, the exile and imprisonment of communist poets like Nazim Hikmet, Orhan Kemal, Pablo Neruda, René Depestre, Faiz Ahmad Faiz, Habib Jalib, and Roque Dalton attested to the transnational commitments of this international communist poetics of dissent.[49]

Arabs have long regarded poetry as their "greatest and most congenial mode of literary expression."[50] The relationship between poetry and history was clear enough for one Jordanian tribal sheikh to declare to an anthropologist that members of a rival tribe "have no history" *because* "they composed no poetry."[51] Shawkat M. Toorawa asserts that almost any Arab from Bahrain to Casablanca would "almost certainly be able to cite or recite some poetry," an indication of the popular resonance of Arabic poetry.[52] Arab poets assumed the role of national spokesmen in the struggle against colonialism, fusing classical aesthetics and modernist ideas to subvert colonial surveillance and popularize new strategies of resistance for mass audiences.[53] Neoclassical genres like the *qasida* (ode) and *marthiyya* (elegy) were conducive to public performance and featured prominently in the emerging print culture of the Arab world, and neoclassical poets articulated new visions of collective national identity and bourgeois class consciousness.[54] While colloquial poets contributed to new formations of subaltern class consciousness among workers and provided the popular slogans that animated political demonstrations in Egypt, these roles were monopolized by neoclassical poetry in the first half of the twentieth century in Iraq.[55] The ideas expressed in their poems enrich our understanding of Iraqi intellectual history, and their confrontations with the state contribute to the global study of the "dangers of poetry" and the radical solidarities forged between poets across both the Arab region and the decolonizing world. It was the contribution of poets to public protests and political scandals, however, that did more than anything else to define the social role of poetry in modern Iraqi history.

## Texts, Acts, and Reception

Most contemporary historians are cognizant of the need to read texts as cultural artifacts of their own peculiar social and political context.[56] Attention to the material conditions in which art is produced compels us to understand the historical context of the author's world. These demands clearly position historians on the materialist side of major debates in literary criticism on the utility of the sociological approach and the social value of "art for art's sake."[57] These debates were familiar to Arab and Iraqi poets of the mid-twentieth century, who accepted the materialist vision of poets as both subject and agent of class interests and ideological agendas in their embrace of literary "commitment."[58] 'Ali al-Hilli reflected the prevailing philosophy of both communists and nationalists when he invoked Sainte-Beuve's sociological approach to literary criticism in defense of committed poetry in October 1959.[59] When Badr Shakir al-Sayyab articulated his own contrarian defense of art for art's sake two years later, he was renouncing the entire corpus of committed literature produced by his friends, rivals, and enemies over the previous decades.[60] Notwithstanding this critique of commitment, which would radically transform both poetry criticism and poetry composition in Iraq and the wider Arab world in subsequent decades, the aesthetics of Iraqi poetry were inextricable from their social context. As Sami Zubaida's ruminations on the "poetry of public spaces" make clear, critical attention to the material conditions of poetry applies not only to biography and social context but also to the spatial landscapes in which poetry was recited.[61]

The universe of political poetry during this period of Iraqi history is simply too expansive for a truly comprehensive treatment, so I have had to make calculated decisions about which poets and poems to include in my analysis. To illustrate the "dangers of poetry" in the cultural politics of anticolonialism and nationalism in Iraq, I have chosen to emphasize the poets whose voices resonated loudest in the political debates, public scandals, and intellectual controversies of the period. In most cases, the strength of this resonance was determined by the poet's location in the nascent public sphere—his links to political patrons, representation in the local press, affiliations with opposition parties, and presence in private salons and public cafés. In other cases, however, the voices of poets with more marginal public personas resonated due to the very marginality and subversiveness of their political positions and poetic innovations. Historical judgments of significance, of course, benefit from the ability to see beyond isolated moments of time and to assess the influence of particular ideas and actions on the unfolding logic of history. This is particularly true of the free verse movement of the late 1940s and early 1950s, when the aesthetic experiments of a modernist avant-garde began making ripples through the Iraqi poetry scene that would later overwhelm the entire neoclassical tradition. One of the central arguments of this book is that despite the tremendous aesthetic virtues of free verse poetry, this movement ultimately spelled the end of the poetry of public spaces by reifying an artificial distinction between high culture and mass culture and transforming poetry from a public medium of social communication to an intellectual discourse of cultural representation.

While the geographic scope of this study is largely defined by the national borders of the colonial and postcolonial Iraqi state, I have neither limited myself to analyzing Iraqi poets nor attempted a balanced analysis of a coherent corpus of "Iraqi poetry." Both the engagements of Iraqi poets with their counterparts in Egypt and Syria and the engagements of Egyptian and Syrian poets with Iraqi poetry and politics have proven relevant to my argument in different places. I have made no attempt to engage with the poetry traditions of Iraqi Kurdistan both because I do not read Kurdish and because the Arab poets of Iraq made little attempt to engage either the poetry or the politics of their Kurdish counterparts. Even among the Arab poets of Iraq, I focus far more extensively on the poetry scenes of Najaf and Baghdad than that of Mosul for three interrelated reasons. The first is that the traditional system of education and linguistic training of important Shiʿi centers of learning in Najaf and Baghdad made those locales more vibrant centers of poetry and ensured that Najafi and Baghdadi poets would be overrepresented in the public sphere.[62] Second, the particular social and intellectual conditions of Najaf inspired a number of young poets to gravitate toward the nationalist, socialist, and communist politics of Baghdad and thus helped to solidify the pointed political subversiveness of the Najafi-Baghdadi poetry axis.[63] The third and final reason for this disproportionate emphasis on the Najafi and Baghdadi poetry scenes is that these cities emerged as the crucible of sectarian politics in the country. While I have taken care not to allow these concerns to overdetermine my analysis of Iraqi history, there is no question that the contentious politics of sectarianism infused much of the poetry of this period and gave rise to several public poetry scandals. One important theme of this book is the relationship between secularism and sectarianism in the cultural politics of nationalism and communism, and I argue throughout the book that poetry was instrumental in the gradual eclipse of the latter by the former.[64]

The diffuse historical archive of poetry from this period is subject to the same restrictions and impediments that have impeded scholarly research on Iraq since the US invasion of the country in 2003.[65] Environmental catastrophe and human error, both ultimately attributable to the action and inaction of the Coalition Provisional Authority in the critical months of March and April 2003, destroyed or damaged rare newspapers, journals, and state documents that would have yielded invaluable evidence about this poetry of public spaces.[66] The India Office Library and British National Archives, however, offer a wealth of information about the role of poetry in World War I and the British Mandate and, to lesser extent, the postcolonial era. Some periodicals in which the poems analyzed in this study originally appeared survived in collections housed by different libraries across the world. Many of the most important and consequential poems subsequently appeared in poetry *diwans* (collections), which frequently included detailed historical context about when and where the poems were recited and how they were received. While improvised poems were sometimes edited and rearranged in these collections, the nature of poetic meter and rhyme made it nearly impossible to substantially transform the original poem and, in any case, significant revisions from the originals were generally noted and contested by Iraqi critics. Additional historical context about these poems can be found in published memoirs and critical studies, which are replete with unknown details about poets and poetry. Some of these published sources are extremely rare and largely untapped by historians, and though they fail to satisfy the archival fetishism of modern historians, they nevertheless contribute not only to our collective historical knowledge of Iraqi culture and society but also to the social history of ideas in the Middle East.[67]

My methodological approach to the popular culture of anticolonialism in this book is shaped by my attention to the historical context, popular reception, and political consequences of popular poems. Poems were social texts that produced cultural meaning and political ideology as much as they reflected the underlying cultural and political struggles of their social context. My reading is less influenced by literary theory and criticism than by the historicist approach of Robert Danton in his study of dissident French poetry. Danton interprets the recitation and dissemination of poems as social acts and explores archival records and published sources to interpret social meaning through historical inquiry, insisting that "the meaning of an act, like the act itself, can be recovered by detective work."[68] In the process of uncovering the meaning of dissident anticolonial poetry, I build on the received historical knowledge about modern Iraqi culture, society, and politics and contribute to ongoing historical debates about the nature of colonialism, modernity, and nationalism in modern Iraq.

A caveat regarding my approach to poetry, aesthetics, and the ethics of translation is warranted here. Translation is an inherently political act, shaped by the translator's intimate relationship to the text and awareness of culture difference and power dynamics, and the act of translating is always burdened by attendant ethical implications.[69] The act of translation is even more difficult for poetry, as the translator is forced to make difficult decisions about how to reconcile semantic accuracy and aesthetic value. Above all else, translators must convey how the poem would have been received and interpreted in its original social and literary context. Tahia Abdel Nasser argues persuasively that "ethically responsible literary translation communicates cultural difference and the conflictual cultural history in which the poem is embedded."[70] My approach to translation throughout this project has been informed by other cultural historians working with poetry and prioritizes the concerns of content over those of form. While both dimensions of translation are important, the task is more difficult in some cases than others. The aesthetics of neoclassical Arabic poetry, for example, are far more difficult to convey in English than those of free verse poetry. Not all of the poems analyzed in this study were beautiful in their original Arabic, but many of them were. I strive to convey the aesthetic value of particularly striking poems in my analysis whenever I feel as though this beauty has been lost in the process of translation.

## The Story of Iraqi Poetry

This book narrates the interplay between culture and politics in modern Iraq through the prism of rebel poetry. It builds on historical scholarship about the role of Arab artists and intellectuals in the construction of popular discourses of nationalism and anticolonialism and contributes a new case study on the evolution of cultural politics.[71] The book also builds on recent scholarship on the life and work of leading Arab poets and their contributions to new cultural discourses of modernity.[72] I view the evolving relationship between poetry and politics in Iraq through the historical lens of what Raymond Williams has called the "long revolution" of modernity.[73] The book documents the centrality of poetry to the emerging popular press and public sphere in colonial Iraq and highlights the desire of young Iraqi poets to "produce poetry that would be agent as well as an effect of cultural and political change."[74] The story of these poets is both tragic and inspiring, revealing the dangers of poetry in both the transformative impact of poets in Iraqi society and politics and their persecution at the hands of rivals and enemies.

The book documents the public careers of roughly three generations of poets who came from very different cultural backgrounds, embraced different forms of political identity, and wrote different types of poetry. These generations are linked by their general ethos of rebellion and belief in the social and political utility of poetry to construct new forms of collective consciousness among their national and regional audiences rather than any common ideological or literary agenda. While some of the poets examined in this book are considered canonical representations of a prestigious literary tradition, many others were far less distinguished, and some were even considered "bad poets." This book began with my research on the lives of the communist poets Muhammad Mahdi al-Jawahiri and Muhammad Salih Bahr al-'Ulum, and while I devote considerable attention in the book to their lives and those of their predecessors and heirs, I have not attempted to write biographies or prosopographies of literary and intellectual cohorts. My attention to the social evolution of poetry and cultural politics in modern Iraqi life has allowed me to locate and untangle the complex historical processes through which political identities, social commitments, and cultural ideologies were transformed.

Three overlapping themes on the contribution of poets to pivotal developments in Iraqi society over the *long durée* emerge over the course of the book. First is the contribution of poets to national identity and the contentious struggle over collective political solidarities in the colonial and postcolonial periods. My analysis of the relationship between poetry and the emerging consciousness of Arab and Iraqi national identity challenges both sectarian and ideological conceptions of Iraqi history. While the various articulations of collective national consciousness by Iraqi poets that evolved over the course of more than half a century illustrate the insufficiency of sectarian determinism, they also reveal that nationalist politics cannot be divorced from the social and cultural context in which it emerged. Second is the position of poets in the political hierarchies and social structures of the modern state. My argument that poets should not be considered merely as one particular subset of the modern intelligentsia is based on both the liminal position of poetry between traditional and modern forms of cultural expression and the cultural particularities of Iraqi society that allowed poetry to resonate across literate and illiterate audiences. Poets were simultaneously the custodians of cultural tradition and the public intellectuals of modern society, and their efforts to navigate the tensions between power and popularity reflected broader constellations of popular opinion and political alienation in colonial and postcolonial Iraq. Third is the commitment of poets to intellectual and aesthetic innovation and their conception of rebellion and revolution as both a political and cultural process. While the iconic neoclassical poets of the late Ottoman generation generally embraced innovation in content and rejected innovation in form, subsequent generations came to view the stylistic innovations of the free verse movement as an integral component of the all-encompassing ethos of commitment (*iltizam*). All of these poets, however, shared a common view of their social responsibility to educate and awaken their audiences to the particular concerns of modernity, anticolonialism, nationalism, and socialism that consumed them.

The book begins by analyzing the engagement of Iraqi poets with the concepts of modernity and nationalism in the Arab Nahda of the nineteenth and early twentieth centuries. While most historical accounts of the Arab cultural revival emphasize the intellectual and literary innovations of new prose genres as the expression of Arab modernity, neoclassical poetry imbued these engagements with modernity with an aura of cultural authenticity essential to their popular legitimacy. The relationships between neoclassical poets like Ibrahim al-Tabataba'i, Muhammad Saʿid al-Habbubi, and ʿAbd al-Muhsin al-Kazimi linked the previously disparate poetry scenes of Najaf and Baghdad in the late nineteenth century, and distinctive classical aesthetics of their poetry produced new conceptions of "Iraqi poetry" in the modern terminology of nationalism. The transnational links between Iraqi conceptions of modernity and nationalism were reinforced by poets' engagement with foreign periodicals like *al-Muqtataf*, *al-Hilal*, and *al-ʿIrfan*. As the young generation of poets who came of age during the Ottoman and Iranian constitutional revolutions struggled to reconcile their new cosmopolitan vision of modernity with their respect for their own historical and literary heritage, they contested the peripheral position allotted to Najaf and Baghdad in the cartography of Arab modernity. Their revisionist reconstruction of the historiography of the Nahda linked poetry to cultural revival in a way that emphasized the cultural authenticity of their vision of Arab modernity and presaged the anticolonial poetry of the coming decades.

The overwhelming concern for cultural authenticity among neoclassical poets in late Ottoman Iraq was reflected in their engagement with anticolonial politics during and after World War I. The untold story of colonial interventions in the nascent press to cultivate and subsidize the political loyalty of poets provoked a bitter cultural backlash among nationalist poets who denounced this poetry of collaboration and redoubled their commitment to poetic dissidence. Poets revolutionized modern conceptions of public protest and political dissent through their public recitations of inflammatory anticolonial poems during the Iraqi Revolution of 1920. While colonial anxiety about the dangers of poetry fueled new regulations of public space and the local press during the British Mandate, poetry rivalries fueled a new spirit of political gamesmanship between poets. Their struggle to win popular approval and cultivate reputations for courageous dissent created a new idealized prototype of the "rebel poet" who voiced the will of the nation in opposition to colonialism and exploitation. The dissident nature of anticolonial poetry did not reflect a nativist cultural reaction against the West, but instead challenged sectarian rivalries, gender hierarchies, and structures of social class in a new spirit of secular and universalist modernity.

The anticolonial spirit of poetry during the mandatory period did not disappear with the dawn of Iraqi independence in October 1932 but was instead displaced onto new partisan rivalries. Iraqi poets supported a number of revolutionary political causes in the 1930s, 1940s, and 1950s in the name of "finishing" the long project of national liberation. Their conviction that the transition to independence denied real sovereignty to the people and enshrined imperial interests and class privileges in the postcolonial state fundamentally transformed "anticolonialism" from a cultural discourse about the presence of foreign troops and politicians on Iraqi soil into a radical critique of the social structure of domination and exploitation imposed by the colonial state. While disagreements about the proper strategies of anticolonial resistance were reflected in the bitter tones of sectarianism and ideological conflict between poets in the late 1930s and early 1940s, the socialization of nationalist and leftist poets in the internment camps of World War II and the shared contribution of both camps to the public protests of the late 1940s and early 1950s contributed to the new spirit of national front politics. This period represented the apex of the poetry of public spaces in Iraq, when the politics of literary commitment and social context of mass politics facilitated the emergence of new horizontal solidarities between classes, sects, and genders in the streets, cinemas, and cafés of Baghdad. That this convergence of political and social forces occurred at the very moment that the new free verse poetry began to eclipse the popularity of the older neoclassical style among young poets and poetry aficionados was an irony of history that helps to explain the relative brevity of this seminal moment when poetry shaped mass politics.

The convergence of socialist and nationalist politics in the poetry of the national front era was abruptly arrested shortly after the revolution of July 14, 1958. Poetry became the contested landscape for the cultural confrontation between nationalists and communists in revolutionary Iraq. The cultural politics of the new "poetry wars" of the Qasim era (1958–1963) transformed the meaning of nationalism and anticolonialism in Iraq. While much attention has been paid to the ideological dimensions of the struggle over Arab unity, the popular poetry of this period was consumed by questions of gender, sexual morality, and violence. The popular culture of communist and anticommunist poetry reveals both the hidden social history of cultural concepts like national identity and the role of poetry and art in constructing and contesting the meaning of social and political acts. The poets who participated in the long anticolonial struggle suffered the horrors of prison and the pain of exile during the descent into political violence. Only the brutal repression of the Ba'thist era finally eliminated the possibility of poetic dissent and brought an end to the unique historical era in which the dangers of poetry transfixed the attention of the nation.

This book narrates the history of these encounters between poetry and politics in a way that links Iraqi cultural history to the global history of anticolonialism, radical politics, and revolutionary culture. While on one level it is a national history of several generations of poets in Iraq, it cannot escape the transnational links and cosmopolitan visions that proved so critical to the experience of modernity by disparate intellectuals, artists, and audiences across the globe.[75] The local, national, and international geographies of anticolonial modernity imagined, articulated, and contested by poets were the product of their efforts to come to terms with these global transformations and realignments. The story of these poets and the circulation of their poems across urban landscapes and national borders reorients the narratives of Iraqi intellectual and cultural history toward the social domain of politics, where the new cosmopolitan horizon of modernity met the sea of popular culture.

❴ CHAPTER 1 ❵

# NEOCLASSICAL MODERNITY
*Poetry, History, and Authenticity, 1876–1914*

In the twilight of his controversial life, Maʿruf al-Rusafi (1875–1945) reflected on his life of poetic dissidence in an interview with the leftist politician and journalist Kamil al-Chadirchi (1897–1968).[1] Rusafi spoke to his relationship with Jamil Sidqi al-Zahawi (1863–1936), with whom he was inextricably linked in the history of secularism and modernity in Iraq.[2] In the late nineteenth century, they shared poems with one another before publishing them in Egyptian newspapers and journals, but Rusafi now insisted that Zahawi's poetry was marred by linguistic errors and denied that it had influenced him in any way.[3] Zahawi had always been sensitive about criticism of his poetry, once ignoring Rusafi for months after a prominent Syrian critic described the latter as the superior poet and then informing the young poets who frequented his salons in Baghdad that Rusafi was "ignorant of the modern sciences."[4] Rusafi noted that both shared a similar religious education and became acquainted with secular modernity through the foreign journals that circulated in Baghdad.[5] "If [Zahawi] became acquainted with modern sciences from journals like *al-Muqtataf* and others," he asked rhetorically, "well I also read these journals, so what is the difference between him and me?"[6] The unspoken answer was that while there was little difference between the modernist content of their poems, Rusafi's superior command of classical form made him a more authentic Iraqi poet and more effective spokesman of the Iraqi cultural renaissance.

The contribution of Iraqi poets to the cultural renaissance of the late nineteenth and early twentieth centuries has passed largely unnoticed in the historiography of the Arab Nahda. The origins of this intellectual, literary, and cultural renaissance of the late nineteenth and early twentieth centuries have generally been located in Egypt and Syria, where Christian and Muslim reformers began to construct modern subjectivities rooted in the tropes of positivism, secularism, and humanism.[7] The new intelligentsia disseminated their ideas in scientific and literary periodicals that championed modern styles of prose and new literary genres adapted from Europe. As Stephen Sheehi argues, the experience of modernity facilitated the emergence of new national subjectivities in opposition to parochial degeneracy and sectarian fanaticism.[8] The promotion of national subjectivities had negative consequences as well, and many Iraqi poets resented the fact that the new Nahda discourse rendered them "backward" in terms of both geography and genre. Though the initial Iraqi response to Nahda periodicals like *al-Muqtataf* and *al-Hilal* was hostile and Iraqi contributions to the prose debates of the Nahda remained limited, Zahawi did publish articles in *al-Muqtataf* and *al-Muqattam*.[9] Young Najafi modernists contributed more substantively to the prose debates of the Lebanese journal *al-ʿIrfan*, established in 1909.[10] Poetry, however, remained the singular Iraqi contribution to the Nahda, the hallmark of Iraqi national culture and the critical medium for reconciling Arab modernity and cultural authenticity. Iraqi poets used the traditional form of the qasida to articulate their neoclassical vision of modernity, invoking the "glorious past to indict the present."[11] Poets like Rusafi and Zahawi could summon verses from classical ʿAbbasid poets to defend science, technology, and secularism.[12] The neoclassical qasida protected them from the traditional hostility to modern and avant-garde culture that confronted intellectuals elsewhere in the region.[13]

Marshall Berman wrote that the experience of modernity represented "a paradoxical unity, a unity of disunity: it pours us all into a maelstrom of perpetual disintegration and renewal, of struggle and contradiction, of ambiguity and anguish."[14] In the Middle East, this "unity of disunity" was perceived through the ruptures with "tradition," that impossibly vague analytical category that cuts across spatial, social, and cultural planes in ahistorical fashion. Tradition and modernity were "enacted performatively," not as objective signifiers of class, education, or urbanism but instead as subjective markers of social capital and cultural loyalty.[15] This struggle between tradition and modernity was marked by pervasive concerns for cultural authenticity throughout the late nineteenth and early twentieth centuries. Muhammad ʿAbduh and the generation of reformers whom he inspired, for example, conceived of Islamic modernism as a project of cultural renewal that avoided both traditionalist stagnation and modernist imitation.[16] While Islamic modernists defended the "authentic" content of Islam in the "modern" form of rational prose, Iraqi poets of the late Ottoman era inverted this dynamic by defending the "modern" content of secularism in the "authentic" form of classical poetry. Yet as Orit Bashkin notes in her analysis of Iraqi reformist discourse in the early twentieth century, "secularism was not an essential prerequisite to a discourse about constitutionalism and democracy."[17] Both secular and pan-Islamic poets contributed to the discourse of "neoclassical modernity" that looked simultaneously to the past and future, critically shaping new cultural epistemologies and national subjectivities in twentieth-century Iraq.

The publication of Iraqi poetry in Nahda periodicals reflected the importance of poetry to the commercial and philosophical mission of the press. Their appearance marked the evolving role of poetry in society and the gradual evolution from oral culture to print culture, but poetry continued to function as an important means of public communication.[18] The overlapping paths of development of oral culture and print capitalism amplified the public reach of poetry, which could be read aloud in cosmopolitan urban cafés and semipublic salons in Arab cities across the Ottoman Empire and British Egypt. The poetry of this period was consumed by the idea of modernity and reflected little interest in the contentious ideological and political partisanship of subsequent decades, but poetry still posed real dangers when poets tested the limits of free expression in the late Ottoman era. Poets did not yet see themselves as inciters of revolution, but they began to view themselves as spokesmen of revolutionary ideas that might herald the dawn of an elusive and contested modernity.

This narrative of poetry and modernity in Iraq begins at the intersection of cultural revivals in Egypt and Iraq, when Iraqi contributions to the Cairo press simultaneously shaped Egyptian and Iraqi perceptions of Iraqi cultural heritage and national subjectivity. At the same time, the reverberation of the Iranian and Ottoman constitutional revolutions produced new forms of engagement between poetry and politics.[19] The relaxation of press censorship fueled the emergence of local public spheres in which poets and intellectuals defended constitutionalism, secularism, and modernity.[20] In Najaf, a new generation of poets articulated their own relationship to modernity by reimagining the history of the Arab Nahda. Their simultaneous celebration of Najafi cultural heritage and the new Egyptian cosmopolitanism, however, produced new anxieties about the reconciliation of past and future. The young Najafi poet ʿAli al-Sharqi compared these anxieties to "the cage of the nightingale," as young poets overcome with "the longing of the preacher for his congregation" yearned to fulfill their destinies as national prophets but found their voices stifled by parochial tradition.[21] This quintessentially modern experience of the "maelstrom of perpetual disintegration and renewal" reflected the new social expectations of poetry in the twentieth century.[22]

## The Neoclassical *Qasida*

"Poetry is the *diwan* of the Arabs," their public register, historical archive, and literary canon, attests a traditional Arabic saying, and the qasida was the pinnacle of classical Arab poetry.[23] The classical qasida proceeded from a nostalgic prelude (*nasib*) to a descriptive desert journey (*rahil*), before culminating with a panegyric (*madih*).[24] It was based on an opening verse (*bayt*) divided into two hemistiches (*masraʿ*) of equal length, which appeared in print as a single line separated by a small gap. Poets could choose between sixteen traditional meters, but each verse of the qasida ended with the same vowel-consonant sequence.[25] In subsequent centuries, the rahil was abandoned and the nasib was elided with the panegyric, which emphasized one of several themes that became distinct subgenres of the qasida. In addition to the autonomous panegyric (madih), there were poems of self-glorification (*fakhr*), elegy (*rithaʾ*), love (*ghazal*), satire (*hijaʾ*), wisdom (*hikam*), and description (*wasf*). The qasida reached its cultural peak in the early ʿAbbasid era, before it was supplanted by new genres like the couplet (*mathnawi*), quatrain (*rubaʿi*), and the strophic *muwashsha* and *zajal*.[26] Whatever the virtues of these new genres, most modern critics agreed that none replaced the grandeur of the classical qasida.

The simultaneous fragmentation of poetry traditions and collapse of Arab political power defined the Age of Decadence (*'asr al-inhitat*). The corruption and stagnation of the Ottoman era, which has been called "the nadir of Arab culture," intensified perceptions of poetic decay and decline.[27] Postclassical poetry was characterized by an obsession with technical prowess, and by the late eighteenth century, it "had become artificial, imitative and sham."[28] Most poetry was not printed before the late nineteenth century, and Arab poets complained of their cultural isolation in the poems they recited to narrow audiences of poets and scholars.[29] Divorced from politics, disinterested in society, and detached from classical aesthetics, they succumbed to frivolous celebration of their own cleverness.

Though the origin of the Arab Nahda is generally traced to the emergence of new literary genres in the early nineteenth century, early historians of Arab nationalism like George Antonius emphasized the role of poets in amplifying this spirit of cultural regeneration and awakening dormant national consciousness. Antonius argued that Ibrahim al-Yaziji's anti-Ottoman appeal of 1868 "did much to foster the national movement in its infancy," noting that the rhythmic cadence, emotion, and "talent of Arabs for memorising poetry" made poetry ideal for fostering political conspiracies.[30] Early scholarship on the Nahda was guided by the assumption that cultural revival was inspired by Arab encounters with European modernity.[31] While these paradigms have been challenged by recent scholarship on Arab cultural vitality in the seventeenth and eighteenth centuries, the general narrative of poetic decline has been largely unchallenged.[32] Some critics even insist that because poetry was more impervious to innovation, the poetic renaissance did not begin until the final decades of the nineteenth century.[33]

The classical qasida never entirely disappeared, and the few poetry collections published in the early nineteenth century reflected the lingering influence of classical aesthetics.[34] The "neoclassical qasida," however, emphasized a conscious commitment to reconcile classical form and modern content. Critics described these poems as *al-qasida al-taqlidiyya* (traditional qasida), *al-qasida al-'amudiyya* (upright *qasida*), *al-shi'r al-hadith* (new poetry), or *al-shi'r al-'asri* (modern poetry).[35] Neoclassical poets rejected the frivolity of the Age of Decadence and instead emphasized the new political and social concerns of modernity. Concern for cultural authenticity made the classical *maqama* and neoclassical qasida particularly compelling genres for articulating new subjectivities of secularism and nationalism.[36]

The Egyptian poet and politician Mahmud Sami al-Barudi (1839–1904) was widely seen as the first genuine neoclassical poet due to his fusion of classical aesthetics with new idioms of anticolonialism, nationalism, and modernism.[37] Barudi inspired fellow Egyptians Ahmad Shawqi (1868–1932) and Hafiz Ibrahim (1871–1932) to publish poems in the seminal Nahda journals. Poetry was not initially seen as an appropriate genre for modern ideas, but editors eventually concluded that it could serve their cultural project by defending modernism in the language of cultural authenticity.[38] The poems of Shawqi and Ibrahim began appearing regularly in *al-Muqtataf* and *al-Hilal* in the late nineteenth and early twentieth centuries.[39] The dissemination of these periodicals in Iraq and the Levant inspired a new wave of neoclassical poets influenced by the radical worldviews of the Nahda press.[40] This chronology and cartography of cultural revival and political awakening emanating from Cairo at the turn of the twentieth century, however, overlooks the cultural vitality of nineteenth-century Iraq.

## Poetry and Society in Late Ottoman Iraq

The principal features of postclassical decline—affected aesthetics, political disengagement, and social marginalization—were less pronounced in Iraq.[41] In contrast to the vibrant colloquial culture in Egypt, the tradition of classical aesthetics in Iraq gave neoclassical poets a virtual cultural monopoly.[42] Poetry thrived in Baghdad and southern towns like Najaf and Hilla, where mosque courtyards provided space for public discussions of poetry and politics.[43] Religious elegies were more popular here than stilted panegyrics, and the diwan of Haydar al-Hilli (1831–1886) included nineteen elegies for Imam Husayn.[44] Shi'i poets were adept at fusing poetry and politics, particularly after the Wahhabi incursions into southern Iraq in the early nineteenth century, which prompted al-Hajj Hashim al-Ka'bi (d. 1817) to ask sarcastically, "Is it true there were no Caliphs after their Prophet / and no Imams who forbid the things that he forbid? / Were they all tyrants, deceivers, and heretics / except for Sa'ud, whose light restores sight to the blind?!"[45] This Wahhabi threat "produced a unique *Iraqi* religious debate" that persisted well into the early twentieth century.[46] Panegyrics continued to flourish in Baghdad, but poets like Salih al-Tamimi (1762–1845) rejected "artificial" flattery and conveyed their frustration with political oppression.⁴⁷ ʿAbd al-Ghaffar al-Akhras (1805–1875) used his panegyric for Daʾud Pasha to complain of the "terror and doom and convulsion" that gripped Ottoman Iraq.⁴⁸ This subversive praise reflected a novel political phenomenon, "the beginning of the poetry of protest in Arabic in modern times."⁴⁹ Panegyrics also reflected new ideas about patronage and the "relation between power and knowledge" as poets claimed the right to speak for the nation.⁵⁰

Iraqi poets emphasized their interest in local politics and society by dating their qasidas so that "the poet became the scribe of history," recording the visits of notable men, the rise and fall of rulers, and the introduction of new technologies in the nineteenth century.⁵¹ The rise of descriptive poetry about modern technology has generally been attributed to Barudi, but ʿAbd al-Baqi al-ʿUmari (1788–1861) wrote about the telegraph, and Ibrahim al-Tabatabaʾi (1832–1901) and Muhammad Hasan Kubba (1853–1918) wrote about the tram line built between Baghdad and Kazimiyya in 1870. In his description of rails plowed into the face of the earth so that a "fortress of steel" could glide along their contours, Tabatabaʾi framed his experience of modernity as the rupture of old conceptions of space and time: "Now the short distance behind is not so short / and the long distance before us is not so long!"⁵² Tabatabaʾi was a religious scholar, and while both Shiʿi mujtahids and Sunni ʿulama considered secular poetry less intellectually important than religious scholarship, the cultural prestige of poets defined social status beyond the confines of the seminary (*al-hawza al-ʿilmiyya*).⁵³

The social stakes of poetry were particularly pronounced in Najaf, where reputations were forged in poetry competitions. Muhammad Mahdi al-Jawahiri (1899–1997) recalled that "from the very beginning, poetry was a grave and dangerous game, for despite the fact that my home was always a house of poetry and literature, like so many houses and families in Najaf, and despite the status that a man of religion or a *faqih* enjoyed, his prestige in my eyes was measured by his prestige as a poet."⁵⁴ Jawahiri saw the reputation of his father, Sheikh ʿAbd al-Husayn al-Jawahiri (1864–1917), suffer when Sheikh Jawad al-Shabibi (1865–1944) mocked the appearance of his pockmarked skull during an infamous poetry battle: "You have a skull adorned and embellished / branches of skin planted on it with yarn / Like a garden filled with budding flowers / chrysanthemums and lilies and violets."⁵⁵ While these verses reflect the decadent frivolity rejected by neoclassical poets, accounts of the competitions emphasize their social significance.⁵⁶

Regardless of their rank in the *hawza* hierarchy, popular poets attracted disciples who cultivated and defended the reputations of their masters. Alongside Ibrahim al-Tabataba'i, Muhammad Sa'id al-Habbubi (1849–1916) emerged as the other leading Najafi poet of the late twentieth century. While most Najafis learned poetry from family members and religious teachers, Habbubi learned from the salons of Najaf and Baghdad before entering the hawza.⁵⁷ He discovered the enduring tension between poetry and *fiqh* (jurisprudence) when the scholar Kazim al-Khurasani (1839–1911) caustically dismissed his question on jurisprudence: "You are a man of poetry, so why concern yourself with these legal principles?"⁵⁸ Habbubi promptly retired from poetry and devoted himself to fiqh, illustrating the dilemma of the ambitious poet-faqih who yearned to advance in the hawza, but his many disciples continued to defend his poetry reputation.

Poetry also cataloged social relations through the correspondence between friends, which was not necessarily private and instead reflected the classical spirit of *fakhr* (self-glorification). Poets transformed quotidian events into transcendent memories, preserving moments of bliss in verses like written analogues of photographs. 'Abd al-Muhsin al-Kazimi (1870–1935), for example, thanked a Najafi friend for sending him a book in Kazimiyya: "Now the song and singing have become delicious / and the sweetness of intoxication and gratitude are a hymn!"⁵⁹ The boundary between affective and romantic attachments was not always entirely clear, and the vague homoeroticism of Habbubi's poetry later became more explicit in the poems of Mullah 'Abbud al-Karkhi (1861–1946) and Ma'ruf al-Rusafi (1875–1945).⁶⁰

The nineteenth century was transitional in the sense that poets expressed tentative commitments to the modern revival of classical aesthetics.⁶¹ In the early twentieth century, young Najafi poets celebrated Tabataba'i and Habbubi as pioneers of modern poetry, praising their restoration of "true poetry."⁶² While this praise exaggerated the gravity of the postclassical poetic decline, Tabataba'i and Habbubi actually had very little to say about decline and revival. The elevation of these poets as neoclassical pioneers was more closely tied to the new national and cultural rivalries of the early twentieth century. Iraqi "neoclassical modernity" was built on the fusion of classical form and modern content, and the insistence of young Najafis that Tabataba'i and Habbubi had a superior grasp of classical tradition reflected their desire to assert a distinctively Najafi claim to custodianship of the past.[63]

## Borders, Crossings, and Networks of Arabic Poetry

There was no such thing as "Iraqi poetry" before the final decades of the nineteenth century. While there were substantial intellectual and cultural links across southern Iraq, links between the poetry scenes of Najaf and Baghdad were limited, and they were virtually nonexistent between Najaf and Mosul. Poetry was rarely published, and there was little engagement between Iraqi poets and their Egyptian and Syrian counterparts.[64] Print capitalism helped to end this cultural isolation, facilitating the movement of poetry across borders and forging new cultural identities in the process.[65] The crystallization of the new concept of "Iraqi poetry" was particularly apparent in the life of 'Abd al-Muhsin al-Kazimi, born in Kazimiyya to a family that claimed descent from Imam Musa al-Kazim.[66] 'Abd al-Muhsin was introduced to poetry by his older brother and spent many youthful evenings at garden poetry salons along the banks of the Tigris. It was here that Kazimi first encountered Ibrahim al-Tabataba'i, who was impressed by the youth's talents and invited him to come with him to Najaf and study poetry.[67] At around the same time, the Kazimiyya poet Muhammad Hasan Kubba (1853–1918) was introducing his Najafi friend Muhammad Sa'id al-Habbubi to the Baghdadi poetry scene.[68] Habbubi's first poetry instructor was Kazimi's older brother, and the relationship between these poets gradually transformed Kazimiyya into a cultural nodal point between Najaf and Baghdad.[69]

Kazimi's life was dramatically affected by his relationship with Jamal al-Din al-Afghani (1838–1897), whose pan-Islamic approach to political and social reform inspired the Kazimi's critique of insular sectarianism.[70] Afghani settled briefly in Kazimiyya after his expulsion from Iran in 1891, and the twenty-one-year-old Kazimi grew so close to him that he aroused the suspicion of Ottoman authorities and was forced to flee into exile.[71] Kazimi migrated between Iran and India, where he struck up a lifelong friendship with the reformist mujtahid Sayyid Muhammad al-Mazandarani, before finally settling in Egypt in 1899.[72] Mazandarani introduced Kazimi to

Muhammad ʿAbduh, the Grand Mufti of Egypt, provided the young Iraqi poet with a modest monthly stipend. Kazimi began attending ʿAbduh's salon, where he met Mahmud Sami al-Barudi, who had just returned from his own exile, along with other popular poets and reformist intellectuals.⁷³ Ahmad Shawqi praised Kazimi's poetry in the Egyptian newspaper *al-Muʾayyad* in 1902, but he was infuriated three years later when Mustafa Sadiq al-Rafiʿi published an article describing Kazimi as "the best poet in Egypt" and relegating Shawqi to the third tier.⁷⁴ ʿAbbas Hilmi Pasha, the khedive of Egypt at that time, agreed to pay Kazimi's stipend after ʿAbduh's death, but Shawqi exploited the khedive's hatred of the late mufti, whispering that Kazimi was "the Imam's poet" and encouraging him to cancel the stipend.⁷⁵ These poetic rivalries indicate both the high regard for Kazimi's poetry in Egypt and the social dangers of poetry.

Given the neoclassical veneration of classical aesthetics, Kazimi's classical sensibilities made him a cultural sensation in Egypt.⁷⁶ He memorized more than twelve thousand lines of classical poetry and could compose hundreds of verses in a single session, which led the Egyptian critic ʿAbbas Mahmud al-ʿAqqad to call him "the poet of spontaneity and improvisation."⁷⁷ His contemporaries marveled at his "bedouin spirit," especially pronounced in his fakhr.⁷⁸ Kazimi wrote traditional religious poems, but he also praised the reformism of Muhammad ʿAbduh, the journalism of ʿAli Yusuf, the nationalism of Mustafa Kamil and Muhammad Farid, and the "modern" poetry of Shawqi, Ibrahim, Barudi, and Rafiʿi.⁷⁹ Most of his poems were composed for salons, but he did publish some in Egyptian newspapers, including an anticolonial poem about the Italo-Ottoman War.⁸⁰ His reputation was enhanced by his appearance in the traditional black *ʿabaʾa* (cloak) and white *ʿimama* (turban) of Najaf, a striking contrast to Egyptian *effendis* around him who wore suits and neckties, either bareheaded or wearing the *tarboush*.⁸¹ Classical sensibilities aside, Kazimi was no conservative, and his poems reflected progressive views about women's reform.⁸² One photograph in his diwan shows the elderly poet flanked by his daughters Karima and Rabab, clad in white dresses with open collars and hemmed at the knees, with bare legs and high heels, unveiled with hair curled fashionably across their foreheads.⁸³ Rabab al-Kazimi became a poet and feminist activist in her own right, publishing dozens of poems in the Egyptian press in the 1920s and 1930s.⁸⁴

## The Awakening of the Iraqi Modernists

'Abd al-Muhsin al-Kazimi remained in Cairo for the rest of his life, but he was nevertheless an integral figure of the Iraqi poetry revival. Young Iraqis were aware of the praise he received from Egyptian poets and longed to publish their own poems in Egypt.[85] Kazimi's presence also shaped Egyptian conceptions of Iraqi poetry, which appeared as an untouched resurrection of classical Arab heritage. The evolution of a regional discourse about national cultures was aided by regional disparities of print markets, as Iraqi writers generally preferred to publish in the "advanced" presses in Egypt and Syria.[86] As Iraqi participation in these markets intensified, Egyptian enthusiasm for the "pure" Iraqi poetry of Kazimi was echoed in the enthusiastic reception of Jamil Sidqi al-Zahawi and Ma'ruf al-Rusafi.

Zahawi's autobiographical account of his intellectual and cultural awakening affirms the centrality of border crossings and new metropolitan landscapes to the Arab "experience of modernity."[87] He was born in Baghdad, where his father served as mufti of Baghdad for nearly forty years, memorizing the Qur'an and studying *sarf* (grammar), *nahw* (syntax), *mantiq* (logic), and *balagha* (rhetoric) at a traditional *kuttab* (religious school).[88] His father was versed in Arabic, Persian, Turkish, and Kurdish poetry and introduced Zahawi to canonical 'Abbasid poetry.[89] His older brother, however, discouraged Zahawi's interest in poetry after he succeeded their father as mufti, and the disillusioned youth grew frustrated with the traditional lifestyle of the 'ulama.[90] Religious opposition to the appearance of the Nahda journal *al-Muqtataf* in Baghdad piqued Zahawi's interest, and he later recalled that when he first read the journal, "I awoke as if I had acquired the treasures of the world."[91] Zahawi had no formal secular education, but he now sought to transform himself into a modern intellectual. He worked as a teacher and journalist in Sulaymaniyya and Baghdad for more than a decade before moving to Istanbul in 1896, an experience that intensified his desire to experience all things modern.[92] While he knew no European languages, he immersed himself in Arabic and Turkish translations of Shakespeare, Goethe, Hugo, Dumas, Tolstoy, Darwin, Spencer, and Le Bon.[93] He became friends with Tevfik Fikret, a Turkish poet and editor of the avant-garde journal *Servet-i Fünun*, whose experiments with new meters and unrhymed verse inspired Zahawi's experiments in Arabic poetry.[94]

Zahawi's association with the Turkish avant-garde brought him under state surveillance and earned him a punitive assignment to Yemen.[95] He was eventually permitted to return to Istanbul, but he provoked another controversy after publicly reciting a poem critical of Sultan Abdülhamid II. The poem accused the sultan of inverting traditional Islamic justice and warned of the rising tide of popular anger that would soon envelop his empire: "Even if your hands have grown, do not be deluded / for they remain small before the looming hand of fate."[96] Zahawi was banished to Baghdad, where leading Wahhabi agitators accused him of harboring *zandaqa* (heretical) beliefs and demanded his execution. He responded to these charges in the anti-Wahhabi tract *al-Fajr al-Sadiq*, couched in effusive praise for Sultan Abdülhamid II, but the humiliated poet privately composed dozens of anti-Ottoman poems over the next three years.[97] These poems invoked the spirit of neoclassical modernity in the wistful historical nostalgia for the revival of ʿAbbasid Baghdad: "Baghdad days used to glimmer in her beauty / shimmer like the radiant stars of heaven / Will that fallen civilization return once more / or is that great civilization now gone forever?"[98] Other poems emphasized the suffering of Arabs living under Turkish rule, complaining that "as soon as [the Turks] fell upon a land, its condition grew grave / as if they were responsible for the plague that afflicted it."[99] While these poems have been described as "Arabist," Zahawi was driven by political grievance rather than nationalist ideology.

It was during this period that Zahawi met Maʿruf al-Rusafi, a fellow product of traditional *kuttab* education in Baghdad. Rusafi entered the Ottoman military academy but failed his examinations and was forced to return to religious study under Mahmud Shukri al-Alusi, a scholar who embodied the ambivalence of the modernist Salafiyya movement in his marriage of reformist principles and sectarian bigotry.[100] While Alusi taught him morphology, grammar, rhetoric, and prosody, Rusafi boasted that his only poetry teachers were classical poets like al-Mutanabbi (915–965) and Abu al-ʿAlaʾ al-Maʿarri (973–1057).[101] He began reading Egyptian journals like *al-Muʾayyad*, *al-Muqtabas*, and *al-Muqtataf*, where he encountered the poetry of ʿAbd al-Muhsin al-Kazim and was inspired to send his own distinctively Iraqi poems to the journals.[102] Rusafi took pride in the enthusiastic reception of his poetry in Cairo, recalling that Muhammad Kurd ʿAli published his poem "The Orphan on the Day of the Festival" on the front page of *al-Muqtabas* under the title "The Best Poetry." His memory failed in this case, as no version of that poem ever appeared in *al-Muqtabas*, but Kurd ʿAli did publish several dozen of his poems between 1906 and 1910, many of which appeared on the front page as "modern" counterparts to "enlightened" classical poets like Maʿarri.[103] Rusafi was always identified in the Egyptian press as a "Baghdadi poet," and many of his poems dealt with explicitly Iraqi themes.[104] While these journals experimented with new genres of literary fiction to narrate the "essential march of modernity," the persistent appearance of Iraqi qasidas on their pages reinforced the significance of cultural authenticity to the evolving conception of neoclassical modernity.[105]

Zahawi published poetry in the same journals, and though the two poets initially shared poems with one another, their rivalry was intensified by foreign debates about Iraqi poetry.[106] The Lebanese journalist Naʿum Labaki published an article in his São Paulo journal *al-Munazir* claiming that "Maʿruf al-Rusafi" was an assumed name, because no Baghdadi poet could criticize the Ottoman Empire as Rusafi did in *al-Muqtabas*. Muhammad Kurd ʿAli responded in *al-Muʾayyad* that both Rusafi and Zahawi were real poets living in Baghdad, but his perceived slight of Zahawi's talents infuriated the older poet and caused him to ignore Rusafi for months.[107] The rivalry intensified in subsequent years, as Zahawi responded to appraisals of Rusafi's superior aesthetic form by emphasizing the superiority of his own intellectual content.

## Constitutionalism and the Iraqi Public Sphere

The modernist current in Iraqi poetry flourished after the Iranian Constitutional Revolution of 1906 and Ottoman Constitutional Revolution of 1908.[108] The generation of poets who came of age during these revolutionary upheavals were swept away by enthusiasm for modernity.[109] Iranian debates reverberated in southern Iraq, where Iranian *mujtahids* (religious scholars) and their supporters inspired "a popular culture" of constitutional politics.[110] At the same time, the restoration of the Ottoman constitution by the Committee of Union and Progress allowed new periodicals and ideas to circulate through the Arab provinces, which "served not only to help 'imagine' the community in universally inclusive terms, but also increasingly in exclusionary and sectarian terms."[111] Iraqi poets from different backgrounds interpreted the revolution as the vindication of their own ideological agendas, with Shi'i poets like 'Abd al-Mutallib al-Hilli (1863–1921) emphasizing the opposition of the constitutionalist mujtahids to Ottoman sectarianism and secularist poets like Zahawi and Rusafi celebrating the arrival of the modernist spirit they had read about in *al-Muqtataf* and *al-Hilal*.[112]

Zahawi had spent the past several years composing brooding poems about tyranny and oppression and dreaming about justice, freedom, and liberty.[113] He argued that the West had eclipsed the East in terms of intellectual progress, but he now saw an opportunity to serve as spokesman of Eastern revival:

> Freedom was proclaimed to all mankind, and so
> the age of forced labor and the whip has passed
> Every last soul has been freed from his chains,
> this is the moment for which they have longed
> It has been said that my poetry writes the history
> of the liberation of people from chains and wants[114]

Rusafi had also grown frustrated with Ottoman rule and complained of social decay in Iraq, which he described as a land of "ignorance and poverty, where the gluttons and drinkers of life are masters."[115] Like many other Ottoman writers, he saw the Japanese triumph in the Russo-Japanese War of 1905 as evidence of an incipient Eastern awakening.[116] His enthusiasm for the Constitutional Revolution was apparent in a poem describing the euphoria in Baghdad: "We went out intoxicated with glory, shouting one / to the other with cries that slayed oppression and injustice / The shimmering freedom of life became visible to us after / our noble army drew back the curtain from her veiled face!"[117]

Zahawi returned to the liberal environment of Istanbul, where he took teaching posts in Islamic philosophy and Arabic literature at the Mekteb-i Mülkiye and Darülfünûn.[118] Rusafi followed after he was invited to edit an Arabic edition of the newspaper *Iqdam*, but funding collapsed and he moved to Salonika at the invitation of Iraqi politicians Hikmat and Khalid Sulayman in April 1909.[119] When he arrived in Salonika, counterrevolutionary forces seeking to restore the absolute authority of Sultan Abdülhamid II had seized power in Istanbul, and Rusafi was denounced as one of the reactionaries because he was still wearing the traditional ʿ*imama* (turban). Saved from the crowd by the intercession of the Sulayman brothers, Rusafi traveled with the Third Army from Salonika to Istanbul as an embedded poet to document the restoration of Committee for Union and Progress (CUP) control.[120] His poems reflected his new enthusiasm for constitutionalism: "This is the voice of equality addressing us as equals / renouncing the preference for some over all others."[121] Rusafi traded his ʿ*imama* for a *tarboush* (fez) to distinguish himself from the "extremists," later recalling his embrace of Western dress (*al-zayy al-afranji*) as a rupture with tradition pivotal to his experience of modernity.[122] As in other accounts of the Arab encounters with modernity, these new sartorial practices reflected the "new aesthetic" of space and society informing the modernist dichotomy between "the tropes of degeneracy and reform."[123]

Zahawi and Rusafi were soon drawn back to Iraq, where they enthusiastically promoted their moral and political agenda of modernism. Rusafi edited the Arabic section of the bilingual journal *Baghdad* and caused a public scandal when he and several friends stormed into the Wazir Mosque and delivered speeches in defense of secularism and liberalism.[124] His critics organized protests and secured a fatwa calling for his execution, and Nazim Pasha, the governor of Baghdad, imprisoned him for several days.[125] Zahawi joined the faculty of the law school in Baghdad but sparked his own scandal when he complained about the oppression of Muslim women and denounced Islamic divorce laws and veiling practices in the Egyptian newspaper *al-Muʾayyad*.[126] Conservatives demanded that Nazim Pasha punish Zahawi's "blasphemy," and the governor obliged by dismissing him from the law school and confining him to house arrest.[127] Months later, Nazim was dismissed from office after a public scandal in which he attempted to kidnap an Armenian teenage girl, Sarah Khatun.[128] Zahawi gloated over Nazim's fall in "The Tyrant of Baghdad," his poem that mocked the hypocritical religious zealotry of the governor and implored him to satisfy his lust with the overflowing chalices and "virginal buxom girls" of Salonika. Lest his satire be seen as contrasting Iraqi honor with Turkish vice, however, Zahawi warned Nazim of abusing the people of Salonika: "But among those people, you will also find fathers / who will not tolerate debauchery, nor their daughters!"[129]

The tremendous popularity of the poem in Baghdad indicated that revolutionary euphoria was beginning to give way to disillusionment.¹³⁰

The fall of Nazim Pasha opened new opportunities for Zahawi and Rusafi to pursue their political ambitions. Zahawi was elected to parliament and returned to Istanbul to publish the Arabic periodical *Sabil al-Rashad*.¹³¹ He hired Rusafi to edit the journal, now renamed *al-ʿArab*, and Rusafi found additional work as an Arabic tutor for the Ottoman minister of interior, Talʿat Pasha, who helped the poet secure his own seat in parliament.¹³² Political office brought prestige but slight compensation, and the poets continued to hold academic and journalism jobs.¹³³ Despite their initial enthusiasm for the CUP agenda, both came to support the opposition Liberal Entente.¹³⁴ While Zahawi showed little interest in the call for decentralization in the Arab provinces, Rusafi embraced decentralization during the Lynch affair of 1910, when the state granted a monopoly over Tigris transport to a British firm.¹³⁵ Rusafi published a poem in *al-Muʾayyad* that described the monopoly as a betrayal of revolutionary ideals: "A complaint for a heart whose blood pulses with grief / to the pillar of the constitution and to justice and right / These three principles stand as kings above all kings / for the people they claim the power of prosperity and repair."¹³⁶ He endorsed the Beirut Reform Committee's appeal for provincial councils in another poem but cut ties with the movement after the group's "treasonous" appeal for European support at the Arab Congress of Paris in June 1913.¹³⁷ Rusafi now denounced decentralization as a smokescreen for Christian sectarian interests, pointedly contrasting the paths of internal reform and external intervention on the path to modernity: "We both set out together, but our journeys soon diverged / moving in different directions, one East and the other West."¹³⁸

## Modernity in the Iraqi Poetry Revival

The constitutional revolutions profoundly changed how poetry was disseminated and interpreted. The only collections published by Iraqi poets over the previous two and half decades were the posthumous diwans of ʿAbd al-Ghaffar al-Akhras and Kazim al-Azri al-Tamimi, neither of which garnered significant attention.¹³⁹ Egyptian editors viewed the poems published by Kazimi, Zahawi, and Rusafi as exotic artifacts of a classical tradition that remained alive in Iraq.¹⁴⁰ The end of press censorship, however, allowed Iraqi poets to publish in the new periodicals that appeared in Iraq, Lebanon, Syria, and Egypt.[141] New voices, new ideas, and new styles reshaped both local and regional perceptions of Iraqi poetry. Iraqi poets began to publish their own curated diwans as a way of establishing their reputations for broader audiences.

The new concerns of Iraqi poets with the relationship between ideas and audiences reflected their preoccupation with material, ideological, and existential "corollaries of modernity" associated with mass society.[142] Their engagement with modernity was reflected in the profusion of poems that appeared in the wake of the constitutional revolutions that obsessively announced the commitment of the poet to secularism, liberalism, reason, science, and technology, sometimes in excruciatingly pedantic fashion and others with more subtlety and nuance. Neoclassical aesthetic constraints restricted their interest in the stylistic experimentation so critical to modernist literature elsewhere, but they embraced limited experiments with vocabulary, rhyme, and repetition as "modern" innovation. The publication of poetry in newspapers and diwans reflected a new interest in using print capitalism to spread their poems to an "imagined community" of Arabs living in the Ottoman Empire and British Egypt. While Benedict Anderson argues that novels fueled the rise of nationalism by popularizing new conceptions of the "homogenous, empty time" of modernity, the new mediums through which neoclassical poetry was disseminated also reflected the emergence of new temporalities in their rigid adherence to dating, which allowed readers to trace the simultaneous movements of diverse poets and ideas through the calendrical time of modernity.[143]

Jamil Sidqi al-Zahawi reflected these new epistemologies and temporalities of modernity when he published his collection *al-Kalim al-Manzum* in Beirut in 1909, becoming the first modern Iraqi poet to use the diwan to promote his reputation. The diwan included poems written before and after the Constitutional Revolution, critiques of Hamidian despotism, and panegyrics for the Young Turks. It was a poetic manifesto of liberalism and modernity, and while his attacks against religious dogma would grow bolder in coming decades, Zahawi was already promoting the ideas of Ernest Renan and Charles Darwin.[144] He showed little interest in anticolonialism, and several poems explicitly praised Britain and British policy in Egypt.[145] Zahawi's vision of modernity was constructed on the three pillars of technological innovation, social reform, and cultural revival, and the poem "People of the Future" expressed his unwavering faith that modernity would "purify man" and usher in a new era of global harmony.[146] Zahawi remained proud of the "principle of simplicity" in his modernist poetics, and the collection reflected his interest in aesthetic experimentation.[147] It included the unrhymed poem "Blank Verse," which he had originally published in *al-Mu'ayyad* in 1905.[148] While critics remain divided about whether Zahawi was the first poet to compose blank verse in Arabic, virtually all regarded the experiment as an aesthetic failure.[149]

Literary journals showed little interest in Zahawi's diwan, but the publication of Rusafi's diwan the following year attracted considerably more attention.[150] Muhammad Kurd 'Ali reviewed the collection in *al-Muqtabas*, proudly describing Rusafi as "the poet of *al-Muqtabas*" and calling his poetry "the highest example of the poetry of this age."[151] The collection reflected prototypically modernist concerns with meaning and transcendence, as in the existential poem "From Whence, to Where," in which the poet contemplated the existence of the afterlife and confessed, "I remain completely lost on this question / trapped between hope and despair."[152] His originality was also reflected in the unconventional organization of the diwan into existential, social, historical, and descriptive categories.[153] Rusafi described Zahawi's blank verse experiments as "unpoetic," but he supported the modernist project of simplicity and later contended that the colloquial poet was "more capable than the poets of classical Arabic of moving the thoughts of the masses, because his poetry is more comprehensible to them than theirs."[154] While his own style was unabashedly classical, his faith in the didactic capacity of poetry was reflected in descriptive poems about the telegraph, telephone, locomotive, airplane, and steamer that displayed his enthusiasm for modernity: "The telegraph is wires that bring the news / in an instant, like the musician plucking a string / Running across the earth and across the sea / to poles that have been planted like trees."[155] These poems were intended to explain the novelty of the modern world, but their didacticism sometimes overwhelmed poetic qualities. While some critics concluded that these "scientific" poems were offered "in imitation of al-Zahawi," Rusafi's belief in the poet's obligation to educate and mobilize the masses attests to the consistency of these experiments with his poetic vocation.[156]

The work of younger Iraqi poets began appearing in foreign newspapers and journals, revealing both the influence of Kazimi, Zahawi, and Rusafi and their own ambitions to propel their country toward the horizon of modernity. Kazim al-Dujayli (1884–1970), a young Shiʻi poet from Baghdad who was inspired by the appearance of poems by Zahawi and Rusafi in the foreign press, published his first poem in the Baghdadi newspaper *al-Irshad* in the weeks after the Ottoman Constitutional Revolution, rejoicing that "this age has filled the horizon with its songs."[157] Dujayli worked under Rusafi at *al-Baghdad* and under Anastas Mari al-Karmali at the literary journal *Lughat al-ʻArab*, embracing Rusafi's secularism and Karmali's support for Arab decentralization.[158] He published prolifically in Iraqi journals like *Lughat al-ʻArab, Dar al-Salam,* and *Layla* and foreign periodicals like *al-Hilal, al-ʻIrfan, al-Muqtabas, al-Muqtataf, al-Mustaqbal,* and *al-Zuhur.*[159] His poems generally echoed the modernist spirit of Zahawi and Rusafi, but Dujayli also wrote romantic poetry, including a long poem about an ill-fated romance between a Muslim boy and Christian girl.[160] He shared Zahawi's interest in experimentation, publishing a poem in *Lughat al-ʻArab* in which the first hemistich of the second verse was repeated for fourteen consecutive verses. The poem ostensibly celebrated technological innovation, but over the course of the repetitive verses, Dujayli's depiction of modernity gradually evolved from unrestrained enthusiasm to more circumspect interrogations of tension and contradiction.[161] His descriptions of modernity as the "era of infidelity and faith," "the era of doubt and certainty," and "the era of enlightenment and stagnation" reflected an increasingly ambivalent vision of the social tension between tradition and modernity that would come to characterize the poems of other young Iraqis from his generation.[162]

## Poetry and the Najafi Nahda

This ambivalent modernity was reflected in the poetry of a new generation of young Najafis who sought to reconcile their pride in the cultural legacy of Najaf with their enthusiasm for the cosmopolitan modernity of the distant urban metropolis. Nearly a dozen of the most prominent Iraqi neoclassical poets were born in Najaf in the late nineteenth century, including Muhammad Hasan Haydar (b. 1888), Muhammad Rida al-Shabibi (b. 1889), Muhammad Baqir al-Shabibi (b. 1889), ʻAbd al-ʻAziz al-Jawahiri (b. 1890),

ʿAli al-Sharqi (b. 1891), Muhammad Mahdi al-Basir (b. 1895), Muhammad ʿAli al-Yaʿqubi (b. 1895), ʿAbbas al-Khalili (b. 1896), Saʿd Salih (b. 1896), Ahmad al-Safi al-Najaf (b. 1897), and Muhammad Mahdi al-Jawahiri (b. 1899). Nearly all came from prominent clerical families, and most were introduced to poetry by their fathers or brothers before entering the *hawza*.[163] They were influenced by the neoclassical poetry emanating from Cairo and the canon of classical poetry, especially the *Luzumiyyat* of al-Maʿarri, which made them receptive to new secular vocabularies of modernism, nationalism, and socialism.[164]

Echoes of the constitutional revolutions reverberated in their discussions of these new secular ideologies.[165] They were introduced to new intellectual and literary currents by foreign journals like *al-Hilal*, *al-Muʾayyad*, *al-Muqtataf*, *al-Muqtabas*, *al-ʿUsur*, and *al-Zuhur*. Equally influential was *al-ʿIrfan*, a new journal based in Sidon that addressed a transnational Shiʿi audience.[166] Typical issues of the journal were fifty pages, with poetry dominating a cultural section of approximately ten pages. Poetry was also interspersed in prose articles to frame modern concepts in familiar terms, similar to the way in which Rifaʿa Rafiʿ al-Tahtawi used ornamental poetry to narrate his "modern experience" in Paris.[167] These journals circulated across southern Iraq, not only in the intellectual hubs of Najaf and Karbala but even in small towns like Suq al-Shuyukh.[168] Radical ideas like Shibli Shumayyil's defense of Darwinism flourished and provoked intense debates among scholars and students in the hawza.[169] The influential scholar and poet Muhammad Rida al-Isfahani composed a lengthy critique of Charles Darwin and Shumayyil that was distinguished by genuine admiration for Darwinist methodology.[170] Isfahani's critique inspired the young poet ʿAbd al-ʿAziz al-Jawahiri to attempt his own reconciliation of Darwinism and Islam in *al-ʿIrfan*.[171]

The Najafi youths first encountered the neoclassical poetry of iconic Egyptian poets in the Nahda periodicals that now appeared in Najaf. The political themes of their poetry introduced new concepts of patriotism, nationalism, and anticolonialism to the Najafi public sphere.[172] While local attitudes toward the Ottoman Empire had long been shaped by political discrimination and sectarian grievances in Najaf, the pan-Islamic agenda and imperial propaganda of Sultan Abdülhamid II mollified these tensions slightly by the turn of the century.[173] Now, however, senior *mujtahids* like Isfahani and their young Najafi disciples sought to advance their own local agendas through the constitutionalist mantra of imperial loyalty. In the ecumenical language of the Nahda secularists and Islamic modernists, they condemned sectarianism and positioned themselves as paragons of Muslim resistance to European encroachment.[174] The lines between the imperial loyalties of Ottomanism, the ethnic affinities of Arabism, and the territorial identities of Iraqism were not yet clearly defined, instead looming as overlapping indexes of defensive priorities that could be mobilized according to the demands of particular political crises.[175] What mattered most was that Najaf was positioned at the center of each emerging constellation of collective identity.

The Nahda periodicals that now appeared in Najaf also included the poems of fellow Iraqis like Kazimi, Zahawi, Rusafi, and Dujayli, which thrilled and inspired the young poets. They yearned to bring their own poetry to the attention of a broader Arab audience, and young Najafis like 'Ali al-Sharqi, 'Abd al-'Aziz al-Jawahiri, Muhammad Rida al-Shabibi, Muhammad Baqir al-Shabibi, 'Abbas al-Khalili, and Muhammad Hasan Haydar began submitting their poems to *al-Hilal*, *al-'Irfan*, *al-Muqtataf*, and other journals.[176] Muhammad Baqir al-Shabibi was so enthusiastic about the press that he published an ode to *al-Muqtataf* and *al-Muqtabas* in the Baghdadi literary journal *Lughat al-'Arab*.[177] Most of their poems dealt with the interrelated themes of Iraqi patriotism, Eastern awakening, and poetic revival. Between the Ottoman Constitutional Revolution and World War I, for example, Muhammad Rida al-Shabibi published patriotic poems in *al-'Irfan* and *al-Barq*, ruminations on Eastern awakening and Western decadence in *al-Zuhur*, and a reflection on the cultural significance of poetry in *al-'Irfan*.[178]

The themes of cultural revival and political awakening reflected the influence of pan-Islamic and pan-Asian intellectuals like Jamal al-Din al-Afghani, Rabindranath Tagore, and Sun Yat-Sen.[179] Shabibi viewed poetry as the spiritual response of the East to the decadent materialism of the West, which he condemned as selfish and antisocial in a poem published in *al-Zuhur*. The poem's critique of capitalism foreshadowed the socialist inclinations that so many Najafi youth would later embrace, including Shabibi's own children: "How many hungry souls now gaze upon merry faces

/ deprived of all nourishment among these gluttons?"[180] Shabibi believed that the restoration of Islamic values and the revival of Arabic poetry were the only means of resisting this epidemic of decadence and isolation and argued in *al-'Irfan* that poetry was so essential to modern society that poets ought to receive salaries, arguing that "[the poet] creates with his tongue the fruit of his vocation / and in this way his craft runs parallel to hands of production."[181] This comparison between the poet's tongue and the hand of production reflected his novel conception of poetry as a means of cultural resistance to capitalism and materialism.

The young Najafis were elated to find their poems published alongside those of prominent Egyptians and Syrians in foreign journals, which began to shape their attitudes toward anticolonialism. When they read Shabibi's contributions to *al-Zuhur*, for example, they encountered in the same issue poems and articles celebrating the Eastern triumph in the Russo-Japanese War, the revolutionary spirit of the Boxer Rebellion, and the life of Jamal al-Din al-Afghani.[182] They found, however, that the cartography of the Nahda relegated Najaf to peripheral status in the cultural revival emanating from Cairo to cosmopolitan cities like Alexandria, Beirut, Damascus, Sidon, and Damascus, and from there to provincial cities like Baghdad, Tunis, Algiers, and Fez.[183] In response, they sought to reconstruct the cultural history of the nineteenth century in a way that reinscribed the importance of Najaf to the Arab Nahda.

The determination of these youths to disseminate "Najafi poetry" to a broader Arab audience was inspired by the publication of the Zahawi and Rusafi diwans in 1909 and 1910. 'Ali al-Sharqi and his cousin 'Abd al-'Aziz al-Jawahiri collaborated to publish the poems of Ibrahim al-Tabataba'i and Muhammad Sa'id al-Habbubi, whom they regarded as the greatest modern Najafi poets. Sharqi portrayed Tabataba'i as the "renaissance man" of the Iraqi Nahda, while Jawahiri described Habbubi as "the best poet of the east yesterday and the greatest of its 'ulama today." Their introductions advanced a novel hypothesis about why the Najafi poets had failed to attain the fame of their Egyptian counterparts. Sharqi contended that the best poets "stand above the dogmas of popular currents and the commercialization of the fruits of their genius . . . they rise and pass, but they do not become famous because they do not sink to the battleground of personal ambition."[184]

While other poets made their reputations with panegyrics, Tabataba'i was distinguished by classical authenticity and spontaneity. Capitalizing on ʿAbd al-Muhsin al-Kazimi's reputation in Cairo, Sharqi argued that his poetry was a "specter of the poetry of Tabataba'i, especially in Kazimi's emulation of [Tabataba'i's] strength of spirit, pace of improvisation, and engagement with classical Arabic verse."[185] Jawahiri likewise portrayed Habbubi's refusal to compose panegyrics for unworthy rulers as evidence of his integrity and contended that his aesthetic similarity to classical Arab poets was far superior to the "modern sensibility" of the Egyptian neoclassical poets.[186]

These persistent efforts to highlight the Iraqi contribution to the neoclassical revival underscored the cultivation of national subjectivities as both a critical component of the reform project and "an effect of modernity itself."[187] Muhammad Rida al-Shabibi reflected the nascent national ideal created by the rupture of modernity in an essay about Habbubi that he published in *al-Zuhur*, celebrating the authenticity of Iraqi classical aesthetics and lamenting that other Arab poets had grown obsessed with fame and fortune, abandoning the "true poetry" of the classical tradition.[188] The editor of *al-Zuhur* was convinced and appended an editorial comment praising the classical aesthetics of both Habbubi and Shabibi, which "remind us of their predecessors, the master Arab poets."[189] The Lebanese poet and journalist Ahmad Rida echoed this appreciation of the Iraqi tradition in his compilation *al-ʿIraqiyyat*, which included biographical sketches and poems from ten Iraqis associated with the poetry revival in the nineteenth century: Sheikh Mulla Kazim al-Azri (1730–1797), Sheikh ʿAbd al-Baqi al-Faruqi (1788–1861), ʿAbd al-Ghaffar al-Akhras (1805–1873), Sheikh ʿAbbas bin Mulla ʿAli al-Najafi (1826–1860), Sayyid Haydar al-Hilli (1831–1887), Sayyid Ibrahim al-Tabataba'i (1832–1901), Sayyid Muhammad Saʿid al-Habbubi (1849–1915), Sayyid Jaʿfar al-Hilli (1861–1898), Sheikh Jawad al-Shabibi (1865–1944), and Sheikh ʿAbd-al-Muhsin al-Kazimi (1871–1935).[190] Rida traced the origins of the poetry revival to eighteenth-century Iraq, long before the emergence of neoclassical poetry in Egypt. The compilation projected a proto-nationalist conception of Iraq by identifying Shiʿi poets from Najaf, Hilla, and Kazimiyya and Sunni poets from Baghdad and Mosul as part of the same distinct tradition of "Iraqi" poetry. Equally significant was the exclusion of Zahawi and Rusafi from the collection, despite the inclusion of their contemporaries Hilli, Shabibi, and Kazimi. Rida was quite familiar with both poets, having met Rusafi in Beirut in 1909 and publishing a review of his poetry in *al-'Irfan*.[191] The Iraqi poetry revival, he seemed keen to assert, did not begin with the appearance of Egyptian periodicals and their influence on the modernist pioneers Zahawi and Rusafi.

While Jawahiri, Shabibi, Sharqi, and others promoted the poetic heritage of Najaf and challenged the historiography of the Nahda, their own poems reflected a cosmopolitan spirit betraying their frustration with the intellectual confines of Najaf. Both Shabibi and Sharqi published poems about the sinking of the *Titanic*, with Sharqi's poem serving as an elegy for the investigative journalist William Thomas Steed, who was widely lauded in the Arab press for his opposition to Italian aggression in the Italo-Turkish War of 1911–1912.[192] Sharqi paid tribute to Steed's memory: "Herald of peace, you have sunk beneath the sea / peace be with you, the peace of soldier's souls / All souls are enchanted with the world until / the body is effaced from the plane of existence."[193] The fact that a young Najafi poet was mourning the death of a British journalist aboard the *Titanic* in a Lebanese journal because of his affiliation with the global pacifist movement simultaneously illustrated the broadened intellectual horizons of the young Najafis and hinted toward the looming conflict between cosmopolitan modernity and provincial traditionalism.

Several months after the appearance of his elegy for Steed, Sharqi published "A Poet in Prison" in *al-'Irfan*. The poem reflected the crisis of modernity in Najafi, where youths struggled to balance their enthusiasm for the new ideologies and aesthetics of the foreign press with their frustration with the intellectual and cultural claustrophobia of their provincial town. The opening verses of the poem articulated the poet's desire to escape the "intellectual prison" of Najaf and experience the cosmopolitan modernity he envisioned beyond its borders through the metaphor of the nightingale's cage:

What town is this whose prison contains me,
confining me like the cage of the nightingale?
The door of his hopes has now been latched,
so he simply hovers around that bolted gate
He flaps his wings, but he finds himself unable

to fly, and so he stares down at his feet below
His heart is pulsing and his wings are flapping,
but bewildered wherever he turns, he fails again
He yearns for nothing but to embrace the dawn,
the longing of the preacher for the congregation . . . [194]

This poetic vision of modernity allowed Sharqi to articulate the "modern desire" that lay at the heart of the intellectual, cultural, and spatial intersection of modernity.[195] Muhammad Rida al-Shabibi echoed this sentiment in a poem addressed to a friend returning from Europe. After rebuking his friend for abandoning his homeland for London, Paris, and Berlin, Shabibi confessed his own cosmopolitan enchantments: "Is there for me, despite my love for my people and my homeland / among mankind some other people and some other homeland?"[196] His younger brother Muhammad Baqir expressed this wistful cosmopolitanism even more clearly in a poem describing his infatuation with a modernity that he could encounter only in the pages of the Nahda periodicals. The poem compared modernity to an impossible romance, reflecting the despair of a young generation facing a dream that lay tantalizingly beyond their grasp: "I struggled to conceal my desire and hide my despair / in the stream tears that cut a trail across my cheeks / Perhaps the east wind will carry this letter to her / for I have grown tired of the tongues of our messengers."[197]

## Conclusion

The neoclassical modernity envisioned by Iraqi poets in the late Ottoman era simultaneously represented a reflection on the past and a dream for the future. Their appropriation of the classical qasida to articulate responses to the paradoxes of modernity was not simply a superficial application of an aesthetic veneer of cultural authenticity to derivative discourses of European modernity. These aesthetic concerns instead reflected a broader response to the implicit and explicit questions of cultural authenticity that infused so many debates of the Arab Nahda. Neoclassical poetics linked the historical grandeur of the Arab cultural tradition to the social and political concerns of modernity in a manner that fundamentally reshaped the relationship of past, present, and future.

The importance of both history and aesthetics in the neoclassical revival played an important role in the emergence of proto-nationalist identities in late Ottoman Iraq. "Iraqi poetry" was first constructed as a distinct aspect of national culture in the late nineteenth and early twentieth centuries, a product of both the discovery of new links and connections between disparate local scenes inside Iraq and the perception of new differences between these collective scenes and their counterparts outside Iraq. The movement of poets like ʿAbd al-Muhsin al-Kazimi between different local and national poetry scenes were liminal journeys that created a new understanding of cultural and political identity.[198] Many of these perceptions of cultural difference were conceived by non-Iraqi critics associated with the Nahda periodicals in Egypt and Lebanon, but they were quickly accepted and internalized by Iraqi audiences as well. Cultural difference became inextricably linked to national pride, which inspired a competition between partisans of the diverse local traditions in Najaf and Baghdad for the right to claim national supremacy. This heated debate over the Iraqi contribution to the Arab Nahda would persist well into the Hashemite era.[199]

Aesthetic authenticity, of course, represented only half of the equation of neoclassical modernity. Enthusiasm for science, technology, democracy, urbanization, and other "corollaries of modernity" came to dominate the content of neoclassical poetry in late Ottoman Iraq. In many cases, the image of modernity presented in neoclassical poetry described the European present as an aspirational Iraqi future. While these visions and dreams of modernity would make legible the "familiar futures" that subsequent generations in Iraq experienced, they also produced temporal and spatial disjunctions between East and West that magnified the contradictions and anxieties of modernity that Iraqis experienced and enacted.[200] The discourse of modernity would soon give way to that of revolution, but these concerns would remain pervasive in Iraqi poetry over the coming decades.

The poems disseminated by Iraqi poets in both the local and regional press reflected the anxieties of the Iraqi engagement with modernity. While young Najafi poets confessed their enchantment with the world that lay beyond the confines of their own hometown, they did not really seek to escape the "cage" of Najaf. They were deeply engaged in a revisionist project to inscribe Ibrahim al-Tabatabaʾi and Muhammad Saʿid al-Habbubi as protagonists in the history of the Arab Nahda, but they yearned for more progress, reform, and regeneration. Their neoclassical vision of modernity privileged the "authentic" language of poetry, and their celebration of classical aesthetics in Iraqi poetry was tinged by self-consciousness about the subordinate role of Iraqi poets and intellectuals in the Arab Nahda. Like Zahawi and Rusafi, the young Najafis yearned for recognition (and perhaps compensation) and to see their poetry transform society. Sharqi's wistful "longing of the preacher for the congregation" continued to gnaw at their conscience, and this imperative to reconcile social commitment and individual ambition would become a driving feature of anticolonial politics during World War I and the British Mandate.

❨ CHAPTER 2 ❩

# REBEL POETRY

*Colonialism and the Poetry of Rebellion, 1914–1920*

On July 22, 1920, the blind poet Muhammad Mahdi al-Basir (1895–1974) ascended the minbar of Haydarkhana Mosque to address the crowd of Sunnis and Shiʻa who came to celebrate the Sunni *mawlid* ceremony celebrating the birth of the Prophet Muhammad in a historic effort to transcend sectarian division.[1] Basir, the "Mirabeau of Iraq," grew up in Hilla and became a popular orator in the *husayniyyas* (Shiʻi religious halls) but was drawn to the revolutionary climate of nationalist politics in Baghdad.[2] He had once published poems in support of the British occupation and now confessed this "collaboration" in public repentance.[3] He declared his willingness to atone by sacrificing his life for the sake of his country: "I wish only that you grant me the honor of death / a death that lets me rest at the side of your martyrs / For God's sake, grant me the death you have chosen / Fatherland, or I am not fit to be one of your sons."[4] The spectacle of the preacher yearning for martyrdom in the vocabulary of nationalism reflected the secularization of anticolonialism.[5] Basir denounced the deception and "voracious appetite" of colonialism before thundering, "Let them bend their necks before you in submission / let your aims and desires now be achieved / Until they acknowledge the corruption they have sown / renounce their sins and submit to your guidance!"[6]

British officials viewed these public gatherings with increasing anxiety and paid local informants to monitor them.[7] While the Foreign Ministry was obsessed with Kemalist and Bolshevik "conspiracies," officials in Iraq were more concerned that "inflammatory" poems might facilitate Sunni-Shi'i cooperation.[8] These fears were confirmed by an informant who confessed apologetically after listening to Basir's poem, "Even I myself felt stirred to do something for the *watan* (fatherland)." Four exclamation points were scrawled in the margin of the report for emphasis.[9] The colonial reaction reflected pervasive fears of poetry as an instrument of popular mobilization, but there was nothing especially novel about Basir's performance. The nationalist mawlids had been taking place daily for nearly two months, and Basir was just one of many poets who participated in them.[10] This was at least the third time that Basir had recited this particular poem, though informants insisted the poem lost none of its effect in repetition.[11]

In some respects, Basir was simply carrying on the long tradition of dissident poetry in Iraq.[12] The real novelty of his performance, however, lay in his articulation of the secular language of nationalism in the sacred space of the mosque, an innovation critical to the new phenomenon of "rebel poetry." More than a mere register of nationalist loyalty, rebel poetry reflected the new ways in which popular politics were shaped by secular modernity.[13] Less than a decade after 'Ali al-Sharqi compared the desire of young Najafi poets for broader audiences to "the longing of the preacher for the congregation," poets like Basir found enthusiasm for their verses overflowing in Baghdad.[14]

While the immense popularity of the rebel poetry scene centered around the Haydarkhana Mosque reflected a shift from "intellectual" concerns of modernity to "popular" enthusiasm for rebellion, these tropes were rarely distinct. Poets advanced modern conceptions of politics, society, and culture through the popular discourse of anticolonial rebel poetry. Basir's show of public repentance underscored the decline of the panegyric, which was now increasingly replaced by protest poems unmoored from older patronage models. Rebel poetry became an act of resistance to colonialism and a public rejection of the "colonial modernity" that portrayed Western progress and Eastern stagnation as consequences of an essentialist "cultural difference."[15] These poems were recited in an emerging public sphere where bourgeois publics and subaltern counterpublics developed a shared interest in the new "plebian culture" of anticolonialism.[16] These public encounters were at times hostile, but they facilitated the rise of an "alternative modernity" in which poets articulated anticolonial arguments in the universal language of modernity.[17] The revolutionary antisectarian nature of the Baghdad mawlids allowed the modern rebel poet to serve as "an agent as well as an effect of cultural and political change" and to participate in the novel construction of the new "social space" of modernity.[18]

The emergence of the new cultural politics and poetics of anticolonial modernity was shaped by the collapse of the Ottoman Empire and rise of the British Mandate. Iraq became a critical theater of World War I in the Middle East in both spatial and ideological terms. Ottoman authorities effectively used poetry as propaganda in the war, emphasizing pan-Islamic loyalties and tribal cultural values to rally their Iraqi subjects to resist the British invasion of November 1914. The initial effectiveness of these appeals was evident in the huge corpus of Iraqi poetry endorsing the Ottoman declaration of jihad and celebrating the Ottoman triumph at Kut in April 1916, but many poets soon grew disenchanted with the Ottoman Empire. As the British army recovered from catastrophe at Kut and pressed toward Baghdad, the Iraqi poetry of war reflected the divided loyalties of Arabs caught between pan-Islamic Ottomanism and the nascent Arabism of the Hashemite Arab Revolt. Some Iraqi poets even celebrated the British "liberation" of Iraq and wrote panegyrics for British military and political authorities. In the prelude to the Great Iraqi Revolution of 1920, however, poetry once again became the critical medium of political dissent in the country as poets forcefully and publicly challenged the rhetoric and practice of colonial modernity and endorsed anticolonial violence in the new vocabulary of secular nationalism. This new phenomenon of rebel poetry linked intellectual conceptions of modernity to the political rhetoric of anticolonial nationalism, reasserting the importance of poetry as the voice of the popular will and the vehicle of national progress.

## World War I and the Poetry of Jihad

The Ottoman Empire entered World War I on the side of the Central Powers in November 1914 in a desperate bid to preserve the territorial integrity of the empire.[19] Germany solicited a declaration of jihad from Sultan Mehmed V in the hope of inspiring a global rebellion among Muslim subjects of the British, French, and Russian empires.[20] While these hopes proved unfounded, the proclamation galvanized popular support within the Ottoman Empire. Fifteen thousand Iraqi tribal irregulars were mobilized, and poets from different ideological camps wrote poems in support of the jihad.[21] Ottomanists like Jamil Sidqi al-Zahawi, Maʿruf al-Rusafi, and ʿAbd al-Mutallib al-Hilli enthusiastically endorsed the jihad to preserve the reforms of the ruling Committee of Union and Progress.[22] Arabists like ʿAbd al-Rahman al-Bannaʾ, Muhammad al-Hashimi, Rashid al-Hashimi Khayri al-Hindawi, ʿAbd al-Muhsin al-Kazimi, Muhammad Hasan Abu al-Muhasin, Muhammad Rida al-Shabibi, and Muhammad Baqir al-Shabibi had already grown disenchanted with the CUP, but they nevertheless wrote poems in support of the jihad.[23]

Iraqi poets contributed to the pan-Islamic propaganda of the Ottoman war effort in both public recitations and state publications. Maʿruf al-Rusafi privately described the war as a wedding feast "marred by misery and misfortune," but he dutifully promoted Arab-Turkish unity in Istanbul by publicly reciting a patriotic poem at the performance of a historical drama about al-Samawʾal b. ʿAdiya, the Arab Jewish warrior famous for his loyalty to Imruʾ al-Qays.[24] Jamil Sidqi al-Zahawi renounced his prior support for Britain and endorsed the jihad in a serialized poem in the Baghdadi newspaper *Sada al-Islam* in November 1914: "This is not the first time in this historical era / that the English saw truth and feigned ignorance / Time after time they coveted, so now they will suffer / the fruits of injustice, for history is repeated!"[25] ʿAbd al-Rahman al-Bannaʾ, an Arabist critic of the CUP, echoed these appeals with pan-Islamist rhetoric: "Rush forward in haste to the battle cry / do not fear the cannons or soldiers / For death is the fate of every soul / but he who dies in defense becomes a martyr."[26] In both newspapers and public spaces, the poetry of jihad became a symbolic marker of Iraqi patriotism and loyalty to the Ottoman Empire.

Ottoman efforts to publicize the jihad among the Arab tribes drew heavily from the poetic tradition of incitement (*shiʿr al-tahrid*).[27] The collapse of Ottoman resistance to the invading British army at Basra in November 1914 pushed Shiʿi mujtahids in Najaf and Karbala to publicly endorse the jihad and mobilize local tribes.[28] They were joined by young poets like ʿAbd al-Mutallib al-Hilli, Muhammad Hasan Abu-al-Muhasin, Muhammad Rida al-Shabibi, Muhammad Baqir al-Shabibi, and ʿAli al-Sharqi, who recited poems to the tribes that fused the vocabulary of jihad with Arabist pride.[29] Muhammad Mahdi al-Qazwini, for example, wrote in anguish to Muhammad Saʻid al-Habbubi, "We are the Sons of Arabs, the lions of mankind / the true religion inside of us gives us a mighty strength / You must be on the march at the head of your troops / to lead them to exterminate the troops of England."[30] Habbubi responded by bringing Abu al-Muhasin, Sharqi, and the Shabibi brothers with him to recite martial poems to the Muntafiq tribes.[31] While tribalism and nationalism are sometimes seen as contradictory and antagonistic expressions of political identity and loyalty, they could also "inform and enhance one another" as expressions of cultural authenticity overlapped with declarations of national pride.[32]

Abu al-Muhasin captured this convergence of loyalties in poems that appealed to tribal pride to resist foreign invasion: "What is glory except to breathe and unsheathe? / What is humiliation except to breathe and sheathe?"[33] His martial poems described resistance as "your duty toward your religion" and condemned collaborators as traitors and infidels.[34] One popular poem condemned a local tribal sheikh as a collaborator for choosing "to forsake the religion of God and appeal / foolishly to that of the Crusaders."[35] The bitter invective of the poem's conclusion articulated the power of poetry as a social mechanism to reward compliance and punish defiance of political expectations: "This verse is nothing more than a piercing pen / a decree condemning you to misery and dishonor / You will soon be stripped of all honor and profit / and clothed in the rags of disgrace before long!"[36]

Thousands of Iraqi tribesmen embraced the Ottoman jihad and joined the forces of Sulayman al-ʻAskari at Shuʻayba in April 1915.[37] While the battle ended in failure, Iraqi poets lauded tribal heroism and blamed the incompetence of Ottoman commanders.[38] Muhammad Saʻid al-Habbubi was mortally wounded in the battle and became the heroic national symbol of anticolonial resistance, but his young poet disciples abandoned the cause and returned to Najaf.[39] Shiʻi enthusiasm for the Ottoman jihad dissipated as scholars and poets began questioning the benefits of imperial loyalty. Muhammad Rida al-Shabibi mocked ʻAskari's bravado and incompetence in a poem that pointedly contrasted the thirst of retreating Arab soldiers and the enticing waters of the Tigris and Euphrates that lay just beyond their reach.[40]

Some Iraqi poets remained loyal to the Ottoman Empire, particularly after the triumph at Salman Pak in November 1915.⁴¹ ʿAbd al-Mutallib al-Hilli reveled in British humiliation during the pivotal siege of Kut in early 1916, describing British "Crusaders" as "common slaughter animals suddenly confined by walls."⁴² When General Townsend surrendered, Hilli mocked him in the poetic vocabulary of religious supremacy: "Townsend submitted to the sword in disgrace / the cross abandoned him under the weight of our blade."⁴³ Abu al-Muhasin blamed the civilians of Kut for aiding British troops and warned of the fate of collaborators: "Do you hope to be saved and leave unharmed / when our soldiers have blocked every exit? / For you can now see our soldiers closing in / on you, like the lion stalking his prey."⁴⁴ The warning was prophetic: hundreds of civilians were executed by Ottoman forces after the British surrender.⁴⁵ Abu al-Muhasin also mocked British prisoners "herded like livestock" toward Baghdad and satirized colonial hubris: "London, do you know the certainty / of the fate that awaits your roving sons / Sent to our land with tender cheeks / that shall before long be turned to dust?"⁴⁶ When Lord Kitchener drowned off the coast of Scotland two months later, Hilli mocked the failure of the would-be colonizer, who "had dispatched together by land and sea / armies whose vast number came to fill the horizon."⁴⁷ These poems of jihad reflected the slow and uneven embrace of the modern vocabulary of anticolonialism, emphasizing the material ambitions of colonialism rather than religious difference.

## Poetics of Collaboration

Iraqi poets were forced to choose between collaboration and silence after General Stanley Maude recovered Kut and then conquered Baghdad on March 11, 1917.⁴⁸ Maude insisted that British troops came to Iraq as "liberators," and many Iraqi political elites celebrated the end of Turkish oppression.⁴⁹ Some poets remained committed Ottoman patriots, including Maʿruf al-Rusafi, who was still living in Istanbul and bitterly reproached the Turkish poet Sulayman Nazif for suggesting that Iraqis betrayed the empire: "I remain loyal and steadfast even if there / are wounds in my heart from the one I love / Today I complain about them and to them / let the wind inform them of my complaints!"⁵⁰ Most poets in Iraq, however, found that patronage relationships with the old Ottoman elites had been severed, and many responded by renouncing the Ottoman jihad and composing poems in praise of Britain. Some of these poems were more restrained than others, but even the most reserved expression of optimism became tainted by the aesthetics of collaboration.

Poets worried about the potential restoration of Ottoman rule and used pseudonyms. Collaboration anxieties diminished the utility of poetry as public communication but amplified the influence of print culture.[51] British officials sought to shape public opinion by subsidizing Razzuq Da'ud Ghannam, and his new newspaper, *al-'Arab*, established with British support in Baghdad in July 1917.[52] Ghannam delegated responsibility to his fellow Christian, Anastas Mari al-Kirmili, the Carmelite priest, linguist, and poetry aficionado who had previously edited the literary journal *Lughat al-'Arab*.[53] Kirmili's anti-Ottoman views were personal: during the war, he had been imprisoned alongside Muslim poets like 'Abd al-Husayn al-Azri.[54] He published an enormous number of pro-British poems in *al-'Arab* and his new literary journal, *Dar al-Salam*.[55] While there is little evidence that British authorities appreciated these poems, his tireless work in soliciting them indicates the importance he attached to poetry.[56]

The poetry of *al-'Arab* and *Dar al-Salam* was published under pseudonyms like Ibn Ma' al-Sama', Ibn al-Furatayn, Ibn al-Saliqa, Ibn al-Ritha', Ibn al-'Arab, Ibn al-Harith, Ibn al-Salam, Ibn Babil, Ibn al-Yara', and Ibn al-'Iraqayn.[57] Each of these pseudonyms reflected the poet's conscious identification with the Iraqi natural landscape, expressing a nascent form of national identity defined in opposition to the broader imperial and religious identities of pan-Ottomanism and pan-Islamism. The quality of the poets varied, with some demonstrating real talent and others resorting to obsequious flattery. The best poems were more anti-Ottoman than pro-British, like those of 'Abd al-Rahman al-Banna' (Ibn Ma' al-Sama'). His poem about the fall of Baghdad was serialized on the front page of *al-'Arab* and portrayed the terror that reigned after the flight of Turkish troops:

> Why has Baghdad fallen to such dejected state?
> Why do people hurry rush from the city in flight?
> Only yesterday, the soldiers were huddled, lurking
> here while people engaged in business and labor
> There was chaos in the haughtiness of the Turks,

but today they are not even the subject of idle talk
For all they possessed in their palaces of tyranny
has this morning become nothing but ruins⁵⁸

The second installment rebuked Iraqi women for lamenting the collapse of Turkish rule, contrasting feminine nostalgia for the past with masculine enthusiasm for national liberation and praising the British as "men who never abandon their friend / not men who ignore the rights of Arabs!"⁵⁹

Anti-Turkish rhetoric dominated most of the poems in *al-'Arab*, like Ibn al-Furatayn's description of urban terror as Turkish forces "set fire to Baghdad in their fit of rage."⁶⁰ Ibn al-Furatayn praised King George V as "Sultan of the Mughals," suggesting his desire to minimize the religious dimension of the war: "The Sultan of the Mughals is the bull that seizes / the skulls of his prey by the throat in subjugation / He is the one whose appearance led the Turks / so feared and fearsome, to destruction in this war!"⁶¹ Muhammad Mahdi al-Basir (Ibn Babil) offered similar criticism of Ottoman rule in *al-'Arab* and *Dar al-Salam*. One poem presented a qualified defense of Shi'i support for the Ottoman *jihad*: "We patiently endured our enemy / to protect our religion, not from fear / But they wrecked this lofty castle / of highest quality that we built for them."⁶² Basir emphasized that the Iraqi Shi'a "endured" Ottoman rule in the name of pan-Islamic solidarity only so long as the empire provided protection from foreign rule.

The most notable contributor to *al-'Arab* was Jamil Sidqi al-Zahawi, who renounced Ottomanism after the execution of Arab nationalists in Damascus and Beirut in May 1916.⁶³ Zahawi described this event as the final rupture of the Arab-Turkish relationship: "What passes has passed and will not return, so listen / to the speaking tongue of history and what it says / Academic tomes will be written as supplications / and these calamities of war will become its chapters."⁶⁴ His poem "The Loyalty of the English," which first appeared in the 1909 collection *al-Kalim al-Manzum*, was reproduced in *al-'Arab* in January 1918. The original poem praised British liberalism in veiled critique of Hamidian despotism, but several lines were now revised to reflect an explicitly anti-Turkish message.⁶⁵ The line "Arabs and Turks, be aware that the / loyalty of some to a nation is a rebuke" was changed to "Arabs and Turks, be aware that the / loyalty of the Turks to a nation is a rebuke," and the line "The scoundrels humiliated you so disgracefully / and in oppression deprived you of your rights" became "The Turks humiliated you so disgracefully / and in oppression deprived you of your rights."⁶⁶ These revisions reflected new vocabularies of ethnic nationalism now invoked to defend the Anglo-Arab alliance.

While Kirmili persuaded several capable poets to write pro-British verses for *al-ʿArab*, the servile flattery and "bad poetry" of many of the contributions made it easy for readers to dismiss the paper as colonial propaganda. Some of the worst poems were attributed to "Ibn al-Saliqa," whose Christian rhetoric was an unhelpful reminder of the disproportionate role of Iraqi Christians in the paper. One poem described King George V as "so lofty that Saturn prostrates before him" and asked rhetorically if "such a just man as he" had ever lived.⁶⁷ Equally galling was Ibn al-Sayyara's melodramatic elegy for General Maude: "The star of good fortune fell from its constellation / and grief encircled them in their depression / A tear flowed from the eye of the Most High / and in the heart of victory there kindled a new fire."⁶⁸ As British subsidies declined with the end of the war, poets like Ibn al-Saliqa and Ibn al-Sayyara simply vanished, but ʿAbd al-Rahman al-Bannaʾ (Ibn Maʾ al-Samaʾ) and Muhammad Mahdi al-Basir (Ibn Babil) reemerged as critics of Britain. Chastened by their experience and disenchanted with colonial rhetoric of liberation, they now renounced the aesthetics of collaboration and refashioned themselves as rebel poets.

## Divided Loyalties of Iraqi Poets

The evolution of many poets from pan-Islamism to Arab nationalism was a tortuous experience that left them exposed to bitter recriminations as they gravitated between pro-Ottoman, pro-British, and pro-Hashemite positions. The crisis of loyalty was driven less by ideological conflict than by divergent perceptions of the "ambiguities of the modern" and different visions of how to resolve the rupture with the past.⁶⁹ The decline of the panegyric and the invocation of new secular motifs of collective identity became symbols of the evolving conception of poetry in modern society. Poets mediated the relationship between the past and present in different ways, but as both pro-Ottoman and pro-British stances became untenable, the pro-Hashemite perspective promised to restore national unity between proponents of different modernist visions under the ambiguous ideological framework of Arab nationalism.

The political evolution from Ottomanism to Arabism was particularly pronounced in the Baghdadi poet Khayri al-Hindawi (1885–1957), an early supporter of the Committee for Union and Progress.[70] Like many other liberal intellectuals and poets, Hindawi slowly gravitated toward the Arab decentralization movement.[71] Concluding that the Young Turks were unwilling or incapable of enacting their own agenda, Hindawi argued that it was up to the Arabs to pursue their own visions of modernity. Despite his frustration with the CUP, Hindawi endorsed the Ottoman jihad in the vocabulary of secular nationalism, invoking the "new glories and the prestige of antiquity" that distinguished Arab "sons of Qahtan" from other nations.[72] His enthusiasm for the war paralleled that of the European futurists who pined for the cultural and spiritual regeneration of modernity.[73] Hindawi was briefly imprisoned for insubordination during the war, escaping only in the chaos of the British occupation. Recanting his past enthusiasm for war, Hindawi now yearned nostalgically for the "stagnation" and "age of immobility" violently displaced by modernity.[74]

Hindawi's experience was shared by Kazim al-Dujayli (1884–1970), a prominent contributor to both Egyptian and Iraqi Nahda periodicals. Dujayli shared Hindawi's disillusionment with the CUP and published a thinly veiled attack against these "oppressors of the people" in *al-Muqtataf* in 1913. The poem appealed to the CUP to satisfy Arab grievances and fulfill its revolutionary platform: "Create for [the Arabs] a true domain of equality / and the nation will open its heart in welcome / Treat them with kindness and justice so that they / and their wealth will be more than a ledger of profit."[75] Even this tepid critique was interpreted as a dangerous expression of sedition, earning Dujayli a six-year prison term. He was released from prison at the beginning of the war, but his "prison poems" preserved an intimate depiction of Ottoman despotism in Baghdad.[76] Like Hindawi, Dujayli's experience of war caused him to express ambivalence about modernity in postwar poems published in *al-Muqtataf* and *al-Hilal*.[77]

Many other poets gravitated toward Arabism after the executions in Damascus and Beirut and celebrated Sharif Husayn's declaration of the Arab Revolt in June 1916.[78] Muhammad Baqir al-Hilli, 'Abd al-Husayn al-Azri, Muhammad Mahdi al-Basir, Muhammad ʿAli al-Yaʿqubi, Munir al-Qadi, and others embraced the Hashemite cause as a symbolic expression of shifting political allegiances.[79] Many of these poets were Shiʿi mujtahids, and their support for the Hashemites was expressed in antisecular terms. Ironically, this religious orientation was shared by Maʿruf al-Rusafi, who continued to invoke pan-Islamic solidarity to *defend* the Ottoman Empire. Rusafi rejected the Arabist alliance with Britain, contrasting the triumvirates of the "Three Pashas" and the Triple Entente with a "third triumvirate" of Arab "traitors," the Egyptian politicians Husayn Kamil and Husayn Rushdi and Sharif Husayn. Rusafi condemned Husayn's alliance with Britain as a betrayal of Islam: "His *fitna* [temptation] did not slake his thirst for injustice / until he found refuge with the enemy of God / If he refrained today from working with England / the evil he has plotted and sown might lessen."[80]

In contrast to both Rusafi and the Shiʿi Arabists, Rashid al-Hashimi and Muhammad al-Hashimi embraced a more explicitly secular vision of Arab nationalism. The Hashimi brothers were born to a prominent family of Baghdadi poets and became engrossed in the intellectual and cultural currents of the Arab Nahda after the Ottoman Constitutional Revolution.[81] Rashid showed some ambivalence toward the Ottoman Empire before the war, but only in veiled language that echoed the Najafi dreams of modernity.[82] His younger brother Muhammad was more daring and caused a scandal when his first poem was published in the local newspaper *al-Riyadh*.[83] The poem complained of Arab-Turkish discord in a relatively anodyne call for pan-Islamic solidarity, but the fifteen-year-old poet was arrested and fined five lira by an Ottoman court. The scandal piqued the interest of Jamil Sidqi al-Zahawi, who sent the poem to Sayyid Talib al-Naqib, a wealthy Basra politician who perceived that cultivating the support of poets through traditional patronage could support his own political ambitions.[84] He funded Muhammad's education in Cairo, and the young poet repaid the favor with an effusive panegyric praising Sayyid Talib as the "Chief of Iraq."[85]

Rashid al-Hashimi remained in Baghdad at the beginning of the war and endorsed the Ottoman jihad, complaining of Iraqi lethargy in the face of British aggression in *Sada al-Islam*: "Has the Holy Qurʾan become merely a toy / in the hands of the children of whores and butchers?"[86] The executions in Beirut and Damascus, however, caused Rashid to embrace the Hashemite cause: "Here we are, here we are for you / we have risen to respond to the crime / This Sharif Husayn has unsheathed / a sword to fall upon their necks!"[87] Subsequent pro-Hashemite poems substituted the rhetoric of jihad with appeals to the "Arab Nation."[88] Rashid al-Hashimi eventually left Baghdad join the Hashemite movement, following Faysal from Mecca to Damascus and reciting dozens of nationalist poems at public rallies.[89]

Muhammad al-Hashimi was studying Arabic literature at the Egyptian University, but he embraced the Hashemite cause around the same time as his older brother did.[90] He was frustrated with Egyptian ignorance about Iraq and contributed a series of articles to *al-Muqtataf* that surveyed the physical geography of Baghdad, the landscape of the countryside, and local dialects and folk culture.[91] Both brothers used panegyrics to win Hashemite approval and elevate themselves into national spokesmen of Iraq. Muhammad praised the Hashemite officer ʿAbd al-ʿAziz ʿAli al-Misri and his commitment to martyrdom, claiming that "more preferable than the death of our souls / is the death that consumes our lifeless corpses."[92] Rashid also praised Misri and implored Iraqis to embrace the Hashemite cause.[93] After Misri's plot to resurrect the Ottoman alliance was uncovered, however, Rashid resorted the new ethnic chauvinism of Arab nationalism, mocking Misri's Circassian origins and asking, "When did ʿAbd al-ʿAziz become among us / an Arab who traces his roots to ʿAdnan?" "By God, if I were a foreigner like him," Rashid insisted, "throw me to mountains of Khuzestan!"[94]

Early support for the Hashemites was more symbolic than ideological, and Rashid al-Hashimi also wrote panegyrics for Ibn Saʿud.[95] Muhammad al-Hashimi denounced the Ottoman era as a "black page of history," but he soon questioned his support for the Anglo-Arab alliance.[96] His participation in the Egyptian Revolution of 1919 intensified his anticolonial sentiments and inspired a poem blaming Britain for the death of student protesters: "[Britain] shed our blood and corrupted the country / neither sparing the weak nor checking the greedy / Lord, what pharaoh is more oppressive than them? / Who has strayed further from justice for sake of oppression?"[97] He moved to Damascus, where he met the Najafi poet Muhammad Rida al-Shabibi and sought to cultivate a Sunni-Shiʿi political alliance. His invocation of the martyrdom of Imam Husayn in his poem about the Egyptian martyrs was largely addressed to Shabibi and his Najafi compatriots, a symbolic rather than ideological use of religious motifs.[98]

Muhammad Rida al-Shabibi and Muhammad Baqir al-Shabibi shared much in common with the Hashimi brothers. Muhammad Baqir also sparked controversy before the war when he published a poem in *al-Raqib* that asked rhetorically, "Have our eastern sons despaired of their East? / Is there not one among them now moved to treachery?" Ottoman authorities tried him for sedition, but he escaped punishment after Mahmud Shukri al-Alusi testified that "treachery" (*khaʾina*) meant "dissent" rather than "betrayal" in this context.[99] The scandal strengthened the Shabibi brothers' reputation as proponents of Arabism, and their recitation of martial poetry to the Middle Euphrates tribes further reinforced their Arabist credentials.[100] After the death of their mentor, Muhammad Saʿid al-Habbubi, however, Muhammad Baqir al-Shabibi recanted the rhetoric of jihad and denounced "the great massacre" of war in *al-Muqtataf*: "This very war, this grave source of evil / will it overflow its banks in the deluge of rain? / For the general rages against his soldiers / and the pilots ascend in their zeppelins / While the current overflows its banks."[101]

The Shabibi brothers enjoyed good relations with Britain before the Najafi uprising of March 1918, when local rebels assassinated a British officer.[102] Muhammad Rida al-Shabibi reflected on the uprising in his poem "Damascus and Baghdad," which marked the fall of Damascus to Britain on October 1, 1918.[103] Shabibi warned Faysal and the Syrians to heed the fate of Iraq and remain wary of British promises:

> This is what led [us] to offer the heritage of Babylon,
> the architecture of the caliphs and their walls of defense
> But they did not leave the walls of Najaf as they were,
> nor her structures as they stood when they first came
> Were it not for my concern for the fate of your country,
> by God, I would I sulk in anguish for the fate of my own![104]

The poem defended Hashemite supporters from charges of colonial collaboration by insisting that Ottoman railway concessions to Germany opened the country to foreign penetration: "They laid iron, but you were untroubled by the expanse / of these railway tracks that lay like shackles on our land

/ But these tracks of iron, twisted and intertwined / become a snare that trapped the honor of Iraq." Weeks later, Gertrude Bell reminisced about past encounters with the poet and expressed her confusion about his sudden turn against Britain: "I knew him in 1918, and then he suddenly went off in a huff (I never knew why) to the Hijaz and Syria, where he wrote very violent anti-British articles in the local press."[105] Bell's failure to comprehend the impact of British actions in Najaf reflected the myopia of colonialism, especially when Shabibi's poetry narrated his grievances with such clarity.

Shabibi's loss of faith was shared by ʿAbd al-Muhsin al-Kazimi, who had enthusiastically backed the Anglo-Arab alliance from exile in Cairo.[106] Shortly after the Balfour Declaration of November 1917, however, Kazimi asked bitterly, "The treaty is sacred to us, but I wonder about [the British] / are they, too, bound by their word in treaties? / Or do you suppose that while we fulfill our bargain / they have now discharged all their promises to us?"[107] Muhammad Mahdi al-Basir, who published pro-British poems in *al-ʿArab* and *Dar al-Salam* under the pseudonym "Ibn Babil," experienced similar disillusionment.[108] Basir contended that the Treaty of Versailles proved that British rhetoric was only intended to "hide the crescent in the shadow of the cross" and warned that "ink would soon be replaced by blood" in the Middle East, where[109] Muhammad Baqir al-Shabibi also condemned the colonial "propagandists of peace" and called on Eastern nations to "come together in struggle to reject the old order / and start working sincerely to safeguard peace."[110] Kazimi and others remained more optimistic about American support for national self-determination, reflecting the fleeting pro-American "Wilsonian moment."[111]

The tensions of Arab nationalism intensified after British officers arrested the Iraqi politician Yasin al-Hashimi in Damascus in November 1919. The hardline Arab nationalist was extremely popular in Syria, and his arrest provoked widespread strikes and demonstrations.[112] Maʿruf al-Rusafi, who came to Damascus along with other Arab refugees from Istanbul, was spotted in the crowds by British intelligence officers, reciting a poem that urged people to rise in rebellion:

Yasin, you have taken hold of our hearts
and become the protector of this dear nation

> They expelled you from the country with tricks,
> but the enraged people remain behind you. . . .
> In your name we rouse this country to rebellion,
> until the number of rebels fills her vast expanse
> Let us rise in fury and rage and determination,
> inspiring even the cowardly nobles who watch
> Together now, let us kindle a burning fire of rage
> until their heads are bowed before your sword![113]

British intelligence reports included an Arabic transcription of the poem, described as "an inflammatory, pan-Arab, revolutionary, anti-ally and especially anti-British qasida urging the people to revolt." The reports' attention to crowd reactions reflected growing colonial anxiety about the dangers of rebel poetry.[114] Less evident to British observers obsessed with pan-Islamic conspiracies was the fact that Rusafi and other poets had almost entirely abandoned the Islamic rhetoric of jihad in favor secular nationalism.

The Hashimi brothers also recited revolutionary poems in Damascus and Aleppo.[115] At Petra in June 1919, Rashid al-Hashimi reminded Hashemite troops that colonial powers were the "true enemy" and denounced the parochial ambitions of politicians who "chase after pennies."[116] Rashid became increasingly critical of Hashemite corruption and subservience and was arrested several weeks later after reciting a poem in Damascus declaring that the waters of the Tigris "would yet run with blood."[117] Muhammad al-Hashimi provoked his own poetry controversy in November 1919 by denouncing Faysal's faith in colonial promises: "You listen to voices from countries of the West / but here in the East you heard from witnesses / The sounds that reach your ears will not be / silenced until you rise in rage and rebellion."[118] Later that month, Muhammad invoked Woodrow Wilson's Fourteen Points to denounce British and French betrayal in a poem he recited to the Arab Club in Aleppo.[119]

The Hashemite struggle in Syria seemed to resolve the problem of divided loyalties in Iraq, as both pro-Ottoman and pro-British poets began embracing anticolonial rhetoric to support the Hashemite cause. 'Abd al-Rahman al-Banna' ("Ibn Ma' al-Sama'") called for an uprising in Syria and declared, "We signed our contract with [France] / with the blood of her noblest youths."[120] His anger was echoed by Muhammad Mahdi al-Basir ("Ibn Babil"), who addressed the Iraqi nation in a poem in *al-Lisan* in April 1920: "I am enslaved, just as they desired / are your, in this vast expanse, still free?"[121] It was it this point that Basir left Hilla for Baghdad to refashion himself as "the poet of the Iraqi revolution." Basir was strongly influenced by the revolutionary poems recited by Iraqi poets in Damascus, which now began to circulate inside Iraq. National pride in Iraqi contributions to the Hashemite cause influenced both the political content and public context of the new rebel poetry that echoed through public spaces in Iraq.

## Rebel Poetry and the Haydarkhana Salon

Basir arrived in Baghdad in late April 1920, weeks after the Syrian National Congress established an independent Arab Kingdom. The formal declaration of the British Mandate remained weeks away, but the British intent to remain in Iraq was obvious. Fearful of a national rebellion, British officials anxiously monitored the steady arrival of Najafi dissidents in Baghdad.[122] These activists viewed mosques as logical sites for coordination because of colonial reluctance to intervene directly in religious affairs, but the effort to secure spaces was obstructed by the subsidies that Britain distributed to mosque custodians. When Sheikh Ahmad Da'ud asked 'Abd al-Rahman al-Gaylani for permission to use the 'Abd al-Qadir al-Gaylani Shrine, for example, Gaylani rebuffed Da'ud and reported him to British authorities.[123]

Nationalist activism was coordinated by Haras al-Istiqlal, a secret society whose leaders included Sunni and Shi'i activists from Baghdad and Najaf.[124] The society organized a series of *mawlids*, Sunni rites celebrating the birth of the Prophet Muhammad, and *ta'ziyyas*, Shi'i rituals marking the martyrdom of the Imam Husayn, to coincide with the month of Ramadan. The two ceremonies were quite different in form and tone, the former cheerful and the latter somber, but both involved the recitation of religious poetry. Activists agreed to hold mawlids in Shi'i mosques and ta'ziyyas in Sunni mosques as a public demonstration of nationalist solidarity, which provoked serious anxiety among British officials.[125] These joint rituals were convened throughout Baghdad, but the Haydarkhana Mosque in central Baghdad became the symbolic center of the movement.[126] The fact that the poetry recited in these religious ceremonies invoked the secular vocabulary of nationalism represented another facet of "neoclassical modernity," as the content of secular modernity now permeated both classical forms of poetry and sacred spaces of religious worship.

Dozens of poets participated in the mawlid celebrations during and after the holy month Ramadan (May 19, 1920–June 17, 1920).[127] Muhammad Mahdi al-Basir was relatively unknown in Baghdad at the beginning of Ramadan but earned considerable notoriety shortly after his public appearance at the opening ceremony for the new Ahliyya secondary school on May 17. The event was designed to promote colonial benevolence, but Basir used the opportunity to challenge Iraqi leaders to resist colonialism: "There are no youths who would not stand firm / and there is no pride in turning to flee in fear / In the jungle, the lion's den will not be protected / From wolves if the lion does not pounce!"[128] His talent as poet and orator impressed other nationalists, and he was invited to participate in the mawlids. Basir later expressed his personal distaste for this type of "platform poetry"—poetry recited to large public audiences and generally connected to contemporary political events.[129] He contended, however, that such literary compromise was necessary because the Iraqi public was more responsive toward poetry than prose.[130]

Three days later, Basir recited the traditional Shi'i ta'ziyya lamentation at a local Sunni mosque. He was paired for the first of several dozen times with the blind Sunni poet Mullah 'Uthman al-Mosuli, a skilled mawlid reciter. The congregation flowed into the street, and British officials noted the sensational impact of Basir and 'Uthman, fretting that "the great object of these *mawluds* [sic] is to reach the lower classes, and excite them to take an interest in political affairs" and noting that "such a thing has never before occurred in Islam."[131] Colonial fears intensified after the May 23 mawlid at Haydarkhana Mosque, where Basir appealed for Sunni-Shi'i unity before the municipal employee 'Isa 'Abd al-Qadir recited a nationalist poem to the crowd of Sunni and Shi'i worshippers:

> Sons of the Two Rivers, descendants of nobility,
> wake up and listen to words of absolute certainty!
> We became separated into sects and we disagreed,
> and so we become, one and all, most contemptible

Until we surrendered ourselves, as a collective,
to a nation of tyrants, these despots of injustice!
They oppressed and tyrannized as they pleased,
for this is the mission of the oppressive tyrant!
But come now, wake yourselves, howl, and rebel,
and then begin, one and all, to cooperate again!¹³²

Iraqi informants emphasized the striking reaction of the crowds to the poem: "After his recitation, ['Abd al-Qadir] was carried shoulder high by the cheering crowd to where the Ulama and notables were waiting where he was congratulated and kissed by all present." Their reports recorded individual reactions, noting, for example, that the applause of Sheikh Ahmad al-Shaykh Da'ud was particularly "vociferous."¹³³

'Isa 'Abd al-Qadir was not a prominent poet, but British authorities moved swiftly to arrest him.¹³⁴ A. T. Wilson, the acting civil commissioner, described the poem as "dangerous to public order," a decision strengthened by unsubstantiated reports that 'Abd al-Qadir had "mentioned a white woman at Clock Tower Barracks in a suggestive way."¹³⁵ The *Haras al-Istiqlal* activist 'Ali al-Bazirgan gathered patrons of neighboring cafés and cinemas to march on the police station where the poet was detained, but when two armored cars tried to prevent their advance, one of the drivers panicked and crashed. Angry crowds threw stones at the disabled vehicle, and in the ensuing melee, the driver of the other car ran over and killed a deaf man, the opening salvo of the Iraqi Revolution of 1920. Ja'far Abu al-Timman, Muhammad Mahdi al-Basir, 'Ali al-Bazirgan, and Sheikh Ahmad al-Shaykh Da'ud were briefly detained the next day by the military governor, while 'Isa 'Abd al-Qadir was transferred to prison in Basra.¹³⁶

The mawlids continued in June and July, and Muhammad Mahdi al-Basir and Mullah 'Uthman repeatedly urged Sunni-Shi'i unity and appealed for Jewish and Christian support.¹³⁷ The two blind poet-preachers traveled between Sunni and Shi'i mosques in Baghdad, A'zamiyya, and Kazimiyya, sometimes together and sometimes separately, with Basir reciting the Shi'i ta'ziyya at Sunni mosques and 'Uthman reciting the Sunni mawlid at Shi'i mosques.¹³⁸ 'Uthman was skilled at crafting his appeals in the religious vocabulary of Shi'i veneration, declaring at a performance in Kazimiyya on

June 7 that "Abu Bakr and 'Umar are mournful / over the fate of the regent, Haydar ['Ali] / The angels of heaven and Gabriel / for his sake are vexed and troubled."[139] The Sunni poet Sayyid Habib al-'Ubadyi al-Mosuli expressed a similar message in another popular mawlid poem:

> The West has have done a most amazing thing,
> for we have known no ruler except ['Ali],
> And I swear by the Holy Quran and Gospel,
> we will not accept a protectorate in his place!
> If they try it, blood will flow like a torrent,
> For after the rule of ['Ali], husband of [Fatima],
> Are we to accept the English as rulers?![140]

The poem ended by imploring Iraqis, "Do not say Ja'fariyya and Hanifiyya / do not say Shafi'iyya and Zaydiyya / For we are united by Islamic Shari'a / which rejects Western protection [*wasiyya*]!"

Public appeals for national unity pressured reluctant notables to abandon their links to Britain. 'Abd al-Rahman al-Kaylani was induced to abandon his previous reluctance and permit a nationalist mawlid attended by Sunnis, Shi'a, Christians, and Jews at the 'Abd al-Qadir shrine on June 10.[141] Mullah 'Uthman and Munir al-Qadi recited nationalist poems, Christian leaders promised to return the hospitality of this "unprecedented spectacle," and all sides thanked Britain "for thus unwilling being the cause of such a union."[142] Basir urged attendees to reassure their Jewish brothers that their property would be protected in the event of an uprising.[143] The dramatic shift in public opinion was reflected in the local press, as journals like *Dar al-Salam* that once published pro-British poems now published invitations to the nationalist mawlid.[144] Cognizant of the fate of 'Isa 'Abd al-Qadir, mawlid participants struggled to balance nationalist fervor and their desire to avoid retribution, and on at least one occasion, Basir warned 'Abd al-Rahman al-Banna' and other poets to tone down their language. This warning reminded the crowd of the presence of spies in their midst, and one observer was denounced and beaten with shoes.[145]

The ability of poets to stir popular emotions was widely respected, but poets were not immune to fear of the masses. After three youths created panic in the market by spreading rumors that a revolt had begun, Muhammad

Mahdi al-Basir sternly warned that such provocations would undermine merchant support.¹⁴⁶ One report noted that "the danger of these *mawluds* [sic] lies in their appeal to the masses—and the certain amount of lawlessness and contempt of authority recently apparent can all be attributed to them."¹⁴⁷ This fear was pervasive, and one account of a poem recited by Basir described the boisterous reaction of crowds "who although they understand not a little of the political position of the day, find it novel and exhilarating to be able to shout without reproof against authority."¹⁴⁸ Another report on a Haydarkhana mawlid described the crowd as the "poor class of the people—coolies, coffee shop riff-raff, and most noteworthy, a goodly number of well known criminals."¹⁴⁹ Suspected spies were routinely beaten, and colonial authorities pointed to this violence in their desperate attempts to convince nationalist leaders to cancel the events.¹⁵⁰

Oratorical skill was highly valued at the mawlids, and accomplished poets like 'Abd al-Razzaq al-Hashimi and 'Ata Effendi al-Khatib had their poems recited by youths with stronger voices.¹⁵¹ Basir used his voice and charisma to elicit emotional responses from the crowds, which rewarded his efforts with donations to the nationalist cause.¹⁵² Tawfiq al-Mukhtar, an ex-Sharifian officer, recited poems that "reduced the audience to moans and tears," even as local informants scoffed that they "could hardly have been his composition."¹⁵³ The young colloquial poet Muhammad Hasan al-Haddad made little impression on Iraqi literary history, but his emotional verses made him a crowd favorite of the mawlid scene.¹⁵⁴ Haddad's poems "made many weep" with their "stirring and inflammatory speech," and crowds frequently "cheered loudly and called for it to be repeated."¹⁵⁵ He was flanked by another poet who shouted, "Long Live 'Abdullah and the Deputies!" after every verse to enthusiastic cheers.¹⁵⁶ Nationalist organizers recognized Haddad's popularity and asked him to address student groups and deliver political sermons.¹⁵⁷ Poetry excerpts appeared frequently in intelligence reports, but prose quotes did not, perhaps a reflection of the greater capacity of Iraqi informants to memorize verse. This feature of Iraqi culture also explains the broad national circulation of rebel poetry beyond mawlid audiences.¹⁵⁸

Poets frequently attacked informants, collaborators, and notables who showed insufficient support for the nationalist cause. Muhammad Hasan al-Haddad and 'Abd al-Rahman al-Banna' warned informants and collaborators of the retribution that loomed "after the revolution."[159] Mullah ʿUthman, ʿAbd al-Karim al-ʿAllaf, and ʿAta Effendi al-Khatib called on the people of Baghdad to emulate the tribal uprising in the Middle Euphrates, praising the resistance of Shiʿi tribes and mocking the hesitance of rival Sunni tribes, an indication of the new intersections of tribalism and nationalism.[160] The prominent Basra politician Sayyid Talib struggled to remain neutral during the revolution and ignored invitations to the Haydarkhana mawlid, but poets like ʿAbd al-Rahman al-Bannaʾ addressed him as though he were present and warned him of the fate of collaborators.[161] Kazim al-Dujayli damaged his reputation as a nationalist poet when he tried to facilitate a reconciliation, informing both Sayyid Talib and the nationalist leader Yusuf al-Suwaydi that the other wished to meet. Suwaydi discovered his subterfuge, and nationalist activists expelled Dujayli from the Haydarkhana Mosque when he appeared on August 5, informing him that the mawlid was for Muslims and "not for heretics"![162]

Though the attacks against Dujayli indicate the limits of secularism at this stage, the poetry of the mawlids nevertheless showed how new vocabularies of secular nationalism were facilitating the emergence of global anticolonial solidarities. After one "seditious speech" in July, ʿAbd al-Rahman al-Bannaʾ led the Haydarkhana crowd in the chant, "Long Live America and Her Consul!"[163] Several months later, as the revolution wound down, the nationalist leaders Sayyid Muhammad al-Sadr and Yusuf al-Suwaydi urged the American consul in Baghdad to intervene. Their narrative of the revolution began with ʿIsa ʿAbd al-Qadir's "patriotic" poem and subsequent arrest for "mentioning the past glory of Iraq [and urging] that the necessary steps be taken towards attaining our past greatness, which we enjoyed when we were united."[164] The arrest of the poet, they argued, caused the Iraqi people to organize a demonstration demanding their legal rights, and the British attack on these patriots in front of the Haydarkhana Mosque caused the ʿulama and tribes of southern Iraq to rise in defense of the urban crowds. While Sadr and Suwaydi were simply responding to the rhetoric about national self-determination in the spirit of the Wilsonian moment,[165] their transformation of the poem into the spark that lit the revolution nevertheless provided an instructive view of their faith in the political power of poetry.

## Poetry and the Tribal Uprising in the Middle Euphrates

The idea that ʿAbd al-Qadir's poem "caused" the Middle Euphrates tribal rebellion was both fanciful and illustrative of the contentious Iraqi debate about the 1920 Revolution. Tribalism and nationalism, however, were far less more antagonistic than is sometimes assumed, and poetry played a critical role even in the tribal dimension of the uprising. British and Iraqi accounts of the revolution have offered widely divergent claims about the role of urban nationalism, religious fatwas, tribal grievances, and foreign propaganda.[166] Most British accounts reflected Orientalist conceptions of the tribes as "noble savages" and assumed that Hashemite, Kemalist, or Bolshevik agents had incited the uprising.[167] Iraqi debates were more contentious, simmering beneath the surface of nationalist politics for nearly three decades before the publication of several memoirs in the 1950s.[168] The most enduring point of contention was the question of whether the tribes were organized and inspired by urban nationalists. While it is impossible to document the causal links between poetry and revolution, the rebel invocation of nationalist poetry suggests the importance of poetry to revolutionary culture in both Baghdad and the countryside.

The most important link between the urban nationalists and southern tribes was Sayyid Hadi Zwain, a tribal sayyid, and Haras al-Istiqlal, an activist from Hilla with close connections to the Shiʿi ʿulama. Zwain traveled to Baghdad in April 1920 to meet with other nationalist leaders, and he met secretly with Muhammad Mahdi al-Basir shortly after the arrest of the poet ʿIsa ʿAbd al-Qadir.[169] Zwain confided that the tribes would soon rise in rebellion and requested that Basir "say in the voice of the Baghdadi mujahidin some verses to awaken the zeal of the noble sons of the Middle Euphrates."[170] Basir responded with an improvised poem appealing to tribal honor and appealing for national solidarity: "Can Baghdad speak a word while she is a prisoner? / Can she remain silent about the freedom she desires? / Can our [Arab] cousins refrain from aiding [Iraq] / While [England] is preparing to tighten the noose?"[171] Zwain returned to Najaf and was "very energetic" in reciting the poem and promoting nationalist views to the tribal leaders of the Middle Euphrates.[172] His solicitation of nationalist poetry indicates the importance that he attached to poetry in the national liberation struggle, which seemed almost incomprehensible without poetry.

Poetry helped mobilize support for the tribal rebels in Baghdad, but its impact was limited by the British presence. In the Middle Euphrates, however, Najafi poets echoed the nationalist solidarity of the Baghdad mawlids and fused the symbolism of jihad with the secular rhetoric of Arab nationalism to rally support for the revolution.[173] Sayyid Qati' al-'Awwadi, a Najafi participant in the Haydarkhana mawlids, convinced Sayyid 'Alwan al-Yasiri and Sheikh 'Abd al-Karim al-Jaza'iri to convene a political meeting disguised as a traditional ta'ziyya at the Hindi Mosque in Najaf in early June.[174] Sayyid Muhammad Baqir al-Hilli recited a nationalist poem praising the Hashemites and denouncing British perfidy: "They demand a protectorate over Iraq / as if our sons had suddenly become orphans / They respect even the Jews and their right / is respected while that of the Muslims is neglected."[175] The poem's content was typical of this historical moment, but its recitation in the *husayniyya* (congregation hall) was striking, as the ta'ziyya ritual involved poetic elegies for Imam Husayn but never secular poetry. The eruption of applause in the sacred space of the husayniyya was a singular event that illustrated the novel political climate of the country.[176]

By the end of June, the rebel movement had spread from Najaf to the Middle Euphrates, and a group of prominent clerics and sheikh met at a tribal *mudhif* (guesthouse) in Mishkhab on June 28, 1920. Muhammad Baqir al-Hilli, whose poetic contributions were worth "hundreds of guns" according to one rebel leader, was again asked to recite a revolutionary poem.[177] The poem urged tribal sheikhs to remember British deception in India and Egypt and played to notions of tribal honor by warning of the "moment of betrayal."[178] Hilli reminded the Khaza'il sheikhs of the Prophet Muhammad's injunction against accepting Christian authority, and tribal delegates responded by drafting letters to fellow sheikhs urging them to join the rebellion. Sayyid Muhsin al-Yasiri carried the message to Sheikh Sha'lan Abu al-Jun in Rumaythah, arriving on July 1 only to find that Sha'lan had been arrested at noon the previous day and freed hours later when his tribesmen attacked the prison, sparking the tribal phase of the Iraqi Revolution.[179]

Poetry continued to foster tribal solidarity and encourage new tribes to join the rebellion, and some fragments of tribal poetry made their way into British intelligence files.[180] On one occasion, a female poet of the 'Awabid tribe improvised an attack on Sheikh 'Alwan al-Hajj al-Sa'dun of the Bani

Hasan, with whom the ʿAwabid had been feuding. The Saʿdun sheikhs were widely resented for their wealth and collaboration with Britain, and ʿAlwan's support for the revolution was ambivalent at best.[181] The poem compared ʿAlwan unfavorably to the poet's own sheikh, Marzuq al-ʿAwad: "Whoever is in touch with ʿAlwan, tell him / that his leadership amounts to the sale of shit / For our Marzuq swallows his insignificance / he was called protector and became salvation."[182] The verses were memorialized in the folk culture of southern Iraq, and while the poem did not force ʿAlwan to reverse course and embrace the revolution, it did show how poetry could be used to contest political legitimacy in both urban and rural areas.

In Najaf, the Shabibi brothers played particularly prominent roles in the Iraqi Revolution of 1920. Muhammad Rida al-Shabibi rallied tribal support in Nasiriyya and was delegated to seek Hashemite support for the uprising in the Hijaz.[183] He was impressed by the nationalism of Sharif Husayn and noted that his faith in Britain had been shaken by events in Syria.[184] The Najafi poet ʿAli al-Bazi memorialized the mission in verse, extolling the virtues of Husayn and Faysal and their implacable commitment to Arab independence and declaring that "Muhammad Rida al-Shabibi was been entrusted / to tell the tale of this historic partnership."[185] This faith in Hashemite opposition to colonialism might seem ironic in retrospect, but the Najafi delegation realized that the tribes required external support and that the anticolonial struggle would require simultaneous action on national and international fronts. While his older brother traveled to the Hijaz, Muhammad Baqir al-Shabibi remained in Najaf, where his recitation of nationalist poetry drew the attention of British authorities.[186] He soon began to circulate revolutionary pamphlets and produced five issues of the revolutionary newspaper *al-Furat* in late September and eight issues of *al-Istiqlal* in October, a critical contribution to the development of an independent national press.[187]

Ayatollah Muhammad Taqi al-Shirazi, the leading Shiʿi religious authority in Iraq, authorized the formation of a civic council in Karbala on July 26, 1920. Sayyid Muhsin Abu Tabikh was elected head of the revolutionary national government in Karbala three weeks later, with the support of both tribes and ʿulama. Abu Tabikh's authority was recognized at a public ceremony in early October, which brought tribal sheikhs, local notables, and urban nationalists like Yusuf al-Suwaydi, ʿAli al-Bazirgan, and Jaʿfar

Abu al-Timman to Karbala.[188] Sayyid Jamil Qutban recited a poem by the Karbala'i poet Khalil 'Azmi praising the Iraqi commitment to national liberation: "Our proud souls rejected injustice and oppression / and surrender to men who did not sire and raise us."[189] There was nothing particularly noteworthy about the poem, but the ceremony showed how ordinary civilians like 'Azmi and Qutban could use poetry as a way to participate in revolutionary culture.[190] This revolutionary movement, however, collapsed within a week after the arrival of reinforcements from India and the intensification of Britain's aerial bombing campaign.[191]

Iraqi nationalists greeted the collapse of the revolutionary movement with a mixture of pride, relief, regret, and resentment. Some religious scholars and tribal sheikhs who supported the revolution now sought to reconcile with colonial authorities, blaming their actions on the "incitement" of the urban nationalists.[192] In contrast, virtually all of the poets who participated in the revolution expressed pride in their actions and insisted that poetry had played a pivotal role in it. Muhammad Mahdi al-Basir bragged to one informant that *Haras al-Istiqlal* orchestrated the tribal rebellion, while 'Abd al-Karim al-'Allaf publicly boasted that it was inspired by the mawlid poems of Baghdad.[193] The poets who participated in the revolution attacked rivals who remained silent, including Jamil Sidqi al-Zahawi and Ma'ruf al-Rusafi. 'Ali al-Sharqi, who participated in the initial rebel meetings in Najaf, was conspicuously silent after the tribal uprising began, and his reputation now suffered as a result.[194]

A. T. Wilson was dismissed as civil commissioner just as the revolution began to collapse in late September 1920 and replaced by Percy Cox, the first high commissioner of the British Mandate. Just before leaving the country, Wilson reflected on the origins of the revolution at a farewell ceremony in Basra hosted by Sayyid Talib al-Naqib and emphasized the role of poets: "In modern times, their influence has been strengthened to the point that they have become more capable, in their spirits and their doctrines, of affecting souls more deeply than any material truths or government agents."[195] Wilson may have been trying to evade responsibility for his own policy failures, but Muhammad Mahdi al-Basir cheered his acknowledgment of the political power of poetry. Poetry did not merely a represent political attitudes and historical events but instead inspired and shaped the cultural construction of revolutionary attitudes and actions, placing poetry "on equal footing with the revolution itself."[196]

## Conclusion

The importance of poetry to the rebel movement was linked to the revolutionary transformation of public space during the events of 1920. Ottoman oppression had largely confined poets to the private spaces of salon gatherings, and while the British occupation once again freed them to publish political poems in newspapers and journals, this freedom was limited by colonial authorities to a narrow range of permissible subjects and opinions. The decline of old patronage models and the public backlash to colonial collaboration simultaneously weakened the panegyric as a poetic genre and strengthened the poetry of incitement as an expression of public dissent. As the rebel movement gained momentum over the course of 1920, Sunni mosques, Shi'i husayniyyas, and tribal mudhifs were transformed into public spaces where the rebel poetry of poets like Basir articulated popular demands and inspired violent resistance.

The significance of this new rebel poetry of public spaces was not limited to the immediate public demands expressed in verse, but also extended to the new secular motifs and discourses that now initiated the secularization of the Iraqi public sphere. The political content of poems and the social context of the spaces in which they were recited became mutually constitutive of the new secular modernity articulated and enacted in the spirit of the anticolonial rebellion. Just as the physical space of mosques and husayniyyas magnified the public reach of rebel poetry, the political cooptation of sacred space and sacred rituals like the mawlid and ta'ziyya brought the modernist discourses of secular poets into greater dialogue with religious publics and further transformed popular understandings of public space. The blurred lines of the religious and the secular in the rebellion hinted toward the new political structures and cultural discourses of anticolonial nationalism that would emerge during the British Mandate.

The political implications of the secularization of language and space were particularly apparent in the gradual shift of political loyalties expressed in poetry. The contentious rivalries between the Ottomanist and Arabist camps dissolved in the face of the new colonial enemy, which inspired a new anticolonial discourse that unified the old proponents of pan-Islamic and nationalist ideologies. Particularly notable in this regard was Maʿruf al-Rusafi, whose slow evolution from Ottomanism to Arab nationalism began with the recitation of rebel poetry in the revolutionary crucible of Damascus in late 1919. The revolutionary convictions of secular nationalism were inherently linked to the dreams of secular modernity that emerged in the late Ottoman period in both discursive content and spatial orientation. Over the coming decade, dozens of young provincial poets from Najaf and the surrounding cities would reenact the journey of Muhammad Mahdi al-Basir from Hilla to Baghdad on their own journeys to satisfy the "longing of the preacher for the congregation" in the urban landscape of nationalist politics.

( CHAPTER 3 )

# DOUBLE-EDGED PRAISE
## *Patronage, Power, and Panegyric, 1920–1932*

Percy Cox arrived at Baghdad West Railway Station on October 11, 1920, to assume his position as the first high commissioner of the British Mandate. He was greeted by a contingent of colonial officers and local dignitaries, but the star of the reception was Jamil Sidqi al-Zahawi, who hailed Cox as the savior of the nation: "Come back to Iraq and reform what is rotten / disperse justice and bring prosperity to the people!"[1] Zahawi criticized those who participated in the recent uprising and insisted that their actions did not reflect popular opinion: "They said that the revolution would bring happiness / to the people, but we see that they are not happy / How unfortunate is this strife of blind rebels / that tormented the bodies and souls of her sons!" He appealed to imperialist nobility, asking Cox to "be firm with this people" and heal a nation "still throbbing from the fever of revolution." Embracing the role of enlightened colonizer, Cox replied in Arabic that he sought only to oversee the emergence of an autonomous Arab government.[2]

The esteemed British orientalist Gertrude Bell, who was then serving the colonial administration as Oriental secretary in Baghdad, cheered the performance of "Jamil Zuhair [sic], the famous Baghdad orator."[3] Most Iraqi poets, however, fumed at his betrayal of the nation.[4] Muhammad Mahdi al-Basir pointed to Zahawi's praise for the rebellion in an earlier elegy for martyrs in Rumaytha as evidence his political opportunism.[5] Basir mocked both Zahawi and Cox in a satirical poem published in the Baghdadi newspaper *al-Istiqlal*:

> The dove turned to the hawk and said to him,
> "I suffer because you have occupied my nest,
> I need to know if you are an honorable guest,"
> and then he turned on his heel, ready to fight,
> But the hawk said, "Not to worry, my friend!
> Rest assured that a real wealth of intelligence
> Has now come to rest in your very nest, but
> in order for me to properly regulate its affairs,
> I will naturally need to turn a healthy profit,
> which will of course drive you back to poverty . . . "[6]

Gertrude Bell was responsible for press surveillance, but she had difficulty understanding poetry and missed the metaphor.[7] ʿAbd al-Husayn al-Azri (1880–1954), a fellow rebel poet of 1920, attacked Zahawi more directly in a poem that circulated among the political exiles in Henjam: "Where can you turn to appeal for relief / when your refuge is the source of suffering? / If the stranger's whip brings you pain / the treachery of your own kin stings worse."[8] Zahawi insisted until his death that he was the true victim of this "treachery" but nevertheless came to regret the panegyric.[9]

The furor over Zahawi's poem demonstrated how competing concerns of patronage and popularity began to transform Iraqi poetry during the British Mandate (1920–1932). The anarchy of 1920 convinced Zahawi that colonial support was necessary to support social reform, and he viewed poetry as a vehicle for securing patronage.[10] Most poets, however, viewed colonial patronage as collaboration and instead cultivated popular approval in their poems. Though many shared Zahawi's modernist vision of social and political reform, they believed that this dream of modernity could only be attained under cover of popular anticolonial politics. These tensions of patronage and popularity forced poets to make difficult decisions about how to reconcile modernity and authenticity in their relationship with the Hashemite monarchy.

The dilemmas of anticolonial modernity were symbolized by the tenuous revival of the panegyric during the British Mandate. The British occupation destroyed old patronage networks and allowed new forms of rebel poetry to fill the cultural vacuum, but surveillance and censorship of poetry intensified after the collapse of the Iraqi Revolution of 1920. Colonial officials remained wary of the public danger posed by anticolonial popular poetry.[11] When Faysal became the first king of Iraq, he sought to harness the power of poetry by cultivating the support of court poets whose panegyrics strengthened the bond between poetry and politics.[12] Poets competed for access to financial stipends, state employment, parliamentary seats, and cabinet posts in the Hashemite Kingdom.[13] Their enduring concern for popular opinion, however, caused them to portray the political elites they praised as the anticolonial leaders of their own fantasies, making their panegyrics into "dangerously double-edged" expressions of public praise.[14] Poetry became a public register of cultural authenticity and perilous political game whose stakes were intensified by whispered accusations of collaboration.

The gradual alienation of popular poets from the Hashemite state during the waning years of the British Mandate inspired new forms of mass politics and popular mobilization. The vibrant cultural politics of anticolonialism were animated by poets who inspired increasingly radical and subversive challenges to the social structures and cultural institutions that sustained colonial rule. Daring articulations of modernity brought these poets into conflict with the custodians of religious tradition and inspired new visions of secular modernity. As in other parts of the colonized world, women's bodies became critical symbols and sites of contestation in both the quest for modernity and the struggle against colonialism.[15] The culture wars of the colonial era left many youths disillusioned with the oppressive social and cultural atmosphere of the colonial state. Anticolonialism became a catalyst for social reform, inspiring poets to pursue their project of "enunciating a new political consciousness" of modernity.[16]

## Prologue to Patronage Wars

While Zahawi endured attacks from fellow poets in Baghdad for praising the virtues of colonialism, his rival, Maʿruf al-Rusafi, was ensnared in a similar scandal in Jerusalem. Their experiences showed the social ramifications of colonial patronage, which became synonymous with collaboration and betrayal. The colonial panegyric was stillborn, and anticolonial concerns continued to transform the nature of panegyrics for local elites. Panegyrics had to satisfy popular expectations by praising the resistance of their subjects to colonialism, but the portrayal of elites as more rebellious than they actually were became subversive and dangerous, burdening patrons with the weight of popular expectations they could not bear.

Rusafi moved from Istanbul to Damascus after the war and participated in public demonstrations against the imposition of colonial mandates on the Arab provinces of the Ottoman Empire. He left Syria shortly after the collapse of Faysal's Arab Kingdom but chose to move to Jerusalem rather than return to Baghdad in the midst of the 1920 Revolution. Rusafi quickly won the patronage of the mayor of Jerusalem, Raghib al-Nashashibi, and recited anti-Zionist poems to thousands of Palestinian youths.[17] His popularity in Palestine, however, collapsed in a scandal that began with a lecture in December 1920 about the history of Islamic Spain delivered by Abraham Shlomo Yehuda, a prominent Jewish historian of Iraqi origin.[18] Herbert Samuel, the British high commissioner of Palestine, was present and announced his intent to aid the resurrection of classical Arab civilization by establishing an Arab college in Jerusalem.[19] Nashashibi asked Rusafi to respond to Samuel, and the poet obliged five days later with a poem that praised Yehuda's lecture and Samuel's pledge to "restore what the hand of time has taken" from the Arabs. He insisted that "it is not true what the other have alleged / that we hate the nation of Israel in public or in private" and described Jews and Arabs as "cousins" who share a "kinship of their tongues." The poem concluded, however, by reiterating opposition to Zionist colonization: "But we [Arabs] remain afraid of expulsion, exile, and / the policies of a state that seized our nation by force."[20] Despite the pointed warning of the final verse, Samuel sent a memo asking editors of local Arabic newspapers to publish the poem.[21]

Most editors complied, but they emphasized the compulsory nature of the request to their readers. Many newspapers included a transcription of the memo above the poem, which worked to portray Rusafi as a colonial collaborator.[22] Even editors sympathetic to Rusafi were unwilling to defend the poem, instead defensively noting his previous criticism of Zionism.[23] The editor of *al-Karmil* printed the poem alongside a retort from Wadiʿ Bustani, which challenged Rusafi's vision of Arab-Jewish harmony by contrasting

Palestinian attitudes toward their Mizrahi "cousins" and the new Ashkenazi immigrants:

> Your poetry is truly unique among the pearls of speech,
> and in the sea of poetry you are truly the master of pearls
> But this sea you have entered is the sea of politics,
> where truth rises with the tide but recedes with the ebb
> The one who crossed the Jordan River was our cousin,
> but we are suspicious of the one who now comes by sea[24]

The poem satirized Rusafi's praise for Samuel: "Are you really our old Samaw'al of yesterday? / Is the land of England now ruled by Banu Fihr? / Should we place our faith in Balfour after Muhammad / and Jesus and Moses, or Aaron who bore his sin?"[25] Invoking the Arab Jewish warrior Samaw'al b. 'Adiya' and the Banu Fihr (Quraysh), Bustani reminded Rusafi that the problem in Palestine had less to do with communal coexistence than colonial relations of power.

Rusafi defended himself, claiming that his poem was not naive flattery but instead intended to amplify pressure on Samuel.[26] Emphasizing his long commitment to social reform and national liberation, Rusafi published several poems about the responsibility of poets.[27] His defense of the double-edged panegyric, simultaneously praising and threatening, failed to repair Rusafi's reputation in Palestine, and so the poet accepted an invitation to return to Baghdad and edit a new anti-Hashemite newspaper funded by Sayyid Talib al-Naqib and 'Abd al-Rahman al-Kaylani. By the time he arrived in Baghdad, however, Rusafi discovered that Sayyid Talib had been exiled to Ceylon, and Kaylani had lost interest in the project.[28]

## Iraqi Poets and the Hashemites

When Rusafi arrived in Baghdad in April 1921, the Iraqi press was consumed by the debate on the Hashemite claim to the throne. When Britain accepted the League of Nations mandate to govern Iraq at the San Remo Conference in April 1920, British officials still intended to govern the country along the colonial model established by the India Office.[29] The Iraqi Revolution of 1920 demonstrated the impossibility of this dream, forcing Britain to accede to public demands and establish an Iraqi national government under the rule of King Faysal (1921–1932), the son of Sharif Husayn and commander of the Arab Revolt who was expelled from Syria by France at the end of July 1920.[30] His expulsion presented both a dilemma and an opportunity for British officials, who felt they owed Faysal for his service during the war and believed that he could simultaneously mollify local opinion, restore stability, and protect colonial interests in Iraq.[31] Britain proceeded cautiously to avoid giving Iraqis the impression that he was a British puppet, but Faysal was given assurances that Britain "would offer no obstacles to his selection" for the Iraqi throne at the Cairo Conference on March 12, 1921.[32] While Faysal returned to the Hijaz to prepare for the campaign, his Iraqi allies, Jaʿfar al-Askari and Nuri al-Saʿid, worked to consolidate the support of local political elites.[33]

Iraqis were divided about whether the coronation of Faysal represented the triumph or defeat of the 1920 Revolution.[34] The fact that Faysal traveled to Basra aboard a Royal Navy cruiser lent credence to the latter view for Maʿruf al-Rusafi, a longstanding critic of the Anglo-Hashemite alliance. Rusafi announced his preference for "an enlightened Iraqi" alternative to Faysal in *al-ʿIraq* before losing the courage of his convictions three days later and denying that he was the "Rusafi" who wrote the letter.[35] Most poets viewed Faysal's arrival as a triumph, pointing to the presence of amnestied rebels like Muhammad al-Sadr and Yusuf al-Suwaydi alongside Faysal.[36] When the entourage arrived in Basra on June 23, 1921, Faysal was serenaded by panegyrics from dozens of Iraqi poets.[37] Kazim al-Dujayli, whose appeal for moderation led to his expulsion from the Haydarkhana rebel poetry scene, sought to reclaim his reputation by linking himself to Faysal.[38] He praised the uprising of 1920 and urged Faysal to lead Iraq to independence: "Iraq sacrificed so many souls for your sake / so come and redeem your cousins from captivity."[39] Faysal appreciated the poem, which seemed to confirm his view of the political utility of poetry.[40]

Faysal's appreciation of poetry increased during his tour of Iraq, as he came to see the panegyrics recited for him in nearly every city and village as an expression of the popular will.[41] He also came to perceive the danger of poetry, however, as other poets challenged his claim to represent the triumph of the revolution. Muhammad Baqir al-Shabibi insisted in Najaf that the Arab "revolution of liberation and emancipation" remained unfulfilled and emphasized Iraqi expectations that Faysal would provide "a safe and loyal hand that would watch over the independence of our country and our interests and our national [*qawmiyya*] and patriotic [*wataniyya*] goals."⁴² Faysal was startled by Shabibi's tone, which he called "dangerously double-edged to the verge of hostility."⁴³ In the following weeks, many poets invoked this "dangerously double-edged" praise to warn Faysal against betraying popular expectations of national liberation.⁴⁴ Shabibi recited another threatening panegyric for Faysal in Baghdad and reinforced these warnings in the political poems he published in the nationalist newspaper *al-Dijla*.⁴⁵

Faysal received a warmer reception in Baghdad, where Khalil Amin declared, "We have invited you to become our king / and will accept no substitute even for a day." The crowd applauded and demanded that he repeat the verse over and over again as they chanted, "We have pledged allegiance to your kingship!"⁴⁶ Jamil Sidqi al-Zahawi had previously shown little interest in the Hashemite cause, but he now declared allegiance to Faysal: "I stand before you to hand to you, King / the throne chosen for you by the King of Heaven / The throne of Iraq is the bond of this country / pledged to you by the people and their Allies." Faysal reciprocated the gesture, praising Zahawi as "one of the most effective agents in the revival of science and literature in these lands."⁴⁷ Muhammad Hasan Kubba described Faysal as "the Napoleon of the ʿAdnanis and Bismarck of the Qahtanis," and Muhammad Baqir al-Hilli declared, "If the East were blessed after Muhammad / with another Prophet, it would be you!"⁴⁸ However slavish their praise, Faysal was thrilled with the performances and expressed his gratitude to the poets.⁴⁹

Faysal began using patronage to secure the allegiance of popular poets, offering Maʿruf al-Rusafi a position in the Ministry of Education on July 3, 1921.⁵⁰ Four days later, Rusafi expressed his gratitude at the home of his old patron, ʿAbd al-Rahman al-Kaylani, ironically explaining his conversion as the product of his new commitment to "social" rather than "individual" interests and reciting a poem of reconciliation to enthusiastic applause.⁵¹ Percy Cox was in the audience, and though he was unaware of Rusafi's identity, he noted his appreciation for this "oriental practice" of using poetry to forge political alliances.⁵² While Rusafi's performance reflected the material benefits of patronage, Jamil Sidqi al-Zahawi solicited Faysal's support for cultural revival in a poem about ʿAbbasid Baghdad, where "civilization was constructed," that he recited on the ruins of Mustansariyya University. Zahawi implored Faysal to show Britain the true spirit of Eastern awakening: "Westerners, I see now upon the horizon / of the easterners a faint light gleaming / Perhaps it heralds the break of dawn / a new day most radiant to our eyes!"[53] Days later, the state announced plans to revive the university and appointed Rusafi to the curriculum committee.[54] Rusafi and Zahawi began competing in their praise of Faysal, drawing considerable press attention. Zahawi was more obsequious than Rusafi, promising Faysal that all Iraqis stood as "slaves to your crown."[55] At the same event, Rusafi recited a poem whose "tedious verses were thought [by Faysal] not to have been sufficiently sympathetic."[56]

Faysal faced more immediate danger with the "dangerously double-edged" praise of rebel poets.[57] Veterans of the Haydarkhana scene recited poems in praise of rebel leaders Sayyid Muhammad al-Sadr and Yusuf al-Suwaydi in July 1921, and the editor of *Lisan al-ʿArab* announced his intent to publish a poetry collection about the Arab Revolt and Iraqi Revolution. The suggestion of a link between the two rebellions was subversive, as Britain sought credit for the former while repudiating the latter.[58] This tension between colonial and anticolonial visions of nationalist history intensified during public debates. A meeting of notables in Baghdad devolved into chaos when anticolonial nationalists denounced Faysal's subservience to Britain. The "agent of provocation" was Muhammad Mahdi al-Basir, the "blind poet who was responsible for the most stirring of the revolutionary odes read in the mosques last summer and has recently emerged from the imprisonment which he earned by his connection with the *Istiqlal* newspaper."[59]

## Nationalist Poets and the Hashemite Monarchy

Iraqi poets continued to produce "dangerously double-edged" praise in both public performances and press publications. In addition to *al-ʿArab*, which was renamed *al-ʿIraq* in May 1920, several new newspapers appeared in Baghdad in late 1920 and early 1921, including *al-Dijla*, *al-Fallah*, *al-Istiqlal*, and *al-Rafidan*.[60] Numerous editors and journalists associated with these papers were vocal anticolonialists, including Sami Khunda of *al-Rafidan* and Hasan al-Ghasibah of *al-Dijla*.[61] They understood the importance of poetry in the cultural politics of anticolonialism and recognized that poetic symbolism and metaphors often eluded the grasp of colonial authorities.

Muhammad Mahdi al-Basir was particularly effective at using poetry in this subversive manner, avoiding punishment for the dozens of nationalist poems he published in *al-Istiqlal* in fall 1920.[62] Gertrude Bell missed the significance of the threats in these poems due to her limited comprehension of Arabic poetry. When Basir began attacking Britain more explicitly in December 1920, he reverted to his old pseudonym, "Ibn Babil." One of these poems drew Bell's attention, and she clumsily translated a long excerpt in her intelligence report.[63] It was the same poem that Basir recited repeatedly at the Haydarkhana mawlids.[64] Although Bell had written extensive reports about the impact of that poem and the danger of Muhammad Mahdi al-Basir just months before, she failed to recognize that "Ibn Babil" was in fact Basir.[65]

Rashid al-Hashimi and Muhammad al-Hashimi joined the newspapers *al-Dijla* and *al-Rafidan* and became embroiled in a number of poetry scandals.[66] Rashid rebuked Ma'ruf al-Rusafi and the "Iraq for the Iraqis" camp for their parochialism and insisted that only the Hashemites could restore national unity.[67] One of his poems imagined the anarchy and chaos of the insular "Iraqi" government that Rusafi envisioned.[68] Several weeks later, however, Rashid expressed his own "double-edge" praise for Faysal, lauding his courage and eloquence but criticizing his deference to Syrian tribes as political weakness.[69] Rashid grew more audacious in the coming months, and at a public ceremony at the Persian School in Baghdad in August 1921, he rose uninvited to recite a poem that subversively called on Faysal to liberate Syria and Lebanon.[70] Gertrude Bell praised Faysal for cleverly "professing to have forgotten [Rashid's] name" and urging Iraqis "to confine themselves to the problems of their own State."[71] Local press accounts, however, described Faysal rebuking the poet by name.[72] At a banquet in Kazimiyya organized by Sayyid Muhammad al-Sadr several weeks later, Rashid congratulated Faysal on his coronation with a pointed qualification: "if you have come in order to liberate [Baghdad]."[73] He stared defiantly at Faysal as he lectured the new king about the danger of colonial alliances:

> Leader of the People, do not corrupt this leadership

and do not seize for yourself the rope of this covenant
Set your sights upon Syria and embed firmly in her head
the lance of Iraq and her neighboring environs in Tikrit
What can I say to that nation among us that has broken
a treaty we considered settled, despite our complaints?[74]

Hashimi fled immediately after he finished reciting the poem and altered the offending verses in *al-Dijla* the next day in order to protect himself from arrest.[75]

The Hashimi brothers embarrassed Faysal again by participating in a memorial ceremony for ʿAbd al-Majid Kanna on September 23, 1921.[76] Kanna, a member of the nationalist society Haras al-Istiqlal, had been hung the previous year for plotting to assassinate local collaborators, and dozens of anticolonial poets now recited poems to honor his sacrifice.[77] Unlike the other poets, Muhammad al-Hashimi had been in Syria during the revolution, but he now sought to inscribe himself into it. He described martyrdom and independence as the desire of all nationalists and promised Kanna, "You achieved the first of the two wishes / and I will pursue the latter until my dying days."[78] The poem brought the crowd to tears, and his brother Rashid wrote a "glowing account of the ceremony" in the new nationalist newspaper, *al-Rafidan*.[79] Muhammad al-Hashimi was a palace employee, and British complaints about his poem earned him a "several rebuke" from Faysal.[80] Three months later, Muhammad published a more veiled poem about a child orphaned by the uprising of 1920, denouncing the greed of the political elite and complaining that "the wealthy now live in opulence / while we dwell in hunger and misery."[81] While the poem aroused only minor interest from colonial officials, the social critique linking class grievances to anticolonial politics would become increasingly prominent over the coming decades.[82]

Colonial anxiety about dissident poetry led to the censorship of nationalist newspapers, and *al-Rafidan* proudly announced in its masthead that it had been suspended six times by the Ministry of Interior.[83] Though the paper published numerous poems linking the Iraqi struggle to national liberation movements in Egypt, Turkey, India, and Ireland, Rashid al-Hashimi's poems attacking rival poets as colonial collaborators were seen as particularly "irresponsible and mischievous."[84] Muhammad Mahdi al-Basir and ʿAbd al-Rahman al-Banna' were imprisoned after publishing anticolonial poems in *al-Istiqlal* in February 1921.[85] Even ostensibly pro-British newspapers like *al-'Iraq* began soliciting poems that condemned both colonialism and collaboration from rebel poets like Basir and Khayri al-Hindawi.[86]

Basir attempted to revive the spirit of rebel poetry at a demonstration marking the anniversary of Faysal's coronation on August 23, 1922.[87] Ten thousand Iraqis chanted against colonialism as he spoke, leading Percy Cox to order his arrest and deportation to Henjam.[88] The nationalist newspapers *al-Rafidan*, *al-Mufid*, and *al-Dijla* were suspended, eliminating the press platform for rebel poetry.[89] Basir was allowed to return only after renouncing politics, and the Hashimi brothers found that they could publish their poems only in foreign newspapers.[90] Journalism was not very lucrative in Baghdad, and the brothers appealed to the Ministry of Education to employ Iraqis like themselves instead of foreigners.[91] These appeals were ironic, given Rashid al-Hashimi's past denunciation of the "Iraq for the Iraqis" movement, but they symbolized the pervasive disillusionment of nationalist poets. "They said that a country had risen anew / with the aid of their policies and treaties," Muhammad al-Hashimi complained in one poem, "But they cheated us of our proper role / saying this is the fate of a subjugated race."[92]

### The Ruba'iyat of Jamil Sidqi al-Zahawi

Unlike the rebel poets of Baghdad, Jamil Sidqi al-Zahawi believed that poets should reject partisan politics and devote themselves to social reform and intellectual liberation. He accepted employment in the colonial administration after the fall of Baghdad in 1917, but public opinion turned against his collaboration only after his infamous panegyric for Percy Cox.[93] Zahawi later protested that the poem was only a plea for stability, but he wrote at least three other poems critical of the rebellion.[94] When he could no longer stand the public criticism, Britain gave him permission to leave for Egypt with his government stipend.[95] Zahawi decided to remain in Baghdad, publishing poems in Egyptian periodicals like *al-Hilal* and reciting countless panegyrics for Faysal in 1921.[96] Faysal asked Zahawi to establish a new literary journal in September 1921, but their relationship soured, and Zahawi was stripped of his government stipend.[97]

Zahawi responded to this turn of fortune in a series of quatrains modeled on the famous *Ruba'iyat* (quatrains) of 'Umar al-Khayyam, which he later translated from Persian to Arabic.[98] Beginning in December 1921, these poems appeared beneath the *al-'Iraq* masthead every morning for several weeks.[99] While Zahawi's later quatrains echoed Khayyam's philosophical and scientific interests, the poems in *al-'Iraq* addressed social and political matters.[100] The poems never explicitly criticized Faysal, but they reflected Zahawi's disillusionment with politics: "The sword ruled over the people / but it did not rule their hearts / For the sword has several properties / both meritorious and disgraceful."[101] One poem blamed social strife on the greed of political elites: "I believe that misery is the measure / by which to judge the joys of life / And I view the huts that stand beside / these opulent palaces as painful groans."[102] Most were addressed to his fictitious lover, Layla, a metaphor for the Iraqi nation.[103] Zahawi melodramatically described Layla's cruelty toward him, but he occasionally expressed optimism that he could win back her affection.[104]

Gertrude Bell noted that the poems were "attracting much interest" in Baghdad and began (poorly) translating them in intelligence reports.[105] Faysal worried that the poems were damaging his reputation and tried to buy Zahawi's silence by making him historian laureate and palace poet, but Zahawi rejected the latter post, insisting that he would write panegyrics only on his own terms.[106] Faysal refused to separate the offers, and Zahawi disengaged entirely from politics, publishing only "intellectual" poems.[107] He developed his own cartography of the Arab Nahda, describing Egypt as the most enlightened nation, followed at a distance by Syria and Iraq, and then the remaining Arab countries "still slumbering in a nighttime of gloomy ignorance without a single star in their sky." This hierarchal vision of enlightenment reflected his belief that "the tide of knowledge rises in the West / while that tide is now ebbing in the East." Zahawi also argued that Arabic poetry "must imitate the example of European poetry while preserving the purity of Arabic poetics."[108] It was precisely the vision of modernity that the young Najafis had worked so hard to challenge in the late Ottoman era.

Zahawi's appeal for imitation did little to burnish his waning reputation in Iraq or the Arab world. His inability to navigate the shifting cultural politics of modernity was particularly apparent during his tour of Egypt in 1924, when he recited poems about modern science and contemporary events.[109]

Most Egyptian poets showed little interest, but Ibrahim al-Mazini wrote to a Baghdadi newspaper that Zahawi's poetry "shocks me and raises doubts in me about his abilities and makes think that the man must have been better than this as a poet."[110] Mazini was a romantic poet and found the contrast between Zahawi's modernist ideas and stale neoclassical aesthetics insufferable.[111] Stung by the criticism of his poetic form, Zahawi renewed his commitment to avant-garde content, reciting a poem questioning the resurrection of souls that infuriated conservative ʿulama and forced him to flee Egypt.[112]

Zahawi finally found a suitable patron in Prime Minister ʿAbd al-Muhsin al-Saʿdun, an astute lover of poetry who appointed the poet to the Iraqi Senate in 1925. Zahawi celebrated this long-awaited national recognition of his own importance with the familiar trope of Layla: "The specter of Layla came in the descent of poetry / becoming one with me after separation and absence / When my eyes fell upon her they shed tears of joy / my heart grew lighter and began dancing in my breast."[113] He attributed his decision to return to Baghdad from Cairo to his patriotic devotion to his beloved Iraq.[114] Zahawi continued to insist that content rather than form was the essence of poetry and modernity and mocked critics who believed that "the essence of poetry is ordered expression / even when that expression is devoid of thought." He argued that "true" poetry required rupture with the past, asking rhetorically, "Can two poets really ever share the same rank / when one represents the past and the other the present?"[115] His own rebellion against the past was reflected in poems challenging Islamic orthodoxy, expressing skepticism about the resurrection of souls and the existence of hell.[116] Describing himself as the original "modernist poet" (*al-shaʿir al-ʿasri*), Zahawi rescinded his call to imitate European poetry, declaring that "imitation is objectionable, whether it is imitation of the classical Arab poets or the modern Western poets."[117] Zahawi again published experimental blank verse poems, this time explicitly linking avant-garde content to formal experimentation to articulate his vision of the Eastern awakening in unrhymed fashion.[118]

Zahawi's experience of patronage as intellectual liberation was short-lived: he lost his Senate seat after his patron, ʿAbd al-Muhsin al-Saʿdun, committed suicide in 1929.[119] Maʿruf al-Rusafi and Anwar Shaʾul joined Zahawi in mourning Saʿdun, who was popular among Iraqi poets for both his patronage of their work and his courage in resisting British dictate.[120] Zahawi's optimism vanished, and his poetry once again became as despondent as it had been in the days when his *ruba'iyat* (a quatrain) graced the front page of local newspapers.[121] He now refashioned himself as an anticolonial nationalist, claiming that Britain had driven Sa'dun to suicide and that the Anglo-Iraqi Treaty of 1930 was a betrayal of the nation: "They stabbed you, my beloved country / stabbed your breast until you died / It was your own sons who killed you / those you draped in flesh and blood."[122] While this political conversion might be indicative of Zahawi's vanity and concern for recognition and praise, it also reflected both the waning legitimacy of the state and the declining value of the panegyric. Like many other poets, Zahawi seemed to conclude that there was little worth praising in Iraqi politics and even less reward for doing so.

### The Political Odyssey of Ma'ruf al-Rusafi

Ma'ruf al-Rusafi searched fruitlessly for a political patron after his return to Baghdad in April 1921, reciting panegyrics for 'Abd al-Rahman al-Kaylani and Faysal before falling out of favor with both men.[123] While Zahawi complained of his unrequited love for Iraq in his cryptic ruba'iyat, Rusafi appealed directly to the public and especially Iraqi youth, telling a student audience in December 1921, "This is your century, more advanced than any / for the sword has now yielded to the pen."[124] Rusafi embraced his rivalry with Zahawi one week later, invoking the famous rivalry between Hammad 'Ajrad and Ibn Burd in the late 'Umayyad and early 'Abbasid era to assert his own importance as the "Ibn Burd of the modern age":

> What am I but a poet with a true purpose,
> sometimes weeping and sometimes warbling
> Between my prattling jaws I have a sword,
> that I draw some days and sheathe on others
> No wonder that I am attacked by that poet
> who recites silly verses in slavish imitation
> Even Ibn Burd, who was the greatest poet,
> was slandered in the poems of Hammad ⊠Ajrad[125]

These two poems revealed Rusafi's ambivalent conception of poetry in modern society. His declaration that "the sword has now yielded to the pen" indicated his faith in the transcendent ideals of poetry, but his boast about the "sword" between his jaws showed his enduring appreciation of the dangers of poetry.

Rusafi believed in the didactic capacity of poetry and composed nationalist poems set to popular tunes for school textbooks.[126] Other poems reflected his vision of neoclassical modernity, appealing to fellow poets to link the glorious past to the glimmering future: "If you recited to us some poems of pride / it would remind us of those halcyon days / And of our ancestors and how they reigned / and how they achieved such vast glory."[127] He became one of the most vocal critics of Faysal, who fumed about the "extremist propaganda" that poets recited in his presence.[128] In September 1922, Rusafi spoke at a banquet honoring Amin al-Rihani, a Lebanese-American poet and confidant of Faysal, who previously criticized the "antiquated" aesthetics of Iraqi poets.[129] Rusafi sarcastically praised Rihani, dedicating his poem "to the pillar of his society, to the pride of his tribe / To the great genius, to the philosopher of his age / to the poet of his nation, the old fox of his generation!" Moving beyond "dangerously double-edged" praise, Rusafi bluntly denounced Hashemite subservience to colonial power:

> Now Amin, do not get angry with me, for I
> have not alleged anything without evidence!
> How can you expect Iraq to move and progress,
> when the path of colonies is no real path at all
> No good comes to a nation when its sword
> is with the coward and money with the miser,
> When its ideas are with the exile, knowledge
> with the foreigner, and power with the stranger?![130]

Faysal understood the term *stranger* (*dakhil*) as a reference to himself, but Rusafi disingenuously insisted that it referred to Britain to avoid punishment. Rihani was infuriated, dismissing Rusafi as a "bedouin" poet and alluding to rumors about alcoholism and homosexuality in his description of Rusafi as "bankrupt in his social, political, and religious beliefs."[131]

As the scandal raged, Rusafi returned to Istanbul and then moved on to Beirut, complaining that Iraq had betrayed him and blaming the "lowly horde" of politicians who denied him the patronage he deserved.[132] He vented his fury in a famous poem that fused self-glorification with anticolonialism: "What hurts me most is that I am among Arabs / who feel no anger about this painful affair / But by God, my right would not have been denied / if I were a foreigner with a reddish beard!"[133] The poem attracted widespread attention, inspiring responses from poets as far away as Tunisia.[134] Rusafi broke his vow never to return to Iraq just months later when ʿAbd al-Muhsin al-Saʿdun invited him to stand for parliament.[135] He repaid Saʿdun's patronage by denouncing an electoral boycott organized by Shiʿi mujtahids and nationalist politicians.[136] Rusafi lost his election but continued to pursue political reconciliation, apologizing to Faysal and returning to his post at the Ministry of Education.[137] When a statue of General Maude was unveiled at the British embassy in December 1923, Rusafi argued that Iraqis should acknowledge "the eternal place of this great leader in Arab history."[138] His declaration shocked the nationalist public, and even Gertrude Bell praised this "remarkable eulogy" from a longstanding critic of Britain.[139]

Rusafi's good behavior did not last, and he was soon satirizing local politicians in popular poems. One poem mocked the impotence of Iraqi officials to punish him for his subversive poems without the approval of their British advisers.[140] Another complained, "Today Indian gentlemen walk among us / while our native sons lack any power / Now India is more noble than my country / and Indians are more noble than my people."[141] Yet another poem described "democracy" as a colonial mirage and insisted that every symbol of national sovereignty masked the reality of domination:

> Flag, constitution, and national assembly,
> each has been corrupted from real meaning
> These names are nothing but words to us,
> while their meanings still remain unknown
> Whoever reads the constitution knows that it
> is but literature according to the mandate deed
> Whoever sees the flag fluttering finds that it
> is not fluttering to the glory of this nation's sons
> Whoever comes to our assembly knows that it
> is composed of men totally despised by voters

>  Whoever watches the cabinets is aware that they
>  are bound by the shackles of foreign advisors . . . [142]

These anticolonial poems bolstered Rusafi's political reputation as the spokesman of nationalist opposition during the struggle over the Anglo-Iraqi Treaty in 1928.[143] He echoed Jamil Sidqi al-Zahawi in blaming Britain for the suicide of their mutual patron, 'Abd al-Muhsin al-Sa'dun, in an elegy that circulated in Lebanese, Palestinian, and Syrian newspapers.[144] When praise no longer paid, poets like Rusafi discovered, popularity provided new paths to power and prestige.

## The Hijab Wars in Iraqi Poetry

Long before Rusafi and Zahawi finally buried their feud in December 1928, the two great modern poets found common cause in support of women's reform.[145] Zahawi's critique of the status of women in Islam inspired rebuttals from conservative poets like 'Abd al-Rahman al-Banna', who responded: "May God humble our kinsmen who wish / for beautiful girls to abandon their protection / And who say that when the veil falls down / it leads girls into the chains of the prisoner."[146] The young Najafi poets generally supported women's education but rarely went so far as to call for unveiling in the late Ottoman era.[147] These debates became entangled with the cultural politics of anticolonialism, as the association of unveiling with Europeanization (*taghrib*) invoked cultural anxiety and inspired defenses of Muslim cultural difference.[148] While Iraqi women participated in public debates about polygamy, education, and health care, arguments about the hijab were voiced almost entirely by men as women's bodies and sartorial practices became symbolic representations of the gendered domain of national culture threatened by colonialism.[149] These debates were conducted largely through poetry, which attracted far more attention than prose arguments about education and veiling.[150]

Most Iraqi poets accepted that women's education was a precondition for national revival. Zahawi expressed this view in one of his famous when he declared, "People advance in two units / both the females and the males / For can the bird really take flight / without using both of his wings?"[151] When Rafa'il Butti compared the status of Iraqi women unfavorably to that of Egyptian women in *al-ʿIraq*, he argued that education should be limited to "tasks that nature has prescribed for her as housekeeper, wife, and mother" and cited Rusafi in defense of this position: "Creatures that have never seen any place / that rears them like the bosom of mothers / For the mother's bosom is on the other side / a school for the instruction of boys and girls."[152] His editorial diluted the poem's progressive sentiment, but it was apparent that Butti considered Rusafi a moral authority whose words could be used to defend social reforms in the language of "cultural authenticity."

Male concern for women's issues became more pronounced in the colonial era, as poems about the status of women became common. Zahawi grew more vocal about women as his political frustrations increased, publishing several poems about the unhappy marital lives of wives.[153] The fact that the ubiquitous Layla of his rubaʿiyat could be read literally as a woman or figuratively as the nation reinforced the political dimensions of his social analysis, as calls for "awakening" and "liberation" could be read in gendered or national terms. Many poems about the status of women appeared in *al-ʿIraq*, including contributions from non-Iraqi poets like Jibran Khalil Jibran, Ilyas Abu Mahdi, and Hafiz Ibrahim.[154] The Iraqi poet Ibrahim Munib al-Pachachi published an ode to the American actress Pearl White that praised Western women and appealed for Eastern reform: "If I were given the chance, I would wish / to see female teachers in all the east / To build up young men and young women / in the knowledge that illuminates both halves."[155] While Pachachi's message was ostensibly about education, his praise for White's unveiled beauty and pointed contrast between Eastern oppression and Western liberation showed the difficulty of disentangling political and social arguments in the looming "hijab wars" of Iraqi poetry.

Poets disagreed about the scope of women's reforms and expressed anxiety about terms like *liberation* and *awakening*.[156] ʿAbd al-Rahman al-Banna' argued for clear limits to reform in an early defense of the hijab, written in response to Zahawi in 1919: "She is protected from all stares so that / she views it as a shelter that provides shade / If not for the hijab obstructing others from her / She would walk the path to their wicked thoughts."[157] Zahawi was largely dismissed by his opponents due to his eccentricity and political irrelevance, but Maʿruf al-Rusafi became a more dangerous proponent of women's liberation even though his libertinism and homosexuality left him susceptible to charges of indecency.[158] His poem "Woman in the East" sparked the "hijab wars" in March 1922 by attributing veiling to a corruption of Islamic scripture: "[Muslims] refused to recognize the rights of women / and kept them confined their whole lives / Compelling them to wear the hijab and denying / that they had the right to remove this veil." The poem also contended that Muslim misogyny made Iraqi women objects of colonial desire:

> They claimed women are suitable for nothing,
> except remaining in the home and copulating,
> So what are they but a pleasure and commodity?
> Even if men are forbidden from buying and selling,
> They demeaned them as mothers and so became
> the lowliest of nations by what they have done
> If they had only left women's honor untouched,
> they would have remained one of the highest!
> Do you not see that they became slaves because
> they grew up in disgrace in dens of slave girls?
> They barely noticed when their women became prey
> to bear the injustice of these Western politicians . . . [159]

Rusafi's protégé, Muhammad Bahjat al-Athari, denounced him as an infidel; his mentor, Mahmud Shukri al-Alusi, issued a fatwa condemning the poem; the editor of *al-Dijla* accused him of blasphemy and "decadent views"; and *al-Istiqlal* was shuttered for "security" reasons within days.[160]

Numerous nationalist poets published poems defending the hijab in *al-Yaqin*, an anticolonial journal edited by Muhammad al-Hashimi.[161] Critical of both secularism and religious traditionalism, they echoed the arguments of those Egyptian nationalists who defended veiling as a defense of national culture from colonial encroachment and insisted that other reforms were more pressing.[162] 'Abd al-Husayn al-Azri responded favorably to Zahawi's plea for women's education but now worried that if unveiling were coupled with an end to gender segregation, it could "only evoke desire" and threaten the "virtue of girls."[163] Azri urged Rusafi to focus on less superficial reforms and suggested that unveiling could come later: "Build schools for them and elevate the level / of their character for the sake of their children / Scrutinize her morality before unveiling her / to be sure that her morals are not a mirage!"[164] Hamzah al-Qaftan rejected Rusafi's argument that Iraqi men "barely noticed when their women became prey / to bear the injustices of these Western politicians," insisting that unveiling would make things worse: "If the result was that women became easy prey / to bear the injustices of these Western politicians / What whoring will come when hijabs are lifted / and she is exposed behind the veil?!"[165]

Rusafi responded to Qaftan in "Freedom in the Politics of Colonialism," which appeared in *al-Mufid* on May 1, 1922. The poem mocked male obsession with women's bodies and sarcastically implored his critics, "Do not bother to try and understand / for there is virtue in your obliviousness / Remain steadfast in your ignorance / for there is only evil in knowledge."[166] More significant, the poem linked the hijab wars to national liberation, complaining that ignorance allowed colonialism to fester in Iraq. Rusafi returned to unveiling repeatedly, complaining that Muslim women were the most oppressed people on earth and declaring, "My biggest complaint with my nation is that they / consider the imposition of the hijab part of Shari'a."[167] Three years later, he praised the Syrian feminist Nazira Zayn al-Din for her critique of the hijab and celebrated her triumph over the "seclusionists."[168] These poems appeared in foreign journals and collections, however, and attracted less attention and controversy in Iraq than his earlier poems. While progressive poets defended Rusafi, his critics were more numerous and vocal.[169]

Jamil Sidqi al-Zahawi implored the Muslim woman to "take from her Western sister the custom of unveiling and tear into pieces the hijab draped over her by ignorance."[170] He later insisted that "this type of hijab was never promoted / by any prophet nor approved by philosophers / Whether in law or nature of common sense / it is objectionable in reason and conscience."[171] His epic poem "Revolt in Hell" included a discussion on veiling with an angel, who asked rhetorically, "How can a people aspire to modern civilization / when half is concealed from view of the other?"[172] Zahawi's involvement in the hijab wars was supplemented by his contributions to Layla, the pioneering women's journal founded by his sister Asma' al-Zahawi in October 1923.[173] In addition to Zahawi and Rusafi, progressive poets like Kazim al-Dujayli, Muhammad al-Hashimi, and Anwar Sha'ul contributed poems in support of women's liberation.[174] Neither male nor female contributors to the journal, however, dared to bring up the subject of veiling lest it be tainted by allegations of blasphemy and immorality.[175] As in Egypt, the veiling controversy seemed less significant at this moment in time than education and marital rights to most female activists.

While Rusafi and Zahawi published their views on women to an increasingly narrow audience in the latter half of the 1920s, a young Najafi poet provoked a new scandal about women's education in his anonymous poem, "The Reactionaries." The education of women was critical to Satiʿ al-Husri's nationalist agenda at the Iraqi Ministry of Education, and many Shiʿi critics of this project resented the intrusion of the state into the lives of Shiʿi women.[176] Conservative Shiʿi ʿulama protested the opening of a girls' school in Najaf in 1929, and the anonymous poem linked this controversy to the broader struggle for social justice:

> These controversies will continue for some time,
> unless their days are shortened by stiff resistance,
> Unless the reformists push some new measures,
> standing firm for what they deem appropriate,
> The people will continue suffering this deception,
> the evil deeds of those still tethered to the past,
> The chains of feudalism that imprison the east,
> oppressing people by dividing them into groups
> Do you not see that collective rights of the people
> have today become possessions of individuals?
> Every ambitious neighbor of Iraq has proceeded,
> and succeeded quite rapidly, without dire effect
> How strange it is that those who are responsible
> for the salvation of people have become the obstacle![177]

The poem condemned the Najafi ʿulama in lurid terms: "What is religion but a tool that they proclaim / an instrument for the end that they seek / While beyond them the youth can see that some / are thieves, and others are pederasts and fornicators." Several mujtahids confided to King Faysal that the anonymous poet was in fact a palace employee and regular fixture in the taverns of Baghdad, who wrote poems in praise of alcohol and female dancers.¹⁷⁸ He was none other than Muhammad Mahdi al-Jawahiri, whose responsibility for compiling the king's daily press digest meant that he was responsible for writing summaries of his own anonymous poem and the vitriolic responses it provoked.¹⁷⁹ Ironically, the poet was at that time best known for his confrontation with Sati' al-Husri, whose agenda of women's education Jawahiri now defended.¹⁸⁰ Jawahiri's political experience in the British Mandate illustrates that the intersection of sectarianism, nationalism, and modernity was often more complicated than might be assumed.

## Jawahiri and the Lure of Bagdad

Muhammad Mahdi al-Jawahiri was born in 1899, a product of the Najafi cultural revival fueled by his older brother 'Abd al-'Aziz and cousin 'Ali al-Sharqi. He studied rhetoric, eloquence, and fiqh in the hawza, but grew bored with Najaf and yearned to escape its confines.¹⁸¹ British repression forced the exodus of many young Najafi poets after the uprisings of 1918 and 1920, and Jawahiri's generation dreamed of following their path.¹⁸² His contemporaries Ahmad al-Safi al-Najafi and Sa'd Salih recounted their isolation in the hawza, where they barricaded themselves in the quarters of the liberal mujtahid Sa'id Kamal al-Din to discuss poetry and politics. Kamal al-Din's death destroyed this "fortress of the liberals," and both poets left Najaf for new cosmopolitan environments in Baghdad, Beirut, Damascus, and Tehran.¹⁸³

Jawahiri shared these cosmopolitan dreams and attraction to the secular politics of Baghdad and later recalled his desire to transform himself from provincial "Najafi poet" to nationalist "Iraqi poet."¹⁸⁴ He wrote nationalist poems celebrating the Najafi contribution to the 1920 Revolution and published them in *al-Istiqlal*.¹⁸⁵ He spent several weeks impatiently scanning the Baghdadi newspapers for some response to the poems and was elated when he found a reply from Muhammad al-Hashimi on the front page of *al-Rafidan*. Hashimi addressed Jawahiri as "the Poetic Genius of Najaf" and pleaded, "Nightingale, come sing for us / and gather our pain into verse / For we are a mournful audience / and we are awaiting a command." He began to feel as though his "ambitions had exceeded the limits of Iraq" and contributed poems to foreign journals like *al-'Irfan* and *al-Hilal*. When he visited Baghdad several months later, he felt "like an apparition" because he was still dressed in the traditional Najafi fashion, wearing the *jilbab* (robe), *ʿabaʾa* (cloak), and *ʿimama*. Jawahiri's encounter with Western dress (*al-zayy al-afranji*) in the metropolitan landscape reified the contrast between past and present and the "new aesthetic of space" in his experience of modernity.[186] When he returned to Najaf two days later, he regaled his friends with stories of the city that emphasized the discourse of progress and civilization: "I continued to talk for months to my friends and acquaintances about my discoveries there. Without any sense of exaggeration, I was telling stories like Columbus narrating his discovery of America—like the 'Najafi Columbus,' I narrated my so-called discoveries in Baghdad."[187] Long before he became a fixture of leftist Iraqi politics, Jawahiri was boasting of the capacity of his poetry to inspire nationalist loyalties in both the local and foreign press.[188]

Jawahiri's own vision of the relationship between poetry and politics was inspired by the actions of Maʿruf al-Rusafi, the Hashimi brothers, and the Shabibi brothers, whose "dangerously double-edged" panegyrics he now emulated. He began attracting colonial attention in early 1922 due to the poems published in support of anticolonial nationalist movements in Egypt and India.[189] Jawahiri published a poem in *al-Rafidan* on May 27, 1922 that denounced Winston Churchill's speech defending the British Mandate in the House of Commons. Ostensibly a panegyric for Faysal, the poem was characterized by threats more than praise, as Jawahiri complained that Faysal had been given "the burden of kings and the power of slaves" and warned him to heed the legacy of the 1920 uprising: "Yesterday they were satisfied by what you did / and called for swords to be returned to sheaths."[190] Gertrude Bell was consumed with the nationalist demonstrations in Baghdad and failed to notice the poem, but she remained wary of Jawahiri and monitored the poems he published in *al-Rafidan* and *al-Dijla*.[191] Jawahiri imitated Maʿruf al-Rusafi's attack on Amin al-Rihani at a banquet in Najaf in September 1922, heaping Rihani with sarcastic praise and mocking his critique of Iraqi poetry: "Who is it that possesses the character to distinguish / the literature of civilization from bedouin aesthetics?"[192]

Jawahiri's struggle to gain national recognition soon became tangled in the politics of sectarianism. His sympathies lay with fellow Shiʿi elites marginalized by the colonial state due to pervasive stereotypes of Shiʿi fanaticism and Persian loyalty.[193] Most cabinets included only one Shiʿi representative, generally one of the "poet-clerics" of Najaf or Karbala as minister of education.[194] These poets clashed with Sati' al-Husri, the pan-Arab ideologue and director general of education, over the preferential employment of non-Iraqi (Sunni) teachers in state schools.[195] At the same time, many Shi'i poets downplayed sectarian grievances by emphasizing shared Sunni-Shi'i opposition to the "fanatical" Wahhabis who threatened Iraqi sovereignty from the Arabian peninsula.[196] 'Ali al-Sharqi wrote panegyrics praising Faysal as an ally of the Shi'a in the struggle against Wahhabism and the anti-Shi'i sectarianism that threatened Arab unity and the "Eastern renaissance."[197] Several years later, however, Sharqi described colonialism and sectarianism as two sides of the same coin.[198] Muhammad Baqir al-Shabibi likewise complained that the "spoils of power" had been appropriated by Britain and the Sunni elites, while the Shi'a, who had sacrificed so much in the 1920 Revolution, remained marginalized.[199] The ambivalence of Shi'i attitudes toward the state reflected a circular conception of history in which reform and renaissance were essential components of the universal struggle against oppression in every age rather than singular characteristics of Hashemite nationalism.[200]

Jawahiri's own intervention in this "filthy schism" of sectarianism was a product of the Nusuli affair, which erupted shortly after Sati' al-Husri hired Anis al-Nusuli, a Sunni Muslim from Lebanon, to teach Islamic history in Baghdad.[201] Nusuli published a history of the 'Umayyad caliphate that was critical of Shi'ism, provoking sustained opposition until he was dismissed by (Shi'i) Minister of Education Sayyid 'Abd al-Mahdi in January 1927.[202] While Husri encouraged students and teachers to protest Nusuli's dismissal, Jawahiri praised the actions of 'Abd al-Mahdi: "If not for you the innocent would be infected by the disease of their propaganda / and the master of the dog's bite would bring down his dogs."[203] Pleased by the poem, 'Abd al-Mahdi ordered Husri to hire Jawahiri to teach Arabic in Baghdad, much to the consternation of the director general.[204] Days after his appointment, Jawahiri published a poem in a local Baghdadi newspaper that included several lines that would spark a new political sandal:

> Here is Persia, whose breeze is morning,
> and whose skies are but branches and leaves . . .
> I have in Iraq my clique, and if not for them,

then Iraq could never be so very dear to me
There is no Tigris without them, no matter
how pleasant, and no Euphrates to be drunk[205]

Jawahiri's poem echoed the sentiment of a poem published by his cousin 'Ali al-Sharqi the previous year, which complained that the Iraqi Shi'a were habitually suspected of harboring "Persian" affinities by their Sunni compatriots.[206] Husri had already developed his own suspicious of Jawahiri's "Persian" affinities and now used the "anti-Arab" message of the poem as an excuse to attack the poet. When Husri later recounted the affair in his memoir, he rearranged the lines of the original poem to strengthen this impression:

I have in Iraq my clique, and if not for them,
then Iraq could never be so very dear to me
There is no Tigris without them, no matter
how pleasant, and no Euphrates to be drunk
There is only Persia, whose breeze is morning,
and whose skies are but branches and leaves

Husri showed the poem to Ma'ruf al-Rusafi, who declared that "this is *shu'ubiyya* in every sense of the word!"[207] Husri used the charge of shu'ubiyya, a derogatory reference to Persian chauvinism from the 'Abbasid era, to formally terminate the poet.[208] Jawahiri protested that Rusafi and Husri had misread the poem to no avail, and the affair intensified the sectarian grievances kindled by the Nusuli affair.[209]

Sayyid Muhammad al-Sadr, the prominent Shi'i mujtahid and nationalist leader, brought Jawahiri's case to Faysal, who gave Jawahiri a palace post in the interest of quelling sectarian tensions.[210] Faysal appreciated Jawahiri's poetry, but his patronage created numerous headaches due to the poet's rebellious spirit and iconoclastic stances.[211] In October 1929, just two months after provoking controversy in Najaf over his attack on clerical opponents of the girls' school in "The Reactionaries," Jawahiri again sparked public scandal by publishing "Lust of a Poet" (later retitled "Try Me").[212] The poem linked religious skepticism and libertinism, denouncing "popular traditions and hypocrisies" and praising the "carnal pleasures of life," infuriating both conservative mujtahids and Faysal's older brother 'Ali and eventually leading to the poet's departure from the palace.²¹³ Navigating the landscape of political patronage remained a difficult and dangerous game for popular Iraqi poets like Jawahiri.

## Conclusion

The visit of the iconic Indian poet Rabindranath Tagore to Baghdad in May 1932, just months before the termination of the British Mandate, served as a fitting coda to the decline of the panegyric in the colonial era. Tagore was well known and well respected among Iraqi poets, and Faysal viewed his visit as an opportunity to demonstrate his interests in the "Eastern revival" through state patronage of poetry.²¹⁴ Jamil Sidqi al-Zahawi was particularly enthusiastic about Tagore's visit, greeting the Indian poet at the Khanaqin rail station and accompanying him to Baghdad.²¹⁵ Tagore addressed a delegation of Iraqi poets, calling for a global "Brotherhood of Letters" that might bring about a new era of peace and harmony between nations.²¹⁶ Zahawi responded with a panegyric for Tagore, praising his "eternal" contribution to the Eastern revival.²¹⁷ Not every poet at the banquet appreciated Tagore's appeal for harmony or Zahawi's praise for this apparently apolitical stance. Muhammad Bahjat al-Athari responded with poem rebuking both Tagore and Zahawi for ignoring the anticolonial struggle in Iraq:

> Please, do not be afraid to tell me what [Tagore] said,
> that he spoke against those of us who took up arms
> As far as we are concerned, you just do not understand,
> and can be forgiven and pardoned for your ignorance
> But resistance has become a sacred command for us,
> and those who embrace it in defense will live forever²¹⁸

Tagore did not understand Arabic and applauded the harangue like everyone else, but if he had understood, he might have protested to Athari that he viewed spiritual and intellectual regeneration as necessary prerequisites for decolonization.²¹⁹ In the absence of such understanding, the tension at the banquet illustrated the declining role of patronage and panegyric in the evolving cultural politics of Iraqi poetry. While Tagore and Zahawi believed that state patronage was necessary to allow poetry to promote the sort of cultural revival necessary for national independence movements, Athari insisted that acceptance was tantamount to collaboration as long as patronage remained linked to the structures and institutions of colonialism.

The "dangerously double-edged" nature of praise embodied by the political panegyric represented an attempt to mediate these competing concerns for patronage and popularity. While the colonial panegyrics published in *al-Iraq* after the fall of Baghdad reflected total disregard for popularity, the experience of the Iraqi Revolution of 1920 and the dawn of the Hashemite Kingdom offered a new opportunity for poets to seek patronage of political elites with some claim to popular legitimacy. The concerns of anticolonialism and the reality of Anglo-Hashemite relations, however, forced poets to take some creative license in their praise for the resistance and independence of figures like Faysal. Exaggeration of this variety was not particularly welcome, as it placed the burden of popular expectation on the shoulders of politicians who were incapable of bearing it or unwilling to do so. The blurred lines between praise and threat intensified the political stakes of the panegyric performance, which ultimately collapsed under the weight of this tension.

The shifting relationship between poetry and patronage had other cultural ramifications apart from the general decline of the panegyric. The movement of poets like Zahawi, Rusafi, the Hashimi brothers, and Jawahiri between political support and opposition depending on the vagaries of state patronage may appear at first glance to reflect the individual vanity and material self-interest of poets, but it also reflected at times their belief in principles and willingness to suffer deprivation for the sake of their reputations. One of the peculiarities of poetry in Iraqi society was the perception of poet as national spokesmen, but he now increasingly began to appear as public dissident. Whether speaking in defense of social reform and women's rights or in opposition to political sectarianism, religious orthodoxy, and cultural tradition, this dissident current was a reflection of the growing gulf between poets and political elites and the gradual alienation of state and society. The "rebel poetry" of the mawlid scene in 1920 was replaced by a new rebellious current that challenged domestic enemies instead of the familiar foreign targets. When these two discursive currents began to merge in the 1930s and 1940s, they gave rise to a truly radical spirit of anticolonial revolution.

The radical cultural politics that emerged in the aftermath of the British Mandate colored the ways in which the colonial period was understood and remembered. When Jamil Sidqi al-Zahawi died in 1936, he was memorialized by numerous Iraqi poets, including Salma ʿAbd al-Razzaq, better known as Um Nizar and the mother of the iconic and pioneering female poet Nazik al-Malaʾika, who praised Zahawi's support for women's freedom in the Baghdadi newspaper *al-Subh*.[220] She was an ardent defender of Arab nationalism and the anticolonial movements in Syria and Palestine, but she now chose to overlook Zahawi's relationship with colonialism.[221] Her silence reflected the grand bargain of nationalist history in the assessment of the "poetry wars" of the 1920s, celebrating the progressive defense of modernity and ignoring the political scandal of collaboration. Forgetting the embarrassing mistakes and missteps of the past in the interest of national unity would prove to be a critical and enduring commitment of anticolonial poetry over the course of subsequent decades.

( CHAPTER 4 )

# PATRIOTS AND TRAITORS
## *The Cultural Politics of Nationalism, 1932–1945*

Nine years after publicly rebuking Rabindranath Tagore, Muhammad Bahjat al-Athari sparked another political scandal with his poems.[1] Athari had emerged as a prominent proponent of pan-Arabism in Iraq during the 1930s and an enthusiastic supporter of the Rashid ʿAli movement in 1941.[2] The nationalist poems he published during the Anglo-Iraqi War of May 1941 led to his internment at Fao after the war.[3] While he had spent the previous five years attacking leftist poets for their "shuʿubiyya," Athari's encounters with anticolonial leftists in the internment camp forced him to rethink his attitudes about partisanship.[4] He reflected on these encounters in the satirical poem "The Tragic Tale of the Rooster of al-Fao," composed after a rooster escaped one night in December 1941 and defecated on the head of one of the prisoners. The rooster was killed in the ensuing melee, and the entire camp convened the next morning for a mock trial.

The dead rooster was convicted of treason, sentenced to death, and hung from miniature gallows as Athari recited his eulogy: "My heart is saddened and my tears pour down / in sorrow for your tragic fate, Rooster / This prison trembled from top to bottom / with sorrow, as people cry, 'Cock-a-doodle-doo!'" Beneath the veneer of absurd prison theater, Athari was making an argument about patriotism by comparing the rooster's "crimes" to colonial accusations against "Nazi" and "Bolshevik" prisoners:

> Did you fight for true freedom or total anarchy?
> Or were you, Rooster, a Bolshevik in this world?
> I cannot say, but the people differ in their views,
> between truth and falsehood, faith and misgiving,
> What was the nature of your sin against the people?
> Was it incitement and zeal, or slander and agitation?

Athari proceeded to accuse the prisoners of internalizing the structures of colonial oppression: "How could we ask moderation from tyrants / when we treat the innocent rooster with suspicion / When we took up residence in the marches of Fao / vanity seized us as if we were Saxons and Sikhs!"[5] The anticolonial introspection had a palpable impact on the diverse factions of political prisoners, and when state officials discovered that it was circulating in Baghdad, they transferred Athari to a new camp in Samarra', where he remained until the end of 1944.[6]

The poem illuminated the evolving cultural politics of anticolonialism in Iraq. Athari previously accused leftists of ignoring the Arab struggle in Palestine, but he came to respect the nationalist commitment of leftist prisoners and fellow poets like Muhammad Salih Bahr al-ʿUlum.[7] While Athari attacked Maʿruf al-Rusafi for his stance on women in the 1920s, his attitude toward social reform now evolved in a more progressive direction.[8] This evolution reflected the broader reconciliation of nationalists and leftists after nearly a decade of bitter partisan disputes on political legitimacy, social justice, and cultural authenticity. Poets had always envisioned themselves as national spokesmen, but their conceptions of social responsibility were now complicated by their new position as organic intellectuals and representatives of particular ideological and class interests.[9] The need to portray these interests as an expression of the national will worked to reinforce the dichotomy between "patriotism" and "treason."

Anticolonial poetry imagined the struggle of a unified nation against the colonial state between the beginning of the British occupation in 1914 and the end of the British Mandate in 1932, but national independence transformed this political calculus by redefining the meaning of colonial and anticolonial. If colonialism did not end with the British Mandate—and virtually everyone agreed that it had not—then anticolonial poets had to define what colonialism meant in the absence of a colonial state. Nationalist poets envisioned the new struggle against colonialism as the liberation of other Arab states from colonial rule. Leftist poets, however, saw the struggle against colonialism as the displacement of political elites and structures of domination established by the colonial state. Each vision of national liberation drew on different conceptions of the nation and imagined different classes of enemies in the same dichotomous rhetoric of "patriot" and "traitor." These bitter ideological conflicts reflected the contested meaning of both "nationalism" and "anticolonialism" in the postcolonial state.[10]

The cultural politics of anticolonial nationalism were critically shaped by the two military coups of October 1936 and April 1941. Though both episodes were engineered by opportunistic and self-interested army officers and political elites, they attracted the support of different segments of the Iraqi intelligentsia and promulgated different visions of national and cultural identity.[11] This clash between the ethnic (qawmi) vision of pan-Arab nationalism and the territorial (watani) vision of Iraqi patriotism became the defining feature of Iraqi cultural politics in the mid-twentieth century. The divide reflected ethnic and religious interests in the demographic landscape of Iraq and the Arab world, but it was also shaped by particular class interests. The qawmi nationalists who prioritized the liberation and unification of their Arab neighbors tended to be more conservative, while the watani nationalists who embraced a cosmopolitan vision of the Iraqi nation were overwhelmingly leftist. Although the qawmi vision of Arab nationalism has been traced to the influence of Germanic romantic nationalism and thus linked to global genealogies of fascism, the qawmi poetry of the 1930s and 1940s reveals little interest in the politics or aesthetics of fascism.[12] Both the qawmi and watani visions of nationalism were shaped by the same anticolonial impulse to finally sweep away the legacies of colonialism, and the Anglo-Iraqi War of 1941 finally allowed each side to perceive their shared interests in this struggle.

Perhaps the most instructive dimension of the qawmi-watani divide in this period was the manner in which each side defined its opponents. In contrast to their own patriotic struggle for national liberation, qawmi and watani nationalists each argued in their own distinct manners that their enemies were traitors to the nation. Qawmi nationalists invoked the language of shuʿubiyya to denounce their rivals as traitors to the Arab nation whose parochial loyalty to the Iraqi homeland (*watan*) sustained the legacy of colonial borders and obstructed Arab unity. Watani nationalists, in contrast, emphasized the superficial qawmi rhetoric of postcolonial elites to argue that their rivals were sustaining the social structures of colonial exploitation in order to satisfy their own lust for wealth and power. Despite their different visions of both national identity and the legacy of colonialism, the poets who waged this bitter debate in the Iraqi public sphere shared more in common than they realized at the time. Their public interventions voiced the lingering desire for national liberation, and their claims to speak on behalf of the nation allowed them to project new ideological and class interests onto the discourse of anticolonial nationalism. The same poets who had previously described a conflict between patriots and traitors for the soul of the nation began fusing qawmi "nationalist" interests and watani "leftist" politics into the postwar cultural discourse of the anticolonial national front. Due in part to the structural transformation of the postcolonial Iraqi press, poetry became the critical battleground of this contested cultural politics of nationalism.

## Independence and Disillusionment

The League of Nations voted to terminate the British Mandate on October 3, 1932.[13] Iraq celebrated the end of colonialism at a series of state banquets, where poets competed in their praise for King Faysal.[14] Muhammad ʿAli al-Yaʿqubi, who had supported the Ottoman jihad and the uprising of 1920, hailed Faysal's consummation of this struggle at the banquet in Najaf. Yaʿqubi described the dream of independence as "the desert mirage that beckons the thirsty" and the Hashemite monarchy as "the mouth of Arabism."[15] His praise of the Hashemite was echoed by Mahmud al-Habbubi: "The Arab nation has rejoiced since this victory / when you became the pride and hope of all Arabs / Rise to unite them and gather their citizens / like your father gathered his lost and roving sons!"[16] This euphoria of independence proved fleeting, as poets soon began complaining that independence was accompanied by no efforts to redistribute colonial power and wealth or to liberate occupied Syria and Palestine.[17] Within months, Habbubi was denouncing the independent state as a pale imitation of colonial rule: "Standing now on your doorstep are / noble Arabs, while infidels surround the throne

/ Every inflamed jugular seethes against / these fools despised by the people / Traitors who know nothing of politics / but how to win the object of their desires."[18]

Muhammad Salih Bahr al-'Ulum, a radical young Najafi poet and grandnephew of the iconic poet Ibrahim al-Tabataba'i, echoed these frustrations in pithy popular poems.[19] One poem satirized politicians who celebrated the end of the British Mandate as the dawn of a new era:

> I undressed the Mandate and beheld it,
> disguised in my own *sidara* [cap] and *'iqal* [rope band],
> Astonished that eyes could be so deceived,
> that clouds could conceal this mirage!
> You who celebrated this false modernity,
> filled with all the old and ragged things,
> What is the difference between the Mandate
> and its genitals on the body of Independence?[20]

Bahr al-'Ulum was known as the "poet of youths" (*sha'ir al-shabab*) because his anticolonial nationalism was so popular among Najafi youths in the 1920s, when children entertained themselves by reciting popular poems and "even grocers knew no means of expressing their [nationalist] sentiments other than poetry."[21] He shared Rusafi's belief in the poet's social responsibility, defending the superiority of poetry to prose because of its capacity for political mobilization.[22] Though he was educated in the hawza, he assailed the conservative 'ulama who declared that "pursuit of knowledge is *haram* [forbidden] / while extortion of money is lawful."[23] While he recited poems at religious festivals in Najaf even after leaving the hawza, these verses were colored by the rhetoric of secular nationalism.[24]

Bahr al-'Ulum's anticolonialism did not distinguish between watani and qawmi nationalism.[25] He wrote poems about the popular protest that erupted when the British Zionist activist Alfred Mond visited Baghdad in 1928, allowing Najafi youths to imagine themselves in the crowds and pretend that their poems were part of the urban nationalist drama.[26] His nationalist vision shaped his frustration with Najafi provincialism, and he joined his uncle and guardian, Sayyid Muhammad 'Ali Bahr al-'Ulum, in appealing for Sunni-Shi'i unity.[27] One poem from 1931 denounced the divisive politics of sectarianism: "There is nothing in [religion] to divide the people / in matters of faith or love or happiness or unity / For religion creates harmony, but it seems / it is now used in this country for quarreling."[28] When Bahr al-'Ulum was arrested for promoting the electoral boycott of 1929, he blamed the "representatives of the nation on one side" of the Tigris River in parliament and "their mother on the other side" in the British embassy.[29] He became secretary of the Najafi branch of the National Brotherhood Party (Hizb al-Ikha' al-Watani) and publicly called for the abolition of the Anglo-Iraqi Treaty during Faysal's visit to Najaf in April 1931.[30] He was promptly arrested but reveled in his new notoriety: "Prison is a blessing of honor / and an offer of tranquility."[31] The party organized protests, and Najafi authorities released the poet two days later.[32]

Bahr al-'Ulum pioneered new methods of poetic dissent, publicly denouncing the "sins of Nuri al-Sa'id" as authorities struggled to contain the danger of his poems.[33] He participated in a banquet for Sheikh Hamad bin 'Isa in Bahrain in 1932, seizing the opportunity to denounce Arab rulers: "The sheikhs allege, like the mules of other men / that flattering their enemies is a form of liberation / That the struggle of anyone who defends his right / is blasphemy and those who struggle are infidels / But as for their treachery in selling our lands / to foreigners, it seems that this sin is blessed!"[34] He was immediately deported, but news of the performance contributed to his rebel reputation in Iraq.[35] His annual poems about the 1920 Revolution linked social grievances to nationalist politics, arguing that the postcolonial state appropriated the sacrifice of anticolonial rebels: "Where is justice and equality and brotherhood / you who promise these delusions and phantoms? / Did you leave them in the gardens of the rich / so they could divide them between their goblets?"[36] On April 12, 1934, he asked a large crowd of peasants in Kufa, "Will the wages of the shoeless workers of Iraq now / be distributed in the colony of greedy foreigners?"[37] His call for the peasants to take up arms violated the limits of dissent, and Bahr al-'Ulum was sentenced to two months in prison. A crowd surrounded the truck that carried him away, chanting against imperialists and traitors with such force that an appellate court overturned the sentence rather than risk making him a symbol of resistance.[38]

Muhammad Mahdi al-Jawahiri, the young Najafi poet whose secular views had already provoked controversy in Baghdad, also began articulating a rudimentary socialist vision.[39] One poem from May 1931 invoked Étienne Lantier, the radical protagonist of Émile Zola's *Germinal*, to warn of labor unrest in Baghdad: "Are you familiar with Lantier and what he did / for the sake of dignity that rose from misfortune? / Is it possible for dignity without hardship and loss / to be as complete as the tattered dignity of toil?"[40] Like Bahr al-'Ulum, Jawahiri became particularly concerned with Iraqi peasants after a series of regressive new land ordinances.[41] He described the impact of these laws in a poem that circulated in 1934, contending that poets had a social responsibility to articulate popular grievances. More notably, the poem described the older generation of poets as traitors for abandoning this responsibility: "Alas, today the poets persist in sowing dissension / and writers have become creatures of their own hardship / So let us call all enlightened men to fulfill their duty / but do not imagine that this task will be easy!"[42]

### Dissident Poetry and the Tribal Rebellion of 1935

By the end of 1934, frustration with the postcolonial state reached a boiling point in Najaf and the Middle Euphrates. Egregious electoral fraud led Muhammad Salih Bahr al-'Ulum to complain, "This is a country where henchmen play their roles / and sinners indulge themselves behind the veil / Thieves who came to power thanks to colonialism / now gather to plot the subjugation of my people."[43] In *al-Ikha' al-Watani*, the newspaper of the reconstructed National Brotherhood Party, Mahmud al-Mallah expressed similar disillusionment with pervasive colonial influence in the "independent" state: "We threw a grand wedding feast, but it / could not be consummated without jewels / So they bound our feet in shackles / and we reckoned them gilded anklets."[44] As opposition to the new government mounted in the nationalist press, a coordinated campaign by tribal sheikhs, nationalist politicians, and army officers forced the resignation of two prime minister in two weeks before King Ghazi relented and appointed National Brotherhood Party leader Yasin al-Hashimi as prime minister on March 17, 1935.[45]

Yasin rewarded his supporters with large estates and parliamentary seats but showed no inclination for real reform, much to the chagrin of erstwhile allies like Ja'far Abu al-Timman.[46] Bahr al-'Ulum was a disciple of Abu al-Timman and organized protests in Baghdad calling on Yasin to fulfill his promises.[47] He denounced politicians as "[opportunists who] are not part of our class, but are / among us only to destroy our consciousness," an indication of his evolving socialist views.[48] He was arrested after reciting an older poem calling on peasants to rebel: "Leave your fields and throw away your sickle / the day has come to drench the soil with blood / Hold the state to account with your sword / for they have seized your rights as plunder."[49] A military tribunal sentenced the poet to death, but the sentence was commuted to twenty years of hard labor and Bahr al-'Ulum was later released in the political amnesty of September 1935.[50] When the poem was finally published two years later, the words *blood* and *sword* were replaced by an ellipsis, even though the rhyme scheme and reputation of the poem removed any ambiguity.[51] His radical vision of poetry and politics was encapsulated by his declaration shortly after his release: "I was a revolution since the day I was born / my revolution is a fire consuming the cities of tyrants!"[52]

While Bahr al-'Ulum was emerging as the public face of dissident poetry, Muhammad Mahdi al-Jawahiri returned to teaching and remained silent.[53] He was appalled, however, by Yasin's brutal repression of the tribal uprising in the Muntafiq.[54] Jawahiri seethed against politicians and sheikhs who "rented scores of their sons out for slaughter for the gratification of the ruling class their appetites."[55] He described the execution of rebel leaders and burning of villages in a poem published on the front page of *al-Islah* on October 12, 1935. The poem denounced the political manipulation of tribal rivalries and complained that the state had betrayed the legacy of 1920: "It was natural that tribal intervention was summoned / for the role of these tribes had been polluted / They had once been a weapon for us but had now / become a weapon against us every now and then."[56] The poem rebuked Yasin, imploring him to "turn against this lifestyle that sates your ambition / do not grow comfortable in the seat of the coward!" The furious Yasin retaliated by suspending Jawahiri from his teaching position and closing *al-Islah*. Yasin seems to have realized the danger in making an enemy of the irascible poet and offered to arrange Jawahiri's election to parliament in exchange for his silence, but the scheme failed and Jawahiri's independence from state employment allowed him to remain a defiant rebel poet.[57]

## The Bakr Sidqi Coup

General Bakr Sidqi overthrew Yasin al-Hashimi and installed Hikmat Sulayman as prime minister on October 29, 1936. The coup was supported by the Ahali Group, an association of social democrats and leftist intellectuals who had grown disenchanted with the postcolonial state and appealed for democracy and "national liberation" in the vague rhetoric of "populism" (*sha'biyya*).[58] The Ahali intellectuals enjoyed minimal influence over Bakr Sidqi, but their support gave the coup a revolutionary aura palpable in the poems recited in public and published in leftist newspapers like *al-Haris* and *al-Inqilab*.[59] Leftist poets like Muhammad Salih Bahr al-'Ulum attributed their support to the Ahali Group and described the coup as the culmination of Iraq's anticolonial struggle.[60] From exile in Damascus, Ahmad al-Safi al-Najafi published a poem in *al-Haris* celebrating the end of Iraqi servitude to Britain and blaming colonialism for obstructing social progress.[61] Nu'man Mahir al-Kan'ani, a student at the Military College in Baghdad, published a poem in the same paper three days later, heralding the new dawn of righteousness that emerged as "the clouds of deception were chased away / overcome by the assault from the light of truth."[62]

None of the poets who backed the coup were members of the Ahali Group or the Iraqi Communist Party (ICP), but both groups mobilized popular support.[63] Muhammad Mahdi al-Jawahiri and Muhammad Salih Bahr al-'Ulum joined the labor leader Muhammad Salih al-Qazzaz in leading huge crowds of workers in revolutionary socialist chants.[64] The Popular Reform League, a new party established by the Ahali Group, became the poets' gateway to communist politics. Bahr al-'Ulum described the coup as a "revolution" (*thawra*) and insisted that Bakr Sidqi was merely enforcing the popular will: "Were it not for the growth of the tyrant's ferocity / that has induced our souls to riot and unrest / The wrath of the rebels would not have burst forth / the 'revolution of the coup' would not have erupted!"[65] His revolutionary commitment was so complete that he transformed himself into a factory worker and union activist, taking a job in a Baghdad cigarette factory.[66] Jawahiri, in contrast, supported the revolution through his newspaper *al-Inqilab* (*The Coup*), which published dozens of leftist and nationalist poems.[67] One poem by Muhammad Rida al-Khatib described the coup as the logical response to colonial exploitation: "What good is a country that denies its own people aid / while its abundant wealth is reserved for foreigners / The bliss of the Tigris and Euphrates flow for them / while our own share was just a torrent of misfortune."[68] Khatib compared Yasin al-Hashimi to past tyrants like Genghis Khan and al-Hajjaj, inflecting his anticolonialism with the new dichotomy between "patriots" and "traitors."

Jawahiri likewise described Yasin al-Hashimi and Rashid ʿAli al-Kaylani as "traitors" responsible for "stirring up bitter feelings" between religious sects.[69] The only poem he wrote about the coup appeared in *al-Inqilab* and celebrated the rebirth of the Iraqi nation: "The tomb stirred and there suddenly burst forth / the shrouds of a nation we thought was buried!"[70] The poem's most striking feature was its appeal to the government to deal violently with the reactionary "traitors" who opposed the Popular Reform League:

> Tighten the rope and pull taut their necks,
> for there may be danger in letting it fall slack
> Do not say that violence only begets hatred,
> for they were already prepared to harm you
> Imagine if it were reversed and take a lesson
> from what they would do if they had triumphed
> Is there any mention of mercy in their dictionary,
> or any report of wisdom and its companions?

Partisan poetry was often caustic even before the coup, but poets had rarely endorsed violence against their opponents so explicitly. Jawahiri's nationalist opponents would remain embittered by these lines, later inverting his dichotomy of patriotism and treason to brand him a traitor to the Arab nation.[71]

Jawahiri's call for violence was echoed two days later in three revolutionary quatrains published by Bahr al-ʿUlum in *al-Inqilab*. The first poem condemned the farce of parliamentary politics, complaining , "These administrations made every effort / to give distant barons unlimited power / But have they reserved even one seat / to honor artists and revere artisans?"[72] Another depicted the struggle of peasants against feudalism and argued that the crimes of the previous era had not yet been punished:

> The lord of the castle prolongs his sleep,

To dream of his return to parliament
The dog and the peasant are at his door,
Without rest until the break of dawn
The first one is barking at all the guests,
While the other cries for his neglected right[73]

It was the third and final poem, however, that went furthest in its appeal for violent social revolution. Its first three lines described an idyllic dawn in the Iraq countryside before abruptly concluding, "If only I had a hut in the countryside / I would use its walls to raise gallows in palaces!"[74] This public plea for vengeance gave rise to the popular slogan "the hut and the palace," which animated contentious debates on rural land reform over the coming months.[75]

Despite these pleas for vengeance, the Popular Reform League lost the support of the government.[76] Bakr Sidqi was terrified by the radical rhetoric of *al-Inqilab* and denounced the Popular Reform League as communists in a speech to parliament in March 1937.[77] On the morning of this speech, ʿAbd al-Qadir al-Zahawi published a panegyric for Bakr Sidqi in *al-Inqilab*. Hoping to win back military support for the radical agenda, Zahawi praised Bakr Sidqi as a national savior in overwrought language: "With the sword of justice the heavens anointed / an avenger to assail every enemy and pharaoh / He is the leader whose every decree dictates / an end to the sanctioned violence of the past."[78] In a series of interviews with *al-Inqilab* the following week, Jaʿfar Abu al-Timman took a different path, denying that he was a communist but insisting defiantly, "If our efforts to reform the country, help the poor, and apply justice are communist acts, then I appeal to God the Almighty and All-Powerful to bring us to the threshold of communism!"[79] Neither tactic worked, and Bahr al-ʿUlum responded more confrontationally, leading his fellow tobacco workers on strike on April 5, 1937.[80]

As the leftist position unraveled, Jawahiri provoked a new confrontation with Amin al-Rihani, with whom he had clashed fifteen years earlier.[81] Jawahiri remained bitter about Rihani's portrayal of his dispute with Satiʿ al-Husri, which described Jawahiri as "an Iranian teacher who composed poetry" and supported Husri's contention that his poem had "ridiculed Iraq and its people."[82] When Rihani visited Baghdad to report on the Bakr Sidqi coup, Jawahiri described him as a "dangerous spy" in *al-Inqilab* and called his hotel to taunt him: "Welcome, Professor Amin al-Rihani. Do you know with whom you are speaking? It is the man born in Iran, the Persian who writes poetry, in Persian of course. It is Muhammad Mahdi al-Jawahiri!"[83] Rihani's complaints to the government were echoed by the British embassy, which protested several weeks later about an article in *al-Inqilab* alleging that Britain was organizing a new tribal rebellion.[84] The final straw came when Jawahiri protested the dramatic increase in the price of kosher meat, raising the plight of poor Jews in a front-page editorial.[85] The chief rabbi of Baghdad filed a formal grievance, and the government seized the opportunity to arrest and silence the provocative poet.[86]

## Regret, Recrimination, and Retaliation

Jawahiri was sentenced to one month in prison for incitement and two more for cursing the judge.[87] Jawahiri boasted about the danger of his poetry, describing prison guards as his "entourage" and declaring that prison was reserved for the "dangerous and the important."[88] After the collapse of the Popular Reform League, Muhammad Salih Bahr al-ʿUlum was more introspective about leftist failure:

> I saw in the market some bulls being led
> by their ambitions for offices and portfolios
> I rushed out to ask, "Where is their trough?"
> and learned that it lay in the next parliament
> Despair shattered the chalice in whose depths
> lay the dregs of faith in some of these men
> I ran to search for a grave in which to bury
> all that remained of my hopes and dreams[89]

Bahr al-ʿUlum insisted that leftists had been betrayed by their faith in these "traitors" who placed greed and ambition above the interests of the masses. When Bakr Sidqi was assassinated in August 1937, he coldly insisted that "whoever calls the people to worship him / will find their response in the bottom of the grave."[90] While both Jawahiri and Bahr al-ʿUlum sought to distance themselves from Sidqi, they now faced charges of "treason" levied against them by their nationalist opponents.

While the new government declared its intention to "close the curtain" on the crimes of the past, many Arab nationalists demanded retribution against the Popular Reform League "communists."[91] Dozens of communist cadres were arrested, and the climate of repression ensured the silence of nearly all leftist poets.[92] ʿAbd al-Husayn al-Azri, a religious poet who had previously attacked Zahawi and Rusafi for their stance on veiling, now vented his fury against Jawahiri and the Popular Reform League: "The League lied to you when they / told you water had become wine / But you rushed to fill your chalice / and dreams increased your intoxication."[93] Even the relatively progressive ʿAli al-Sharqi chided his cousin Jawahiri for embracing the revolutionary rhetoric of political "charlatans." His description of Bakr Sidqi and Hikmat Sulayman, neither of them ethnically Arab, as "strangers" echoed nationalist efforts to link leftist ideas to foreign plots: "Leaders and patrons of this country were startled / to see relatives and kin replaced by strangers."[94] In contrast to the shuʿubiyya narratives promoted by other nationalists, however, Sharqi was less interested in condemning leftists as "traitors" and maintained a distinction between the leftist ideals of the Popular Reform League and the selfish actions of political elites.

Maʿruf al-Rusafi made similar arguments to challenge the false dichotomy between socialism and nationalism. Rusafi had always been sympathetic to Marxism, and he now defended the Popular Reform League against anti-communist attacks.[95] In a famous parliamentary speech in June 1937, Rusafi challenged opponents to rebut the "communism" of the Prophet Muhammad and declaring provocatively, "I am a communist!"[96] Despite his socialist sympathies, Rusafi nevertheless viewed the coup as a British conspiracy against Yasin al-Hashimi and Arab nationalism:

> If you asked me who in the army was the one
> who was responsible for overthrowing [Yasin]?
> I would say, ask [the embassy], for they followed
> orders that came from [the British Middle East Office]
> For until now in Palestine and among her rebels
> [Yasin] played a hand that Cairo knew too well
> There they hatched the conspiracy against him
> until the bureau's orders were ready for the army[97]

This suggestion that Britain orchestrated the coup as a response to Yasin's support for the Arab Revolt in Palestine reflected the prevailing dichotomy of patriots and traitors.[98] The juxtaposition of the communist speech and nationalist poem, however, revealed Rusafi's desire to differentiate between national and social objectives and to show that nationalism and communism were not mutually incompatible.

The contentious memorial ceremonies for Yasin al-Hashimi in February 1938 indicated that most nationalist poets were not as interested in nuance. Yasin died in Damascus while Bakr Sidqi was still in power and received a state funeral in Syria when Iraq blocked the repatriation of his remains.[99] The Iraqi government now sought to honor the late nationalist icon with state memorials in Basra and Baghdad. Jawahiri recited an elegy in Basra, striving to heal the wounds of the past by describing Yasin as the "most brilliant star" of the anticolonial struggle, praising his contribution to Arab nationalism, and blaming Britain for partisan rivalries in Iraq.[100] This plea for reconciliation was rejected eleven days later by Muhammad Bahjat al-Athari at the memorial in Baghdad. Athari denounced Jawahiri and the Popular Reform League, describing their slogan of shaʻbiyya (populism) as a cover for shuʻubiyya (ethnic parochialism):

> That rotten platform of shuʻubiyya has clothed
> the body of the nation as libertines and traitors
> Vile creatures of undetermined race assaulted
> with injustice the noblest of nations and intentions
> In full pursuit of their evil plan, they conspired
> for the rule of tyrants behind the black of night
> Inciting the fleeting greed of the common people
> they are lowly born, violent, and aggressive[101]

Athari fused ideological, class, and racial grievances in this assault on leftist "libertines and traitors" and veneration of the noble lineage, chivalry, and honor of qawmi nationalism. His invocation of shuʻubiyya was particularly striking, as Iraqi poets like Muhammad al-Hashimi had previously described the qawmi veneration of pan-Arab nationalism over and above Iraqi nationalism as the "new shuʻubiyya."[102] The public impact of the poem was striking, and just days after his performance, the government voted to rescind immunity for those who participated in the coup.[103]

These shuʿubiyya accusations made leftist poets sensitive to the political content of their poetry.[104] Jawahiri refrained from commenting on politics except in nationalist poems about the Palestine struggle.[105] His vivid description of rural poverty and inequality in "Feudalism," however, circulated widely among leftists in the late 1930s.[106] The thinly veiled warning of the poem reflected his growing awareness of Marxist theories of revolution: "I do not dread the revolution of the greedy / for it will be followed by the revolution of the angry!"[107] The influence of communism on Bahr al-ʿUlum was even more explicit in the poems he recited to fellow workers and communists. One poem from October 1937 celebrated the twentieth anniversary of the Bolshevik Revolution: "The memory of October will remain for eternity / poetry that grants the people consciousness / The joy of this holiday is not only for Russians / but has come as a herald for the human race."[108] This leftist struggle to balance cosmopolitan internationalism with the demands of nationalist cultural politics would be tested again in the Rashid ʿAli movement in April 1941.

## The Rashid ʿAli Movement and the Poetics of Nationalism

While the Rashid ʿAli movement of 1941 has frequently been described as an eruption of pro-Nazi sentiment among the Iraqis, recent scholarship has noted the proliferation of anti-Nazi voices in the Iraqi public sphere and indicated that many supporters of the movement were more strongly motivated by anti-British than pro-Nazi sentiment.[109] Intellectuals like Yunis al-Sabʿawi and Yunis Bahri did express enthusiasm for Nazism, and the pan-Arabist Muthanna Club and its Futuwwa youth movement embraced "fascist imagery" in the late 1930s.[110] Iraqi opposition to backing the British campaign against Nazism, however, was mostly driven by the practical concerns of anticolonialism. Chamberlain's concession at Munich reinforced popular perceptions that antifascism was empty colonial rhetoric and that Britain only respected strength.[111] The British embassy in Baghdad appealed for the support of the Iraqi public by emphasizing fascist colonialism in Libya and Ethiopia, but propaganda could not force Iraqis to ignore the reality of Allied colonialism in Palestine and Syria.[112] Many Iraqis began to "look forward to the day when both Germany and the Allies will be so weakened in a long drawn-out struggle that foreign influence in the East must relax its grip."[113]

Ma'ruf al-Rusafi reflected this stance in an apocalyptic poem that gleefully predicted the destruction of Europe and urged Iraqis to "consummate this revolution of the ages."[114]

Like their African, Asian, and Arab counterparts, many Iraqi poets opposed fascism but adopted a transactional view of the European conflict.[115] Muhammad Salih Bahr al-'Ulum was a longstanding critic of fascism and had written poems denouncing Nazism and Hitler as early as 1934.[116] He condemned the Italian invasion of Ethiopia in 1935, contrasting the principled stand of Soviet ambassador Maxim Litvinov with European appeasement: "Litvinov told the truth but was denounced / by heads of governments lacking conscience / They shed hypocritical tears for Ethiopians / while courting the greedy conqueror."[117] His attitude toward the war generally followed the communist line, but he continued to blame Nazi aggression even after the Molotov-Ribbentrop Pact: "War erupted and the land tasted her poison / as stars fell and darkness concealed her martyrs / The living and dead burned in their flames / it began in the Reich and there it will end!"[118] Muhammad Mahdi al-Jawahiri was also a critic of Nazism, but he began denouncing both sides of a war waged to defend colonial territories and urging Arab neutrality in his new newspaper, *al-Ra'i al-'Amm*.[119]

As the public debate on Iraqi neutrality raged, Rashid 'Ali al-Kaylani returned to power in a coup orchestrated by the four colonels of the "Golden Square," a cell of nationalist army officers who were actively engaged in politics, on April 1, 1941.[120] While Nuri al-Sa'id and Crown Prince 'Abd al-Ilah fled to Jordan, Britain landed thousands of troops in Basra, insisting that they be allowed to move toward Palestine in accordance with the Anglo-Iraqi Treaty but clearly stalling their movement in preparation for a confrontation in Iraq. Spontaneous demonstrations in support of Rashid 'Ali erupted across the country, with nationalist and leftist poets pledging their allegiance. Muhammad Salih Bahr al-'Ulum, a longstanding critic of Rashid 'Ali, declared his enthusiasm for the latter's "declaration of revolution" in a poem he recited in a demonstration in Najaf on May 1. Recalling the tribal ambush of British trains in the 1920 uprising, Bahr al-'Ulum thundered, "Tell those who received their homes as compensation / for my homeland and the violation of my honor / 'Go and ask the train that is supposed to carry you / about the Euphrates and the day it was attacked!'"[121] Bahr al-'Ulum may have been welcoming Rashid ʿAli to his own side of the anticolonial struggle, but the poem clearly indicated the enduring dichotomy between patriots and traitors that shaped his vision of colonialism and nationalism.

The Anglo-Iraqi War began the next day, when Winston Churchill ordered the British Army to fire on the Iraqi units that surrounded the British Royal Air Force station at Habbaniyya.[122] Nationalist newspapers like *al-Bilad*, *al-Istiqlal*, and *al-Zaman* published scores of nationalist poems during the brief war. In one of these poems, Muhammad Bahjat al-Athari described the Nazi assault on Britain as divine retribution for the sins of colonialism, mocking pathetic British appeals for American aid and ridiculing the "feeble and lame" President Roosevelt.[123] Most poets, however, ignored the Nazi role in the conflict and instead described the war as the culmination of Iraq's long struggle against British colonialism. ʿAbd al-Karim al-ʿAllaf asked rhetorically in *al-Istiqlal*, "Shall we protect the rights of the English and these / designs of theirs whose veil has now been drawn? / We have been quiet about the oppression of our nation / but when we are silent, our vengeance only rises."[124] ʿAbd al-Sahib al-Dujayli echoed this line in the same paper, complaining that Britain "humiliated the Arabs until they could not bear it / and made them taste every flavor or injustice."[125] Ahmad al-Safi al-Najafi remained in Syrian exile but sent a picture of himself reciting nationalist poems at a Damascus demonstration to *al-Istiqlal* and published one of those poems in *al-Bilad*. Safi had previously endured Athari's shuʿubiyya accusations due to his Shiʿi background, Persian ancestry, and leftist sympathies, but he embraced the rhetoric of pan-Arabism in his insistence, "You were always one Arab nation / so do not ever say `two nations' / You are now the object of the hope / of every nation in this Arab East!"[126] These nationalist tropes would continue to define his political poetry after the war, a clear indication of the new links between nationalists and leftists forged in the war.[127]

While the press was an important platform for nationalist poetry, Baghdad Radio broadcast dozens of poems that reached even larger audiences in urban cafés.[128] Despite their antipathy for Rashid ʿAli, most leftist poets followed the example of the Iraqi Communist Party, which voiced its support for the regime even before formal Soviet recognition.[129] Bahr al-ʿUlum absolved the left of blame for aligning with Nazis, insisting in a public poem that British actions proved that the war was motivated by colonialism rather than antifascism: "What do the English really want, for they have / left their own wealth open for Hitler to count / Berlin is terrorizing London with her eagles / while the flies of London play like eagles in our sky."[130] He insisted that "national defense is a religious duty" and left Najaf to support the struggle in Baghdad, reciting his long poem, "History, Record!," on Baghdad Radio on May 21. The poem linked the Iraqi struggle to anticolonial movements in Egypt, Palestine, and the Balkans and bluntly declared that colonialism could only be defeated with violence: "Speak to [the English] through the mouth / of your machine guns for time is short / And they do not hear the voice of truth / unless it comes in a whizz of bullets."[131]

Ma'ruf al-Rusafi had already retired to Falluja to work on his controversial biography of the Prophet Muhammad, but he broke his silence with a popular poem praising the "exalted Rashid 'Ali" that was broadcast repeatedly by Baghdad Radio.[132] The poem invoked the familiar nationalist dichotomy of patriotism and treason, mocking the flight of Nuri al-Sa'id and 'Abd al-Ilah to Jordan and declaring that they "became infidels" when they abandoned Iraq and "left their countrymen to bear their burden." Rusafi remained in Falluja for the duration of the war and described the destruction of the city by British troops and Assyrian mercenaries, who were accused of raping Muslim women and other "wicked offenses in the homes of Falluja."[133] These crimes, Rusafi observed, were consistent with the colonial logic of divide-and-rule employed by Britain in the Middle East: "You have derided and scorned Muslims as fools / while making Jews your advisers and confidants."[134] Rusafi returned to Baghdad after the war to stay with Khayri al-Hindawi, the poet who had defended him during the hijab wars of the 1920s, and while he could not publish "Day of Falluja," he recited it numerous times to his admirers in the cafés.[135]

Rashid 'Ali and his allies fled Baghdad on May 29, 1941, while Nuri al-Sa'id and 'Abd al-Ilah returned three days later.[136] Muhammad Salih Bahr al-'Ulum watched the "bloody procession" of troops retreating to their barracks and mourned the Iraqi defeat: "The city of Falluja was deluged with blood / her noble breaths smothered and stifled / While Englishmen returned to dance / with whores and harlots at Habbaniyya."[137] As the sad scene unfolded before him, a procession of Iraqi Jews celebrating the return of the crown prince was attacked by soldiers, the beginning of the violent urban riots known colloquially as the Farhud, which claimed the lives of nearly two hundred Iraqi Jews during the first two days of June 1941.[138] Bahr al-ʿUlum regretted this violence but insisted that it was the fruit of colonial policy in Iraq: "You divided the people into sects and parties / until you opened the door to their colonization / You suppressed and ignored the spirit of truth / a politics that transformed enemies into lovers."[139] Furious that Iraqi patriots were now branded Nazis and accused of treason, Bahr al-ʿUlum began reciting a satirical poem about a simple baker caught in the midst of this absurd witch hunt:

> The inspector asked Fatuma the Baker,
> "When did Nazism [*Naziyya*] enter this shop?"
> She moaned over her deplorable fortune,
> wailing in the face of this horror and dread:
> "Do you not know my name or occupation?
> Your food comes from my delicious bread!"
> We can see ourselves in this simple woman,
> wronged while our beloved Iraq is distressed[140]

The bizarre and irrelevant invocation of Nazism symbolized the bitter irony of "traitors" challenging the nationalism of "patriots." This irony that was reinforced several weeks later when Bahr al-ʿUlum, the great antifascist poet of the 1930s, was arrested as a "Nazi sympathizer."[141] This British emphasis on Nazism to conceptualize and discredit Iraqi nationalists who supported the Rashid ʿAli movement appeared patently absurd to the many Iraqis who embraced the movement for entirely different reasons and in the end undermined any attempt to emphasize the very real crimes perpetrated against Iraqi Jews.

## Prison Poetry and Public Apologies

State efforts to invert the nationalist rhetoric of "patriots" and "traitors" in their prosecution of the partisans of the Rashid ʿAli movement were undermined by incompetence and incoherence. The trials of "Nazis" were subjected to public ridicule, as defense attorneys were threatened with prosecution when they argued too forcefully and ordinary citizens used the courts to settle personal scores.[142] British officials at the Ministry of Interior scoured back issues of *al-Bilad, al-Istiqlal,* and *al-Zaman* to identify "Nazis," but state employees intervened repeatedly to protect family, friends, and allies.[143] Unprotected "traitors" were nevertheless located, and disease and overcrowding grew rampant as the internment camps filled with scores of politicians, journalists, poets, teachers, and students.[144] Poets like Muhammad Salih Bahr al-'Ulum pointed to reports of rape and looting by Indian troops in the Iraqi countryside to portray these internees as innocent brothers, husbands, and fathers whose only crime was defending their land, women, and honor against foreign invasion and exploitation.[145]

Beyond these questions of innocence and guilt, however, was the historical incoherence of the state campaign against treason. Poets and politicians implicated as "traitors" invariably denied sympathy for Nazism and defended their support for Rashid 'Ali on nationalist grounds.[146] Muhammad Bahjat al-Athari declared that the sight of the "flag of the Thames" flying over the internment camps at Fao and 'Amara vindicated his stance in the war.[147] His prison poetry defended the patriotic nationalism of the internees and insisted that death was preferable to the dishonor of those who now supported the state.[148] These arguments resonated in the botched prosecution of Muhammad Mahdi al-Jawahiri, who had opposed the Rashid 'Ali movement and fled the country to avoid becoming entangled with it. Jawahiri nevertheless discovered that he was slated for internment because Yunis Bahri had recited his poetry on Radio Berlin. He appealed for help from Muhammad al-Sadr, insisting that Bahri had recycled older poems about the Iraqi Revolution of 1920, and escaped interment only after the Minister of Interior Salih Jabr consulted his own copy of Jawahiri's diwan to confirm.[149] The fact that the state interpreted the same poem as "patriotic" with respect to the 1920 uprising and "treasonous" with respect to the 1941 conflict underscored the incoherent historical evolution of Hashemite "nationalism." British and Iraqi officials clashed repeatedly about the difference between "legitimate" nationalism and "treasonous" anticolonialism, with the former now complaining that any public criticism of the British role in Iraq amounted to the "falsification of history."[150]

The ultimate effect of these efforts to blur the lines between nationalism and anticolonialism was predictable enough. Internment not only failed to break the spirit of the political prisoners, it also facilitated the emergence of new alliances between the nationalists and leftists lumped together as traitors. These shifts were particularly apparent in Athari's elegy for the "Rooster of al-Fao," which offered an implicit critique of the vicious partisan conflicts between the two camps over the preceding five years.[151] Bahr al-'Ulum also promoted these new alliances in the desert prison camp at Nuqrat al-Salman, where he recited nationalist poems to fellow prisoners and organized the first prison hunger strike in Iraqi history.[152] His prison poems reflected the new anticolonial consensus that the political elite were "traitors" who persecuted loyal "patriots" with no differentiation between nationalists and leftists:

> They sold their nation to the mother of Cornwallis
> and rushed to spoil themselves with their bounty
> With this blood money they arrested every free man,
> whom they imprisoned without crime or conviction
> But here in Nuqrat al-Salman, we see our tribulation
> as something far stranger than those that came before
> For the slave rules over us at every single second,
> domination that departs from custom and convention,
> Yet this is our government, erected for us by tyranny,
> if only it had not been erected and did not now exist![153]

He began invoking pan-Arab rhetoric more pointedly in prison, declaring in one poem, "We were sent to raise the lofty flag / to finally establish an Arab state / To gather all who speak the language / of the *daad* [a distinctive Arabic consonant] and to build a free life."[154] Yet even as he embraced nationalist rhetoric, Bahr al-'Ulum never shied away from emphasizing his antifascist politics and continued to denounce Hitler and mourn Nazi military triumphs like that at al-'Alamayn before his fellow prisoners.[155]

Interment became a nonpartisan marker of patriotism for poets, a "crown of honor" awarded in recognition of "service to the homeland" in the words of Ahmad al-Safi al-Najafi.[156] Safi was arrested in Beirut after British authorities notified the Free French that he had published "Nazi propaganda" in *al-Bilad* and composed a series of poems that ridiculed these accusations.[157] While he always denied any sympathy for Nazism and contended that his stance was driven entirely by anticolonial sentiment, Safi worried in one poem that Britain might lose the war, depriving him of his opportunity for vengeance and leaving him "half a Muslim."[158] Ma'ruf al-Rusafi complained that Britain had deprived him of the honor of arrest and internment for the "noble crime" of nationalism and tried to provoke the government into doing so by taunting the spies who monitored his salon discussions.[159] This was certainly the intent behind his public circulation of the poem "The English in Their Colonial Policies," which condemned the colonial legacy in Iraq:

> How often have they plowed the soil of their colonies
> with black injustices that ruined their fertile soil?
> How often have they roused the people from slumber,
> inciting strife like darkness that looms over hardship?
> They feast on the butter produced through machination,
> and throw the leftover scraps to the native inhabitants
> They take from the colonies the gems that eluded them,
> and give them back nothing but rubbish and refuse
> Go visit India and take a look around, and you will see
> nothing but dust and rubble scattered across the ground[160]

The cabinet nearly collapsed when an official at the Ministry of Transportation and Public Works publicly praised the poem in June 1941. C. J. Edmonds, the British adviser to the minister of interior, demanded that Jalal Baban fire his employee but was rebuffed.[161] Rusafi began publicly goading Edmonds, mocking his inability to silence him in popular poems that circulated in the cafés of Baghdad and Falluja. One poem complained directly of Edmonds's role in the state's crusade against political dissent: "You take your salary from us like an employee / and by God this is the most painful part / For today we bear the burden of your tyranny / and for the privilege dole your wages in cash."[162] The provocation backfired: Rusafi's state subsidies were withdrawn and newspapers were warned not to publish his poems, but he was not arrested due to the government's fear that his public profile would generate protests and only underscore the failure of the internment campaign.

While Edmonds blacklisted poets, the mayor of Baghdad argued that the state should exploit the public utility of poetry in order to combat anticolonial nationalism.[163] Mustafa al-'Umari approached 'Abd al-Husayn al-Huwayzi, a distinguished Najafi poet and cleric who had praised Rashid 'Ali during the war.¹⁶⁴ Huwayzi was now induced to apologize for this poem to ʿAbd al-Ilah in the Baghdadi newspaper *al-Akhbar*. His new poem blamed Rashid ʿAli for inciting what Huwayzi now called a national "fitna": "The politicians deluded and misled the nation / while creeping away like cowards in the morning / He said in his speech, 'All who die are martyrs' / but those who lived are more fortunate / For were his speeches any use to our soldiers?"¹⁶⁵ This public recantation was echoed by Muhammad ʿAli al-Yaʿqubi, a fellow Najafi poet who had praised the Rashid ʿAli movement as the culmination of the 1920 Revolution: "Tyranny led [Britain] to the banks of oblivion / for this the fate of every domineering nation / Have you forgotten what once befell her army / at our hands, for I do not think she ever has!"¹⁶⁶ Yaʿqubi now offered his "penitent apology and renunciation" and begged for ʿAbd al-Ilah's forgiveness in *al-Akhbar*. The new poem also contended that Iraqis had been duped by deceitful politicians: "We thought hardship would end when you left / that adversity would vanish when you were gone / But the moment you left, the pillars of morning / cracked under the misfortune of blackened night."¹⁶⁷ Dozens of other poets, including Kazim Al Nuh, ʿAbd al-Muhsin al-Hashimi, and Mahmud al-Habbubi, published similar recantations in *al-Akhbar* in fall 1941. Iraqi critics like Raʾuf al-Waʿiz have noted that the poets' diwans almost always included the panegyrics for Rashid ʿAli and never the subsequent recantations, arguing that this showed their patent insincerity.¹⁶⁸ Most of these poets were elderly, and their recantations tended to be viewed more with pity than contempt, further reinforcing the declining value of the political panegyric in the postcolonial era.

## Stalingrad and the Triumph of the Iraqi Left

Two months after these recantations, Muhammad Mahdi al-Jawahiri extolled Soviet heroism in the Battle of Moscow in his newspaper *al-Raʿi al-ʿAmm*. It was a grandiose celebration of communist strength, addressed to future generations who would learn of Soviet exploits in school: "The giant cut off the nose of the proud / and the tyrant burned in his lofty fires / History saw what was never seen before / in this struggle of pain of endurance."¹⁶⁹ The first line of the poem had originally read, "The East cut off the nose of the West," but Jawahiri changed it at the last minute to avoid provoking the ire of C. J. Edmonds.¹⁷⁰ British officials had initially conflated "national socialism" and "national communism" as two sides of the same anticolonial coin, but they soon came to recognize communists as the more vocal and effective critics of fascism and Nazism in Iraq.[171] They noted the propaganda value of antifascist poetry and allowed Jawahiri to publish freely in *al-Raʿi al-ʿAmm*, much to the chagrin of Iraqi opponents, who argued disingenuously that the paper's pro-Soviet line masked "Nazi" subversion.[172] His ode to "Stalingrad" praised the Soviet ideals of "freedom and prosperity and brotherhood" and insisted that committed leftist poets must "respond to the spirit of the call" and illuminate the new horizon of socialist utopia.[173]

British officials slowly came to realize how effective Jawahiri was becoming in his promotion of increasingly popular communist ideas.[174] Communist youths were soon fighting Nazi sympathizers in the streets and cafés and painting over swastikas chalked on the walls of university buildings.[175] While leftist poets and intellectuals were attacked by their nationalist opponents as "sycophants and opportunists," they maintained their principled stance against the "grave danger" of fascism.[176] Their position sometimes resulted in strange compromises that would leave them open to charges of collaboration in later years. The Jewish poet Anwar Shaʾul published five poems in the local press celebrating Allied victories in the war, and while he judiciously balanced praise for Churchill with praise for Stalin, the enthusiastic response of the British embassy to the poems indicated the stakes of war poetry.[177] British officials leaned on Nuri al-Saʿid to convince Jawahiri to write a poem in honor of the British triumph at El Alamein to complement his ode to Stalingrad and produced the pro-British poem "Tunis."[178] Jawahiri acknowledged that he accepted Nuri's request out of political expedience, understanding that his support for the British war effort was necessary to facilitate freedom of expression for the Iraqi Left. He always insisted, however, that his own antifascist politics were more sincere than those of the "collaborationist" politicians who struggled "for the sake of British and American interests."[179] Aside from the strange saga of the pro-British "Tunis," Jawahiri's war poems promoted his vision of communist internationalism in support of the Soviet military victories.[180] While he did not criticize Britain during the war, his pointed praise for Soviet anti-imperialism and anticapitalism reflected the ideological weight of this silence. As communism began to supplant fascism in the public sphere, British officials began to worry that their tolerance of the antifascist Left had backfired and came to view *al-Ra'i al-'Amm* as the most dangerous newspaper in the country.[181] The oscillating British perspective on the stakes of Jawahiri's poetry reflected the shortsighted colonial view of political alliances. Jawahiri and the communists were seen as strategic allies when the radical nationalists were strong and dangerous adversaries when they were weak.

The divide-and-rule tactics of colonialism were proving less effective in Iraq, partly because the communists and leftists were becoming more adept at building broader alliances by fusing class grievances with anticolonial rhetoric. When British and Iraqi officials tried to channel popular anger with inflation against Jewish merchants, the communists worked instead to blame landowners, politicians, and the British army.[182] The extent to which these arguments permeated popular opinion was apparent in the wartime poetry of Jawahiri's cousin 'Ali al-Sharqi, who had previously criticized leftist naiveté in the days of the Popular Reform League. Sharqi now described the traumas of war as a product of capitalist exploitation: "Workers are sacrificed by their country / life becomes death and profit becomes loss / The factory explodes into machines / as the capitalist glimpses his destruction." In contrast to this depiction of capitalist society, Sharqi described the Soviet Union as a land of brotherhood and equality for all men and women and praised the leadership of Stalin: "A union that rejects all distinction / between the wealthy and wretched / Guided by a cool and collected leader /whose character is crafted from iron."[183] While Sharqi's evolution from critic of the Popular Reform League to defender of Stalin in a span of less than ten years illustrated the growth of communist influence during the war, he had neither abandoned pan-Arabism nor become a communist.[184] This was not an indication of individual conversion between the two ideological currents, but instead a reflection of the general convergence of interests between the two currents. Liberated from the ideological and tactical constraints of politicians and intellectuals, poets like Sharqi were constructing a new national political consensus that would prove critical to the national front politics of the 1950s.

## Conclusion

Amid the litany of poems published in praise of the Soviet Red Army in *al-Ra'i al-'Amm* during the war was a poem that appeared in May 1944.

dedicated by Muhammad Mahdi al-Jawahiri to Ma'ruf al-Rusafi.[185] The poem praised Rusafi's social convictions and political courage: "You were bold when some thought moved you / from the ideas that summoned you to danger / Certain there was none other among the people / who could be even half as courageous as you."[186] Rusafi was suffering from poverty and depression in the final years of his life, but he was touched by the tribute and responded in kind to Jawahiri two weeks later in *al-Ra'i al-'Amm*: "Today poetry flourishes in you and not me / But before today I was a real poet like you."[187] The public exchange cemented the affinity between the poets and echoed an exchange between the two poets in Rusafi's newspaper, *al-Amal*, in 1923, when Jawahiri defended Rusafi's critique of veiling and defense of women's liberation.[188] The relationship between the two poets, however, soured in the intervening two decades, after Rusafi supported Sati' al-Husri's "shu'ubiyya" accusation against Jawahiri and the poets found themselves on opposing sides of the nationalist debates in 1936 and 1941. The final reconciliation between the two poets reflected their shared commitment to the new cultural politics of anticolonial nationalism that would transcend partisan rivalries in the coming decade.

The cultural politics of nationalism that inflected the poetry of the postcolonial period was initially a divisive force in Iraqi politics and society. The partisan poetry of this period was characterized by a pervasive dichotomy between "patriots" and "traitors" to the nation among both watani and qawmi nationalists. Nearly all poets who invoked this dichotomy did so in order to portray their own side as authentic custodians of the anticolonial legacy in the country. Their differing points of emphasis about what this legacy really meant, however, served to cement new distinctions between "leftist" anticolonialism and "nationalist" anticolonialism. The former current was focused on domestic politics and the struggle against the institutions of domination and exploitation bequeathed by the colonial states, while the latter was focused on foreign politics and the struggle against the artificial borders imposed by colonial edicts. While historical scholarship on the watani/qawmi divide has emphasized the very real differences between the basic conception of the nation as "Iraqi" or "Arab," it has tended at times to obscure the equally real ambiguities and affinities of the debate. The poetry of the period offers a better window into these debates precisely because it diminishes the importance of conventional political platitudes.

As the response of poets like ʿAli al-Sharqi and Maʿruf al-Rusafi to the nationalist campaign against the leftist Popular Reform League indicates, the dichotomy between "leftists" and "nationalists" was never as rigid as it may seem in retrospect. Both poets insisted that the two approaches to the colonial legacy in Iraq and the Arab world need not be considered mutually exclusive, a stance that was also apparent in the "nationalist" themes invoked by "leftist" poets like Muhammad Mahdi al-Jawahiri and Muhammad Salih Bahr al-ʿUlum. It was the experience of World War II that gave real weight to these hidden or contested alliances, however, as the experience of Muhammad Bahjat al-Athari in the Fao internment camp attests. The softening of partisan stances was made possible by the realization that the Hashemite state represented the colonial legacy inveighed against by both anticolonial currents. The tacit agreement between leftists and nationalists that they could both be "patriots" in their struggle against the "traitors" who controlled the levers of power in the postcolonial state laid the groundwork for the postwar politics of the "national front."

Another notable line in Jawahiri's May 1944 tribute to Maʿruf al-Rusafi declared in admiration, "In all of those panegyrics you were really cursing / surrounded by lords who were busy blaspheming."[189] This appreciation of Rusafi's ability to scandalize the ruling class with his poems was reflected to an even greater extent by his own public life in the postwar period. Rusafi died on March 16, 1945, but he managed to inspire one final scandal two months after his death, when *al-Bilad* published one of his poems to commemorate the end of the war. The poem denounced Britain for betraying promises to Sharif Husayn and the Arabs and proved so popular that the government instituted new press restrictions.[190] In the context of the general political alienation between the Iraqi public and the postcolonial state, the scandal pointed toward new uses of the revolutionary power of poetry in the postwar era. Dissident poetry would become a way to challenge the state and embarrass political elites, not only in the columns of newspapers but in public spaces. There is little doubt that Rusafi would have been proud to see a "real poet" like Muhammad Mahdi al-Jawahiri carry forward his rebellious legacy in this way.

( CHAPTER 5 )

# POETRY OF PUBLIC SPACES
## *Mass Politics and New Horizons, 1946–1958*

On January 5, 1946, the Iraqi government held a memorial at the Ghazi Cinema in Baghdad for Jaʿfar Abu al-Timman.[1] Muhammad Salih Bahr al-ʿUlum had already eulogized Abu al-Timman after his death forty days earlier, praising his influence on both nationalist and leftist politics, but he now appeared at the memorial service to publicly condemn Nuri al-Saʿid for betraying his mentor's anticolonial legacy.[2] Bahr al-ʿUlum denounced the use of martial law to prosecute nationalists and leftists after the Anglo-Iraqi War, complaining, "These palaces are for traitors and their successors / while gallows and graves are reserved for patriots." This rhetoric of treason pervaded his attack on the political elite, who he argued had betrayed not only the nation but also their own souls: "Even the hearts of those who dragged the country / to this fate cry out that they were dragged as well." As Nuri and his supporters stormed out of the theater in anger, Bahr al-ʿUlum improvised a memorable rebuke:

> You who flee this judgment, try to understand,
> the final settlement with tyrants is harsh indeed
> They knew the harshness of the penalty and that
> their power to halt its harsh judgment was weak
> You who flee, drink from the cup of this complaint,
> for you will find in it that the blame is all for you

> Linger a bit, for the people have issued a judgment,
> and the verdict they render is excommunication![3]

Over the past two decades, most poetic attacks on the state had been published in party newspapers or recited to partisan audiences, but Bahr al-ʿUlum now drew on the legacy of rebel poetry to renew his commitment to the dangers of poetry and emphasize the stakes of public dissidence.[4]

Nuri returned to the cinema after Bahr al-ʿUlum finished his poem but left again during Muhammad Mahdi al-Jawahiri's elegy.[5] Jawahiri praised Abu al-Timman and the Iraqi Revolution of 1920 before complaining about the postcolonial state's appropriation of this anticolonial legacy:

> Twenty-five years have passed as if they were,
> with their personalities, an item from the news
> We tired of them like a prisoner tires of shackles,
> so far in excess of any crimes they committed . . .
> Noble youths grew older, but they only renewed
> the youthfulness of the old leader of the wicked
> Suddenly the face of grandson and grandfather,
> seemed to observers to be one and the same
> Who could have imagined it would last so long,
> a government constructed on flawed foundation?! . . .
> A novel whose chapters were so jumbled by time
> that the roles seem to have been transformed
> How evil is this drama contrived by the author,
> in artifice collected under the cover of a book
> Puppets are staged, while behind them stands
> a puppet master concealed behind the curtain
> The roles of different sects and ethnic groups
> are put on display by this policy of colonialism[6]

Jawahiri published the poem on the front page of his newspaper the next morning and waited arrest, while Bahr al-ʿUlum went into hiding.[7] The minister of interior at the time, however, was Saʿd Salih, a fellow Najafi poet sympathetic to Bahr al-ʿUlum and Jawahiri who refused to order their arrest.[8]

This public articulation of dissent foreshadowed a new era of political poetry in which poets became active participants in new revolutionary currents of mass politics.[9] The cultural politics of nationalism were transformed by the two seminal popular uprisings of the postwar era, the Wathba of January 1948 and the intifada of November 1952, which brought hundreds of thousands of disenchanted Iraqi students, workers, and activists into the streets to protest colonialism and dictatorship.[10] Leftist poets like Bahr al-ʿUlum and Jawahiri, along with a new generation of nationalist and communist comrades and rivals, revived older forms of rebel poetry to contest a political order now characterized as the "black regime."[11] Their poetic contributions to the revolutionary culture of the period reflected the subordination of partisan conflicts to the new revolutionary project of national liberation. Poets from both the nationalist and communist camps embraced the Sartrean ethos of commitment (iltizam) as a revolutionary "doctrine of cultural action" against the state.[12] The political reconciliation forged in the internment camps of World War II was evident in the national front politics of the postwar era, as leftist poets increasingly embraced nationalist rhetoric and nationalist poets adopted socialist slogans. The enduring desire of poets to speak for the nation had never been as tangible and visceral as it was in these heady days of public protest.

The new cultural politics of revolution was reflected not only in the political content of poetry but also in the radical aesthetics of the modernist free verse movement in Arabic poetry, which first emerged in the fertile cultural arena of postwar Baghdad. A new generation of young poets, driven by Jabra Ibrahim Jabra's maxim that "everything had to change," embraced avant-garde aesthetics as a way of expressing their commitment to overturning the traditional modes of thinking that left Iraqis and Arabs vulnerable to colonial domination.[13] Free verse poetry eventually drove both the neoclassical qasida and the traditional practice of platform poetry into virtual extinction, but the two styles of poetry coexisted during the 1950s.[14] Numerous critics have argued that the modernist aesthetics of free verse poetry expanded the cultural and intellectual horizons of a new generation of poets, liberating them from the stagnant traditions and conventions of the past.[15] However valid this judgment remains as an index of beauty and innovation, the gradual eclipse of neoclassical poetry also restricted the social utility of poetry. The eventual triumph of free verse poetry reified an artificial distinction between mass culture and high culture by privileging avant-garde aesthetics over the "cultural authenticity" of the anticolonial qasida. The types of poems once recited from platforms and public squares were now published in trendy journals and beautifully illustrated collections, and poets were transformed from national spokesmen into mere intellectuals.

This cultural transformation took time, and the neoclassical qasida remained the dominant form of postwar poetry. The public dissidence of rebel poets like Muhammad Salih Bahr al-'Ulum and Muhammad Mahdi al-Jawahiri facilitated the growth of mass politics and the rise of a new "horizon illuminated with blood."[16] Their poems mobilized crowds and articulated revolutionary demands for national liberation, and their socialist internationalism allowed them to link their own struggle to contemporary decolonization movements throughout the Third World and articulate new "geographies of liberation."[17] Like communist poets in Europe, their embrace of mass politics was "aimed at the collective construction of a new world."[18] Their revolutionary politics were animated by subversive intrusions in the struggle to control public space and shape nationalist narratives. The effectiveness of their heroic acts of dissent and defiance was apparent above all else in the dramatic intensification of state persecution against rebel poets in the postwar period. The intensification of state repression and the challenge of free verse aesthetics limited the scope of this poetry of public spaces to a specific moment in time and space, but it nevertheless worked to translate cultural politics of commitment into concrete social action.[19]

## Poetry and Mass Politics in Iraq, 1946–1948

The refusal of Sa'd Salih to arrest Muhammad Salih Bahr al-'Ulum and Muhammad Mahdi al-Jawahiri in January 1946 presaged further poetic interventions in political affairs. When Tawfiq al-Suwaydi became prime minister in February 1946, he ended martial law, restored press freedom, and allowed five new political parties to be licensed, including the leftist National Democratic Party, National Unity Party, and People's Party.[20] Bahr al-'Ulum and Jawahiri served on the central committee of the National Unity Party and urged the cooperation of all leftist parties.[21] At one party meeting, Bahr al-'Ulum implored his comrades not to fall victim to the divisive partisanship of the past: "Despite our shared grief, our division into factions / was an evil consequence that doubled our shared curse / But the triumph of Iraq will come through this Union / our struggle will be salvaged from the jaws of defeat!"[22] This appeal for national unity would become the dominant trope of postwar national front poetry.

Jawahiri took advantage of new press freedoms to finally publish "Tartara" on March 24, 1946.[23] He had written the poem to protest the suspension of his newspaper, *al-Ra'i al-'Amm*, in August 1945 but was unable to publish it at the time. The satirical poem attacked Salih Jabr and Arshad al-'Umari, prominent members of the previous cabinet, for suspending the paper for misleading reasons:

> What prattle is this chattering to me,
> pushing me forward, holding me back,
> Making me first Shi'i and then Sunni,
> turning me Jewish and then Christian,
> Fashioning me Kurdish and then Arab,
> flinging at me false charges of racism
> Rendering me cosmopolitan and then British,
> Picturing me as rational and then delusional
> My own being, as their eminences desire,
> From my very face to the seat of my ass
> Stands open for benefit like Salih [Jabr],
> Splendidly furnished like [Arshad] al-'Umari![24]

Jabr and 'Umari demanded the arrest of Jawahiri, but Sa'd Salih again refused to arrest his friend. The enraged politicians retaliated by withdrawing support for Suwaydi's cabinet, the second time in six months that Jawahiri played a role in the collapse of a cabinet.[25] Unfortunately for the poet, the next three prime ministers had all been targets of Jawahiri's satire and vowed to silence his dangerous dissent.[26]

Bahr al-'Ulum was elected to lead the Cigarette Workers Union and emphasized the links between poetry and labor in one poem recited to workers in Mosul in May 1946: "If poetry were not inspired by your revolution / it could not be appreciated by those who hear it / One line of poetry that helps to build your unity / is mightier than a house of one thousand floors."[27]

The poet's nationalist reputation made him an effective spokesmen of the communist effort to link capitalism and colonialism, particularly after Iraqi police massacred striking oil workers in Gawurpaghi in July 1946.[28] Bahr al-ʿUlum narrated the events to fellow workers in Baghdad in language dripping with anger: "In the tragedy of Gawurpaghi, injustice struck me in the gut / I yearned to bleed for the slaughter of sons and brothers / Victims were cleansed not with water but their own blood / Butcher of Kirkuk, await the resurrection of these corpses!"[29] The poet pleaded to fellow workers to demand "retaliation for every atrocity" and ridiculed the government's appeal for patience: "What is neutrality when the blood / of workers runs in the streets?"[30]

Prime Minister Arshad al-ʿUmari responded by suspending newspapers and arresting publishers, editors, and journalists, which only amplified the underground communist press.[31] Bahr al-ʿUlum led his tobacco union on strike three weeks later and organized a national boycott of Ahliyyah cigarettes, but the financial precarity of the workers brought the strike and boycott to an end on October 19, 1946.[32] Bahr al-ʿUlum linked the strike to anticolonial politics in a poem he recited at a National Unity Party meeting, linking the suppression of the recent Anti-Zionist League demonstration in Baghdad, the oil strike in Gawurpaghi, and the tobacco boycott on the tyranny of "John Bull."[33] The poem's seamless integration of Arab nationalist rhetoric and communist concerns symbolized the new cultural politics of the anticolonial national front and reflected growing cooperation between nationalist and leftist factions.[34] Dissident poetry, articulating increasingly radical social and political messages, reached new audiences. Terrified that the radical politics of Baghdad would "infect" other cities, Nuri al-Saʿid took the extraordinary step of preventing Bahr al-ʿUlum from visiting his hometown of Najaf, which caused the poet to protest bitterly that he was "torn from my home and people"[35] State efforts to physically constrain the public reach of poets and poetry, however, could not suppress the revolutionary spirit of cultural dissidence that gave birth to the new poetry of public spaces.

## Poetry and the Cultural Politics of the Wathba

The massive Wathba protests of January 1948 transformed Muhammad Mahdi al-Jawahiri and Muhammad Salih Bahr al-ʿUlum from rebel poets into nationalist icons. The protests erupted in response to the renegotiation of the Anglo-Iraqi Treaty, which simply confirmed core British interests in the country in exchange for some minor symbolic concessions. Jawahiri was in London with a delegation of journalists during the negotiations and recalled Crown Prince ʿAbd al-Ilah explaining dejectedly, "What can we do? They frighten us, Jawahiri, by bringing up the [communist] bogey every now and then."[36] The Portsmouth Treaty was signed on January 15, 1947, and public protests in Baghdad were organized by nationalist law students, including the poets Kazim Jawad, Hilal Naji, and ʿAdnan al-Rawi.[37] Jawahiri had finally been awarded his long-coveted seat in parliament several months earlier, but he leaped to the defense of the law students when Nuri al-Saʿid accused them of undermining the Arab struggle against Zionism.[38] When his cousin ʿAli al-Sharqi asked why he risked his seat in this manner, Jawahiri explained that he was incapable of remaining silent in the face of injustice, describing himself as a "bedouin in Paris."[39]

While Jawahiri confined himself primarily to press commentary, Bahr al-ʿUlum joined the protests in Baghdad. He recited fiery anti-British poems to students and workers: "Did you forget the days of the Euphrates / and return in disgrace to face another day? / The Tigris will show you that she is a tyrant / the face of a rebellious people to her enemies."[40] As protesters clashed with police on January 20 and 21, Bahr al-ʿUlum's poems became anthems that the crowds chanted: "The treaty came to prepare our land for invasion / sanctioning this assault against its own nation / Using the language of bullets to impose itself / compelling support from these barking dogs!"[41] Protesters soon overwhelmed police, halting traffic and blocking bridges, and looting the offices of the Criminal Investigations Division and the pro-British newspaper, *Iraq Times*.[42] ʿAbd al-Ilah admitted defeat on the evening of January 21, announcing over the state radio that the government had "unanimously agreed" to oppose ratification of the treaty.[43]

The repudiation of the Portsmouth Treaty failed to assuage the crowds, who demanded more radical reforms. On January 22, ten thousand protesters marched behind the casket of Shamran ʿAlwan, a Jewish communist student killed by police two days earlier.[44] The crowds hoisted Bahr al-ʿUlum on their shoulders as he improvised defiant poems and declared on behalf of the nation, "We stand ready to wade into the deluge of death / as we sing to the people a hymn of immortality!"⁴⁵ Jawahiri appeared in the street for the first time, urging the crowds to honor martyrs like Shamran through revolutionary political action:

> Every one of us envies you, for you achieved
> the honor of the moment from this intrigue
> Every one of us now walks at your heels,
> in pursuit of sacrifices both trivial and heavy
> Every one of us surrenders to your inspiration
> in compliance with the will of the free nation
> For if you will it, we shall march in anguish
> and if you will it, we will march in full haste
> If you will it, we will dye this road with blood,
> a coat of paint to herald the stage of transition⁴⁶

Bahr al-'Ulum echoed this appeal for martyrdom and sacrifice, reciting poems that appealed to labor unions and the army to "erect victory arches for your workers."⁴⁷ Bahr al-'Ulum insisted that these heroic acts of resistance would inspire future generations and boasted that his own poems would memorialize their contributions to the future revolution: "In my mouth is an anthem that will be recounted / to you by Iraqis, generation after generation."⁴⁸

Bahr al-'Ulum's poem "The People's Leap" ("Wathbat al-Sha'b") gave the protests their famous name. He improvised the poem from the shoulders of protesters on January 22, urging them to defeat a treaty their own government had already renounced: "Wathba of the People, tear apart / this treaty of fools with your curses / The Portsmouth Treaty is a shackle / enjoining unconditional occupation."⁴⁹ The term *wathba* reflected his belief that the people were finally "leaping" from the stage of bourgeois revolution to true popular revolution. Thousands of students and workers embraced his vision the next morning, chanting for a "people's revolution" as they carried Bahr al-'Ulum and the leftist lawyer Kamil Qazanchi on their shoulders. Reports of poems that "wrought [the crowds] up to vehement passion" led police to arrest Bahr al-'Ulum that evening.⁵⁰ The poet was interrogated by the notorious CID chief Bahjat Atiyya, who brought up his poem from the previous day: "Are you the one who said: '*Wathba* of the People, tear apart / this treaty of fools with your curses / The Portsmouth Treaty is a shackle / enjoining unconditional occupation'?" Atiyya taunted the poet that he would now learn "whether the fools are you and that rabble" or the politicians, to which Bahr al-'Ulum retorted in verse: "If they cut me up into a thousand pieces / and burn me in the most wicked flame / I will not be hindered from a people who / take precedence in my moral universe / For I did not drink from life to be kept away / from them and my nation as cupbearer."[51] Furious with the poet's impudence, Atiyya ordered Bahr al-'Ulum back to his cell, where his hands were bound and hung from the ceiling as guards poured cold water on him throughout the cold night.

While Bahr al-'Ulum suffered in prison, protests continued to rage in Baghdad. When students tried to cross al-Ma'mun Bridge to join workers on the other side of the Tigris River on January 27, police opened fire from rooftops, leaving hundreds dead on the bridge and in the river below.[52] Among the fallen was Muhammad Mahdi al-Jawahiri's younger brother Ja'far, who died a week later.[53] Thousands came to his memorial service at the Haydarkhana Mosque in Baghdad on February 14, watching as Jawahiri climbed a ladder amid the sea of mourners in front of the mosque, raised a loudspeaker, and began reciting the most famous poem in Iraqi history:

> Do you know or do you not know,
> that the wounds of the fallen are a mouth?
> A mouth not like that of the charlatan,
> nor like the mouth of those who beg
> It calls to the hungry and the wretched,
> to spill their blood to feed themselves
> And shouts at the band of sycophants,
> curse these villains and reclaim your honor!

The British ambassador was caught in the traffic standstill, complaining that it was "intolerable" that he "should be forced to make a detour which took ten or fifteen minutes longer" and demanding that police disperse the crowds.[54] The poem was published on the front of nearly every newspaper the next day, its memorable climax articulating the revolutionary vision of the Wathba:

> I see a horizon illuminated with blood,

as the stars now vanish from our sight
A rope from the earth ascended by men,
as the stairs hurl off those who climb them
If a hand reaches out, it is only in betrayal,
interfering to obstruct their final victory
Heaped around it all is a pile of corpses,
whose size is eclipsed only by its honor
A hand now stretches from behind the veil,
and draws upon the horizon what is to be
One generation passes and another rises,
while the fire they face continues to burn[55]

While Jawahiri's poetry was characterized by "ornate language and strict metrics," his performances always affected his audience, even when it was composed primarily of illiterate workers and peasants.[56] The poem's place in the collective memory of the Wathba owed as much to the story of the performance as it did to the memorable phrases preserved on paper.[57] More than any other poem, "My Brother Ja'far" symbolized the poetry of public spaces and the link between poetic language and social performance.

The solidarity of nationalists and leftists was tested by the crisis in Palestine and clashes over the future of Iraqi Jews.[58] On April 14, Jawahiri led a huge demonstration against Zionism and in support of Iraqi Jews and recited another elegy for the Wathba martyrs in al-Saba' Square.[59] The poem appealed for national unity and religious harmony "if after the long separation there was a meeting / between the sheikh, the rabbi, and the priest / and if we agreed on how to raise our voices / and to unfurl our national flags."[60] Dozens of young leftist poets participated in these demonstrations, including the college student Lami'a 'Abbas 'Amara, whose own elegy for martyrs was one of the first public recitations of political poetry by a female poet.[61] The optimism of the Left faded soon after Iraq joined the war against Israel on May 15, 1948, however, as the government used martial law to arrest communists and manipulate elections.[62]

Leftist parties boycotted the June 1948 elections, but the nationalist Independence Party won four seats. Jawahiri, who had surrendered his own seat on principle, contrasted his own "righteous abstention" with nationalist collaboration and described Independence Party leader Muhammad Mahdi Kubba as "but filth to me!"63 The poem reflected both the waning political legitimacy of the state and the dedication of rebel poets to public dissidence. Jawahiri's poem "The Balcony," published in *al-Raʿi al-ʿAmm* in August 1948, became a manifesto of this commitment, attacking poets who wrote from the comfort of cafés, "shouting to one another about foolish things / like the whooping of storks showered with pebbles." He invoked the rebel poetry of 1920 to complain about modern poetry devoid of political resonance:

> How embarrassed they would be if they compared
> their own lives to those of their predecessors,
> Who gave their land blood from which to drink,
> whose slogans were this blood that was shed,
> Those men worked only to feed their stomachs,
> so why do these not heed the pleas of bellies?
> What a disgrace to don the guise of litterateurs,
> which real poets are more honorable without64

While this attack on "café poets" predated debates on "commitment," Jawahiri introduced a novel dimension of the Iraqi poetic tradition in his argument that the committed content of modernist poetry was worthless when it was divorced from the committed form of public performance.65

## The Evolution of Public Poetry, 1948–1952

The communist tropes of Jawahiri's poetry were popular among workers, and when *al-Raʿi al-ʿAmm* experienced financial difficulty, Bahr al-ʿUlum and fellow workers lent him money to keep the paper afloat.66 Jawahiri was deeply shaken by the February 1949 execution of the communist leaders Yusuf Salman Yusuf, Zaki Muhammad Basim, Yahuda Ibrahim Siddiq, and Husayn Muhammad al-Shabibi.67 The climate of oppression was reflected in poems like "Descend, Darkness," a prayer for damnation, retribution, and destruction of "disfigured wretches" who tortured Iraq.68 On July 4, 1949, months after this despondent curse, Jawahiri renewed his commitment to public dissidence with the scandalous poem for Hashim al-Witri that introduces this book.69

Jawahiri's poetry reflected both national front cultural politics and the socialist internationalism of the Peace Partisans. He went to Poland in August 1948 as the sole Iraqi delegate to the World Congress of Intellectuals in Defense of Peace, where he met European leftist poets like Aragon, Brecht, and Eluard.[70] The conference led Jawahiri to become formally involved in communist politics for the first time, and he worked with Muhammad Salih Bahr al-ʿUlum and the leftist politician ʿAziz al-Sharif to establish the Iraqi branch of the World Committee of Partisans for Peace, an international movement that adhered closely to the line of the Soviet Cominform.[71] While the organization was later renamed the World Peace Council, both supporters and opponents in Iraq continued to refer to it as the "Peace Partisans" (*Ansar al-Salam*).[72] None of the three Iraqi leaders of the movement ever joined the Iraqi Communist Party, but they were all sympathetic fellow travelers. While communist cadres described Sharif with more than a hint of contempt as "a nationalist today, a Marxist-Communist tomorrow," many came to realize that leftist nationalists like Sharif could advance the communist agenda.[73] Leftist poets were equally critical to this agenda in Iraq, as their calls for "national liberation" and "world peace" linked anticolonial nationalism and communist internationalism.[74]

The most important contribution of the Peace Partisans poets to the cultural politics of the 1950s was their novel anti-American and anticapitalist rhetoric.[75] Bahr al-ʿUlum wrote poems describing Chiang Kai-shek and the Kuomintang as "servants of America" and portraying Mao's triumph as an omen for U.S. defeat in the Cold War: "It was the day of reckoning for their masters in the United States / who know that their own arrow will come from the same quiver."[76] Another poem emphasized the link between capitalism and imperialism, appealing to the Peace Partisans to "prepare yourself to save this region / tyrannized by the guinea and the dollars!"[77] Bahr al-ʿUlum responded enthusiastically to the Stockholm Appeal in March 1950, joining a global campaign of poets who rallied popular support for the communist World Peace Council.[78] Bahr al-ʿUlum viewed the campaign as an opportunity to demonstrate the political utility of poetry, declaring in July 1950, "I am at your service, World Peace Council, with poems / suitable for the consideration of all conscious masses."[79]

The pacifism of Peace Partisans poetry was characteristic of the new Third Worldist poetics of decolonization.[80] Hymns of "peace" were particularly striking from a poet like Bahr al-ʿUlum, famous for his poems of violent resistance, but pacifism was a useful framework for anti-Americanism. Bahr al-ʿUlum denounced America's "savage aggression" against the "heroic Korean revolution" and compared President Truman to Hitler: "He did not realize that the rights of the people / could not be defeated by injustice of tyrants / But the methods of the leader of these savages / will finish in failure just like those of Hitler."[81] Another poem linked capitalist frivolity to imperialist racism, mocking Truman for imagining that war would be like "the game of golf" and emphasizing Third World solidarity: "The West now sees that the future belongs to the East / unlike white cowards, the black masses are lions."[82] Jawahiri also denounced American "savagery" in Korea, graphically describing the barbarity of American imperialism: "Nourishing its children with this oppression / behind the curtain of gloom and darkness / Feasting on the bones and their marrow / the dregs of the blood that once flowed."[83] The support of both poets for the World Peace Council aroused considerable interest and anxiety in Iraq and the United States.[84]

The gradualist Marxists of the Peace Partisans understood that anti-American tropes gave poets the nationalist credibility needed to advance their radical social agenda. Realist descriptions of poverty and exploitation had been dominant tropes in Iraqi poetry since the neoclassical revival, but the new school of socialist realism emphasized the revolutionary struggle of the masses against the alliance of imperialism and capitalism.[85] While socialist realism is generally linked to modernist poetry, its impact was equally apparent on neoclassical poetry.[86] Jawahiri, for example, portrayed social exploitation as the main concern of revolutionary politics in his viciously satirical poem "Lullaby for the Hungry":

> Sleep, you hungry people, sleep!
> So that you are free from vice and blame
> Sleep, for the most precious unity
> of the nation demands that you sleep
> Sleep, you hungry people, sleep!
> for sleep is one of the virtues of peace
> The political parties are united in sleep
> and sought shelter from the violent clash

> The masses are made tranquil by sleep
> and their ranks have no need for division
> So it is foolish for you to be unhappy
> and to rise and to disturb this harmony . . . [87]

Jawahiri was now explicitly calling for popular revolution rather than appealing to political elites to initiate social reforms, as he had done in poems like "Feudalism."[88] Bahr al-'Ulum was equally influenced by socialist realism, and one Iraqi writer recalled that his poem "Where Is My Right?" was more popular than the *Communist Manifesto* among young Marxists in Baghdad.[89]

The World Peace Council viewed the anticapitalist, anti-imperialist, and anti-American tropes of socialist realism as a counter to the bourgeois "cosmopolitanism" of American popular culture.[90] Ironically, however, socialist realism inspired a new form of leftist cosmopolitanism in Iraq. This was particularly apparent in "Dawn of Peace," written by the young communist poet Badr Shakir al-Sayyab and published with the support of Jawahiri, Bahr al-'Ulum, and the Peace Partisans.[91] The poem denounced the American arms trade and the "lust for death" that fueled capitalist and imperialist designs on the Third World, complaining that the brunt of this burden "fell on the backs of those who did not purchase / commodities that traverse the globe in dollars."[92] The poem was written in conventional neoclassical style, but Sayyab was already engaged in the aesthetic experimentations that would revolutionize Arabic poetry in the coming decade.[93] The rhythm and cadence of neoclassical poetry were better suited for the popular campaign of the Peace Partisans, but avant-garde free verse poetry was becoming increasingly enmeshed in the debates on socialist realism and commitment in Baghdad cafés.

## The Free Verse Revolution in Iraqi Poetry

Badr Shakir al-Sayyab was part of a new generation of poets in Baghdad whose worldview was shaped by the twin historical traumas of 1948, the Iraqi Wathba and Palestinian Nakba. Their fusion of socialist realism and commitment with the avant-garde aesthetics of free verse revolutionized the Iraqi poetry scene in the 1950s.[94] The "commitment generation" included several dozen poets born in the 1920s, most of whom were educated at the University of Baghdad. Nazik al-Mala'ika (1923–2007), Badr Shakir al-Sayyab (1926–1964), 'Abd al-Wahhab al-Bayati (1926–1999), Buland al-Haydari (1926–1996), 'Atika Wahbi al-Khazraji (1926–1997), Shadhil Taqa (1928–1974), and Lami'a 'Abbas 'Amara (b. 1929) studied at the Higher Teachers' Training College.[95] Khalid al-Shawwaf (1924–2012), 'Adnan al-Rawi (1925–1967), Kazim Jawad (1928–1984), Hilal Naji (1929–2011), and 'Ali al-Hilli (b. 1930) studied at the College of Law in the same period.[96] Only a few poets of this generation, like the "vagabond poet" Husayn Mardan (1927–1972) and the Najafi poet Talib al-Haydari (b. 1928), honed their craft elsewhere. Poets from the Higher Teachers' Training College generally embraced modernist aesthetics and communist politics, while those from the College of Law were more conservative and inclined toward neoclassical aesthetics and nationalist politics.

Most Western critics use the term *free verse* to describe poetry free from meter and rhyme.[97] In Arabic, free verse poetry (*al-shi'r al-hurr*) was both metrical and rhymed, but poets now varied the meter and rhyme established in the first two hemistiches of the poem.[98] It was this rejection of rigid pattern that distinguished al-shi'r al-hurr from previous experiments in Arabic poetry, which adhered to a common pattern within the poem or stanza. For example, the Mahjar poets used different meters and rhymes between stanzas but never within a single stanza, and the blank verse experiments of Jamil Sidqi al-Zahawi (1863–1936), 'Abd al-Rahman Shukri (1886–1958), and Ahmad Zaki Abu Shadi (1892–1955) were unrhymed but still metered. The prose poetry (*al-shi'r al-manthur*) of Amin al-Rihani (1876–1940) and Khalil Gibran (1883–1941) was genuinely free of pattern, meter, and rhyme, but it was considered "poetic prose" and hence largely ignored by poetry critics.[99]

The first free verse poem was published by Nazik al-Mala'ika in the Lebanese magazine *al-'Uruba* in December 1947. "Cholera" described the postwar epidemic that engulfed Egypt and Iraq, its opening lines representing a striking visual and rhythmic departure from classical tradition:

Dawn appears,
   listen to the footsteps of the passersby,
   in the silence of dawn, listen, look at the procession of mourners,
ten dead, twenty,

do not count, listen to the mourners,
hear the voice of the bereaved child,
dead, dead, the number is lost
dead, dead, there is no tomorrow,
in every place is a body mourned by the grieved,
there is neither a moment of peace nor silence,
this is what the hand of death did,
Death, death, death,
mankind laments, laments what was perpetrated by death. . . . [100]

Badr Shakir al-Sayyab's first collection of poetry was printed several days later in Cairo and also included a free verse poem.[101] Sayyab insisted that his poem was written first, later dating it November 1946, and many Iraqi poets felt obliged to choose sides in the dispute.[102] Mala'ika and Sayyab were acquainted with one another, and their experiments were neither independent nor derivative, but the debate reflected the stakes of poetic innovation.[103] 'Abd al-Wahhab al-Bayati, Buland al-Haydari, Kazim Jawad, Lami'a 'Abbas 'Amara, Husayn Mardan, and other young Iraqis became enthusiastic proponents of free verse poetry.[104] Virtually all of these poets supported either the Iraqi Communist Party or the nationalist Independence Party and embraced the radical poetics of Third Worldism.[105] Their literary influences, however, were mostly drawn from British romanticism, French decadence, and Soviet socialist realism.[106]

In the premier issue of the Beirut avant-garde literary journal *al-Adab*, Suhayl Idris declared that "the literature that this magazine invites and encourages is the literature of 'commitment' that springs from Arab society and flows through it."[107] Modernist Iraqi poets applied abstract debates about socialist realism and commitment to their poems about the lives of common people. Bohemian poets like Buland al-Haydari published poems reflecting ambivalent modernist visions of urban alienation and rural nostalgia.[108] 'Abd al-Wahhab al-Bayati transformed oral stories of peasant migrants in Baghdad into poems about the misery of village life and the pain of urban migration.[109] One poem contrasted rural poverty with the urban trauma of capitalist exploitation: "What a blind beast / whose victims are our corpses, the bodies of our women / and the pleasant dreamers."[110] Badr Shakir al-Sayyab's nostalgic poems about peasant life in his village of Jaykur reflected T. S. Eliot's vision of the city as an urban wasteland.[111] Jaykur became a metaphor for the precolonial past, linking rural decline to colonialism and folk culture to socialist realism.[112]

The "vagabond poet" Husayn Mardan showed no such nostalgia for his own village of Hindiyya, instead repudiating every facet of rural life.[113] When his first collection of poetry, *Qasa'id 'Ariya* (*Naked Poems*), was published in 1949, its obscene eroticism attracted immediate attention. Mardan's flamboyant dedication of the collection "To the revolutionary poet and free thinker / to . . . Husayn Mardan" reflected an individual subjectivity outrageously out of step with the collective orientation of socialist realism.[114] When he was tried for crimes against public decency in June 1950, his lawyer compared Mardan to Gustave Flaubert, arguing that both writers were simply "representing vice in order to spread virtue."[115] The judge was sympathetic to poetic freedom, inviting Muhammad Mahdi al-Jawahiri to testify for the defense and acquitting Mardan.[116] Mardan's countercultural celebration of the self was flamboyant, but it was inspired by Sartrean existentialism and reflected his own interpretation of commitment.[117] Some of his poems were explicitly political, including one that compared the attitudes of Iraqi politicians toward their subjects to "the tyrant's fear of his slave."[118] Mardan was not a communist, but his bohemian lifestyle and association with countercultural communist circles made him a "cultural communist" to many observers.[119]

The young poets who continued to write neoclassical poetry were equally influenced by the politics of commitment, embracing the Third Worldist poetics of national liberation and substituting revolutionary rhetoric for aesthetic innovation. The nationalization of the Anglo-Iranian Oil Company in March 1951 was particularly inspiring to young Iraqis like Talib al-Haydari, who had just published a book of poetry and prose that portrayed the martyrdom of Imam Husayn as a revolutionary political act.[120] His radical theology shaped the radical poetics of his collection *Tahiat Iran* (*Long Live Iran*), which described nationalization as inspiration for revolutions that would soon sweep across the Middle East:

> One of these nights must come for the East
> to sweep away this injustice and this evil

To sweep away every one of these despotic
tyrants and every single greedy colonizer
To sweep away every one of these overseers
and every single employer of hired labor
To sweep away every one of these profiteers
who tamper with the wheat and the barley
To sweep away every one of these libertines
who seek pleasure in the despair of the poor
To sweep away every one of these misers
who greedily covet the most trivial things
Selling your people for the sake of money—
which one is cheaper, the money or the bed?![121]

The book was widely distributed in Baghdad and Tehran, and both Muhammad Musaddaq and Ayatollah Kashani sent notes of appreciation to Haydari.[122] Haydari's fusion of anticolonialism and anticapitalism was embraced even by nationalist poets like ʿAli al-Hilli, whose poems dedicated to Iranian martyrs of the nationalization struggle reflected the pervasive socialist cosmopolitanism of the commitment generation.[123]

## Poetry and the Intifada of November 1952

Most of the young committed poets participated as students in the Wathba of January 1948, but they played a larger role in the Iraqui intifada of November 1952. The protests were organized by the national front alliance of the Peace Partisans, National Democratic Party, Independence Party, and United Popular Front.[124] The willingness of the nationalist parties to cooperate with their socialist counterparts reflected their suspicion that "anticommunism" was being invoked to criminalize all forms of political dissent. Even conservative figures like the old Najafi poet Muhammad Rida al-Shabibi now denounced the government in speeches cheered by the Peace Partisans.[125] Iraqis were inspired by the Iranian oil saga, and Muhammad Mahdi al-Jawahiri's elegy for Iranian martyrs became a revolutionary anthem for Iraqi protesters: "Their blood flowed to impose their will / the martyrs fell to raise their plight / Their bloody submission worked to implant / their banner among those of the people."[126]

Opposition demands for electoral reform were dismissed by the government, inflation intensified political grievances, and nationalists and socialists began competing with one another in their demands for sweeping social reform.[127] On November 20, 1952, students clashed with police at the University of Baghdad, demanding electoral reform, land redistribution, release of political prisoners, abrogation of oil concessions, and rejection of foreign defense treaties.[128] Over the next week, tens of thousands of students, workers, and communists marched in the streets and chanted revolutionary slogans.[129] Crowds chanted for a national salvation government led by the social democratic politician Kamil al-Chadirchi and the poet Muhammad Mahdi al-Jawahiri, who was arrested preemptively when the protests began.[130] Demonstrations spread across the country, and protesters repeatedly invoked Jawahiri's name as they chanted anti-American and anti-British slogans.[131]

Muhammad Salih Bahr al-'Ulum had been imprisoned the previous year, but by sheer coincidence, he was released the same day that the intifada began.[132] The great poet of the Wathba now appeared again in the crowd, pale and gaunt as he was "carried on the shoulders of the masses, reciting poetry as the masses repeated his anthem."[133] Bahr al-'Ulum enjoyed just three days of freedom before fleeing underground after a military court sentenced him in absentia to three more years in prison for his role in the protests.[134] Younger communist poets like Badr Shakir al-Sayyab and 'Abd al-Wahhab al-Bayati also played leading roles in the intifada. Sayyab was in the crowd that looted the US Information Services office on November 23, recalling that it felt "as if they were destroying colonialism itself rather than tape recorders and burning exploitation rather than cinema reels." He climbed an electrical pole and recited a poem that delighted the crowds sacking the building: "The martyr grew hungry and opened his mouth for blood / so wring out your heart or the hearts of the criminals."[135] Like Bahr al-'Ulum four years earlier, Sayyab was carried by the crowd as he recited rebel poems, but he recoiled when he saw his comrades murder two police officers, douse the corpses in gasoline, and set them on fire.[136] Sayyab fled into exile in Iran, but Bahr al-'Ulum was arrested while trying to cross the border at Khanaqin in March 1953.[137] He recalled proudly that "people from different backgrounds and classes looked after me" while he was in hiding and that "every house of the people became the house of their poet."[138]

Despite the role Bahr al-ʿUlum and Sayyab played in the intifada, the episode also symbolized the new limits of the poetry of public spaces. Baha al-Din Nuri, first secretary of the ICP, argued happily in his postmortem analysis of the uprising that poets had been supplanted by workers in public protests.[139] The eclipse of poets in the intifada protests, however, was due precisely to the fact that the state was now more aware of the dangers of poetry and arrested Jawahiri, Bahr al-ʿUlum, Sayyab, and other rebel poets much more rapidly. The poetry of public spaces was possible only when dissident poets were allowed access to those spaces. State repression grew more intense between 1948 and 1952, but poets like Jawahiri also severed their remaining links to political elites. Without any claim to the politics of loyal opposition, their access to the public sphere evaporated. Modernist poets like Sayyab and Bayati faced different difficulties among the crowd due to their avant-garde aesthetics, which lacked the rhythm and cadence of neoclassical platform poetry. The political commitment of the modernist poets simply did not resonate with the mass culture of public spaces and popular demonstrations in the same way.

## Communists, Nationalists and National Front Poetry

The political repression that followed the intifada may have tempered the transgressions of public poetry, but nationalist and leftist poets redoubled their commitment to the cultural politics of the national front in their published work. Old partisan disputes seemed almost inconsequential in light of the pressing demand for national solidarity in the struggle against the monarchy and its imperialist backers. Young nationalist poets embraced leftist appeals for radical social reform and appropriated leftist rhetoric about the global struggle against colonialism. Leftist poets reciprocated these nationalist contributions to the national front and emphasized their shared political interests. The political context of the "Arab Cold War," which pitted progressive anticolonial republics against conservative pro-Western monarchies, provided both sides with ample opportunities to voice shared interests and sympathies.[140]

In the immediate aftermath of the intifada, leftist poets looked to the oil nationalization campaign in Iran as a model for revolutionary action.[141] In the wake of Operation AJAX, the CIA operation that overthrew Prime

Minister Muhammad Musaddaq in August 1953, the leftist poet Talib al-Haydari praised the fallen Musaddaq for "[leading] the slumbering people to bring to an end / the era dominated by bondage and colonialism" and called on Arabs to either seize or destroy their own oil wells.[142] Kazim Jawad described the scene from Baghdad, where radical students sat silently in cafés and listened to radio reports of the coup. Jawad linked the nationalization campaign to the anticolonial struggle in India and compared the weapons of General Zahedi's troops to the "whips of Indian rajas inlayed with pearls." The leftist trope of the new revolutionary horizon broke through the despair of failure, as Jawad described crowds of Iranian workers and communist cadres chanting, "From here / the star of morning / will surely reach the horizon of the people!"[143] This revolutionary fervor was infectious, and Iraqi workers at the Basra Petroleum Company struck at Zubayr on December 5, 1953.[144] When local police attacked the striking workers, rumors spread that they had been ordered to do so by "Mr. Tissow," the firm's British manager. Tissow became a target of anticolonial anger in protest chants and popular poems, including one by Kazim Jawad: "Mr. Tissow, the number of your Tissowians is countless / so lift your nose in the air as you plunder our wealth!"[145] The poem invoked the new revolutionary horizon that loomed "after tomorrow," and while it was not published at the time, it helped to cement the image of Tissow as a symbol of neocolonialism in café culture.[146] When numerous Iranian army officers were executed in October 1954 due to their clandestine involvement in the communist Tudeh Party, the Iraqi female communist poet Hayyat al-Nahr honored their martyrdom in a poem linking the struggles for national liberation and social justice: "We will build a happy and free homeland safe from harm / Whose only concern is justice and only dream is peace."[147]

While leftist poets like Talib al-Haydari, Kazim Jawad, and Hayyat al-Nahr dreamed that the events in Iran would inspire communist revolution in Iraq, the same events caused Badr Shakir al-Sayyab to question his faith in communism. Sayyab fled to Iran to evade arrest after the intifada and participated in the Tudeh demonstrations in Tehran during the events of Operation AJAX in August 1953.[148] When ordered by Tudeh leaders to stand down as General Zahedi seized power in order to avoid entangling the Soviet Union in a military conflict with the United States, Sayyab recalled protesting, "But you are Iranians not Soviets, and your duty is to defend the interests of your people, the Iranian people, and not the interests of the Soviet Union and her people!" One Tudeh member laughed at Sayyab's naiveté, admonishing him that "the first duty of every communist party in the world in this period is to defend peace before national interests."[149] Sayyab would point to this communist betrayal of the nation to explain his conversion from communism to pan-Arabism, and his poetry began to invoke nationalist rhetoric.[150] His 1956 poem "The Informant," for example, described a police informant concluding that Iraqi dissidents were "awakening" to the Arab nationalist struggles in Tunisia, Algeria, and Egypt:

> Why do they read: because Tunisia is awakening to the struggle?
> Because the rebels of Algeria are weaving, from the sand
> and from the storms and floods and from the gasps of the hungry,
> the funeral shrouds of tyrants? All while the bombs of the volunteers
> whistle in the dusk of the [Suez] Canal?[151]

Despite Sayyab's later anticommunist polemics, these nationalist poems co-existed comfortably with his commitment to leftist internationalism, and he continued to publish poems in praise of iconic socialists like Messali al-Hadj and Federico García Lorca.[152]

Communist betrayal in Tehran was far less important than communist commitment in Baghdad to nationalist poets like 'Adnan al-Rawi, a graduate of the College of Law who gained notoriety for his role in establishing several underground nationalist organizations in the early 1950s.[153] Rawi fled to Cairo in 1954 and was sentenced to death in absentia, but he gained an even larger audience as a broadcaster on Nasser's Voice of the Arabs radio station.[154] In the introduction to his 1957 poetry collection, *al-Naft al-Multahib*, Rawi praised the anticolonial commitment of communist poets like Muhammad Mahdi al-Jawahiri, Muhammad Salih Bahr al-'Ulum, 'Abd al-Wahhab al-Bayati, and Kazim Jawad and even compared the courageous rebel poetry of Bahr al-'Ulum to that of Ma'ruf al-Rusafi, who remained the hero of most nationalist poets in Iraq.[155] One poem in the collection described these committed communist poets as "spokesmen of the nation" and contrasted them with apolitical poets who "distract the people with trivial verses."[156] Rawi's new poems linked the political and social struggle for national liberation, portraying the nationalist struggle against British imperialism and the struggle of the hungry masses against "feudalism" as two sides of the same coin.[157] Above all else, his poems used the oil question as fuel for a revolutionary movement that no longer distinguished between colonialism and the Hashemite state: "We shall set ablaze the oil that beguiles Iraq / and once again reclaim it as our usurped right / We will reclaim it from the blood of that clique / when our anger descends upon them tomorrow!"[158]

The influence of socialism on the nationalist poets was even more pronounced in the case of ʿAli al-Hilli, a former classmate of ʿAdnan al-Rawi at the College of Law. Hilli was a partisan of the conservative Independence Party during the Wathba of January 1948, but he showed an early appreciation for leftist poetics in a poem about that uprising that consciously modeled Jawahiri's famous "My Brother Jaʿfar." Hilli's invocation of wounds, victims, mouths, and ropes symbolized the internalization of leftist cultural politics and embrace of leftist tropes about the revolutionary horizon that loomed before them: "The exalted horizon reveals a revolution / longing for the afterglow of the Wathba."[159] Hilli became interested in the plight of the rural poor and took inspiration from the American writer Erskine Caldwell, a communist fellow traveler whose stories Hilli translated from English into Arabic.[160] He wrote poems about the martyred Tunisian labor activist Farhat Hached and the leftist National Union Committee in Bahrain that combined leftist social critique with Arab nationalist commitments.[161] When Hilli attended the Arab Writers' Conference in Damascus in September 1956, he was so impressed by peasant support for the Arab Socialist Baʿth Party that he became a member.[162] He published a poem attacking Nuri al-Saʿid in the party newspaper *al-Baʿth* in Damascus, describing himself as a "prisoner" and yearning for violent revolution: "Tomorrow we clap our hands and venerate the blood of the martyr / when we shatter our chains and roast the sinners in the harvest fire."[163] When he returned to Baghdad, Hilli was tried for insulting the government and dismissed from his job at the Agricultural Bank of Baghdad.[164] Hilli's radical social outlook was scarcely distinguishable from that of the communists by late 1957, when he called for the "bloodied quill and ink of the poet" to inspire a revolution of peasants and workers and even invoked the "moaning of the weary sickle" to appeal to his communist allies.[165]

The leftist turn of the nationalist poets was reciprocated to a lesser extent by communist poets, who now invoked pan-Arabist rhetoric on certain occasions. Muhammad Mahdi al-Jawahiri moved to Damascus to escape political repression in 1955 and gained considerable fame and notoriety there when he recited a poem in honor of the Baʿthist army officer ʿAdnan al-Maliki, who was assassinated by inoperative of the Syrian Social Nationalist Party (SSNP) rumored to be working with British and American intelligence agencies in March 1955.[166] Jawahiri's elegy for Maliki echoed these rumors, alleging that Western operatives orchestrated the assassination because Maliki opposed the Baghdad Pact. Jawahiri boasted of the new national front solidarity between leftists and nationalists against "this joke of an alliance between the oppressor / and oppressed, between master and slave girl!"[167] He intended to return to Baghdad after this performance, but the crowd implored him to remain in Damascus, and he acquiesced to their demand.[168] Jawahiri recited another elegy for Maliki the following year to a massive crowd at the Municipal Stadium where he had been assassinated, proclaiming in his most famous lines of poetry, "I am Iraq, my tongue is her heart, and my blood / is her Euphrates, my very being is cleaved by her."[169]

The cultural politics of the national front were perhaps most evident in the poetry of Kazim Jawad, a classmate of ʿAdnan al-Rawi and ʿAli al-Hilli at the College of Law who moved between the nationalist and leftist camps in the early 1950s.[170] Like his fellow law students, Jawad had been a partisan of the nationalist Independence Party in the late 1940s, but he began to fuse nationalist and communist rhetoric in his valorization of the Wathba and intifada as popular revolutions of the working masses against "the rulers of America, those masters of war and gods of destruction / Whose wealth supports the Zionist wolves."[171] Before long, Jawad became a socialist himself and began writing poetry about non-Arab communist figures like the Chinese leader Mao Zedong and the anti-Nazi Czech journalist Julius Fučík.[172] His nationalist past made him particularly attuned to the cultural politics of pan-Arabism, and he emphasized his solidarity with Arab national liberation movements in Palestine and Algeria. One poem invoked the anticolonial legacy of Arab nationalism to describe contemporary Arab struggles for national liberation, connecting Syrian resistance to French rule at Maysalun to the current Algerian struggle: "Yusuf al-ʿAzma / leader of armies, poem of refuge / has returned to lead the people's army to victory in battle."¹⁷³ Jawad criticized the "narrow chauvinist provincialism" of pan-Arabist poets but insisted that pan-Arabism was "nothing more than anticolonial solidarity" in Arab countries.¹⁷⁴ In pursuit of this solidarity, Jawad praised Egyptian resistance at Port Saʿid in November 1956, declaring, "Truly, truly, from the blood of Port Saʿid / the world will be born anew."¹⁷⁵ After he was forced into exile in Aleppo, pan-Arab rhetoric and allusions became even more pronounced in poetic declarations of solidarity with Baʿthist "comrades" in the anticolonial struggle.¹⁷⁶

The fusion of communist internationalism and pan-Arabism was particularly pronounced in the poetry of ʿAbd al-Wahhab al-Bayati, who was beginning to supplant Muhammad Mahdi al-Jawahiri as the idol of young communist poets in Iraq.¹⁷⁷ Bayati's communist internationalism had been apparent since the early 1950s, when he wrote enthusiastic poems about the Mau Mau and Vietcong.¹⁷⁸ Like his fellow modernists, Bayati was influenced by avant-garde aesthetics and translated communist poets like Vladimir Mayakovsky, Paul Éluard, Louis Aragon, Howard Fast, and Nazim Hikmet into Arabic.¹⁷⁹ His translation of Fast's dedication to Hikmet became a statement of his membership in the international brotherhood of communist poets and a declaration of his faith in a new world that "will awaken yet."¹⁸⁰ Bayati was fired from his teaching post in Baghdad due to his communist affiliations in 1954 and spent the next four years moving between Beirut, Cairo, and Damascus.¹⁸¹ His poetry from this period connected the Arab struggle for national liberation to movements in Asia and Africa, and he wrote several memorable poems about the Arab nationalist struggle in Palestine and North Africa.¹⁸² Perhaps most notable was "A Song from Iraq to Gamal ʿAbd al-Nasser," the opening poem to his 1956 collection, *al-Majid lil-Atfal wa al-Zaytun*. In a mirror image of the "communist" rhetoric of ʿAli al-Hilli and the Baʿthists, the nationalist rhetoric of Bayati and the communists was becoming indistinguishable from the genuine article:

Your name, in our remote and verdant village
in Iraq,
in the country of gloomy gallows,
night and prisons,
death and loss,

was heard by my nephews, and they become devoted to your name,
their eyes were ransomed to you,
who brings spring to desert wasteland,
and sends down rain to our verdant village.
Your name, Gamal,
was heard by the sons of my dead brother—
in the bullets
of the band of henchmen
in Iraq—
they heard your name and become devoted,
their eyes were ransomed to you,
who makes both peace and men,
Gamal,
who brings the lost Arabism,
and sends down rain to the desert,
who is the hope in our desolate life,
and our new world,
and our sweet new dawn[183]

The communist poet Hayyat al-Nahr also took a break from her celebrations of Ho Chi Minh and the Vietcong to endorse Nasserism and the Arab struggle at Suez and to declare, "We will write in blood a writ of liberation / for our peoples, and we will protect them."[184] Nationalist critics voiced their approval of these poems as effective communist contributions to the new cultural politics of the national front.[185] While the alliance would fall apart shortly after the July Revolution of 1958, the revolutionary cultural politics of anticolonialism and national liberation had succeeded for the moment in forging a genuine political affinity between communist and nationalists.[186]

## Conclusion

While the young modernist poets competed to express their commitment to anticolonial causes in literary journals and published collections, the ageing neoclassical communist poet Muhammad Salih Bahr al-'Ulum took a different path. The leftist poet had been returned to prison in May 1953 and organized a prison hunger strike that summer in Ba'quba in protest of the massacre of communist prisoners in Baghdad and Kut.[187] The surviving communists were eventually transferred to Ba'quba, and several Jews among them convinced Bahr al-'Ulum to dedicate a poem to Shmuel Mikunis, leader of the Israeli Communist Party. The poem described Israel and Iraq as "two nations brought together by brotherhood" and pledged solidarity in the communist struggle against the respective oppressive states: "Followers of Mikunis, may God protect your struggle against this invasion / the strength of your stance against your rulers is the same as my own / my fist and your fists, each one of them, will be the death of tyrants / and thanks to these workers we shall solve the problems of life!"[188] The poem was smuggled to Israel, where the young Iraqi Jewish communist Sasson Somekh translated it into Hebrew.[189] It was published as a pamphlet by the Israeli Communist Party (Maki) in 1955 and was received enthusiastically by Israeli communists, inspiring a friendly response from the poet Alexander Penn.[190] The poem did not appear in Arabic until it was published in the Kuwaiti journal *al-Bayan* thirteen years later, and there is no evidence that Iraqi nationalists were aware of its existence before then.[191]

This contrast between the communist internationalism of Bahr al-'Ulum and his fellow leftist poets and the racial and religious chauvinism of many of the nationalist poets always lurked beneath the surface of the national front. The anti-Zionist poetry of nationalists like 'Adnan al-Rawi could barely mask anti-Semitic visions of Jewish conspiracies, and there is little reason to think that Rawi and other nationalists would not have lambasted Bahr al-'Ulum for his friendly missive to Mikunis if he had known about it.[192] When the leftist poet Talib al-Haydari declared in his ode to the Peace Partisans that "equality is a right for everyone / for both the white man and the black / for mythologies of centuries past / have vanished before eternal truth," his racial cosmopolitanism was mistaken as a strategic expression of anticolonial unity by nationalist poets.[193] This uneasy coexistence between the two ideological currents could not endure forever, but the poems of this period remain testaments to the vibrant cultural politics of the national front.

The anticolonial solidarity between nationalist and leftist poets was partly a function of the new poetry of public spaces that reshaped the social role of poetry in the postwar era. The flamboyant recitation of dissident poetry by Muhammad Salih Bahr al-'Ulum and Muhammad Mahdi al-Jawahiri was not simply a celebration of contrarian attitudes and subversive politics for their own sake. These public performances were instead designed to inspire revolutionary fervor and mobilize the enthusiasm of crowds. The emotional content of these poems and the courageous context of their public recitation became inseparable from one another, a perfect testament to the symmetry of revolutionary thought and revolutionary action in postwar Iraq. The fact that this poetry of public spaces predated the emergence of "commitment" as the guiding philosophy and poetic praxis of the young modernists remains deeply ironic, given the far greater utility of the former phenomenon in revolutionary politics. Nevertheless, the commitment of the older generation of neoclassical poets to public dissidence worked to illuminate the new revolutionary horizon articulated by Jawahiri and then echoed by Kazim Jawad, 'Ali al-Hilli, and other young poets. This horizon symbolized the dawn of mass politics, the political awakening of the exploited masses, and their embrace of revolutionary political action, all of which "played an important part in preparing the Iraqi people emotionally for the advent and the eruption of revolution."[194]

While the ideologies of commitment embraced by the young modernist poets of Baghdad took inspiration from the neoclassical poetry of public spaces, their aesthetic innovations also contributed to the rapid decline of this cultural phenomenon. Just months after his missive to Shmuel Mikunis, Muhammad Salih Bahr al-'Ulum wrote his most famous poem, "Where Is My Right?"[195] This vicious critique of political oppression and religious hypocrisy was never published, but possession of handwritten copies was considered evidence of political dissidence and earned many leftist poetry enthusiasts decades-long prison terms.[196] Like Jawahiri's famous poem, "My Brother Ja'far," many Iraqi dissidents committed "Where Is My Right?" to memory, a testament to the pneumonic features of neoclassical poetry and a suggestion of how the poetry of public spaces must have circulated among the wider Iraqi public. For all of its aesthetic beauty and intellectual ingenuity, free verse poetry could not compete with neoclassical poetry in this domain. Better suited for books and journals than platforms and more appropriate for reading than chanting, the rise of the free verse movement gradually transformed poetry from an expression of mass culture to an emblem of high culture and poets from national spokesmen to alienated intellectuals. These transformations, however, took time to develop; neoclassical and modernist poetry coexisted throughout the 1950s and 1960s, and even free verse poetry remained extremely popular in comparison to the position of poetry in the United States and Europe. When the new revolutionary horizon finally arrived in July 1958, poets remained well positioned to take advantage of their social status and cultural prestige and once again advance their claims to speak on behalf of the nation.

{ CHAPTER 6 }

# CULTURAL HEGEMONY

*The Politics of Class, Gender, and Nation, 1958–1963*

In October 1961, Badr Shakir al-Sayyab delivered a lecture on commitment (*iltizam*) at a Congress for Cultural Freedom conference in Rome.[1] His defense of "art for art's sake" and criticism of communist "commitment" reflected the anticommunist line promoted across the globe by the CCF.[2] As evidence of communist crimes against poetry, Sayyab selected "two verses from a poem written by an Iraqi communist poet on the Palestinian cause, before the Soviet Union adopted its well-known [support for partition]."[3] He did not mention the poet's name, but the verses he quoted were written by Muhammad Salih Bahr al-'Ulum: "Palestine, the glory is yours / the glory is yours, Palestine / From the East to the West / You are saluted by millions."[4] Sayyab declared that it "cannot ascend even to the level of bad poetry" and complained that "the poet of this very verse was graced by the thunder of applause and acclamation as if it were a [proper] verse of poetry!"[5] Sayyab's contempt for communist aesthetics and envy of Bahr al-'Ulum's popularity were balanced by his grudging acknowledgment that low literacy rates made poetry, which could be recited aloud at party meetings and demonstrations, particularly useful for communists.[6]

The lecture reflected the political crisis that engulfed Iraqi poetry after the revolution of July 14, 1958.[7] Both communist and nationalist poets celebrated the end of the Hashemite monarchy, but the cultural politics of the revolutionary national front collapsed under the weight of the political violence that engulfed the country.[8] The idea of popular culture became an obsession in the struggle for political and cultural hegemony, permeating intellectual debate and inspiring new forms of contestation.[9] Sayyab played a critical role in this crisis in the editorials narrating his evolution from communism to pan-Arabism published in *al-Hurriyya* in fall 1959.[10] He linked communist aesthetics and political loyalties to the problem of cultural authenticity, insisting that both the poetry and politics of Iraqi communists represented a betrayal of the Arab nation. For Sayyab, the very popularity of communist poetry became a threat to the cultural and political sensibilities of middle-class Arabs. The "bad poetry" of communist poets like Bahr al-'Ulum was dangerous precisely because it appealed to the base aesthetic tastes of the unlettered masses. This fear and revulsion of communist popular cultural was a cultural reflection of the economic anxiety that fueled the anticommunist discourse of middle-class nationalists.[11]

Sayyab's bitter invective against popular communist poetry reflected the divergent paths of pan-Arab nationalism (*qawmiyya*) and Iraqist nationalism (*wataniyya*) in postrevolutionary Iraq.[12] Poets from both camps embraced the Sartrean ethos of literary commitment (iltizam) in the 1950s, but Sayyab now declared that "commitment" was a communist ideal that betrayed the true spirit of poetry.[13] He insisted that this ethos was tainted by the hypocritical communist subordination of Arab national liberation to the Soviet internationalist agenda.[14] Sayyab's critique of communist culture reflected the contentious social politics of race and sect in revolutionary Iraq. Nationalist denunciations of the Jewish, Kurdish, and "Persian" presence in the Iraqi Communist Party revived the old critique of shu'ubiyya and inspired the derisive pun *Shi'i-Shuyu'i* (Shi'i-Communist), which portrayed communism as a threat to Sunni Arab nationalism.[15] While racism and sectarianism have tainted the historical reputation of pan-Arab nationalists in comparison to their cosmopolitan communist rivals, these chauvinist dimensions of nationalist cultural discourse were by no means monolithic among the qawmi poets and intellectuals of the Qasim era (1958–1963).[16]

Iraqi pan-Arabism has generally been seen as a reactionary phenomenon that aimed to protect the vested economic and sectarian interests of a privileged minority.[17] There is a great deal of validity in this historical analysis, particularly given the devolution of Ba'thist attitudes toward their religious and ethnic opponents over the final decades of the twentieth century. Most qawmi voices, however, remained committed to a progressive vision of the political, social, and cultural renaissance of the Arab nation. Their anticommunist polemics reflected new concern for women's honor and women's bodies, moving beyond old debates about veiling and education toward new discussions of sexual liberation and public visibility.[18] Nationalist poets depicted women as custodians of an inner domain of national culture besieged by communist sexual aggression and depicted themselves as the chivalrous guardians of their liberated-yet-chaste nationalist sisters.[19] While this cultural project of middle-class feminism was closely tied to their struggle against communism in the social sphere, it also venerated the individual autonomy of Iraqi women as a way of highlighting the hypocrisy of communist rhetoric about women's liberation.[20]

Communist poets were more inclined to ignore the anticommunist critique of their nationalist rivals than to publicly defend their own vision. They denounced their nationalist opponents as traitors and imperialist stooges, but they continued to defend the principle of the revolutionary national front long after it was stripped of practical value. Despite the unmistakable "cultural hegemony" of the communists in revolutionary Iraq, many communists remained hesitant to jeopardize their cultural prestige by engaging contentious debates on race and gender.[21] The sectarianism and chauvinism of the pan-Arabists pushed many young Shi'a and Kurds to embrace communist cultural cosmopolitanism, but communist poetry and propaganda downplayed these issues rather than directly challenging shu'ubiyya narratives.[22] Communists were committed to feminism and sexual liberation, but they hesitated to make their radical gender and sexual politics explicit lest they draw attention to their atheism and provoke a cultural backlash. This was particularly true of female communists, who insisted that in both their behavior and rhetoric about gender and sex, "they were very careful—almost puritanical—precisely because their opponents invoked religion and popular culture against their supposed godless immorality."[23] The contrast between nationalist attacks and communist silence contributed to the asymmetrical nature of revolutionary cultural politics and allowed nationalist arguments about race and sex to overwhelm communist rhetoric about capital and class.

Poetry remained the pivotal arena of revolutionary culture, in which comrades, rivals, and enemies waged their struggle for cultural hegemony. Communist and nationalist poets shaped popular opinion and rendered partisan politics meaningful by constructing new cultural narratives of violence. As the anticolonial solidary of national front politics and poetics gave way to partisan conflict, new patterns of state patronage and repression underscored the significance of revolutionary poetry. The previous convergence of communists and nationalists only intensified the cultural vitriol of political poetry in the Qasim era, which was soon consumed by political and sexual violence. While communists pointed to their long record of activism in support of women's liberation, their nationalist rivals defended new middle-class concerns of "muscular nationalism" and "nationalist feminism."[24] Anticommunist poetry warned of communist threats to women's bodies and defended the nationalist commitment to women's liberation to challenge the communist claim to cultural hegemony.

## Revolutionary Poetics and Political Conspiracies

On July 14, 1958, the Iraqi "Free Officers," a secret cell of roughly two hundred members of the army officer corps, launched a military coup that deposed the Hashemite monarchy and executed the entire royal family.[25] Nuri al-Saʿid was killed while trying to flee Baghdad in women's clothing, leading the communist poet ʿAli Jalil al-Wardi to mock his cowardice: "A donkey ridden by colonizers as they pleased / until he finally sank to his own colonial terror / Where is your courage now, Nuri Incognito / is your refuge disguised like a women too?"[26] As British and American troops landed in ʿAmman and Beirut to prevent the spread of revolutionary fervor, nationalist and communist poets celebrated their triumph.[27] Muhammad Mahdi al-Jawahiri was summoned to the Ministry of Defense on July 24, where ʿAbd al-Karim Qasim and other officers told him that his poems had inspired the revolution.[28] Jawahiri confessed that revolutionary euphoria had rendered him speechless for once in a poem that he recited on Baghdad Radio: "You struck the blow, so I no longer dream of striking / you thrust the sword, so I no longer yearn to thrust / You have made the final and decisive statement / captivating the mind until there was nothing left for me to say."[29] Jawahiri forged a close friendship with Qasim and began publishing political panegyrics again for the first time in more than two decades.[30]

Despite Jawahiri's stronger reputation as poet, most leftists viewed Muhammad Salih Bahr al-'Ulum as the living symbol of rebel poetry. The communist writer Dhu al-Nun Ayyub recalled seeing Bahr al-'Ulum in demonstrations "carried on top of the shoulders of the masses, reciting poetry as the masses repeated his anthem," and described him as "the poet of all those who could not easily understand the sublime poetry of Jawahiri."[31] In the days following the revolution, Bahr al-'Ulum recounted three decades of struggle in a poem he recited on Baghdad Radio: "My duty carried me to prisons that sampled / the message of two generations in one poet / There I saw the revolution in pains of labor / that would soon be born from a pure womb."[32] The poem appeared on the front page of most newspapers the next morning, and even nationalist journalists like Rafa'il Butti, who came to know Bahr al-'Ulum in the internment camps of World War II, declared triumphantly that the poet was "totally free for the first time."[33] Bahr al-'Ulum recited poems in demonstrations in both Najaf and Baghdad, rejoicing that "the era of darkness has vanished in the night / while justice appeared with the break of dawn."[34] The pervasive presence of his poems in protests, newspapers, and radio broadcasts illustrated the enduring popularity of neoclassical poetry, which imparted a strikingly traditional form to the revolutionary culture of the period.

Rafa'il Butti later apologized privately to US officials for publishing the "communist propaganda" poems of Bahr al-'Ulum in al-Bilad, explaining that it was necessary "if he was to sell his papers in present day Baghdad."[35] His ambivalence toward his old friend underscored the tensions of national front politics in the revolutionary atmosphere of Baghdad, as both communists and nationalists struggled to represent the revolution as the culmination of their own ideological agenda. Exiled communist poets like 'Abd al-Wahhab al-Bayati and Kazim Jawad rushed back to Iraq, publishing poems that celebrated the new dawn of political and cultural freedom and linked Iraq's struggle to the international communist struggle.[36]

The Ba'thist poet 'Ali al-Hilli offered a more insular vision of Arab nationalism in his hymn for the "revolution of resurrection" (*thawrat al-ba'th*), which glorified the mutilation of corpses and yearned for the construction of a new society on the blood-drenched soil of Arab lands.[37] As the tensions between these divergent revolutionary visions intensified, leaders from the nationalist Independence Party and socialist National Democratic Party appealed for unity and solidarity. They resurrected the old National Unity Front in November 1958, organizing a huge rally in Baghdad where Jawahiri and Bahr al-ʿUlum recited revolutionary poems.[38] Many nationalists however, concluded that Iraq was caught between the "devil of Nasser and the deep blue sea of Communism" and sided decisively with the former.[39]

The nationalist poet ʿAdnan al-Rawi, who had recently returned to Baghdad from his exile in Cairo, began organizing covertly against Qasim and his communist supporters, appealing to Baʿthists and other nationalist to join his Nationalist Union Alliance (Mithaq al-Rabita al-Qawmiyyin).[40] When Colonel ʿAbd al-Salam ʿArif, the most prominent nationalist among the Iraqi Free Officers, was arrested in November 1958, Rawi began plotting a coup with the old nationalist icon, Rashid ʿAli al-Kaylani.[41] The plot was discovered, and Qasim now allowed the communist Popular Resistance Forces to man checkpoints across the country.[42] Rawi and his fellow conspirators were tried by the Special Supreme Military Tribunal, better known as the "People's Court," under the leadership of the flamboyant Colonel Fadhil ʿAbbas al-Mahdawi.[43] In his prison poems, Rawi described the plot as an extension of Rashid ʿAli's long struggle against colonialism and asked with feigned incredulity whether the "rebels" were arrested simply "because they are Arabs until the Day of Judgment / and vengeance pushes them on the path to unity / wretched Arab Unity?"[44] The poems also linked Arab nationalism to the struggle against "feudalism," an indication that nationalists had no intention of conceding the communist appeal to the urban and rural poor.[45]

Muhammad Mahdi al-Jawahiri addressed the Rashid ʿAli conspiracy in his lecture on commitment at the Arab Writers Conference in Kuwait in December 1958, where he read a note Qasim pledging Iraqi support for liberation movements in Algeria, Palestine, Oman, and Yemen.[46] When he returned to Baghdad, Jawahiri warned of colonial efforts to divide nationalists and leftists, arguing that politicians like Nuri al-Saʿid had used empty nationalist slogans to justify reactionary policies and imperialist alliances.[47] He established the Iraqi Writers Union with state support in January 1959, but most nationalist poets and writers refused to join.[48] Even in this climate of intense partisanship, nationalist and communist students still fought over seats to hear Jawahiri recite his iconic poem, "My Brother Ja'far," at a massive public rally in Baghdad on January 27, 1959.⁴⁹ As Jawahiri sought to unify poets and partisans, 'Adnan al-Rawi complained of communist attempts to marginalize their nationalist rivals through the "red terror" that was now enveloping Baghdad.⁵⁰ His polemics increasingly incorporated racist and anti-Semitic themes, as in one prison pamphlet mocking the "lorry loads of Peace Partisans who fired shots and brandished sticks like they were bound for a foray on Tel Aviv" and comparing communists to Jews who followed Lenin's injunction to "lie, lie, lie until the people believe you."⁵¹

Fears of the communist "red terror" were reinforced at the People's Court, where Colonel Mahdawi echoed communist rhetoric in his denunciation of nationalist conspirators as American agents.⁵² Posters of Qasim and Mahdawi were soon plastered on buildings across Baghdad, while those of nationalist icons like Nasser, 'Arif, Rashid 'Ali, and the "Four Colonels" of 1941 disappeared entirely.⁵³ Nationalists sought to link their opponents to Britain, alleging that Colonel Mahdawi had personally executed Yunis al-Sab'awi and the "Four Colonels" in 1942.⁵⁴ Mahdawi rejected these accusations, but his denunciation of nationalist defendants as "Nazis" reinforced nationalist efforts to link their struggle to the Anglo-Iraqi War and the long history of the anticolonial struggle.⁵⁵ Mahdawi's anti-American rhetoric inspired huge crowds to hurl garbage and rocks at the motorcade of the American diplomat William Rountree in December 1958.⁵⁶ Muhammad Mahdi al-Jawahiri denounced Rountree as the "Son of the Tribe of Sheikh Dulles / whose very name means deception [*dalas*]" on the front page of *al-Ra'i al-'Amm* on December 16.⁵⁷ While this pun on "Dulles" emphasized American efforts to undermine the unity of the national front, it infuriated the nationalist conspirators whom he portrayed as American agents.⁵⁸

In late January 1958, Muhammad Salih Bahr al-'Ulum joined fellow communists 'Aziz al-Hajj, Kamil Qazanchi, and Da'ud al-Sayyigh to testify against Bahjat al-Atiyya, the notorious leader of the Iraqi CID.⁵⁹ The "People's Poet" began with an improvised poem for the "People's Court": "Judges of the people, listen to the voice of a poet / who has spent half a century in battle with the wolf / I waited a generation for you, while my nation / watched the whip fall down across my sides / I cried to my executioner, 'Our day will come / for my army is on the road toward the July Revolution!'"⁶⁰

Each verse was interrupted by applause, a scene repeated nearly a dozen times during the course of his meandering testimony. As Bahr al-ʿUlum testified about the crimes of the old regime, ʿAdnan al-Rawi watched with other prisoners from the other side of the courtroom.[61] He disputed Bahr al-ʿUlum's repeated claims to the anticolonial legacy of the 1920 revolution and dreamed of vengeance in his prison poems: "The tyrant has returned to his refuge / and no good will come from reunion / The land of Rumaytha still remains / thirsty for that most precious drink / Blood to dye her river valley / and make a ravine of sovereignty."[62]

## The Mosul Revolt in the Nationalist Imagination

Whatever spirit of national unity remained was shattered by the violence that engulfed Mosul in March 1959. The Peace Partisans organized rallies across southern Iraq in January and February, infuriating nationalists with their chants against the United Arab Republic and Baʿth Party.[63] Muhammad Mahdi al-Jawahiri spoke at most of these rallies, lending his cultural prestige to the proceedings.[64] When nearly 250,000 Peace Partisans supporters convened in Mosul on March 6, 1959, Colonel ʿAbd al-Wahhab al-Shawwaf announced a nationalist rebellion, ordering the execution of Kamil Qazanchi and other Peace Partisans and causing the death of more than five hundred soldiers and civilians.[65] Rallies in support of Qasim erupted throughout the country, as crowds burned effigies of Gamal ʿAbd al-Nasser and fought with nationalists.[66] Kazim Jawad was at the Mosul rally and dedicated a poem to his fallen comrade Kamil Qazanchi: "So it came to pass that he walked behind the prison and darkness / across the plains of dawn, happiness, and peace / two shots resounded / and he fell to the ground / collapsing on the soil, the dream flowed / from his heavy tears with love and fire / and as he died, from behind his eyes / the new day rose."[67]

While communist poets celebrated their "triumph," nationalist poets made Mosul their rallying cry. ʿAbd al-Hadi al-Fakiki's "Song of Liberation," set to music by the Syrian musician Mahmud al-Sharif, defiantly proclaimed, "We rebelled for righteousness / and challenged those tyrants / We raised the banner of justice / above the corpses of despots / We challenged the face of death / and avenged ourselves in blood."[68] The poem illustrated the new nationalist emphasis on gender, portraying nationalist women as innocent victims and communist women as savages who mutilated nationalist corpses.[69] ʿAdnan al-Rawi likewise described communists massacring children and raping both virgins and old women in their fervor to destroy "Arabism":

> Do not leave the suckling child,
> for tomorrow he will grow bigger and shout the hymns of the faithful,
> for tomorrow he will grow bigger and have faith in the aspirations of Arabism
> Do not leave the suckling child,
> for in his heart is the filth of the aspiration of Arabism
> Before Jerusalem comes calling,
> child of Babylon, foolish one,
> I shall crush your skull with rocks,
> so Forward!
> Partisans ... Partisans of Peace
> Let us crush the skull of the child in March, in the bosom of spring,
> Forward! ...
> Do not leave the woman, over there, do not leave those pure virgins,
> do not leave the fertile among them, do not leave the sterile,
> for perhaps the sterile will give birth,
> for bosoms in March nurse their child upon the milk of exploits,
> the milk of the struggle, for the great union, and the liberation of Algeria,
> and from the ocean to the sea!!
> What foolishness, comrades!
> Forward![70]

This appeal for the defense of (nationalist) female bodies against communist predation inspired Hilal Naji's treatise about Mosul, which denounced the communist "thirst for blood."[71] The centerpiece of his narrative was the story of Hafsa al-ʿUmari, a virgin girl killed by communists who invaded her home, murdered her father, and then tried to rape this "Ornament of Mosul," only to discover that she "preferred to die virtuous, free, and chaste."[72] His description of Hafsa's naked corpse dragged through the streets and hung from a light pole encapsulated the anticommunist nexus of class, gender, religion, and ideology. Nationalists portrayed communists as barbarians violating the private space of middle-class homes, sexual predators defiling chaste virgins, atheists attacking pious Muslims, and hypocrites spilling blood in the name of peace. In contrast, Hafsa became the symbol of nationalist honor through her chastity, courage, and fidelity.[73]

Both communists and nationalists rejected sectarianism in theory, but the new anticommunist narratives began reshaping the modern politics of sectarianism. Some nationalists, like Naji al-Qashtini, appealed for cross-sectarian solidarity by comparing communist violence at Mosul to Yazid's slaughter of Imam Husayn: "The captives every day are given to Yazid / and the victims entrusted to the new Hulagu / The world has never seen such blood spilled / as the blood of the martyred Iraqi people."[74] Others, however, used the sectarian language of shuʿubiyya to emphasize the "Persian" and Kurdish ethnicity of communists and to portray Peace Partisans as enemies of Arab nationalism.[75] ʿAbd al-Hadi al-Fakiki published a treatise describing communists as shuʿubi opponents of Arab nationalism and agents of imperialism.[76] Neither his poetry nor polemics were explicitly sectarian, but Fakiki defined communist shuʿubiyya as "a sect that denies the superiority of the Arabs to foreigners," and nationalists increasingly characterized Iraqi Shiʿa as "Persians."[77] Yunis Bahri, who worked for Radio Berlin during World War II, complained that nationalist prisoners were forced to listen to Muhammad Mahdi al-Jawahiri recite communist poetry in his "Persian dialect" on the radio. Without a hint of irony, Bahri decided to demonstrate the superiority of true Arab diction to the prison guards by reciting an old speech of Adolf Hitler from memory.[78]

Within weeks of the Mosul rebellion, the anticommunist narrative was reverberating beyond Iraqi borders. The Syrian poet Sulayman al-ʿIsa published a graphic poem from the perspective of a young girl killed by communists in Baghdad: "I am but a husk of skin in al-Karkh / lying in a pool of flesh and blood / I am stained of warm reddish blood / cut down and drained as they smiled . . . / I am just a little girl, do you fear my fate / do you not fear death, terror, nothingness?"[79] Two months later, nationalist poets denounced Iraqi communists at the first Arab poetry festival in Damascus.[80] Several of the poems recited in Damascus were published in *al-Adab*, alongside an anticommunist manifesto written by the Palestinian poet Faʾiz Sayigh, which contrasted nationalist "love" with communist "rage, disgust, resentment, and hatred."[81] The "muscular nationalism" of this narrative was apparent in the stark contrast between graphic descriptions of female victims and glorification of masculine resistance.[82]

Women were not only portrayed as victims like Hafsa al-'Umari in nationalist discourse, but also as virtuous guardians of national honor. Hilal Naji made the story of the nationalist officer Nafi' Dawud, who was blinded in Mosul and executed for his role in the rebellion, and his fiancée, Layla Ayyub, a symbol of communist indecency, insisting that "however much this perverted government deviated from basic humanity, [nobody that they would] dare carry out the sentence against a blind man!"[83] The Egyptian poet Jalila Rida imagined Layla Ayyub responding to Dawud's suggestion that she end the engagement while he awaited execution: "I am angry with you, for how you can permit / such doubt and suspicion to overtake you? / How could you possibly order me to abandon you / when I abhor such thoughts of desertion? / Is it because they deprived you of sight / that you harbor such doubts about my fidelity?"[84] This depiction of nationalist fidelity spoke to popular apprehensions of communist sexual mores and reinforced the nationalist defense of middle-class morality.[85]

## Communists, Nationalists, and the Violence of Kirkuk

Leftist poets generally ignored the gendered dimensions of this anticommunist cultural discourse and instead emphasized the feudal-imperial alliance cultivated by their nationalist rivals. Muhammad Salih Bahr al-'Ulum greeted Peace Partisans returning from Mosul at the Baghdad Railway Station, reciting a fiery poem portraying the nationalist rebellion as a colonial plot: "Welcome home to these heroes of the war who preserved Iraq from these plots / Who held the defense against Nasser, colonial agent and servant of Dulles!"[86] Jawahiri responded with his poem "Song of Peace," which he recited to nearly 1 million supporters in Baghdad in early April.[87] The poem declared that the Peace Partisans would triumph in their struggle against the nationalist "beasts":

An army held back from peace by its victory,
a procession that unfolds like the rays of dawn
A breeze sent down from the heavens of truth,
noble angels whose guidance the people seek

> The bearers of evil will be felled by righteousness,
> and injustice will fall to the strength of the free
> The deluge of spilled blood that is now lapped
> by the tongues of the roving and greedy beasts
> Will begin to fertilize the soil so that there grows
> and flourishes an olive branch for the sake of peace
> And the phantoms of lost souls that flutter above
> will be blown from their heights by the wild falcon
> The doves of peace have returned, so bow in fear
> before them when the eagle and the vulture appear![88]

Bahr al-ʿUlum spoke at the rally as well, praising the Peace Partisans and denouncing nationalists as "those who defend the breasts of Miss [Gertrude] Bell and the sanctity of her forbidden milk."[89] The two poets were joined by female comrades like Hayyat al-Nahr, who voiced her own fury with the nationalist assault against the communist "dawn of peace."[90]

The tense political climate was compounded by new communal violence between Turkmen and Kurds at Kirkuk in July 1959, which left thirty-one dead and more than one hundred wounded.[91] This violence had little connection to Arab nationalism and evoked little interest from Egyptian and Syrian poets, but the Iraqi qawmi poets wrote nearly as many poems about Kirkuk as they did about Mosul.[92] Walid al-Aʿzami mocked communist rhetoric of peace in his graphic description of an elderly victim butchered by Kurdish communists.[93] ʿAbd al-Jabbar Daʾud al-Basri defended middle-class morality in his dedication to the Turkmen victims at Kirkuk: "In the name of the child slaughtered by the bands of assailants / In the name of the sheikh torn to pieces under cover of darkness / In the name of the mother whose child did not return in peace."[94] Many of the poems rejected sectarian shuʿubiyya rhetoric in favor of an anticommunist moral narrative of honor, praising "honorable" Kurds who resisted their communist brethren.[95] Hilal Naji wrote fourteen poems about Kirkuk, all consumed by gruesome depictions of dead children, defiled women, and desecrated bodies. One poem described communists jubilantly butchering their victims as they mocked God and the prophets, culminating with the description of a young female victim: "a little girl just beginning to bloom / her braided pigtails blossoming on both sides / is seized now by the talons of wolves / and torn apart by the pillaging gang / swaddled by greenery now submerged / in blood and groans and anger / and a tuft of blonde hair cast aside."[96] While his narrative of the Mosul violence was an ideological treatise defending the legitimacy of the nationalist rebellion, his poems about Kirkuk abandoned narrative pretense and simply bombarded readers with graphic descriptions of sexual violence and mutilated corpses.[97]

Qasim tried to relieve tensions by amnestying ʿAdnan al-Rawi and other nationalist prisoners in August 1959.[98] Two months later, however, nationalist poets exploded in anger after thirteen army officers implicated in the Mosul rebellion were hung in front of Um al-Tabul Mosque in Baghdad.[99] Rawi fled to Cairo, denouncing the executions in a poem that warned of nationalist retribution against the "remnants of hammers and sickles."[100] Nuʿman Mahir al-Kanʿani, who had supported the "Iraqist" Bakr Sidqi coup in 1936, now commemorated the martyrs of Um al-Tabul as victims of communist treachery and declared, "As for Arabism, its dominion will soon be recognized / and soon it will prosecute every last tyrant."[101] Muhammad Jamil Shalash described the martyred officer Fadhil al-Shukra singing a patriotic ode as he ascended the gallows: "Dawn of my country / cradle of heroism and valor / rope of the gallows / I will not wish for anything / other than the liberation of my country / so take me as an offering!"[102] Shalash was implicated in the plot to assassinate Qasim three weeks later and endured a humiliating interrogation at the People's Court.[103] Hilal Naji, who dreamed allegorically of Qasim's assassination in an anonymous poem published in *al-Hurriyya* two months earlier, was also implicated in the plot and sentenced to death in absentia after fleeing to Egypt.[104] ʿAli al-Hilli paid tribute to his nationalist comrades in *al-Adab*, praising Naji's commitment to defending Arab countries from "foreign imperialism and global Judaism."[105] These nationalist poems were extremely popular among Baʿthist cadres in Baghdad and Mosul and contributed to resurgent nationalist effort to contest communist cultural hegemony.[106]

## Badr Shakir al-Sayyab and the Struggle for Cultural Hegemony

Badr Shakir al-Sayyab began publishing his anticommunist tracts in *al-Hurriyya* during the brief thaw after the Kirkuk violence in July 1959.[107] He wrote prolifically, publishing dozens of poems in journals like *al-Adab*, *Shi'r*, *Aswat*, and *al-Hiwar*, along with his collection *Unshudat al-Matar* (*Rain Song*) in 1960. Sayyab's symbolism and mythological references allowed him to evade press censorship in ways that his "committed" nationalist counterparts could not.[108] "Cerberus in Babylon," for example, used the mythical figure of Cerberus as a metaphor for communists who preyed on the bodies of nationalist women: "Cerberus in the hell of Babylon / loves to run behind her through the trails / tearing her shoes with his claws, biting / her supple legs, snapping at her hands, or tearing her gown / staining her scarf with dried blood / as fresh blood fuels his howl."[109] This nightmarish imagery of sexual violence conveyed anticommunist polemics in the language of middle-class morality.[110]

Sayyab resurrected the controversy surrounding his famous 1954 poem, "The Blind Whore," in *al-Hurriyya*. The epic poem detailed the tragic life of Salima, a peasant girl forced into prostitution after her father was murdered by his landlord. The poem satirized Salimah's desperate attempts to maintain her dignity in the face of this degradation:

> No man who makes love to a dark Arab girl will die a loser,
> for your skin is like the color of wheat, daughter of the Arabs,
> like the dawn between the grape arbors,
> like the surface of the Euphrates reflecting,
> the mildness of the earth and rapacity of gold.
> Do not leave me, for the morning reveals my lineage:
> I am descended from a conqueror, a holy warrior, and a prophet!
> I am an Arab: My nation is their blood,
> the best of all blood, as my father used to say.
> In the filthiest parts of my body, in my revealing breasts,
> flows the blood of the conquerors. So come and defile it, men![111]

Sayyab recalled indignantly that when he was hiding in Iran, his Tudeh compatriots voiced their pleasure with this description of defiled Arab honor. He argued that the true meaning of nationalism (qawmiyya) had been "lost between the internationalists (*shu'ubiyyin*) and the chauvinists (*shufiniyyin*)" and called for an inclusive and nonsectarian vision of nationalism. In the same article, however, he criticized miscegenation and endorsed the crude chauvinism of Baʿthist Arab nationalism: "Is it not disgraceful for us as Arabs that our daughters have become whores who sleep with people from every race and color?"[112] Sayyab's anticommunist polemics were animated by concern for racial purity, critique of communist immorality, and attacks on Kurds and Jews, whom he described as Zionist agents who lusted after Iraqi women.[113] While "The Blind Whore" was critical of sexual oppression and commodification, Sayyab's reinterpretation of the poem in *al-Hurriyya* showed his lack of interest in pursuing these themes in his nationalist phase.[114]

Sayyab's critique of miscegenation was linked to his obsession with communist sexual violence.[115] One of his editorials in *al-Hurriyya* accused the communist leader Baha al-Din Nuri of raping the Jewish communist Madeleine Mir.[116] Another recounted the tragic fate of a communist girl impregnated by an older comrade who refused to marry the girl because she belonged to a different sect. He protested that while communists "do not believe in gods or religions" and reject sectarianism, they could not contest social realities. Sayyab claimed that Comrade Fahd refused to intervene and instead mocked the religious beliefs of the community, the girl's father and brother killed her to prevent public scandal.[117] In stark contrast to Nazik al-Malaʾika's critique of "honor killing," Sayyab's opprobrium was directed entirely at the girl's lover rather than her killers.[118] The solution to sexual oppression in this nationalist vision of middle-class morality was not the sexual liberation of women but the revival of masculine chivalry.

After the assassination attempt against Qasim in October 1959, *al-Hurriyya* and other nationalist newspapers were suspended, and Sayyab returned to symbolic anticommunism.[119] He published "The City of Sindbad" in Adonis's literary journal, *Shiʿr*, in April 1960, invoking the specter of communist violence at Mosul and Kirkuk in his nightmarish depiction of Qasim's Iraq.[120] His condemnation of communists as violent "Tatars" and bleak descriptions of crucifixions, severed limbs, and rotting corpses punctuated the darkest statement of political despair from this period: "Death in the streets / sterility in the fields / and everything that we love dies."[121] Three months later, he reinforced this anticommunist narrative in the poem "A Prophecy of 1956," which appeared in *al-Adab* and linked the Babylonian goddess ʿIshtar to Hafsa al-ʿUmari, the young nationalist girl crucified by communists in

Mosul: "'Ishtar is at the trunk of the tree / they crucified her, hammered the nails / in the home of the birth womb / 'Ishtar is concealing Hafsa / inviting her to drink the rains / inviting her to drink until oblivion."[122]

## The Nationalist Struggle for Feminist Legitimacy

While Sayyab portrayed communists as sexual predators, many women supported the Communist Party. More than forty thousand women joined the Iraqi Women's League, an organization linked to the Communist Party that actively campaigned against imperialism, economic injustice, and the oppression of women in the 1950s.[123] The league encouraged women to join the Popular Resistance Forces, endorsed Qasim as "Sole Leader," and celebrated the new Personal Status Law passed in December 1959.[124] The experience of female communist poets like Lami'a 'Abbas 'Amara and Hayyat al-Nahr illustrated the cultural dilemmas that these women faced. Because their nationalist opponents portrayed communism as an affront to both popular culture and religious faith, communist women were always careful to locate their attitudes on sex and gender in the cultural discourse of nationalism.[125] Hayyat al-Nahr, for example, made a concerted effort to link the struggle of Iraqi women to Arab nationalist causes in Algeria, Palestine, Egypt, and Oman.[126] When Lami'a 'Abbas 'Amara praised the contribution of female workers to Mao's Great Leap Forward in a poem that she recited during a cultural expedition to China, her arguments were grounded entirely in economic logic and remained silent about sexual liberation.[127]

The sexual propriety of communist poetry did little to dissuade nationalists from attacking the morality of female communists, and Hayyat al-Nahr was often described as a promiscuous drinker by her opponents.[128] While nationalists denounced communist promiscuity as a threat to middle-class values and religious faith, they framed their stance as a secular defense of sexual morality.[129] Nationalist intellectuals like Shakir Mustafa Salim emphasized communist hypocrisy on women's liberation in his satirical anticommunist tract *Min Mudhakkirat Qawmi Muta'amir* (*From the Memoirs of a Nationalist Conspirator*). Salim described the "black apparitions" of veiled women in the communist crowd who greeted nationalist prisoners in Kut: "They were the (respectable women) from among the wives and sisters of the (noble strugglers), come to welcome us in the (novel and peerless) manner decreed in the final instructions of the late Comrade Fahd.... These women (respectable and secluded) were equipped with rubbish and refuse in buckets to hurl upon us they might scatter roses and basil on distinguished guests."[130] Salim's sarcastic use of parentheticals in the passage mocked communist boorishness and hypocrisy, fusing class and gender grievance to contrast communist and nationalist attitudes toward women. Female communists like Lami'a 'Abbas 'Amara criticized veiling conventions, but nationalists contrasted their own sincere opposition to veiling with the hypocritical behavior of communist men, whose own wives, mothers, and sisters remained veiled.[131] Salim also mocked communist masculinity in his depiction of the communist prison commissioner as an "effeminate little fairy" who reveled in his "disgusting and degenerate morality."[132] His fellow nationalist prisoner, Shadhil Taqa, echoed these themes in poems written to his wife, who smuggled them out of prison and circulated them among nationalist cadres.[133]

This discourse of "muscular nationalism" and "nationalist feminism" inspired nationalist poets to challenge the collective valorization of communist women by promoting individual feminist icons of their own. Communists made little effort to promote female politicians like Naziha al-Dulaymi or poets like Lami'a al-'Abbas 'Amara, Sabriyya al-Hassu, Maqbula al-Hilli, Hayyat al-Nahr, and Wafiyya Abu Qalam, and most female communist poets were reluctant to speak openly about women's causes.[134] Nationalists extolled the poet Nazik al-Mala'ika and political activist Yusra Sa'id Thabit.[135] Mala'ika was never as vocal as her male counterparts in nationalist politics and even briefly joined the leftist Iraqi Writers Union in 1959.[136] By the following year, however she was publishing poems mocking communist obsessions with nationalist conspiracies: "When night descends on these hills, stand up, Comrade / we can watch through dark slits in this deep silence / for perhaps dusk is plotting in secrecy / perhaps it is just by the starlight and night silence / for these hills and that path / and this darkness are agents, one and all!"[137] Even Mala'ika, however, was unwilling to serve as the symbol of feminist nationalism in Iraq and retreated into political silence, which male nationalists explained as state repression.[138] Mala'ika's views on gender, however, had always been more progressive than those of Badr Shakir al-Sayyab and other nationalist poets, and her refusal to criticize communist rivals on gender issues was striking.[139] While communist women exercised considerable self-censorship on women's topics, the voices of nationalist women were drowned out by their male comrades. In both cases, the cultural politics of gender were shaped by male poets speaking about women's bodies.

The Algerian revolutionary Jamila Buhayrid captured the attention of nationalist poets across the Arab world after she was arrested by French authorities and sentenced to death in 1957, inspiring a special edition of *al-Adab* in April 1958.[140] Two months later, ʿAli al-Hilli promised that the fires of Arab nationalism would cleanse the blood of "a thousand Jamilas" and a "thousand Joan of Arcs."[141] Communists poets like ʿAbd al-Wahhab al-Bayati, Lamiʿa ʿAbbas ʿAmara, and Hayyat al-Nahr also dedicated poems to Jamila, while Muhammad Salih Bahr al-ʿUlum reflected the collectivist mentality of the communists in poems that praised female Algerian rebels without mentioning the name of Jamila or the other Algerian heroines.[142] Thousands of women participated in demonstrations in Baghdad to demand Jamila's release from French custody, including the teenage communist activist Haifa Zangana, who recalled that "it was Jamilah, not a pop singer or a supermodel, who served as our role model."[143] Several years later, the Iraqi state brought Jamila Buhayrid and Zahra Zarif to Baghdad after the Algerian triumph and commissioned a bust of Jamila from the sculptor Khalid al-Rahal.[144]

Despite this political consensus of support, nationalist poets transformed the Algerian heroine into a symbol of their struggle against communism. Nazik al-Malaʾika had mocked the superficial feminism of the tributes to Jamila in a poem from January 1959:

> With malice in their hearts, they cut her with their knives,
> while we cut her with a smile and the best intentions,
> with the wounds of callous and foolish rhetoric.
> How deep are her wounds from the fangs of France!
> But the wound of her kin is deeper and more painful than any other,
> so we should be twice as ashamed to face Jamila![145]

Even communists appreciate the poem as a critique of state passivity toward the Algerian revolution.[146] Iraqi devotion to Jamila, however, took on new meanings for nationalist poets after the violence at Mosul in March 1959. The Syrian poet Talʿat al-Rafaʿi connected Jamila to the Mosul resistance in the poem that she recited at the Arab poetry festival in Damascus, declaring, "In the name of Jamila, whose bones are chewed by fire / in the name of Paradise, guarded by Raja' and Maryam / We are Arabs even if not a drop of blood remains / and Baghdad is ours however much they destroy!"[147] Shadhil Taqa wrote poems about Jamila languishing in a French prison cell, singing songs of love and revolution to strengthen the resolve of male comrades.[148] Badr Shakir al-Sayyab likewise linked Jamila and the Algerian struggle against France to the anticommunist struggle in Iraq in his poem "Jamila Buhayrid," connecting the Algerian revolutionary to the Babylonian goddess ʿIshtar, just as he had done with Hafsa al-ʿUmari.[149]

Yusra Saʿid Thabit, a young Baʿthist activist implicated in the plot against Qasim, was soon championed as an "Iraqi Jamila Buhayrid."[150] Her passionate defense of the nationalist cause in the face at the People's Court made her a symbol of feminist honor and nationalist virtue.[151] Colonel Mahdawi mocked Yusra's honor and intelligence, peppering her with confusing questions and encouraging the audience to laugh when he noted an inconsistency. When Yusra acknowledged that her Syrian husband, Hamid Mariʿ, sometimes spent the night at Baʿth Party headquarters rather than coming home, Mahdawi implied that Mariʿ was sleeping with other women and ridiculed her naiveté as the audience laughed. Yusra fought back against Mahdawi and the communist students who testified against her, insisting they were lying and launching into a spirited denunciation of colonial borders that thrilled the nationalists.[152] Hilal Naji portrayed Yusra as a noble sister and daughter who took up arms after her brother was killed by communists in Mosul and her father died of grief and contended that she was raped and tortured in prison, a clear parallel to the Algerian revolutionaries Jamila Boupacha and Jamila Buhayrid.[153] ʿAdnan al-Rawi wrote poems celebrating Yusra as a nationalist heroine and promising her that she would be liberated once the nationalists destroyed colonial borders: "By God, little sister / we will finish a brilliant star / to light your path, Yusra / and tomorrow comes the great unity."[154] ʿAli al-Hilli hailed Yusra as the "sister of Jamila Buhayrid" and described her as "a tune from the lyre of purity / erupting in the revolutionary melody," simultaneously articulating the nationalist defense of feminine honor and valorization of revolutionary womanhood.[155] Yusra's plight became such a cause célèbre among the nationalists that the government eventually agreed to release her, along with her husband and brother, in the political amnesty of December 1961.[156]

## Commitment, Debauchery, and Cold War Politics in Iraqi Poetry

ʿAbd al-Wahhab al-Bayati returned to Baghdad from his brief sojourn in the Soviet Union after the revolution of July 1958.[157] His stay in Moscow coincided with the national furor over the publication of Boris Pasternak's anti-Stalinist novel, *Doctor Zhivago*, which was awarded the Nobel Prize for Literature on October 23, 1958.[158] Bayati published a poem about the controversy in the cultural journal *al-Thaqafa al-Jadida* and his poetry collection *Kalimat La Tamut* (*Immortal Words*), defending the Soviet Union and threatening political reactionaries with violence:

> My sisters,
> you green-eyed girls,
> we shall make from the skulls
> of oil barons
> and agents
> and conspirators
> a game for the laughing children of tomorrow.
> So let them make a thousand Zhivagos,
> and one thousand effigies
> and counterfeiters of history and cookers of meat.
> We shall make from their skulls
> an ashtray for cigarettes.
> My sisters,
> you green-eyed girls[159]

These lines paid homage to the great Soviet poet Vladimir Mayakovski's declaration in "150,000,000": "Let's kill the old people, / and turn their skulls into ashtrays."[160] Bayati returned to Moscow to serve as the Iraqi cultural attaché, but controversy over the poem consumed nationalist poets and critics.[161] When Muhyi al-Din Ismaʿil and Hilal Naji published their anti-communist poetry manifesto *Jinayyat al-Shuyuʿiyyan ʿala al-Adab al-ʿIraqi* (*Communist Crimes against Iraqi Literature*), Yusuf al-Sibaʿi denounced Bayati in his introduction to the book, describing him was "one poet from among those [Soviet] agents who threatens his noble countrymen who support the Arab nationalist cause with his declaration, 'We shall make from their skulls an ashtray for cigarettes.'"¹⁶² This misreading of the poem as an attack on Arab nationalists led Bayati to excise the poem from future editions of *Kalimat La Tamut*.¹⁶³

Whether the misreading was deliberate or accidental, it signaled an evolution of anticommunist discourse, and communist poets were now condemned for their lack of political commitment (iltizam).¹⁶⁴ While nationalist poets like ʿAli al-Hilli, Hafiz Jamil, Shafiq al-Kamali, Nuʿman Mahir al-Kanʿani, Nazik al-Malaʾika, Hilal Naji, ʿAbd al-Qadir al-Nasiri, ʿAdnan al-Rawi, Hazim Saʿid, and Muhammad Jamil Shalash had written dozens of poems about the Palestinian Nakba, Iraqi Wathba, Algerian Revolution, Baghdad Pact, Suez Crisis, Jabal Akhdar War, and United Arab Republic, Ismaʿil and Naji argued that communists wrote only about internationalist causes. Communist poets had produced a vast body of nationalist poetry over the previous three decades, and arguments about their lack of "commitment" required creative explanations about why these poems did not count. Hilal Naji claimed that he once heard Jawahiri explain to fellow poets at the Hasan Ajami Café that he felt compelled by nationalists to write his famous Wathba poem, "My Brother Jaʿfar," and had cribbed the famous opening line, "Do you know or do you now know," from the Arabic translation of Shakespeare's *Julius Caesar*. Naji declared triumphantly that Jawahiri's poetry was inspired by ambition and vanity, not "the *Wathba* of January or the blood of the martyrs that covered the expanse of Baghdad or anything of the sort." He also noted that Jawahiri had recited a poem at the coronation of Faysal II in 1953 in which he praised the hated crown prince, ʿAbd al-Ilah: "It is an honor for uncles to be as you see / intimate with fear and attentive to a leader / ʿAbd al-Ilah is a partner in these noble deeds / You have shared the traits of the sole king!"¹⁶⁵ Jawahiri was embarrassed by the poem and later called it "a lapse and then some," but his relationship with the Hashemites was well known.¹⁶⁶ Ismaʿil and Naji also noted that communist poets Lamiʿa ʿAbbas ʿAmara and Baqir Samaka had written poems in praise of the monarchy, which they viewed as proof of communist treachery.¹⁶⁷

Nationalists condemned communist internationalism as evidence of shuʿubi sympathies and complained of the betrayal of poets who had previously praised Nasser as "hero" but now condemned him as a "conspirator."[168] Isma'il and Naji mocked 'Abd al-Wahhab al-Bayati for describing the horrors of Buchenwald while ignoring the fate of Jaffa, Baghdad, and Algeria and for denouncing Nasser as "the heir of Hitler and the Tatars" while describing the Soviet Union as "the land of bread and peace and flowers."[169] His poems about Nasser, Algeria, and Palestine in the years before the revolution were simply ignored.[170] Muhammad Salih Bahr al-'Ulum's visit to Moscow during his trip to Tashkent for the Afro-Asian Writers' Conference in October 1958 inspired a number of poems in praise of the Soviet Union, which contrasted sharply with his attacks on Nasser as an American agent and "servant of Dulles."[171] This socialist internationalism was echoed by Lami'a 'Abbas 'Amara, who published poems in praise of Mao's Great Leap Forward and in solidarity with the civil rights movement in the United States.[172] Her vision of anti-Americanism had once been a shared feature of the anticolonial politics of the national front, but nationalists now began to see globalist sympathies as subversive and treacherous.[173] Despite their condemnation of communist internationalism, nationalist poets remained committed to the spirit of Bandung and published poems in support of Patrice Lumumba and other non-Arab leaders.[174]

Perhaps the most striking feature of the nationalist assault on the communist poets was their condemnation of communist morality and sexuality. While Sayyab criticized communists for valuing political "commitment" over "art for art's sake," Naji and Isma'il argued that communist "commitment" was undermined by their love of alcohol and women.[175] While nationalist poets supported Arab causes, Baqir Samaka "pursued Señorita Isabella in the taverns of Madrid" while studying in Barcelona.[176] When Sa'di Yusuf fled to Bulgaria, he could not finish his ode to the "workers of Iraq" without describing his "flirtation with the wretched young Bulgarian girls in Sofia."[177] Kazim Jawad said nothing about women or alcohol in his description of Peace Partisans conferences in Stockholm and Berlin, but his old friend Hilal Naji accused him of being "so drunk he could barely open his eyes."[178] Even the elderly Muhammad Mahdi al-Jawahiri was condemned for his hedonist lifestyle: "When one of the feudalists put a bundle of cash in his pocket, he made straight for the taverns of Batawin and Karrada to gulp down liquor and recite his poem 'Anita,' which describes the intimate parts of women that lie between their thighs!"[179] Worst of all was the bohemian poet Husayn Mardan, whose deviant communist morality could be seen in poems about the gratification of his own "feverish lust."[180]

These critiques of communist hedonism were linked to the nationalist defense of middle-class values. 'Abd al-Razzaq Muhyi al-Din alleged in *al-Hurriyya* that communist poets sexually harassed Nazik al-Mala'ika in Jawahiri's home and the elder poet watched silently as Mala'ika fled in humiliation.[181] Bayati's poem about the Pasternak affair was written two months before the Mosul Rebellion, but Naji and Isma'il argued that he was endorsing that violence when he wrote, "We shall make from their skulls / an ashtray for cigarettes."[182] Bahr al-'Ulum was condemned for supporting political violence in a poem that declared, "The people are masters in the elimination of rights / their ropes around the necks of every reckless fool / And when the ropes finally seize hold of some traitor / they dispatch him and move on to hunt for the next!"[183] In their own rendering of the poem, Naji and Isma'il changed the word *traitors* to *rebels* to imply that communists opposed all forms of nationalist resistance and derisively described the "People's Poet" as the "Rabble's Poet" to emphasize the communist threat to bourgeois values.[184]

Communist poets struggled to respond to these assaults on their ideology and morality. They distanced themselves from the violent rhetoric of the "red months" of March and April 1959, refrained from writing about alcohol and sexuality, and expressed support for the Arab struggle in Algeria, Oman, and Palestine.[185] Hayyat al-Nahr was still insisting wistfully in March 1960 that "those who have planted will harvest / and will preserve their victory in the end / and fill the plains with love and bread and peace."[186] In his speech to the Iraqi Writers Union in June 1960, Muhammad Mahdi al-Jawahiri struck a conciliatory tone in his appeal to the communists to "seize the banners of poetry and thought and literature to push the ranks of evil and depravity backward and to propel the soldiers of good and virtue forward."[187] Salah Khalis defended the union's commitment to both "patriotism" (wataniyya) and "nationalism" (qawmiyya), dismissing nationalist poets who refused to join the union as individualists and opportunists and praising recent poetry collections of communists and fellow travelers like Lami'a 'Abbas 'Amara, Muhammad Salih Bahr al-'Ulum, 'Abd al-Wahhab al-Bayati, Buland al-Haydari, Zahid Muhammad, al-Farid Sam'an, Baqir Samaka, and Sa'di Yusuf.[188] Even in this golden age of communist poetry, Khalis remained particularly proud that the Iraqi Writers Union had organized a festival to commemorate the life of the iconic nationalist poet Ma'ruf al-Rusafi.[189]

## Conclusion

The Rusafi Festival took place in Baghdad in April 1959, less than six weeks after the Mosul Rebellion. Dozens of communist poets portrayed Rusafi as the patron saint of communist cultural politics in Iraq, a controversial project of revisionism given Rusafi's pronounced nationalist sympathies.[190] Lami'a 'Abbas 'Amara described Rusafi as the "Poet of the Wretched," and Muhammad Salih Bahr al-'Ulum and Baqir Samaka recited poems that functioned more as panegyrics for Qasim than elegies for Rusafi, though Jawahiri remained focused on the legacy of the poet in his own elegy.[191] The Iraqi Writers Union solicited speeches in praise of Rusafi from global communist poets like Mirzo Tursunzoda.[192] Only Muhammad Mahdi al-Jawahiri remained focused on the legacy of poet, comparing the "immortal Rusafi" to the "great Mutanabbi" and declared that the young generation of Iraqi poets influenced by Rusafi began their revolutionary march on the day that the poet died in his shabby room in Baghdad.[193]

Nationalist poets bitterly denounced this communist effort to appropriate Rusafi's legacy. 'Adnan al-Rawi recalled Rusafi's elegy for the martyrs of the Rashid 'Ali movement: "The covenant of manhood will be absolved from us / if we forgot or pretend to forget the day of your hanging." He now protested that if Rusafi were alive to witness the execution of nationalist officers at Um al-Tabul, he would have declared, "The covenant of Arabism will be absolved from us / if we forgot or pretend to forget the day of your hanging."[194] Fa'iq al-Samarra'i echoed this invocation of Rusafi in his retort to Colonel Mahdawi's habit of quoting Rusafi at the People's Court, reminded the Iraqi people of Rusafi's famous quip, "How many times has the blind mouse / come to be called by us a ferocious lion!"[195] Like their communist rivals, nationalist poets and politicians believed that the spirit of anticolonial nationalism embodied by Rusafi belonged to them. There was a grim irony in the fact that the cultural politics of anticolonialism that shaped Iraqi poetry for nearly five decades was now consuming its own children, forcing them into silence or exile.[196] The legacy of anticolonialism had become little more than a symbolic stance cynically deployed to support or oppose the power of the state.

Gender and sexuality went largely unmentioned by either the communist poets who praised Rusafi or the nationalist poets who condemned their "appropriation." This silence might seem surprising, given Rusafi's public support for women's liberation and well-known homosexual proclivities and the intense interest in gender and sexual politics in this period. It revealed, however, several important dimensions of the contested cultural politics of revolutionary Iraq. Communist poets were silent about Rusafi's libertine social views because libertinism had become a taboo topic of public discussion for them. They did not need to prove to anyone that they were liberated from traditional social and religious mores, but they did seek to prove that their political agenda was consistent with Rusafi's anticolonial nationalism. Nationalist poets, for their part, were silent because they had little interest in defending traditional social and religious mores. They were not opposed to Rusafi's vision of women's liberation or even to the private desire for intoxication and illicit sexual gratification. Their critique of communist sexuality required them to portray communism as a foreign attack against local culture, not an evolution of the modernist outlook of respectable nationalists like Rusafi. This mutual silence illustrated the ironic convergence of both factions on the issues of women's liberation and sexual liberation. Every poet who fashioned himself or herself a revolution agreed about the need for modern and progressive attitudes on these questions.

The heated nature of gender and sexual politics in revolutionary Iraq masked the fact that these discourses were really about something else entirely. Feminist nationalism shaped the cultural politics of revolution because nationalists saw it as their only hope of challenging communist cultural hegemony. Given the relative popularity of the communist economic and political agenda, the new gender cultural war allowed nationalists to portray themselves as chivalrous defenders of middle-class morality against the menacing communist rabble. Realizing that they could not convincingly attack the communists for being too "progressive" in the new revolutionary climate, nationalist poets seized on communist hypocrisy toward women to outflank their rivals in the cultural domain. In this upside-down world of revolutionary Iraq, the middle class flocked to the nationalist bandwagon and embraced the vision of middle-class modernity as a way of reconciling the radical politics of the Baʿth Party with the traditional values and class interests of the bygone era.[197] As custodians of national honor and cultural pride, poets once again asserted themselves as spokesmen of the nation and contested the new horizon of revolutionary politics in the poetry wars that followed the political violence of the "red months" of 1959.

The gender culture war of 1959 and 1960 receded somewhat during the final years of the Qasim era, but the symbolism of women's bodies remained integral to nationalist cultural discourse. When the nationalist poet Shadhil Taqa was released from prison after the Baʿthist coup d'état of February 1963, he wrote a poem addressed to the Algerian heroine Jamila Buhayrid. Hailing her as "star of the Revolutionaries / my sister, Jamila," Taqa invited the anticolonial icon to share the victory of the nationalist forces: "I see the remnants of tyranny, defeated / behind them lie ruins / while in front are new peaks / where light and victory rise above / in the unity of our noble sons and our destiny!"[198] Jamila had been released from prison after the liberation of Algeria from French rule in July 1962, but Taqa's invocation of her name as a symbol of Arab national liberation hearkened back to the feminist nationalism promoted by fellow nationalist poets like ʿAli al-Hilli, Hilal Naji, ʿAdnan al-Rawi, and Muhammad Jamil Shalash in prior years. Just as the cultural politics of the hijab war in the 1920s had masked underlying tensions over the relationship between poetry and patronage under colonial rule, the new cultural politics of gender masked underlying tensions of race, sect, and class in revolutionary Iraq. And yet, however much these poems represented the superficial desires to use women's bodies as symbols of cultural authenticity and revolutionary legitimacy, they also illustrated the capacity of poetry to shape national discourse and cultural attitudes. This cultural power ensured that poetry would remain a dangerous game in Iraq for years to come.

CONCLUSION

# "WE ARE WHAT FLOWS THROUGH EVERY SOUL AND SPIRIT"

The historical legacy of rebel poetry in Iraq unraveled after the bloody Ramadan Revolution, the Baʿthist coup d'état against ʿAbd al-Karim Qasim on February 8, 1963. In a span of days, nationalist troops arrested and massacred thousands of communist cadres and sympathizers in methodical house-to-house sweeps.[1] In the epilogue to his anti-Qasim tract, the nationalist poet ʿAdnan al-Rawi celebrated the carnage, proclaiming that the triumph of Arab nationalism "will be written by everyone who suffered the most grievous pain under the shadow of terror, and these cruel agonies will vanish in the exuberance of the great victory of 14 Ramadan, 1963."[2] On February 16, 1963, as nationalists celebrated their triumph over their communist rivals, Baghdad Radio broadcast a statement authorizing the confiscation of the property and assets of thirty-five individuals accused of having "misused their influence." The poets Muhammad Mahdi al-Jawahiri, Muhammad Salih Bahr al-ʿUlum, and Lamiʿa ʿAbbas ʿAmara were on this list.[3] The announcement was the opening salvo in a long campaign of state repression against dissident poets, artists, and intellectuals that dwarfed that of the past. As one journalist confessed in the months after the coup, "We used to talk about and publish things that irritated Nuri [al-Saʿid] and the palace, knowing that we might go too far and lose our jobs, have our papers closed, or the like. But we knew Nuri wouldn't *hang* us for this. These people (the Baathists) will."[4]

Muhammad Mahdi al-Jawahiri was already living in exile, having fled

Baghdad after he was arrested and charged with "violating public order and inciting the people against the government" in March 1961.[5] The decision to purge Jawahiri was part of Qasim's ill-fated effort to assuage nationalist anger by marginalizing their communist enemies.[6] Jawahiri settled in Prague, where he was soon joined by fellow communist poets and writers like ʿAbd al-Wahhab al-Bayati, Dhu al-Nun Ayyub, and Ghaʾib Tuʿama Farman.[7] These leftist exiles formed the Higher Committee for the Defense of the Iraqi People's Movement Abroad immediately after the Ramadan Revolution and began broadcasting appeals for solidarity on East German radio.[8] As the head of the Higher Committee, Jawahiri earned fawning coverage in the European communist press, which pointedly noted the lack of party credentials among the poets and intellectuals to emphasize the "democratic" nature of their resistance to Baʿthist rule.[9] In his own appeal to fellow travelers and "intellectuals of the world," Bayati likewise emphasized that the Baʿthist victims included "known noncommunists" and even "confirmed anticommunists" and compared the situation in Iraq to the "fascist terror in Spain, Portugal, Greece, and elsewhere."[10] Jawahiri even appealed privately for British support in the struggle against the "tyrannical despotic junta," though his call was ignored.[11] Though Baʿthist authorities were unaware of his plea to Britain, they retaliated against his campaign in the foreign communist press by broadcasting (false) reports that Jawahiri was seeking the aid of the Israeli Communist Party to overthrow the "revolutionary, progressive, and socialist Iraqi regime."[12]

Those communist poets who were still living in Iraq at the time of the coup faced more difficult dilemmas and more tortuous tribulations. While some communist women were arrested and even sentenced to death, Lamiʿa ʿAbbas ʿAmara was spared further reprisals after she agreed to stop writing about politics.[13] Buland al-Haydari was sentenced to death, but while his cousin Jamal al-Haydari was executed in July 1963, the poet was saved by the intercession of a sympathetic Kurdish politician and allowed to leave for exile in Beirut.[14] Perhaps unsurprisingly, the poet who suffered the most was Muhammad Salih Bahr al-ʿUlum, who endured two more years in Nuqrat al-Salman, the desert prison where he had spent so many years for the crime of poetry in the 1940s and 1950s.[15] The existentialist poet and novelist Fadhil al-ʿAzzawi was also arrested due to his communist links and later recalled finding Bahr al-'Ulum in a Baghdadi jail cell three days after the coup. The "People's Poet" was now "hung from the window by his hands, with only his outstretched toes touching the floor of the little room.... He remained like that throughout the night without uttering a single groan."[16] The torture Bahr al-'Ulum endured was typical of the violence that the new regime used against communist poets, artists, and intellectuals.[17]

In the midst of this depressing era for Iraqi communists, Muhammad Mahdi al-Jawahiri recited a poem commemorating the Wathba of January 1948 at a gathering of Iraqi exiles in Prague in January 1965. He dedicated the poem to his old friend and comrade Bahr al-'Ulum, who had played such a pivotal role in that popular uprising, reciting poetry from the shoulders of protesters before he was arrested and tortured. Jawahiri now recalled with bittersweet nostalgia those days when he and Bahr al-'Ulum, better known to friends and comrades by the *kunya* (honorific) Abu Nazim, had stood together at the forefront of national resistance to colonialism and dictatorship:

> Abu Nazim, we are the leaders of a generation,
> we guide it along the path of life, and we chant
> As dear partners, we begin anew this journey,
> whose terrors we know and yet suffer again. . . .
> Abu Nazim, we are the most delicate of people,
> and by our very nature are the slaves of our art
> We are what flows through every soul and spirit,
> expelling the drowsiness for every last eyelid
> How strange that we are still treated so unjustly
> and so cruelly, that we are sold out in this deceit,
> How strange that we defeated that criminal rule,
> only to suffer at the hands of its new imitators![18]

Bahr al-'Ulum was released from prison just weeks later, but the two great communist poets would remain outcasts under the new regime, the leaders of a generation of rebel poets whose time had now passed.[19] Poetry remained politically committed and extremely popular in Iraq, but poets were no longer participants in political events, and their poetry ceased to be dangerous.

## CONCLUSION

## Poetry and the Politics of History

While repression and censorship curtailed the ability of leftist poets and writers to publish anything remotely critical of the state for decades, nationalist poets reveled in their new freedom.[20] ʿAli al-Hilli, Hilal Naji, ʿAdnan al-Rawi, Muhammad Jamil Shalash, and Shadhil Taqa all rushed to publish new collections of nationalist poems or republish anticommunist collections published abroad during the Qasim years.[21] The most prominent of the nationalist poets, Badr Shakir al-Sayyab, had already rejected literary commitment (iltizam) as derivative of communist aesthetics and never allowed his nationalist politics to transform his own poetry into the crude propaganda published by the Baʿthist poet-cadres, but he was dead of complications from amyotrophic lateral sclerosis by December 1964.[22] Even the Baʿthist poets suffered from renewed repression in the five-year interregnum of President ʿAbd al-Salam ʿArif and his brother ʿAbd al-Rahman ʿArif after November 1963.[23] The return of Baʿthist rule in July 1968 restored the political importance of poetry through ostentatious ceremonies of state patronage.[24] The nationalist poetry promoted by the state was slavish and crude, the political inverse of the vibrant rebel poetry scenes of decades past.

State patronage became the complement to state repression, the carrot of collaboration to the stick of punishment in the battle to harness the power of poetry. The communist poet Muzaffar al-Nawwab emerged as perhaps the most prominent dissident poet in the country, composing popular poems in vernacular verse about how to steel the resolve of political prisoners.[25] His most famous poem from this era was "The Recantation," which described the pleas of a distraught mother and sister to a communist prisoner.[26] Turning the tables on the nationalist tropes of sexual honor and shame that pervaded the Qasim period, Nawwab depicted the male prisoner's "recantation" of communist ideals as the true source of disgrace for his steadfast female relatives. The poem circulated widely among communist prisoners, and a delegation of communist workers presented the poet with a copy of the poem written in gold ink during his long stint in prison at Hilla.[27] When Nawwab was released from prison after the second Baʿthist coup in July 1968, he was offered a government job but declined and left for exile in Beirut.[28] Other leftist poets, however, eventually recanted and agreed to compose panegyrics for the state, including Yusuf al-Sayigh, Fawzi Karim, and ʿAbd al-Razzaq ʿAbd al-Wahid.[29] Even the eternally unrepentant Muhammad Salih Bahr al-ʿUlum succumbed to the ravages and torture and reconciled with the nationalist regime after 1968; he even composed panegyrics for Ahmad Hasan al-Bakr and Saddam Hussein to commemorate the "progressive national front" between the Communist Party and Baʿth Party facilitated by the Soviet Union.[30]

The reconciliation of dissident poets and the state forced new reckonings with the contentious historical legacy of the Qasim era. Bahr al-ʿUlum was finally allowed to publish his collected works in fall 1968, but only on the condition that his entire 1959 collection, *Aqbas al-Thawra*, was excluded.[31] The stridently antinationalist tone of those poems would have exposed the contradictions of the new political rehabilitation of communists, and so the partisan conflicts of the past were expunged from history as though they had never happened.[32] ʿAbd al-Wahhab al-Bayati made a similar compromise with the state, emphasizing his nationalist loyalties in the panegyrics he composed for Gamal ʿAbd al-Nasser while living in exile and accepting a position as cultural adviser to the Ministry of Culture and Information after 1968.[33] When a new edition of his celebrated 1960 collection, *Kalamat La Tamut*, appeared in 1969, the controversial poem "Boris Pasternak," which had enraged Arab nationalists with its declaration that "we shall make from their skulls / an ashtray for cigarettes," was simply excised to erase his role in this painful chapter of cultural violence from the historical record.[34] Even Buland al-Haydari, who remained in exile in Beirut and London and never returned to Iraq, opted to forget his role in those poetry wars and never republished his 1960 collection of communist poems, *Jiʾtum maʿ al-Fajr*.[35] His own collected works of poetry appeared in 1992 and included the other nine of the ten volumes of poetry that he had published in his lifetime, but *Jiʾtum maʿ al-Fajr* was not even mentioned in the Preface, as though it had never existed.[36]

Muhammad Mahdi al-Jawahiri, the public face of the exiled Iraqi poets and intellectuals in Prague, also succumbed to the spirit of the "progressive national front" after 1968. When the Baʿthist minister of interior, Salih Mahdi ʿAmmash, issued his infamous "miniskirt edict" requiring schoolgirls to wear longer skirts, Jawahiri wrote a poem in praise of Iraqi legs and sent it to the Iraqi newspaper *al-Ittihad*.[37] ʿAmmash was amused and published his own poem in response, precipitating a cultural thaw that allowed Jawahiri to return to Baghdad and resume his past role as head of the Iraqi Writers Union.[38] Like other communist poets who had once been enemies of the nationalists, including Muhammad Salih Bahr al-ʿUlum, Lamiʿa ʿAbbas ʿAmara, and ʿAbd al-Razzaq, ʿAbd al-Wahid, Jawahiri enjoyed a generous state stipend during the 1970s.[39] The reconciliation did not last, and Jawahiri left Iraq again in 1979, retiring to Damascus, where he once again became an opponent of Saddam Hussein and the Iraqi Baʿth Party. When he died on July 26, 1997, Salih J. Altoma observed that "perhaps no other modern Arab poet has captured in his poetry the tribulations of the entire Arab World in this century as faithfully and vividly as al-Jawahiri."[40] The major change in the world of Iraqi poetry during the final decades of that century was that these tribulations could be captured and narrated only from the safety of exile.

The recession of rebel poetry from the public sphere was also reflected in the life of Saʿdi Yusuf, one of the leading modernist poets in Iraq. Yusuf owed little to Jawahiri aesthetically, but he also linked to the Iraqi Communist Party and became Jawahiri's chief lieutenant in the Iraqi Writers Union.[41] He was arrested along with other communist poets in February 1963 and later that year escaped into a decade of exile in Beirut and Algiers. In 1972, four years after the reconciliation of Jawahiri, Bahr al-ʿUlum, and Bayati with the new Baʿthist regime, Yusuf returned to Baghdad to take a position in the Ministry of Culture and edit the cultural journal *al-Turath al-Shaʿbi*.[42] His own period of reconciliation with the Baʿthist regime ended at the same time as that of Jawahiri, and Yusuf heeded the advice of his friend ʿAbd al-Rahman Munif and returned to a life in exile in 1979.[43] Like so many of the Iraqi exiles, he remained deeply attuned to the problems that his country faced and hopeful that poetry could somehow provide a way forward. When the United State occupied Iraq in 2003, Yusuf reflected nostalgically about the relationship between poetry and politics in Iraq and recalled the role of Muhammad Saʿid al-Habubi, Maʿruf al-Rusafi, and Muhammad Mahdi al-Jawahiri in the long anticolonial struggle. "Now Iraqis expect me to speak," Yusuf observed, "People keep sending me emails. But, in fact, over the last weeks I have stopped writing articles and am returning to my poetry. And people want to read my poems: they are not separate from what is going on in Iraq now, but they are not politically activated. My poems are artistically activated, that is, I write from an artistic standpoint. Other people can write about the details of war. My essential responsibility is writing poetry."[44] Neither the political conditions inside Iraq nor the cultural transformations wrought by the free verse revolution, however, would allow Sa'di Yusuf or any other poet to play a role akin to that Habubi, Rusafi, and Jawahiri had played in the past.

## The Dangers of Poetry

What made poetry dangerous in modern Iraqi history was first and foremost its popular resonance. While poetry certainly contributed to the political, cultural, and intellectual prestige of poets in the elite terrain of high culture, it was the capacity of poets to mobilize mass audiences and shape mass culture that forced political authorities to recognize the threat posed by poets. The danger of poetry was historically contingent, shaped by the structural convergence of singular political, social, and cultural conditions in the early twentieth century. The phenomenon of rebel poetry was set in motion by the dawn of the colonial era, as the decline of state patronage networks in the colonial era and the alienation of popular poets from political elites in the postcolonial period made rebellion and dissidence more attractive to poets than it had previously been. Poetic dissidence was made relevant by the emergence of mass politics and the historical processes of urbanization, coupled with the liberal constraints against excessive state repression, which made protest poetry viable and amplified the public voice of rebel poets. Finally, the lingering appeal of the neoclassical qasida and the modern practice of platform poetry made rebel poetry an effective and authentic form of cultural resistance to colonialism and authoritarianism. These conditions were mutually dependent on one another, and the absence of one or another in different times and places explains why the rebel poetry scenes discussed in this book were rarely replicated elsewhere.

The relentless pursuit of dissidence and danger by rebel poets in modern Iraq may have represented a psychological disposition toward rebellion, but this contrarian impulse was always subordinate to broader concerns of politics and ideology. In the introduction to his first collection of political poetry in 1935, Muhammad Mahdi al-Jawahiri described his own commitment to danger as "the spirit of the rebel poet against many of the customs of the society that surrounds him, who despairs of reforming them through patch and repair and instead calls for them to be created anew."[45] Several months later, his comrade and friend Muhammad Salih Bahr al-ʿUlum was somewhat blunter when he boasted, "I was a revolution since the day I was born / my revolution is a fire consuming the cities of tyrants / In the view of me and my fellow revolutionaries / honor is found in rejecting peace with traitors."[46] For both poets, the revolutionary spirit of rebel poetry was a necessary component of their faith in poetry to transform society and liberate both the individual and the nation from the external forces that restricted their freedom. While their own experiences led them to dedicate their poetry to the promotion of communist ideology and politics, the commitment of Jawahiri and Bahr al-ʿUlum to rebellion and revolution as poetic vocation was bequeathed by the neoclassical pioneers of the late Ottoman era and broadly accepted even by rivals in the nationalist camp. For the better part of nearly six decades in modern Iraqi history, poets enthusiastically grasped the mantle of national spokesmen and "inscribed in poetry the struggles of their people."[47]

The dangers of poetry in modern Iraqi history were always constructed both within and against the domain of elite politics and the complex structures of patronage and panegyric. When Jawahiri reflected on the relationship between poetry and social prestige in late Ottoman Najaf, he contended that "from the very beginning, poetry was for me a grave and dangerous game."[48] For Jawahiri and the other young Najafi poets of the early twentieth century, this "grave and dangerous game" existed entirely apart from the world of politics and patronage that consumed the pioneers of neoclassical poetry in Egypt. Indeed, the very refusal of the great nineteenth-century Najafi poets Ibrahim al-Tabatabaʾi and Muhammad Saʿid al-Habbubi to lend their reputations and poems to inferior politicians and rulers in the form of servile panegyrics made them authentic practitioners of "true poetry" to their young disciples.[49] This aversion to the corrupting influence of political patronage did not survive into the colonial era, but the complicated relations of patronage and praise between the Najafi poets and the Hashemite monarchy nevertheless reflected this spirit of poetic independence and authenticity. The "dangerously double-edge praise" that greeted Faysal during his tour of Iraq in the summer of 1921 showed how poets sought to balance integrity and prestige through their selective engagement with nationalist politics, but it also revealed how both colonial authorities and local elites came to fear the dangerous unpredictability of public poetry. The oscillation of iconic poets like Jamil Sidqi al-Zahawi, Maʿruf al-Rusafi, Rashid al-Hashimi and Muhammad al-Hashimi, Muhammad Rida al-Shabibi and Muhammad Baqir al-Shabibi, and Muhammad Mahdi al-Jawahiri between composing panegyrics in service of the state and reciting dissident poems critical of the state symbolized the ambiguity of patronage politics, which were shaped simultaneously by the state's desire for poetry that might endorse its legitimacy and its fear of poetry that might challenge it. The imbrication of poetry in the partisan politics of anticolonial nationalism critically shaped the cultural politics of revolution in the pivotal events of 1936 and 1941, transforming poets into the spokesmen of new and contentious ideologies that pitted nationalists against leftists. While the dedication of poetry to the service of state politics in these crises was echoed again in the cultural wars of the Qasim era, the absolute discrediting of the national political elite following the Anglo-Iraqi War of May 1941 transformed the precise dangers of poetry by divorcing the practice from traditional patronage networks.

While rebel poetry devoted to the contestation of both colonial occupation and cultural stagnation had established the danger of modern poetry over the preceding decades, it was the new phenomenon of the poetry of public spaces that emerged in the wake of World War II that most clearly manifested the magnitude of this danger. Public poetry was dangerous precisely because it allowed poets to bypass political elites entirely and take their message directly to the public. The "dangerously double-edged praise" of the public poetry of past decades was intended to embarrass and manipulate political elites with the threat of public criticism and exposure. Now, however, when poets like Jawahiri and Bahr al-ʿUlum embarrassed political elites in public as they did to Nuri al-Saʿid at the state memorial service for Jaʿfar Abu al-Timman in January 1946, the performative nature of their critique was directed entirely toward the audience. Even more striking was the role of these poets in the massive public demonstrations of 1948 and 1952, which became possible only due to the historical dynamics of urbanization and the emergence of new forms of mass politics stewarded by the Iraqi Communist Party. The dynamic forms of protest poetry that emerged from these demonstrations reflected both the coincidental convergence of political alienation and social mobilization and the equally fortuitous emergence of national front politics, which allowed the voices and messages of poets to resonate broadly among the relatively unified crowds. It did not take long for the state to perceive the new dangers of this poetry of public spaces and monitor and regulate these rebel poets, but the liberal ideology espoused by the political elite restrained their hand. Public acts of dissidence remained the ever present goal of committed rebel poets throughout the 1950s. The ability to lay claim to public space and articulate dissident messages to captive audiences of poetry enthusiasts was a remarkable development in the history of mass culture in the Middle East, a moment when culture could truly mobilize action rather than simply narrate events and when poetry was always pregnant with danger.

The death of rebel poetry in modern Iraq was spelled not only by the triumph of authoritarianism under the Baʿthist regimes of 1963 and 1968 but also by the aesthetic transformation of poetry in this period. Most evaluations of modern Arabic poetry tend to prioritize intellectual and aesthetic experimentation and innovation as symbolic markers of cultural dynamism. While this tendency is only natural given modern notions of art and aesthetics, it also tends to obscure the political importance of poetry by reading poems as texts instead of events. One of the central contentions of this book has been that Iraqi poetry in this period should not be understood simply as art, and poets should not be seen simply as intellectuals. Aesthetic form and intellectual content were certainly important to poets, but they also viewed poetry as a critical form of public communication with the public and grappled seriously with how to fulfill the social responsibility demanded of them. The modernist proponents of free verse poetry, who were introduced in the late 1940s and gradually monopolized the terrain of poetry over subsequent decades, also talked about social responsibility and embraced the Sartrean ethos of commitment. While they saw aesthetic innovation as a cultural extension of the politics of commitment, the attempt to theorize and modernize poetry also brought the practice of poetry more in line with other modern forms of intellectual and literary culture and in the process sacrificed some of what had made poetry truly unique in modern Iraq. Poets became ordinary intellectuals, and although Iraqi poetry was still read aloud far more frequently than the poetry of most Western cultural traditions, it was now more restricted to salons and cafés and less suitable for platform sermons and protest chants. Beautiful and moving though these verses may have been, they were more avant-garde than popular and tended to reify an artificial distinction between "high culture" and "mass culture" that had not previously existed in Iraqi poetry. The bitter resentment of the popularity of Muhammad Salih Bahr al-'Ulum expressed by Badr Shakir al-Sayyab did not just reflect nationalist animosity toward communist culture; it also demonstrated an ironic modernist suspicion of neoclassical popularity that belies most assumptions about modernism and mass culture. When the short story writer Dhu al-Nun Ayyub described Bahr al-'Ulum in 1959 as "the poet of all those who could not easily understand the sublime poetry of Jawahiri," he expressed the other side of this debate and reflected the prevailing attitude of the communists toward popular culture.[50] Perhaps it was all a moot point, given the fate of Bahr al- Ulum after February 1963, but the evolution of poetry seemed to ensure that poetry could remain dangerous as only an aesthetic expression of dissident ideas, divorced from the social context that had once been so integral to the very notion of rebel poetry.

## The Legacy of Rebel Poetry

On February 22, 2019, the popular singer Taqi al-Husaynawi delivered a blistering performance at a cultural festival in Najaf. Elegantly dressed in a handsome slim-fit black pin-striped suit with the spikey hairstyle that has become so popular among young Iraqi men, Husaynawi looked every bit the part of the pop star and modern dandy. The song that he sang, however, was a musical interpretation of Muhammad Salih Bahr al-'Ulum's famous poem, "Where Is My Right?" (*"Ayn Haqqi?"*). Composed some time after his release from prison in 1956, the poem was never published, but it was "learnt by heart" and "committed to memory by many people" at the time.[51] The lyrics now sung by Husaynawi brought to life Bahr al-'Ulum's blistering attack on the oppressive dictatorial state, exploitative capitalist economy, and corrupt religious establishment:

You wolves have trampled the people for thousands of years,

so leave me to my religion, for what business is it of yours?
Have you received a writ from God to intervene in my affairs,
when God's Book cries from the mosque, "Where is my right?!"
These hypocrites shamelessly deceive God in full public view,
for what is duping God for those who fill the world with deception?
If they could seize all power, they would leave none for God,
and God would be next to me crying out, "Where is my right?"
Taxes are extracted by force from the very poorest of people,
who have performed a thousand tasks and never won their right
The losses fall on them, while their sheep are stolen by politicians
but the "criminal" is the poor man who cries, "Where is my right?!"
A young girl found nothing but swirling dust to cover herself,
so she serviced the whole neighborhood but did not own an inch
She longed for death so that she could at long last own a tomb,
but then the gravedigger above her cried, "Where is my right?!"
What is this and the like except an open field of prostitution
where this land is sold in the most despicable trading markets?
If our religion says to hurl eighty stones at the prostitute,
but the judge who decrees is the culprit, "Where is my right?!"
Liberate this nation, if you are truly preachers of sincerity,
from the chains of ignorance, for freedom will repel the greedy!
Throw your weight toward securing the rights of workers,
bless the huts ever crying to the palaces, "Where is my right?!"[52]

The performance was electrifying, and the video of the performance quickly garnered nearly a million views across various social media platforms and inspired thousands of comments and engaging discussions among Iraqi citizens and expatriates.[53]

There were some echoes of the dissident poetry of public spaces of the past in the discussion of the striking incongruence between the anticlerical lyrics of the song and the sacred space of Najaf. More striking from a historical standpoint, however, was the timelessness of Bahr al-'Ulum's verses, which nearly everyone agreed applied equally to the Iraq of the 1950s as to the Iraq of 2019. Poetry remains a vital force in modern Iraqi society, and the spirit of the rebel poetry lives on even as the voices, aesthetics, and spaces of poetry performance continue to evolve. In Turki al-Hamad's recent novel, *al-Karadib*, the young communist protagonist, Hisham, looks to Bahr al-ʿUlum as the paragon of revolutionary commitment and contrasts his dissident poetry with the frivolous love poems of Nizar Qabbani.[54] This lionization of Bahr al-ʿUlum is borne out by the historical record of his poetry and his life, as this book has made clear. Even after the poet's recantation and reconciliation with the Baʿthist regime, possession of handwritten copies of "Where Is My Right?" was considered evidence of dissidence and earned many leftists lengthy prison terms.[55] Rebel poetry always drew strength from its illicit nature, and in the current climate of public protest and political violence, poetry may very well again fulfill this critical cultural function.

As Baghdad fell to American troops in May 2003, Saʿdi Yusuf's reflections on the legacy of poetry in modern Iraq indicated the enduring importance of imperialism, violence, and tragedy for the rebel poetry tradition. His thoughts were echoed by one of his younger disciples, the poet and novelist Sinan Antoon, in a poignant essay published in the *Nation*. Antoon was born in Baghdad in 1967 and left the city in 1991, but he now recalled the influence of the communist poet Muzaffar al-Nawwab on the dissident youth of the city: "His fiery and banned poems were smuggled into Iraq on cassettes by exiles and circulated secretly among friends." He also reflected on the death of Muhammad Mahdi al-Jawahiri in Damascus six years earlier, noting that the poet's longstanding desire to be buried in Baghdad, the city that he loved more than any other, went unfulfilled and that the orchards along the Tigris that he wistfully recalled from his exile in Prague in the 1960s were now demolished by American bombs. Recalling the prophetic lines of Jawahiri's famous poem, "My Brother Jaʿfar," Antoon concluded, "It is mourning time for me, and Baghdad is now enveloped in a long, cruel and starless night. She will wake up once more and try to forget, as she has done in the past. Meanwhile, I will tend to her scars, ward off future nightmares and shower her with kisses and love from afar."[56]

# NOTES

## Introduction

1. Muhammad Mahdi al-Jawahiri, *Diwan al-Jawahiri*, vol. 1 (Najaf: Matbaʿat al-Ghari, 1935), 3.

2. Muhammad Mahdi al-Jawahiri, *Dhikrayati*, vol. 2 (Damascus: Dar al-Rafidayn, 1991), 57–66.

3. Jawahiri, *Dhikrayati*, 2:22–27.

4. Jawahiri, *Dhikrayati*, 2:58–59, and Johan Franzén, *Red Star over Iraq: Iraqi Communism before Saddam* (New York: Columbia University Press, 2011), 55–56.

5. Muhammad Mahdi al-Jawahiri, *Diwan al-Jawahiri*, vol. 3 (Beirut: Bisan, 2000), 247–252.

6. Muhsin al-Musawi, "Muhammad Mahdi al-Jawahiri (1901–1997)," in *Essays in Arabic Literary Biography*, vol. 3, ed. Roger Allen (Wiesbaden: Harrassowitz Verlag, 2010), 172, and Rula Jurdi Abisaab and Malik Abisaab, *The Shiʿites of Lebanon: Modernism, Communism, and Hizbullah's Islamists* (Syracuse, NY: Syracuse University Press, 2014), 70–73.

7. Jawahiri, *Dhikrayati*, 2:60–66.

8. Jabra Ibrahim Jabra, "al-Shaʿir wa al-Hakim wa al-Madina," in *Muhammad Mahdi al-Jawahiri: Dirasat Naqdiyya*, ed. Hadi al-ʿAlawi (Baghdad: Matbaʿat al-Nuʿman, 1969), 45–46.

9. Sami Zubaida, "Al-Jawahiri: Between Patronage and Revolution," *Revue des mondes musulmans et de la Méditerranée* 117–118 (2007), 81–97.

10. Muhammad Salih Bahr al-ʿUlum, *Diwan Bahr al-ʿUlum*, vol. 1 (Baghdad: Matbaʿat Dar al-Tadamun, 1968), 109.

11. On national front politics in Iraq and the Arab world, see Hanna Batatu, *The*

*Old Social Classes and Revolutionary Movements of Iraq: A Study of Iraq's Old Landed and Commercial Classes and of Its Communists, Ba'thists, and Free Officers* (Princeton: Princeton University Press, 1978), 574–596, and Franzén, *Red Star over Iraq*, 42–48.

12. Cemil Aydin, *The Politics of Anti-Westernism in Asia: Visions of World Order in Pan-Islamic and Pan-Asian Thought* (New York: Columbia University Press, 2007), and Pankaj Mishra, *From the Ruins of Empire: The Intellectuals Who Remade Asia* (New York: Farrar, Straus and Giroux, 2012).

13. Ann McClintock, "The Angel of Progress: Pitfalls of the Term 'Post-Colonialism,'" *Social Text* 31/32 (1992), 84–98.

14. Reinhart Koselleck, *Futures Past: On the Semantics of Historical Time*, trans. Keith Tribe (New York: Columbia University Press, 2004); David Scott, *Conscripts of Modernity: The Tragedy of Colonial Enlightenment* (Durham, NC: Duke University Press, 2004); and Gary Wilder, *Freedom Time: Negritude: Decolonization, and the Future of the World* (Durham, NC: Duke University Press, 2015).

15. Eric Davis, *Memories of State: Politics, History, and Collective Identity in Modern Iraq* (Berkeley: University of California Press, 2005); Orit Bashkin, *The Other Iraq: Pluralism and Culture in Hashemite Iraq* (Stanford: Stanford University Press, 2009); and Maha Nassar, *Brothers Apart: Palestinian Citizens of Israel and the Arab World* (Stanford: Stanford University Press, 2017).

16. Antonio Gramsci, *Selections from the Prison Notebooks*, ed. and trans. Quintin Hoare and Geoffrey Nowell Smith (New York: International Publishers, 1971), 3–24.

17. Hala Fattah, *The Politics of Regional Trade in Iraq, Arabia, and the Gulf, 1745–1900* (Albany: State University of New York Press, 1997), 13–62, and Hilla Peled-Shapira, *The Prose Works of Gha'ib Tu'ma Farman: The City and the Beast* (Lanham, MD: Lexington Books, 2018), 6–8.

18. Yasmeen Hanoosh, "Contempt: State Literati vs. Street Literati in Modern Iraq," *Journal of Arabic Literature* 43:2/3 (2012), 372–408.

19. Yitzhak Nakash, *The Shi'is of Iraq* (Princeton: Princeton University Press, 1994), and Meir Litvak, *Shi'i Scholars of Nineteenth-Century Iraq: The 'Ulama' of Najaf and Karbala'* (Cambridge: Cambridge University Press, 1998).

20. Elie Kedourie, "Reflexions sur l'histoire du Royaume d'Irak (1921–1958)," *Orient* 11:3 (1959), 55–79; Matthew Elliot, *"Independent Iraq": The Monarchy and British Influence, 1941–58* (London: Tauris, 1996); Samira Haj, *The Making of Iraq, 1900–1963: Capital, Power, and Ideology* (Albany: State University of New York Press, 1997); Toby Dodge, *Inventing Iraq: The Failure of Nation Building and a History Denied* (New York: Columbia University Press, 2003); Peter Sluglett, *Britain in Iraq: Contriving King and Country, 1914–1932* (New York: Columbia University Press, 2007); and Susan Pedersen, "Getting Out of Iraq—in 1932: The League of Nations and the Road to Normative Statehood," *American Historical Review* 115:4 (2010), 975–1000.

21. Batatu, *The Old Social Classes*, 180–184.

22. Edward Said, *The World, the Text, and the Critic* (Cambridge, MA: Harvard University Press, 1983), 24–25; Hamid Dabashi, *Islamic Liberation Theology: Resisting the Empire* (London: Routledge, 2008), 157–159; and Jason Bahbak Mohaghegh, *Insurgent, Poet, Mystic, Sectarian: The Four Masks of Eastern Postmodernism* (Albany: State University of New York Press, 2015), 39–43.

23. Amal Vinogradov, "The 1920 Revolt in Iraq Reconsidered: The Role of Tribes in National Politics," *International Journal of Middle East Studies* 3:2 (1972), 123–139; Pierre-Jean Luizard, *La formation de l'Irak contemporain: Le rôle politique des ulémas chiites à la fin de la domination ottomane et au moment de la creation de l'État irakien* (Paris: CRNIS Editions, 1991); and Nakash, *The Shi'is of Iraq*, 49–72.

24. Ibrahim al-Wa'ili, *Thawrat al-'Ishrin fi al-Shi'r al-'Iraqi* (Baghdad: Matba'at al-Iman, 1968); 'Abd al-Husayn Mubarak; *Thawrat Alf wa Tisa' Mi'a wa 'Isrhin fi al-Shi'r al-'Iraqi* (Baghdad: Dar al-Basri, 1970); and Abbas Kadhim, *Reclaiming Iraq: The 1920 Revolution and the Founding of the Modern State* (Austin: University of Texas Press, 2012).

25. Yusuf 'Izz al-Din, *al-Shi'r al-'Iraqi al-Hadith wa Athar al-Tiyarat al-Siyasiyya wa al-Ijtima'iyya fihi* (Cairo: al-Dar al-Qawmiyya lil-Taba'a wa al-Nashr, 1965), and Yusuf 'Izz al-Din, *al-Ishtirakiyya wa al-Qawmiyya wa Atharuhuma fi al-Adab al-Hadith* (Cairo: Jami'at al-Duwal al-'Arabiyya, 1968).

26. Reeva S. Simon, *Iraq between the Two World Wars: The Creation and Implementation of a Nationalist Ideology* (New York: Columbia University Press, 1986), and Peter Wien, *Iraqi Arab Nationalism: Authoritarian, Totalitarian, and Pro-Fascist Inclinations, 1932–1941* (London: Routledge, 2006).

27. Bashkin, *The Other Iraq*, 87–121.

28. Sami Zubaida, "The Fragments Imagine the Nation: The Case of Iraq," *International Journal of Middle East Studies* 34:2 (2002), 205–215; Davis, *Memories of State*; Wien, *Iraqi Arab Nationalism*; Bashkin, *The Other Iraq*; and Orit Bashkin, "Hybrid Nationalisms: *Watani* and *Qawmi* Visions in Iraq under 'Abd al-Karim Qasim, 1958–61," *International Journal of Middle East Studies* 43:2 (2011), 293–312.

29. Ra'uf al-Wa'iz, *al-Ittijahat al-Wataniyya fi al-Shi'r al-'Iraqi al-Hadith, 1914–1941* (Baghdad: Wizarat al-I'lam al-Jumhuriyya al-'Iraqiyya, 1974), and Majid Ahmad al-Samarra'i, *al-Tayyar al-Qawmi fi al-Shi'r al-'Iraqi al-Hadith mundhu al-Harb al-'Alamiyya al-Thaniyya 1931 hatta Naksat Haziran 1967* (Baghdad: al-Jumhuriyya al-'Iraqiyya, 1981).

30. Abdul-Salaam Yousif, "The Struggle for Cultural Hegemony in Iraq," in *The Iraqi Revolution of 1958: The Old Social Classes Revisited*, ed. Robert A. Fernea and William Roger Louis (London: I. B. Tauris, 1991, 173–196.

31. Ami Ayalon, *The Arabic Print Revolution: Cultural Production and Mass Readership* (Cambridge: Cambridge University Press, 2016), 177–193.

32. Gertrude Bell to Dame Florence Bell and Sir Hugh Bell, June 5, 1921, Gertrude Bell Archive, http://gertrudebell.ncl.ac.uk.

33. al-Musawi, "Muhammad Mahdi al-Jawahiri (1901–1907)," 166–175.

34. Natalie Zemon Davis, *Society and Culture in Early Modern France: Eight Essays* (Stanford: Stanford University Press, 1975); Peter Burke, *Popular Culture in Early Modern Europe* (London: T. Smith, 1978); Said S. Samata, *Oral Poetry and Somali Nationalism: The Case of Sayyid Mahammad 'Abdille Hasan* (Cambridge: Cambridge University Press, 1982); and Pierre Bourdieu, "Structures, Habitus, Power: Basis for a Theory of Symbolic Power," in *Culture/Power/History: A Reader in Contemporary Social Theory*, ed. Nicholas B. Dirks, Geoff Eley, and Sherry B. Ortner (Princeton: Princeton University Press, 1994), 180–182.

35. Bertolt Brecht, "On Poetry," in *Brecht on Art and Politics*, ed. Tom Kuhn and Steve Giles (London: Methuen, 2003), 47–50; Theodor Adorno, "On Lyric Poetry and Society," in *Poetry in Theory: An Anthology, 1900–2000*, ed. Jon Cook (Malden, MA: Blackwell, 2004), 342–349; and Clare Cavanagh, *Lyric Poetry and Modern Politics: Russia, Poland, and the West* (New Haven: Yale University Press, 2009).

36. Edward P. Thompson, "Patrician Society, Plebian Culture," *Journal of Social History* 7 (1974), 384–205; Raymond Williams, *Marxism and Literature* (Oxford: Oxford University Press, 1977), 199–205; Geoff Eley, *A Crooked Line: From Cultural History to the History of Society* (Ann Arbor: University of Michigan Press, 2005), 54–59; Kristin Ross, *The Emergence of Social Space: Rimbaud and the Paris Commune* (London: Verso, 2008), 3–31; and Roland Bleiker, *Aesthetics and World Politics* (New York: Palgrave Macmillan, 2009).

37. Ziad Fahmy, *Ordinary Egyptians: Creating the Modern Nation through Popular Culture* (Stanford: Stanford University Press, 2011), 3–5.

38. See also Walter Armbrust, *Mass Culture and Modernism in Egypt* (Cambridge: Cambridge University Press, 1996), and Lucie Ryzova, *The Age of the Efendiyya: Passages to Modernity in National-Colonial Egypt* (Oxford: Oxford University Press, 2014).

39. Salma Khadra Jayyusi, *Trends and Movement in Modern Arabic Poetry*, vol. 1 (Leiden: E. J. Brill, 1977), 26–33, and Leslie Tramontini, "Poetry in the Service of Nation Building? Political Commitment and Self-Assertion," in *Writing the Modern History of Iraq: Historiographical and Political Challenges*, ed. Jordi Tejel, Peter Sluglett, Riccardo Bocco, and Hamit Bozarslan (Hackensack, NJ: World Scientific, 2013), 459–474.

40. Nakash, *The Shi'is of Iraq*, 68–70.

41. Bashkin, *The Other Iraq*, 44–48.

42. Davis, *Memories of State*, 200–226.

43. One notable exception is Leslie Tramontini, "Fatherland, If Ever I Betrayed You . . . : Reflections on Nationalist Poetry of Thawrat al-'Ishrin," *al-Abhath* 50–51 (2002–20003), 161–186.

44. Mike Sanders, *The Poetry of Chartism: Aesthetics, Politics, History* (Cambridge: Cambridge University Press, 2009); James Gregory, *The Poetry and the Politics: Radical*

*Reform in Victorian England* (London: I. B. Tauris, 2014); Patrick McGuinness, *Poetry and Radical Politics in fin de siècle France: From Anarchism to Action française* (Oxford: Oxford University Press, 2015); and Colin Wells, *Poetry Wars: Verse and Politics in the American Revolution and Early Republic* (Philadelphia: University of Pennsylvania Press, 2018).

45. Christopher Caudwell, *Illusion and Reality: A Study of the Sources of Poetry* (New York: International Publishers, 1973), 298–329; Paul Peppis, *Literature, Politics, and the English Avant-Garde: Nation and Empire, 1901–1918* (Cambridge: Cambridge University Press, 2000); Mark Antliff, *Avant-Garde Fascism: The Mobilization of Myth, Art, and Culture in France, 1909–1939* (Durham, NC: Duke University Press, 2007); Geert Buelens, *Everything to Nothing: The Poetry of the Great War, Revolution and the Transformation of Europe*, trans. David McKay (London: Verso, 2015); and Jay Winter, *War beyond Words: Languages of Remembrance from the Great War to the Present* (Cambridge: Cambridge University Press, 2017), 92–115.

46. Edward J. Brown, *Mayakovsky: A Poet in the Revolution* (Princeton: Princeton University Press, 1973); Edith Rogovin Frankel, *Novy Mir: A Case Study in the Politics of Literature, 1952–1958* (Cambridge: Cambridge University Press, 1981); Ronald Hingley, *Nightingale Fever: Russian Poets in Revolution* (New York: Knopf, 1981); Kathleen F. Parthé, *Russia's Dangerous Texts: Politics between the Lines* (New Haven: Yale University Press, 2004); and Marci Shore, *Caviar and Ashes: A Warsaw Generation's Life and Death in Marxism, 1918–1968* (New Haven: Yale University Press, 2006).

47. Barbara Harlow, *Resistance Literature* (New York: Methuen, 1987); Saadia Toor, *The State of Islam: Culture and Cold War Politics in Pakistan* (London: Pluto Press, 2011); Nosheen Ali, "Poetry, Power, Protest: Reimagining the Muslim Brotherhood in Pakistan," *Comparative Studies of South Asia, Africa, and the Middle East* 32:1 (2012), 13–23; Alain Badiou, *The Age of the Poets: And Other Writings on Twentieth-Century Poetry and Prose*, trans. Emily Apter (London: Verso, 2014), 93–109; and Sunyoung Park, *The Proletarian Wave: Literature and Leftist Culture in Colonial Korea, 1910–1945* (Cambridge, MA: Harvard University Asia Center, 2015).

48. Antony Beever, *The Battle for Spain: The Spanish Civil War, 1936–1939* (New York: Penguin Books, 2006), 88–101, 157–165; Jean-Michel Palmier, *Weimar in Exile: The Antifascist Emigration in Europe and America*, trans. David Fernbach (London: Verso, 2006), 353–358; Gayle Rogers, *Modernism and the New Spain: Britain, Cosmopolitan Europe, and Literary History* (Oxford: Oxford University Press, 2012), 163–198; Claudio Pavone, *A Civil War: A History of the Italian Resistance*, trans. Peter Levy (London: Verso, 2013), 615–621.

49. Martin Munro, "Exile, Deterritorialization, and Exoticism in René Depestre's 'Hadriana dans tous mes rêves,'" *Journal of Haitian Studies* 9:1 (2003), 23–38; Orhan Kemal, *In Jail with Nazim Hikmet*, trans. Bengisa Rona (London: Saqi, 2010); Saadia Toor, *The State of Islam: Culture and Cold War Politics in Pakistan* (London: Pluto Press,

2011), 89–94; Mutlu Konuk Blasing, *Nazim Hikmet: The Life and Times of Turkey's World Poet* (New York: Persea, 2013), 111–179; Joaquín M. Chávez, *Poets and Prophets of the Resistance: Intellectuals and the Origins of El Salvador's Civil War* (Oxford: Oxford University Press, 2017), 183–188; and Mark Eisner, *Neruda: The Poet's Calling* (New York: Ecco, 2018), 357–420.

50. M. M. Badawi, *A Critical Introduction to Modern Arabic Poetry* (Cambridge: Cambridge University Press, 1975), 14.

51. Andrew Shryock, *Nationalism and the Genealogical Imagination: Oral History and Textual Authority in Tribal Jordan* (Berkeley: University of California Press, 1997), 162–163.

52. Shakwat M. Toorawa, "Poetry," in *The Cambridge Companion to Modern Arab Culture*, ed. Dwight F. Reynolds (Cambridge: Cambridge University Press, 2015), 97.

53. Hussein N. Kadhim, *The Poetics of Anti-Colonialism in the Arabic Qasidah* (Leiden: Brill, 2004), and Atef Alshaer, *Poetry and Politics in the Modern Arab World* (London: Hurst, 2016), 49–93.

54. Yaseen Noorani, *Culture and Hegemony in the Colonial Middle East* (New York: Palgrave Macmillan, 2010).

55. Joel Beinin, "Writing Class: Workers and Modern Egyptian Colloquial Poetry (Zajal)," *Poetics Today* 15:2 (1994), 191–215, and Elliott Colla, "The Poetry of Revolt," in *Dawn of the Arab Uprisings: End of an Old Order?* ed. Bassam Haddad, Rosie Bsheer, and Ziad Abu-Rish (London: Pluto Press, 2012), 77–82.

56. Nassar, *Brothers Apart*, 9–10. See also Raymond Williams, *Culture and Materialism: Selected Essays* (London: Verso, 1980), 47–49; Edward W. Said, *The World, the Text, and the Critic* (Cambridge, MA: Harvard University Press, 1983), 31–53; and Michael Denning, *Culture in the Age of Three Worlds* (London: Verso, 2004), 189–190.

57. Léopold Sédar Senghor, "L'esprit de la civilisation ou les lois de la culture négro-africaine," *Présence Africaine* 8/10 (1956), 51–65; Frederic Jameson, *Marxism and Form: Twentieth-Century Dialectical Theories of Literature* (Princeton: Princeton University Press, 1974), 306–416; John Sturrock, *The Word from Paris: Essays on Modern French Thinkers and Writers* (London: Verso, 1998), 100–110; and Walter Benjamin, "The Work of Art in the Age of Mechanical Reproduction," in *Illuminations: Essays and Reflections*, ed. Hannah Arendt and trans. Harry Zohn (New York: Schocken Books, 2007), 217–251.

58. Yoav Di-Capua, *No Exit: Arab Existentialism, Jean-Paul Sartre and Decolonization* (Chicago: University of Chicago Press, 2018), 77–107.

59. 'Ali al-Hilli, "Saq 'ala Danub: Shi'r Hilal Naji," *al-Adab* 7:10 (1959), 68–69

60. Badr Shakir al-Sayyab, "al-Iltizam wa al-La-Iltizam fi al-Adab al-'Arabi al-Hadith," in *al-Adab al-'Arabi al-Mu'asir: A'mal Mu'tamar Ruma al-Mun'aqid fi Tishrin al-Awwal Sanat 1961*, ed. 'Abd al-Hamid Jidah and Khalil al-Duwayhi (Tripoli: Dar al-Shamal, 1990), 220–234.

61. Zubaida, "Al-Jawahiri," 81–97.

62. See, for example, the rich descriptions of Najafi poetry in ʿAli al-Sharqi, *al-Ahlam* (Baghdad: Shirkat al-Tabaʿ wa al-Nashr al-Ahliyya, 1963), and ʿAli Khaqani, *Shuʿaraʾ al-Gharri aw al-Najafiyyat*, 12 vols. (Qum: Maktabat Ayat Allah al-ʿUzma al-Marʿashi al-Najafi, 1988).

63. Sylvia Naef, "Shiʿi-Shuyuʿi or: How to Become a Communist in a Holy City," in *The Twelver Shia in Modern Times: Religious Culture and Political History*, ed. Rainer Brunner and Werner Ende (Leiden: Brill, 2001), 255–267, and Fouad J. Kadhem, "Communism in Najaf: The Rise and Fall of a Secular Movement between 1918 and 1963," in *Najaf: Portrait of a Holy City*, ed. Sabrina Mervin, Robert Gleave, and Géraldine Chatelard (Paris: UNESCO, 2017), 295–331.

64. On the relevance and irrelevance of sectarianism to the history of Hashemite Iraq, see Zubaida, "The Fragments Imagine the Nation," 205–215, and Bashkin, *The Other Iraq*, 169–177.

65. Mona Dumluji, Arbella Bet-Shlimon, Alda Benjamen, Saleem Al-Bahloly, Haytham Bahoora, Caecilia Pieri, Bridge L. Guarasci, Zainab Saleh, and Peter Sluglett, "Roundtable: Perspectives on Researching Iraq Today," *Arab Studies Journal* 23:1 (2015), 236–265.

66. Nabil al-Tikriti, "'Stuff Happens': A Brief Overview of the 2003 Destruction of Iraqi Manuscript Collections, Archives, and Libraries," *Library Trends* 55:3 (2007), 730–745.

67. Dominick LaCapra, *History and Criticism* (Ithaca, NY: Cornell University Press, 1985), 71–94.

68. Robert Danton, *Poetry and the Police: Communication Networks in Eighteenth-Century Paris* (Cambridge, MA: Belknap Press of Harvard University Press, 2010), 143.

69. Gayatri Chakravorty Spivak, "The Politics of Translation," in *Outside in the Teaching Machine* (New York: Routledge, 1993), 179–200.

70. Tahia Abdel Nasser, "Revolutionary Poetics and Translation," in *Translating Dissent: Voices from and with the Egyptian Revolution*, ed. Mona Baker (New York: Routledge, 2016), 110.

71. Bashkin, *The Other Iraq*; Noorani, *Culture and Hegemony in the Colonial Middle East*; Fahmy, *Ordinary Egyptians*; and Yasir Suleiman, *Arabic in the Fray: Language, Ideology, and Cultural Politics* (Edinburgh: Edinburgh University Press, 2013).

72. In addition to Musawi, *Reading Iraq*, and Alshaer, *Poetry and Politics*, see Terri DeYoung, *Placing the Poet: Badr Shakir al-Sayyab and Postcolonial Iraq* (Albany: State University of New York Press, 1998); Khaled Furani, *Silencing the Sea: Secular Rhythms in Palestinian Poetry* (Stanford: Stanford University Press, 2012); Khaled Mattawa, *Mahmoud Darwish: The Poet's Art and His Nation* (Syracuse, NY: Syracuse University Press, 2014); and Terri DeYoung, *Mahmud Sami al-Barudi: Reconfiguring Society and the Self* (Syracuse, NY: Syracuse University Press, 2015).

73. Raymond Williams, *The Long Revolution* (Orchard Park, NY: Broadview Press, 2001).

74. Ross, *The Emergence of Social Space* 27.

75. Benedict Anderson, *Under Three Flags: Anarchism and the Anti-Colonial Imagination* (London: Verso, 2007); Michael Goebel, *Anti-Imperial Metropolis: Interwar Paris and the Seeds of Third World Nationalism* (Cambridge: Cambridge University Press, 2015); and Raymond B. Craib, *The Cry of the Renegade: Politics and Poetry in Interwar Chile* (New York: Oxford University Press, 2016).

## Chapter 1

1. Ma'ruf al-Rusafi, *al-Risala al-'Iraqiyya fi al-Siyasa wa al-Din wa al-Ijtima': Yalihi Kamil al-Jadirji fi Hiwar ma' al-Rusafi* (Cologne: Manshurat al-Jamal, 2007), 215–243.

2. Yusuf 'Izz al-Din, "Tasdir al-Kitab," in *al-Zahawi: Dirasat wa Nusus*, ed. 'Abd al-Hamid Rushdi (Beirut: Dar Maktabat al-Hayat, 1966), 7–13, and Fatima al-Muhsin, *Tamaththulat al-Nahda fi Thaqafat al-'Iraq al-Hadith* (Beirut: Manshurat al-Jamal, 2010), 175.

3. Rusafi, *al-Risala*, 231. For negative critical evaluations of Zahawi's poetry, see also Amin al-Rihani, *Qalb al-Iraq: Siyaha wa Siyasa wa Adab wa Ta'rikh, Muzayyan bi al-Rusum*, 2$^{nd}$ ed. (Beirut: Dar al-Rihani, 1957), 240, and Salma Khadra Jayyusi, *Trends and Movements in Modern Arabic Poetry*, vol. 1 (Leiden: Brill, 1977), 184–193.

4. Jamil Sidqi al-Zahawi, "Risala al-Zahawi ila' al-Ustadh Ahmad Muhammad al-'Aysh," in Rushdi, *al-Zahawi*, 25–28, and Rusafi, *al-Risala*, 232.

5. On these periodicals, see Ilham Khuri-Makdisi, *The Eastern Mediterranean and the Making of Global Radicalism, 1860–1914* (Berkeley: University of California Press, 2010), 35–59.

6. Rusafi, *al-Risala*, 232.

7. Albert Hourani, *Arabic Thought in the Liberal Age, 1798–1939* (Cambridge: Cambridge University Press, 1983), and Abdulrazzak Patel, *The Arab Nahdah: The Making of the Intellectual and Humanist Movement* (Edinburgh: Edinburgh University Press, 2013).

8. Stephen Sheehi, *Foundations of Modern Arab Identity* (Gainesville: University Press of Florida, 2004), 44–45.

9. Hourani, *Arabic Thought*, 246–247, and Dina Rizk Khoury, "Looking for the Modern: A Biography of an Iraqi Modernist," in *Auto/Biography and the Construction of Identity and Community in the Middle East*, ed. Mary Ann Fay (London: Palgrave, 2001), 114–116.

10. Tarif Khalidi, "Shaykh Ahmad 'Arif az-Zayn and *al-'Irfan*," in *Intellectual Life in the Arab East, 1890–1939*, ed. M. R. Buheiry (Beirut: AUB Press, 1981), 385–397, and Sylvia Naef, "La presse en tant que moteur du renouveau culturel et littéraire: La revue chiite libanaise al-'Irfan," *Asiatische Studien/Études Asiatiques* 50:2 (1996), 385–397.

11. Muhsin J. al-Musawi, *Arabic Poetry: Trajectories of Modernity and Tradition* (London: Routledge, 2006), 8.

12. Ma'ruf al-Rusafi, *Diwan al-Rusafi* (Cairo: Dar al-Kitab al-'Arabi, 1949), 189, 217, and S. Somekh, "The Neo-Classical Arabic Poets," in *Modern Arabic Literature*, ed. M. M. Badawi (Cambridge: Cambridge University Press, 1992), 57.

13. Patrick Kane, *The Politics of Art in Modern Egypt: Aesthetics, Ideology, and Nation-Building* (London: I. B. Tauris, 2012), 21–52, and Amal Ghazal, "'Illiberal' Thought in the Liberal Age: Yusuf al-Nabhani (1849–1932): Dream Stories and Sufi Polemics against the Modern Era," in *Arabic Thought beyond the Liberal Age: Towards an Intellectual History of the Nahda*, ed. Jens Hanssen and Max Weiss (Cambridge: Cambridge University Press, 2016), 214–233.

14. Marshall Berman, *All That Is Solid Melts into Air: The Experience of Modernity* (London: Verso, 1983), 15.

15. Lucie Ryzova, *The Age of the Efendiyya: Passages to Modernity in National-Colonial Egypt* (Oxford: Oxford University Press, 2014), 10–18.

16. Samira Haj, *Reconfiguring Islamic Tradition: Reform, Rationality, and Modernity* (Stanford: Stanford University Press, 2009), 67–108.

17. Orit Bashkin, "The Iraqi Afghanis and 'Abduhs: Debate over Reform among Shi'ite and Sunni 'Ulama' in Interwar Iraq," in *Guardians of Faith in Modern Times: 'Ulama' in the Middle East*, ed. Meir Hatina (Leiden: Brill, 2009), 145.

18. Sasson Somekh, *Genre and Language in Modern Arabic Literature* (Weisbaden: Otto Harrassowitz, 1991), 51–52.

19. Abbas Kadhim, *Reclaiming Iraq: The 1920 Revolution and the Founding of the Modern State* (Austin: University of Texas Press, 2012), 50–52.

20. Leila Hudson, *Transforming Damascus: Space and Modernity in an Islamic City* (London: Tauris Academic Studies, 2008), 117–138, and Michelle U. Campos, *Ottoman Brothers: Muslims, Christians, and Jews in Early Twentieth-Century Palestine* (Stanford: Stanford University Press, 2011), 59–92.

21. 'Ali al-Sharqi, "Sha'ir fi Sijin," *al-'Irfan* 4:8 (1912), 308–309.

22. Berman, *All That Is Solid Melts into Air*, 15.

23. Renate Jacobi, "The Origins of the Qasida Form," in *Qasida Poetry in Islamic Asia and Africa*, vol. 1: *Classical Traditions and Modern Meanings*, ed. Stefan Sperl and Christopher Shackle (Leiden: E. J. Brill, 1996), 21–34.

24. Reynold A. Nicholson, *A Literary History of the Arabs* (New York: Scribner's, 1907), 77–78.

25. John A. Haywood, *Modern Arabic Literature, 1800–1970: An Introduction, with Extracts in Translation* (London: Lund Humphries, 1971), 5–6.

26. Roger Allen, *The Arabic Literary Heritage: The Development of Its Genres and Criticism* (Cambridge: Cambridge University Press, 1998), 123–138.

27. Hourani, *Arabic Thought*, 34–42; M. M. Badawi, *A Critical Introduction to Modern Arabic*

*Poetry* (Cambridge: Cambridge University Press, 1975), 6–7; and Ibrahim Abu-Lughod, *The Arab Rediscovery of Europe: A Study in Cultural Encounters* (London: Saqi Books, 2011), 18–26.

28. Jayyusi, *Trends and Movements*, 1:25.

29. Somekh, "The Neo-Classical Arabic Poets," 36–37, and Muhammad Lutfi al-Yousfi, "Poetic Creativity in the Sixteenth to Eighteenth Centuries," in *The Cambridge History of Arabic Literature*, vol. 6: *Arabic Literature in the Post-Classical Period*, ed. Roger Allen and D. S. Richards (Cambridge: Cambridge University Press, 2006), 63–67.

30. George Antonius, *The Arab Awakening: The Story of the Arab National Movement* (New York: Paragon Books, 1979, 54–55.

31. Ibrahim Abu-Lughod, *Arab Rediscovery of Europe: A Study in Cultural Encounters* (Princeton: Princeton University Press, 1963), and Hisham Shirabi, *Arab Intellectuals and the West: The Formative Years, 1875–1914* (Baltimore: Johns Hopkins University Press, 1970), and Hourani, *Arabic Thought in the Liberal Age*.

32. Patel, *The Arab Nahdah*, 1–11, and Khaled el-Rouayeb, "Opening the Gate of Verification: The Forgotten Arab-Islamic Florescence of the 17$^{th}$ Century," *International Journal of Middle East Studies* 38:2 (2006), 263–281.

33. Somekh, "The Neo-Classical Arabic Poets," 36–37, and Mir Basri, *A'lam al-Adab fi al-'Iraq al-Hadith*, vol. 1 (London: Dar al-Hikma, 1994), 28–31.

34. Patel, *The Arab Nahdah*, 53–55.

35. S. Moreh, *Modern Arabic Poetry, 1800–1790: The Development of its Forms and Themes under the Influence of Western Literature* (Leiden: E. J. Brill, 1976), 49–50, and *Studies in Modern Arabic Prose and Poetry* (Leiden: E. J. Brill, 1988), 32–33.

36. Hourani, *Arabic Thought*, 104; Musawi, *Arabic Poetry*, 6–9; and Sheehi, *Foundations of Modern Arab Identity*, 115–122.

37. Mounah A. Khouri, *Poetry and the Making of Modern Egypt (1882–1922)* (Leiden: E. J. Brill, 1971), and Terri DeYoung, *Mahmud Sami al-Barudi: Reconfiguring Society and the Self* (Syracuse, NY: Syracuse University Press, 2015).

38. Elizabeth Kendall, *Literature, Journalism, and the Avant-Garde: Intersection in Egypt* (London: Routledge, 2006), 21–22.

39. Hafiz Ibrahim, "Shakwa wa Hanin," *al-Muqtataf* 21:10 (1897), 760; Ahmad Shawqi, "Allah wa al-'Ilm," *al-Muqtataf* 27:8 (1902); 767–768; Hafiz Ibrahim, "Lisan Hal al-Lugha al-'Arabiyya," *al-Hilal* 11:17–18 (1903), 528–529; and Ahmad Shawqi, "al-'Usur wa al-'Usfur," *al-Hilal* 18:6 (1910), 338–340.

40. Khuri-Makdisi, *The Eastern Mediterranean*, 35–59.

41. Jayyusi, *Trends and Movements*, 1:26–33.

42. Jayyusi, *Trends and Movements*, 1:182–183, and Ziad Fahmy, *Ordinary Egyptians: Creating the Modern Nation through Popular Culture* (Stanford: Stanford University Press, 2011).

43. 'Ali al-Sharqi, *al-Ahlam* (Baghdad: Shirkat al-Taba' wa al-Nashr al-Ahliyya, 1963).

44. Haydar al-Hilli, *Diwan Haydar al-Hilli* (Najaf: Matba'at al-Haydariyya, 1950).

45. Hashim al-Ka'bi, *Diwan al-Ka'bi* (Najaf: Matba'at al-Haydariyya, 1964), 48–52, and Jayyusi, *Trends and Movements*, 1:28.

46. Bashkin, "The Iraqi Afghanis and 'Abduhs," 141. See also Yitzhak Nakash, "The Conversion of Iraq's Tribes to Shi'ism," *International Journal of Middle East Studies* 26:3 (1994), 443–463.

47. Salih al-Tamimi, *Diwan al-Tamimi* (Najaf: Majallat al-Bayan, 1947), 101. There are more examples in Ibrahim al-Wa'ili, *al-Shi'r al-Siyasi al-'Iraqi fi al-Qarn al-Tasi' 'Ashar* (Baghdad: Matba'at al-'Ani, 1961), 152–178.

48. 'Abd al-Ghaffar al-Akhras, *Diwan al-Akhras* (Beirut: Maktabat al-Nahda al-'Arabiyya, 1986), 56–60.

49. Jayyusi, *Trends and Movements*, 1:29.

50. Tarek El-Ariss, *Trials of Arab Modernity: Literary Affects and the New Politics* (New York: Fordham University Press, 44–45.

51. 'Abd al-Husayn Mubarak, *Thawrat 1920 fi al-Shi'r al-'Iraqi* (Baghdad: Matba'at Dar al-Basri, 1970), 24.

52. Ibrahim al-Tabataba'i, *Diwan al-Tabataba'i: Wa Huwa Diwan al-Sayyid Ibrahim al-Tabataba'i Sha'ir al-Iraq al-Shahir al-Mutawaffin Sinat 1319 Hijri* (Sidon: Matba'at al-'Irfan, 1914), 71.

53. Wa'ili, *al-Shi'r al-Siyasi*, 104–108.

54. Muhammad Mahdi al-Jawahiri, *Dhikrayati*, vol. 1 (Damascus: Dar al-Rafidin, 1988), 65.

55. Ja'far al-Khalili, *Hakadha 'Araftuhum: Khawatir 'an Unasin Afdhadhin 'Ashu Ba'd al-Ahyan li-Ghayrihim Akthar Mimma 'Ashu li-Anfusihim* (Baghdad: Matba'at al-Zahra', 1963), 59–62.

56. 'Ali al-Khaqani, *Shu'ara' al-Gharri, aw al-Najafiyyat*, vol. 10 (Qum: Maktabat Ayat Allah al-'Uzma al-Mar'ashi al-Najafi, 1988), 143.

57. Basri, *A'lam al-Adab*, 51–60.

58. Basri, *A'lam al-Adab*, 58.

59. 'Abd al-Muhsin al-Kazimi, *al-A'mal al-Shi'riyya al-Kamila li Sha'ir al-'Arab 'Abd al-Muhsin al-Kazimi* (London: Dar al-Hikma, 2002), 32–33.

60. Muhsin, *Tamaththulat al-Nahda*, 311.

61. Basri, *A'lam al-Adab*, 28–31.

62. 'Abd al-Karim al-Dujayli, *Muhadharat 'an al-Shi'r al-'Iraqi al-Hadith* (Cairo: Jami'at al-Duwal al-'Arabiyya, Ma'had al-Dirasat al-'Arabiyya, 1959), 30.

63. Muhammad Rida al-Shabibi, "al-Adab fi al-'Iraq: al-Sayyid Muhammad Sa'id al-Habubi al-Iraqi," *al-Zuhur* 4:1 (1913), 19–27; 'Abd al- 'Aziz al-Jawahiri, introduction to *Diwan al-Sayyid Muhammad Sa'id al-Habubi al-Najafi Ash'ar Shu'ara' al-Sharq Ams wa Akbar 'Ulama'ihi al-Yawm*, by Muhammad Sa'id al-Habubi (Beirut: al-Matba'a al-Ahliyya, 1913), 5–16; and 'Ali al-Sharqi, introduction to *Diwan*

*al-Tabataba'i: Wa Huwa Diwan al-Sayyid Ibrahim al-Tabataba'i Sha'ir al-Iraq al-Shahir al-Mutawaffin Sinat 1319 Hijri,* by Ibrahim al-Tabataba'i (Sidon: Matba'at al-'Irfan, 1914), 2–7.

64. Paul Starkey, *Modern Arabic Literature* (Edinburgh: Edinburgh University Press, 2006), 35–36.

65. Khuri-Makdisi, *The Eastern Mediterranean,* 16–18.

66. Jayyusi, *Trends and Movements,* 1:176–178

67. Yusuf 'Izz al-Din, *Shu'ara' al-'Iraq fi al-Qarn al-'Ishrin* (Baghdad: Matba'at As'ad, 1969), 34, and Basri, *A'lam al-Adab,* 51.

68. Basri, *A'lam al-Adab,* 56.

69. Basri, *A'lam al-Adab,* 57–58

70. Hourani, *Arabic Thought in the Liberal Age,* 103–129, and Nikki R. Keddie, *Sayyid Jamal al-Din "al-Afghani": A Political Biography* (Berkeley: University of California Press, 1972).

71. Kazimi, *al-A'mal al-Shi'riyya al-Kamila,* 26–30, and Keddie, *Sayyid Jamal al-Din "al-Afghani,"* 328–334.

72. 'Izz al-Din, *Shu'ara' al-'Iraq,* 34–35.

73. DeYoung, *Mahmud Sami al-Barudi,* 20–21.

74. 'Izz al-Din, *Shu'ara' al-'Iraq,* 36–38.

75. 'Abd al-Qadir al-Maghribi, "Sadiqi al-Kazimi," in Kazimi, *al-A'mal al-Shi'riyya al-Kamila,* 302–304.

76. 'Izz al-Din, *Shu'ara' al-'Iraq,* 39.

77. Kazimi, *al-A'mal al-Shi'riyya al-Kamila,* 11–16, 295.

78. Jayyusi, *Trends and Movements,* 1:177–178.

79. Kazimi, *al-A'mal al-Shi'riyya al-Kamila,* 104–107, 267–270, 276–280, 324–327, 328–329, 333–339, 340–348, 349–358, 359–360, 376–382, 401–402, 519–522, 529–533, 608–611, 616–620, 628–629, 630–631, 644–645, 646–650.

80. 'Abd al-Muhsin al-Kazimi, "al-Shi'r al-'Arabi," *al-Muqtabas* 2:1 (1907), 19–20, and "Harb al-Majd wa al-Sharaf," *al-Mu'ayyad,* November 29, 1911.

81. Kazimi, *al-A'mal al-Shi'riyya al-Kamila,* 710–714.

82. Kazimi, *al-A'mal al-Shi'riyya al-Kamila,* 490–495.

83. Kazimi, *al-A'mal al-Shi'riyya al-Kamila,* 711.

84. Rabab al-Kazimi, *al-Majmu'a al-Adabiyya al-Kamila: Dirasa wa Shi'r wa Nathr* (London: Dar al-Hikmah, 2000), 32–104.

85. Rafa'il Butti, "'Abd al-Muhsin al-Kazimi," in Kazimi, *al-A'mal al-Shi'riyya al-Kamila,* 297.

86. Bashkin, "The Iraqi Afghanis and 'Abduhs," 141–142, and Ami Ayalon, *The Press in the Arab Middle East: A History* (New York: Oxford University Press, 1995), 91–95.

87. El-Ariss, *Trials of Arab Modernity,* 21–22.

88. Jamil Sidqi al-Zahawi, "Tarjamat Hayati Mulakhkhasah," in Rushdi, *al-Zahawi*, 46–67.

89. Jamil Sidqi al-Zahawi, "Risaʾil al-Zahawi," in Rushdi, *al-Zahawi*, 25–45, and Sadok Heskel Masliyah, "The Life and Writings of the Iraqi Poet: Jamil Sidqi al-Zahawi," (PhD diss., UCLA, 1973), 64–65.

90. Jamil Sidqi al-Zahawi, *al-Kalim al-Manzum* (Beirut: al-Matbaʿa al-Ahliyya, 1909), 166–167; Jamil Sidqi al-Zahawi *al-Lubab: Wa Huwa al-Mukhtar mima Qaradhuha min al-Shiʿr fi Awakhir Hayatihi* (Baghdad: Matbaʿat al-Furat, 1928), 232–233; and Ahmad Hasan al-Zayyat, "al-Zahawi bi-Munasabat Dhikrahu al-Awla," in Rushdi, *al-Zahawi*, 205–213.

91. Dawud Fatu, "al-Falsafah al-ʿUlya," *al-Muqtataf* 20:5 (1896), 365.

92. Rafaʾil Butti, *al-Adab al-ʿAsri fi al-ʿIraq al-ʿArabi: Kitab Taʾrikhi Adabi Intiqadi, Yahwa Tarajim Udabaʾ al-ʿIraq wa Rusumihim wa Nukhbah min Atharihim bayna Manshur wa Manzum*, vol. 1 (Baghdad: al-Maktaba al-ʿArabiyya, 1923), 7–8.

93. Jamil Sidqi al-Zahawi, "Risaʾil al-Zahawi," in Rushdi, *al-Zahawi*, 31.

94. Masliyah, "The Life and Writings," 70–73.

95. Jamil Sidqi al-Zahawi, *Rubaʿiyat al-Zahawi* (Beirut: Matbaʿat al-Qamus al-ʿAmm, 1928), xiv–xv.

96. Butti, *al-Adab al-ʿAsri*, 1:8.

97. Butti, *al-Adab al-ʿAsri*, 1:8.

98. Zahawi, *al-Kalim al-Manzum*, 163–166.

99. Zahawi, *al-Kalim al-Manzum*, 6–9.

100. Bashkin, "The Iraqi Afghanis and ʿAbduhs," 143–144.

101. Rusafi, *al-Risala*, 227–229.

102. Qasim al-Khattat, "Hayat al-Rusafi," in *Maʿruf al-Rusafi Shaʿir al-ʿArab al-Kabir: Hayatuhu wa Shiʿruhu*, ed. Qasim al-Khattat, Mustafa ʿAbd al-Latif al-Saharti, and Muhammad ʿAbd al-Munʿim Khafaji (Cairo: al-Haya al-Misriyya al-ʿAmma lil-Taʾlif wa al-Nashr, 1971), 321–322.

103. Maʿruf al-Rusafi, "Mayt al-Ahyaʾ wa Hayy al-Amwat," *al-Muqtabas* 1:11 (1906), 513–514; "Alikni ya Dhiya," *al-Muqtabas* 2:7 (1907), 377–378; "al-Majlis al-ʿUmumi," *al-Muqtabas* 3:11 (1908), 665–666; and "Baʿd al-Bayn," *al-Muqtabas* 4:4 (1909), 216–217.

104. Maʿruf al-Rusafi, "Suʾ al-Munqalab," *al-Muqtabas* 2:8 (1907), 419–421, and "Jalinus al-Arab aw Abu Bakr al-Razi," *al-Muqtabas* 3:10 (1908), 605–609.

105. Sheehi, *Foundations of Modern Arab Identity*, 112–115.

106. Rusafi, *al-Risala*, 231.

107. Rusafi, *al-Risala*, 231–232, and Khattat, "Hayat al-Rusafi," 46–47.

108. Dujayli, *Muhadharat*, 11.

109. Mubarak, *Thawrat 1920*, 20–21.

110. Kadhim, *Reclaiming Iraq*, 51.

111. Michelle Campos, *Ottoman Brothers: Muslims, Christians, and Jews in Early Twentieth Century Palestine* (Stanford: Stanford University Press, 2010), 134.

112. Kazimi, *al-Aʿmal al-Shiʿriyya al-Kamila*, 405–411, and Dujayli, *Muhadharat*, 25.

113. Zahawi, *al-Kalim al-Manzum*, 24–73, 175–178.

114. Zahawi, *al-Kalim al-Manzum*, 183–185.

115. Rusafi, *Diwan al-Rusafi*, 388.

116. Rusafi, *Diwan al-Rusafi*, 367–369, and Cemil Aydin, *The Politics of Anti-Westernism in Asia: Visions of World Order in Pan-Islamic and Pan-Asian Thought* (New York: Columbia University Press, 2007), 71–92.

117. Rusafi, *Diwan al-Rusafi*, 113.

118. Butti, *al-Adab al-ʿAsri*, 1:9.

119. Rusafi, *al-Risala*, 234–235.

120. Rusafi, *Diwan al-Rusafi*, 382–385.

121. Rusafi, *Diwan al-Rusafi*, 388–389.

122. Rusafi, *al-Risala*, 235.

123. Sheehi, *Foundations of Modern Arab Identity*, 189–197.

124. Rusafi, *al-Risala*, 235.

125. Khattat, "Hayat al-Rusafi," 52–55.

126. Jamil Sidqi al-Zahawi, "al-Marʾa wa al-Difaʿ ʿanha," *al-Muʾayyad*, August 7, 1910, in Rushdi, *al-Zahawi*, 112–117.

127. Butti, *al-Adab al-ʿAsri*, 1:9.

128. Justin Marozzi, *Baghdad: City of Peace, City of Blood—A History in Thirteen Centuries* (Boston: Da Capo Press, 2014), 269–271.

129. Jamil Sidqi al-Zahawi, *Diwan al-Zahawi* (Cairo: al-Matbaʿah al-ʿArabiyyah, 1924), 73–76.

130. ʿAli al-Wardi, *Lamahat Ijtimaʿiyya min Taʾrikh al-ʿIraq al-Hadith*, vol. 3 (London: Kufan lil-Nashr, 1991), 179–184.

131. Butti, *al-Adab al-ʿAsri*, 1:9–10.

132. Rusafi, *al-Risala*, 236–237.

133. Moreh, "Maʿruf al-Rusafi," 615.

134. Rusafi, *al-Risala*, 237, and Butti, *al-Adab al-ʿAsri*, 1:9.

135. Hasan Kayali, *Ottomanism, Arabism, and Islamism in the Ottoman Empire, 1908–1918* (Berkeley: University of California Press, 1997), 100–102.

136. Rusafi, *Diwan al-Rusafi*, 397–399.

137. Rusafi, *Diwan al-Rusafi*, 399–401, and Kayali, *Ottomanism, Arabism, and Islamism*, 126–141.

138. Rusafi, *Diwan al-Rusafi*, 402–405, and *al-Risala*, 238.

139. ʿAbd al-Ghaffar al-Akhras, *al-Tiraz al-Anfas fi Shiʿr al-Akhras* (Istanbul: Matbaʿat al-Sharika al-Martabiyya, 1887), and Kazim al-Azri, *Diwan Shaykh Kazim al-Azri al-Baghdadi* (Bombay: al-Matbaʿa al-Mustafawiyya, 1902).

140. Shabibi, "al-Adab fi al-'Iraq,'" 27.
141. Ayalon, *The Press in the Arab Middle East*, 65–69.
142. Keith David Watenpaugh, *Being Modern in the Middle East: Revolution, Nationalism, Colonialism, and the Arab Middle Class* (Princeton: Princeton University Press, 2006), 9–10.
143. Benedict Anderson, *Imagined Communities: Reflections on the Origin and Spread of Nationalism* (London: Verso, 2016), 9–36.
144. Zahawi, *al-Kalim al-Manzum*, 116–121.
145. Zahawi, *al-Kalim al-Manzum*, 14–16 and 178–181.
146. Zahawi, *al-Kalim al-Manzum*, 182–183.
147. Zahawi, *al-Lubab*, 163, and Shawqi Dhaif, "Jamil Sidqi al-Zahawi," in Rushdi, *al-Zahawi*, 330–345.
148. Zahawi, *al-Kalim al-Manzum*, 171–175.
149. Moreh, "Town and Country," 128–137.
150. Rusafi, *Diwan al-Rusafi*, 27–31.
151. "Diwan al-Rusafi," *al-Muqtabas* 4:10 (1909), 620–622.
152. Ma'ruf al-Rusafi, "Min Ayn ila' Ayn?" *al-Muqtabas* 2:4 (1907), 210–212.
153. Rusafi, *Diwan al-Rusafi*, 5.
154. 'Abbud Karkhi, *Diwan al-Karkhi*, vol. 1 (Baghdad: Matba'at al-Karkh, 1933), xix–xx.
155. Rusafi, *Diwan al-Rusafi*, 250.
156. Jayyusi, *Trends and Movements*, 1:188.
157. 'Izz al-Din, *Shu'ara' al-'Iraq*, 105–106.
158. Reidar Visser, "Sectarian Coexistence in Iraq: The Experiences of the Shi'a in Areas North of Baghdad," in *The Shi'a of Samarra: The Politics and Heritage of a Community in Iraq*, ed. Imranli Panjwani (London: I. B. Tauris, 2012), 168–169.
159. 'Izz al-Din, *Shu'ara' al-'Iraq*, 106–110.
160. Kazim al-Dujayli, "Ulahu wa Ukhrahu," *al-Zuhur* 3:9 (1913), 471, and "Maryam wa Hasan," *al-Muqtataf* 45:3 (1914), 259–261.
161. Kazim al-Dujayli, "Ya Zaman al-Bukhar," *Lughat al-'Arab* 1:6 (1911), 204–205
162. Muhsin, *Tamaththulat al-Nahda*, 202–204.
163. Basri, *A'lam al-Adab*, 107–113, 114–126, 171–180, 180–186, 189–193, 227–231, 235–241.
164. Basri, *A'lam al-Adab*, 172, and Sinan Antoon, "Abu 'l-'Ala' al-Ma'arri (973–1058)," in *Essays in Arabic Literary Biography, 925–1350*, ed. Terri DeYoung and Mary St. Germain (Weisbaden: Harrasowitz Verlag, 2011), 228–234.
165. Basri, *A'lam al-Adab*, 191.
166. "Fatihat al-Sana al-Khamisa," *al-'Irfan* 5:1 (1913), 1.
167. El-Ariss, *Trials of Arab Modernity*, 19–23.
168. Khalili, *Hakadha 'Araftuhum*, 81.

169. Shibli Shumayyil, *Falsafat al-Nushu' wa al-Irtiqa'* (Cairo: Matba'at al-Muqtataf, 1910).

170. Abu al-Majid Muhammad Rida al-Isfahani, *Kitab Naqd Falsafat Darwin*, (Baghdad: Matba'at al-Wilaya al-'Amira, 1912).

171. 'Abd al-'Aziz al-Jawahiri, "al-Intikhab al-Tabi'i," *al-'Irfan* 4:8 (1912), 304–307.

172. On the emergence of nationalism and anticolonialism in neoclassical poetry and the Nahda press, see Khouri, *Poetry and the Making of Modern Egypt*, 7–36, and DeYoung, *Mahmud Sami al-Barudi*, 7–10.

173. Selim Deringil, "The Struggle against Shiism in Hamidian Iraq: A Study in Ottoman Counter-Propaganda," *Die Welt des Islams* 30:1/4 (1990), 45–62, and Meir Litvak, *Shi'i Scholars of Nineteenth-Century Iraq: The 'Ulama' of Najaf and Karbala'* (Cambridge: Cambridge University Press, 1998), 165–169.

174. Yitzhak Nakash, *The Shi'is of Iraq* (Princeton: Princeton University Press, 1994), 50–61.

175. Sami Zubaida, "The Fragments Imagine the Nation: The Case of Iraq," *International Journal of Middle East Studies* 34:2 (2002), 208–210.

176. Khalili, *Hakadha 'Araftuhum*, 81.

177. Muhammad Baqir al-Shabibi, "al-Suhuf," *Lughat al-'Arab* 2:3 (1912), 81–82.

178. Muhammad Rida al-Shabibi, "al-Tammadun al-'Asri," *al-Zuhur* 3:7 (1912), 363–364; "Fi Sabil al-Sharq," *al-Zuhur* 4:2 (1913), 82–83; and *Diwan al-Shabibi* (Cairo: Matba'ah Lajnat al-Ta'lif wa al-Tarjama wa al-Nashr, 1940), 53–55, 56–57, 96–97.

179. Aydin, *The Politics of Anti-Westernism*.

180. Shabibi, "al-Tammadun al-'Asri," 363–364.

181. Shabibi, *Diwan al-Shabibi*, 96–97.

182. Dawud 'Amun, "Yawm Vladimir," *al-Zuhur* 3:3 (1912), 146–148; Niqula Rizq Allah, "'Irs fi Mu'arakah," *al-Zuhur* 4:2 (1913); 78–81; and Shibli al-Shumayyil, "Jamal al-Din al-Afghani," *al-Zuhur* 3:8 (1912), 411–423.

183. Yoav Di-Capua, "*Nahda*: The Arab Project of Enlightenment," in *The Cambridge Companion to Modern Arab Culture*, ed. Dwight F. Reynolds (Cambridge: Cambridge University Press, 2015), 54–74.

184. Sharqi, introduction to *Diwan al-Tabataba'i*, 4.

185. Sharqi, introduction to *Diwan al-Tabataba'i*, 6.

186. Jawahiri, introduction to *Diwan al-Sayyid Muhammad Sa'id al-Habubi*, 6–16.

187. Sheehi, *Foundations of Modern Arab Identity*, 46–47.

188. Shabibi, "al-Adab fi al-'Iraq," 20.

189. Shabibi, "al-Adab fi al-'Iraq," 27.

190. Ahmad Rida, Sulayman Zahir, and Ahmad 'Arif al-Zayn, eds., *al-'Iraqiyyat, al-Juz' al-Awwal: Wa Huwa Mukhtar min Shi'r 'Asharat Shu'ara' min Mashahir Shu'ara' al-'Iraq* (Sidon: Matba'at al-'Irfan, 1912).

191. "al-Qism al-Adabi: al-Rusafi wa Shi'ruhu," *al-'Irfan* 1:4 (1909), 158–160.
192. "William Steed," *al-'Irfan* 4:4 (1912), 172–173.
193. 'Ali al-Sharqi, "Dami'at 'ala Steed," *al-'Irfan* 4:4 (1912), 264–266.
194. 'Ali al-Sharqi, "Sha'ir fi Sijin," *al-'Irfan* 4:8 (1912), 308–309.
195. El-Ariss, *Trials of Arab Modernity*, 50–52.
196. Shabibi, *Diwan al-Shabibi*, 128–129.
197. Muhammad Baqir al-Shabibi, "Alam Tur an al-Dahr Yaktabu Ma Tamli," *Lughat al-'Arab* 3:4 (October 1913), 200–202.
198. Anderson, *Imagined Communities*, 47–66.
199. Orit Bashkin, *The Other Iraq: Pluralism and Culture in Hashemite Iraq* (Stanford: Stanford University Press, 2009), 140–149.
200. Sara Pursley, *Familiar Futures: Time, Selfhood, and Sovereignty in Iraq* (Stanford: Stanford University Press, 2019).

## Chapter 2

1. Muhammad Mahdi al-Basir, *al-Majmu'a al-Shi'riyya al-Kamila: al-Burkan wa Zabad al-Amwaj* (Baghdad: Wizarat al-I'lam, al-Jumhuriyya al-'Iraqiyya, 1977), 45–47, and Yitzhak Nakash, *The Shi'is of Iraq* (Princeton: Princeton University Press, 1995), 66–72.
2. 'Ali al-Wardi, *Lamahat Ijtima'iyya min Ta'rikh al-'Iraq al-Hadith*, vol. 5, pt. 1 (Baghdad: Matba'at al-Ma'arif, 1977), 189; Muhsin J. al-Musawi, *Reading Iraq: Culture and Power in Conflict* (London: I. B. Tauris, 2006), 53–56; and Ali A. Allawi, *Faisal I of Iraq* (New Haven: Yale University Press, 2014), 357.
3. 'Abd al-Husayn Mubarak, *Thawrat 1920 fi al-Shi'r al-'Iraqi* (Baghdad: Matba'at Dar al-Basri, 1970), 50–56.
4. Basir, *al-Majmu'a al-Shi'riyya al-Kamila*, 45–47.
5. Leslie Tramontini, "Fatherland, If Ever I Betrayed You . . . : Reflections on Nationalist Iraqi Poetry of Thawrat al-'Ishrin," *al-Abhath* 50–51 (2002–2003), 175–176.
6. Basir, *al-Majmu'a al-Shi'riyya al-Kamila*, 45–47.
7. Mesopotamian Police, "Abstract of Intelligence," no. 21, May 22, 1920, IOR/L/PS/10/839/7611, no. 22, May 29, 1920, IOR/L/PS/10/839/7611, and no. 23, June 5, 1920, IOR/L/PS/10/839/7611. See also Arnold Wilson, *Mesopotamia, 1917–1920: A Clash of Loyalties* (London: H. Milford, 1931), 253.
8. Priya Satia, *Spies in Arabia: The Great War and the Cultural Foundations of Britain's Covert Empire in the Middle East* (New York: Oxford University Press, 2008), 201–238.
9. Mesopotamian Police, "Abstract of Intelligence," no. 30, July 24, 1920, IOR/L/PS/10/839/6931.
10. Eliezer Tauber, *The Formation of Modern Syria and Iraq* (London: Frank Cass, 1995), 286–305; Pierre-Jean Luizard, *La formation de l'irak contemporain: Le rôle politique des ulémas chiites à la fin de la domination ottoman et au moment de le creation de l'État irakien* (Paris: CNRS Éditions, 2002), 385–402; and Musawi, *Reading Iraq*, 44–59.

11. Mesopotamian Police, "Abstract of Intelligence," no. 30, July 24, 1920, IOR/L/PS/10/839/6931.

12. Salma Khadra Jayyusi, *Trends and Movements in Modern Arabic Poetry*, vol. 1 (Leiden: E. J. Brill, 1977), 26–33.

13. James L. Gelvin, *Divided Loyalties: Nationalism and Mass Politics at the Close of Empire* (Berkeley: University of California Press, 1998), 51–86.

14. 'Ali al-Sharqi, "Sha'ir fi Sijin," *al-'Irfan* 4:8 (1912), 308–309.

15. Homi K. Bhabha, *The Location of Culture* (London: Routledge, 1994); David Scott, *Conscripts of Modernity: The Tragedy of Colonial Enlightenment* (Durham, NC: Duke University Press, 2004); and Leela Gandhi, *Affective Communities: Anticolonial Thought, Fin-de-Siècle Radicalism, and the Politics of Friendship* (Durham, NC: Duke University Press, 2006).

16. Nancy Fraser, "Rethinking the Public Sphere: A Contribution to the Critique of Actually Existing Democracy" in *Habermas and the Public Sphere*, ed. Craig Calhoun (Cambridge, MA: MIT Press, 1997), 109–142; Geoff Eley, "Nations, Public, and Political Cultures: Placing Habermas in the Nineteenth Century," in Calhoun, *Habermas and the Public Sphere*, 289–339; and Dyala Hamzah, *The Making of the Arab Intellectual (1880–1960): Empire, Public Sphere and the Colonial Coordinates of Selfhood* (London: Routledge, 2013), 9–10.

17. Dilip Parameshwar Gaonkar, "On Alternative Modernities," in *Alternative Modernities*, ed. Dilip Parameshwar Gaonkar (Durham, NC: Duke University Press, 2001), 1–23.

18. Kristin Ross, *The Emergence of Social Space: Rimbaud and the Paris Commune* (London: Verso, 2008), 25–28.

19. M. Şükrü Hanioğlu, *A Brief History of the Late Ottoman Empire* (Princeton: Princeton University Press, 2008), 167–182.

20. Eugene Rogan, *The Fall of the Ottomans: The Great War in the Middle East* (New York: Basic Books, 2015), 50–52.

21. Amal Vinogradov, "The 1920 Revolt in Iraq Reconsidered: The Role of Tribes in National Politics," *International Journal of Middle East Studies* 3:2 (1972), 132–133, and Rogan, *The Fall of the Ottomans*, 124–127.

22. Mesopotamian Police, "Abstract of Intelligence," no. 1, January 3, 1920, IOR/L/PS/10/839/7611.

23. Mubarak, *Thawrat 1920*, 41–50.

24. Rusafi, *Diwan al-Rusafi*, 392, 394–397.

25. Mubarak, *Thawrat 1920*, 54.

26. Mubarak, *Thawrat 1920*, 44.

27. Marlé Hammond, "'If Only al-Barraq Could See . . .': Violence and Voyeurism in an Early Modern Reformulation of the Pre-Islamic Call to Arms," in *Warfare and Poetry in the Middle East*, ed. Hugh Kennedy (London: I. B. Tauris, 2013), 215–240,

and Osman Latiff, *The Cutting Edge of the Poet's Sword: Muslim Poetic Responses to the Crusades* (Leiden: Brill, 2018).

28. Wardi, *Lamahat Ijtima'iyya*, 4:232–234, and Luizard, *La formation de l'irak contemporain*, 320–321.

29. Mir Basri, *A'lam al-Adab fi al-'Iraq al-Hadith* (London: Dar al-Hikmah, 1994), 1:110, and Luizard, *La formation de l'irak contemporain*, 320–321.

30. Muhammad Mahdi al-Basir, *Ta'rikh al-Qadiyya al-'Iraqiyya* (Baghdad: Matba'at al-Falah, 1923), 33.

31. Yitzhak Nakash, *Reaching for Power: The Shi'a in the Modern Arab World* (Princeton: Princeton University Press, 2006), 37–38.

32. Yoav Alon, *The Making of Jordan: Tribes, Colonialism, and the Modern State* (London: I. B. Tauris, 2007), 156.

33. Muhammad Hasan Abu al-Muhasin, *Diwan Abi al-Muhasin al-Karbala'i* (Najaf: Matba'at al-Baqir, 1963), 48–50.

34. Abu al-Muhasin, *Diwan Abi al-Muhasin al-Karbala'i*, 17–19.

35. Mubarak, *Thawrat 1920*, 46–47.

36. Abu al-Muhasin, *Diwan Abi al-Muhasin al-Karbala'i*, 13–14.

37. Charles Townshend, *Desert Hell: The British Invasion of Mesopotamia* (Cambridge, MA: Belknap Press of Harvard University Press, 2011), 83–94, and Rogan, *The Fall of the Ottomans*, 124–127.

38. Vinogradov, "The 1920 Revolt in Iraq Reconsidered," 132.

39. Nakash, *Reaching for Power*, 37–38.

40. Muhammad Rida al-Shabibi, *Diwan al-Shabibi* (Cairo: Matba'at Lajnah al-Ta'lif wa al-Tarjama wa al-Nashr, 1940), 47–48.

41. Ra'uf al-Wa'iz, *al-Ittijahat al-Wataniyya fi al-Shi'r al-'Iraqi al-Hadith, 1914–1941* (Baghdad: Wizarat al-I'lam, al-Jumhuriyya al-'Iraqiyya, 1974), 36–38.

42. Wa'iz, *al-Ittijahat al-Wataniyya*, 24–25.

43. Wa'iz, *al-Ittijahat al-Wataniyya*, 36–37.

44. Abi al-Muhasin, *Diwan Abi al-Muhasin*, 59.

45. Rogan, *The Fall of the Ottomans*, 262–273.

46. Wa'iz, *al-Ittijahat al-Wataniyya*, 33.

47. Wa'iz, *al-Ittijahat al-Wataniyya* 37.

48. Ian Rutledge, *Enemy on the Euphrates: The Battle for Iraq, 1914–1921* (London: Saqi Books, 2015), 97–106.

49. Rutledge, *Enemy on the Euphrates*, 132–133, 171–172.

50. Rusafi, *Diwan al-Rusafi*, 418–419.

51. Rogan, *The Fall of the Ottomans*, 262–273.

52. Wardi, *Lamahat Ijtima'iyyh*, 4:370–371; Orit Bashkin, *The Other Iraq: Pluralism and Culture in Hashemite Iraq* (Stanford: Stanford University Press, 2009), 38; and

Abbas Kadhim, *Reclaiming Iraq: The 1920 Revolution and the Founding of the Modern State* (Austin: University of Texas Press, 2012), 97–103.

53. Nissim Rejwan, *The Last Jews in Baghdad: Remembering a Lost Homeland* (Austin: University of Texas Press, 2004), 109, and Bashkin, *The Other Iraq*, 38.

54. Justin Marozzi, *Baghdad: City of Peace, City of Blood—A History in Thirteen Centuries* (Boston: Da Capo Press, 2014), 274.

55. Anwar G. Chejne, *The Arabic Language: Its Role in History* (Minneapolis: University of Minnesota Press, 1969), 116.

56. Basri, *A'lam al-Adab*, 1:267–268.

57. Mubarak, *Thawrat 1920*, 50–51.

58. Ibn Ma' al-Sama', "Layla Suqut Baghdad," *al-'Arab*, September 7, 1917, 1.

59. Ibn Ma' al-Sama', "Um al-Tifl fi Mu'atark al-Salb wa al-Hariq fi Baghdad," *al-'Arab*, September 8, 1917, 1.

60. Ibn al-Furatayn, "Baghdad wa al-Hariq wa al-Nahb," *al-'Arab*, August 5, 1917, 2.

61. Ibn al-Furatayn, "Khayal Turan wa Khutbat Jinkiz," *al-'Arab*, August 28, 1917, 1–2.

62. Mubarak, *Thawrat 1920*, 44.

63. Leila Tarazi Fawaz, *A Land of Aching Hearts: The Middle East in the Great War* (Cambridge, MA: Harvard University Press, 2014), 233–274.

64. Rafa'il Butti, *al-Adab al-'Asri fi al-'Iraq al-Hadith*, vol. 1 (Baghdad: al-Maktabah al-'Arabiyyah, 1923) 18–27.

65. "al-Akhbar al-Mahliyya," *al-'Arab*, January 18, 1918, 3.

66. See Jamil Sidqi al-Zahawi, *al-Kalim al-Manzum* (Beirut: al-Matba'a al-Ahliyya, 1909), 16.

67. Ibn al-Saliqa, "Fi Madh Malik al-Muluk Sahib al-'Adala Hadhrat Jalalat 'Jurj al-Khamis' Damat Shawkatuhu," *al-'Arab*, September 22, 1917, 1.

68. Ibn al-Sayyara, "Fadihat al-Itifaq bi Mawt 'Fatih al-'Iraq'," *al-'Arab*, November 27, 1917, 1.

69. Dina Rizk Khoury, "Ambiguities of the Modern: The Great War in the Memoirs and the Poetry of the Iraqis," in *The World in World Wars: Experiences, Perceptions and Perspectives from Africa and Asia*, ed. Heike Liebau, Katrin Bromber, Katharina Lange, Dyala Hamzah, and Ravi Ahuja (Leiden: Brill, 2010), 313–340.

70. Wa'iz, *al-Ittijahat al-Wataniyya*, 50–52.

71. Hasan Kayali, *Arabs and Young Turks: Ottomanism, Arabism, and Islamism in the Ottoman Empire, 1908–1918* (Berkeley: University of California Press, 1997), 81–143.

72. Yusuf 'Izz al-Din, *Khayri al-Hindawi: Hayatuhu wa Diwan Shi'rihi* (Baghdad: Matba'at al-Sha'b, 1974), 188.

73. Geert Buelens, *Everything to Nothing: The Poetry of the Great War, Revolution and the Transformation of Europe*, trans. David McKay (London: Verso: 2015), 1–36.

74. 'Izz al-Din, *Khayri al-Hindawi*, 62–63, and Khoury, "Ambiguities of the Modern," 315.

75. Kazim al-Dujayli, "Masir wa Masir," *al-Muqtataf* 43:4 (1913), 343–346.

76. Butti, *al-Adab al-'Asri*, 1:188–189, and Khoury, "Ambiguities of the Modern," 334–335.

77. Kazim al-Dujayli, "al-Zaman al-'Atid," *al-Muqtataf* 54:6 (1919), 542–543, and "al-Harb al-'Uzma," *al-Hilal* 27:8 (1919), 748–750.

78. David Fromkin, *A Peace to End All Peace: The Fall of the Ottoman Empire and the Creation of the Modern Middle East* (New York: Owl Books, 1995), 96–115; Fawaz, *A Land of Aching Hearts*, 233–274; and Rogan, *The Fall of the Ottomans*, 275–309.

79. Mubarak, *Thawrat 1920*, 62.

80. Ittihad al-Udaba'' al-'Iraqiyyin, *Mihrajan al-Rusafi 1959* (Baghdad: Matba'at al-Ma'arif, 1959), 72–73.

81. Muhammad Bahjat al-Athari, "al-Muqaddama," introduction to *Diwan Rashid al-Hashimi*, by Rashid al-Hashimi (Baghdad: Matba'at al-Ma'arif, 1964), 11–12, and 'Abdullah al-Jabburi, "Muqaddamat al-Diwan," introduction to *Diwan al-Sayyid Muhammad al-Hashimi al-Baghdadi*, by Muhammad al-Hashimi (Baghdad: Wizarat al-I'lam, 1977), 16–17.

82. Hashimi, *Diwan Rashid al-Hashimi*, 51–52.

83. Sadr al-Din Sadr, "Ta'rikh Waqa'i' al-Shahr fi al-Iraq wa Ma Jawarahu," *Lughat al-'Arab* 2:4 (1912), 166, and Hashimi, *Diwan al-Sayyid Muhammad al-Hashimi*, 252–255.

84. Jabburi, "Muqaddamat al-Diwan," 16–17, and Reidar Visser, *Basra, the Failed Gulf State: Separatism and Nationalism in Southern Iraq* (Münster: Lit, 2005), 38–50.

85. Hashimi, *Diwan al-Sayyid Muhammad al-Hashimi*, 198–200.

86. Hashimi, *Diwan Rashid al-Hashimi*, 116–117.

87. Hashimi, *Diwan Rashid al-Hashimi*, 99–103.

88. Hashimi, *Diwan Rashid al-Hashimi*, 67–68.

89. Athari, "al-Muqaddamah," 13–15.

90. Hashimi, *Diwan al-Sayyid Muhammad al-Hashimi*, 278–279, and Butti, *al-Adab al-'Asri*, 2:17–18

91. Muhammad al-Hashimi, "Akwat al-Iraq," *al-Muqtataf* 48:2 (1916), 166–167; Muhammad al-Hashimi, "Baghdad al-Hadhira," *al-Muqtataf* 50:4 (1917), 373–382; Muhammad al-Hashimi, "Baghdad al-Hadhira," *al-Muqtataf* 51:2 (1917), 143–149; and Muhammad al-Hashimi, "Baghdad al-Hadhira," *al-Muqtataf* 51:4 (1917), 323–330.

92. Hashimi, *Diwan Rashid al-Hashimi*, 11–12.

93. Hashimi, *Diwan Rashid al-Hashimi*, 130–132.

94. Hashimi, *Diwan Rashid al-Hashimi*, 75–77.

95. Hashimi, *Diwan Rashid al-Hashimi*, 78–80.

96. Hashimi, *Diwan al-Sayyid Muhammad al-Hashimi*, 180–186.

97. Hashimi, *Diwan Rashid al-Hashimi*, 71–72.

98. Hashimi, *Diwan Rashid al-Hashimi*, 18–19, and Butti, *al-Adab al-'Asri*, 2:7–18 and 46–46.

99. 'Abd al-Razzaq al-Hilali, *al-Sha'ir al-Tha'ir: al-Shaykh Muhammad Baqir al-Shabibi 1889–1960* (Baghdad: Maktabat al-Nahda, 1965), 35–37.

100. Muhammad Rida al-Shabibi, *Mudhakkirat al-Shaykh Muhammad Rida al-Shabibi wa Rihlatuhu* (Beirut: Dar al-Rafidayn lil- Taba'a wa al-Nashr wa al-Tawzi', 2011), 45–74.

101. Muhammad Baqir al-Shabibi, "al-Majzarah al-'Uzama," *al-Muqtataf* 50:6 (1917), 586–588.

102. 'Ali Khaqani, *Shu'ara' al-Ghari, Aw, al-Najafiyyat*, vol. 1 (Najaf: al-Matba'ah al-Haydariyya, 1954), 36; Hassan Asdi, *Thawrat al-Najaf: aw al-Shirarah al-Awla li Thawrat al-'Ishrin* (Baghdad: Manshurat Wizarat al-I'lam, 1975), 349–351; and Abbas Kadhim, "The Najaf Revolt of 1918: Its Importance and Potential, and the Cause of Its Collapse," in *Najaf: Portrait of a Holy City*, ed. Sabrina Mervin, Robert Gleave, and Géraldine Chatelard (Paris: UNESCO, 2017), 277–294.

103. Rogan, *The Fall of the Ottomans*, 373–380.

104. Shabibi, *Diwan al-Shabibi*, 33–38.

105. Gertrude Bell to Sir Hugh Bell, December 4, 1920, Gertrude Bell Archive, http://gertrudebell.ncl.ac.uk.

106. Wa'iz, *al-Ittijahat al-Wataniyya*, 62–63.

107. 'Abd al-Mushin al-Kazimi, *al-A'mal al-Shi'riyya al-Kamila li Sha'ir al-'Arab 'Abd al-Muhsin al-Kazimi, 1870–1935* (London: Dar al-Hikmah, 2002), 148–151.

108. Originally published in *Dar al-Salam* 4:2 (1919), 164, in Mubarak, *Thawrat 1920*, 81.

109. Basir, *al-Majmu'a al-Shi'riyya al-Kamila*, 32.

110. Hilali, *al-Sha'ir al-Tha'ir*, 40–41.

111. Wa'iz, *al-Ittijahat al-Wataniyya*, 68–69, and Erez Manela, *The Wilsonian Moment: Self-Determination and the International Origins of Anticolonial Nationalism* (Oxford: Oxford University Press, 2007), 197–213.

112. Allawi, *Faisal I*, 229–294.

113. Rusafi, *Diwan al-Rusafi*, 459.

114. "Abstract of Intelligence," no. 1, January 3, 1920, IOR/L/PS/10/839/7611, and "Abstract of Intelligence," no. 9, February 28, 1920, IOR/L/PS/10/839/7611.

115. Athari, "al-Muqaddama," in Hashimi, *Diwan Rashid al-Hashimi*, 14–15, and Tauber, *The Formation of Modern Iraq and Syria*, 219–225,

116. Hashimi, *Diwan Rashid al-Hashimi*, 53–55.

117. "Intelligence Report," no. 19, August 15, 1921, CO 730/4/46069.

118. Hashimi, *Diwan al-Sayyid Muhammad al-Hashimi*, 250–251.

119. Hashimi, *Diwan al-Sayyid Muhammad al-Hashimi*, 259–262.

120. Mubarak, *Thawrat 1920*, 91.

121. Originally published in *al-Lisan* 10 (1920), 282, in Mubarak, *Thawrat 1920*, 82.

122. "Abstract of Intelligence," no. 14, April 3, 1920, IOR/L/PS/10/839/7611, and "Abstract of Intelligence," no. 20, May 15, 1920, IOR/L/PS/10/839/7611.

123. "Abstract of Intelligence," no. 22, May 29, 1920, IOR/L/PS/10/839/7611.

124. Hilali, *al-Sha'ir al-Tha'ir*, 43–45.

125. "Abstract of Intelligence," no. 20, May 15, 1920, IOR/L/PS/10/839/7611, and "Abstract of Intelligence," no. 21, May 22, 1920, IOR/L/PS/10/839/7611.

126. Aula Hariri, "The Iraqi Independence Movement: A Case of Transgressive Contention (1918–1920)," in *Contentious Politics in the Middle East: Popular Resistance and Marginalized Activism beyond the Arab Uprisings*, ed. Fawaz A. Gerges (New York: Palgrave Macmillan, 2015), 97–124

127. 'Ali al-Bazirkan, *al-Waqa'i' al-Haqiqiyya fi al-Thawra al-'Iraqiyya: Risala Tatadamman Munaqasha wa Tahlilan li Hawadith Thawrat al-'Iraq Sanat 1920 Warada Ma Ulsiqa bihi min Muftarayat wa Tashih Ma Dara Hawlaha min Akhta'* (Baghdad: Matba'at As'ad, 1954), 189.

128. Basir, *al-Majmu'a al-Shi'riyya al-Kamila*, 39–40.

129. Jayyusi, *Trends and Movements in Modern Arabic Poetry*, 2:585-594.

130. Basir, *al-Majmu'a al-Shi'riyya al-Kamila*, 13–14, and Mubarak, *Thawrat 1920*, 80–81.

131. "Abstract of Intelligence," no. 21, May 22, 1920, IOR/L/PS/10/839/7611.

132. Mubarak, *Thawrat 1920*, 74.

133. "Abstract of Intelligence," no. 20, May 15, 1920, IOR/L/PS/10/839/7611.

134. "Abstract of Intelligence, Appendix A" no. 39, September 25, 1920, IOR/L/PS/10/839/8046.

135. Rutledge, *Enemy on the Euphrates*, 184.

136. "Abstract of Intelligence," no. 22, May 29, 1920, IOR/L/PS/10/839/7611.

137. "Abstract of Intelligence," no. 22, May 29, 1920, IOR/L/PS/10/839/7611, and no. 23, June 5, 1920, IOR/L/PS/10/839/7611.

138. "Abstract of Intelligence," no. 29, July 17, 1920, IOR/L/PS/10/839/6931, and" no. 30, July 24, 1920, IOR/L/PS/10/839/6931.

139. Wardi, *Lamahat Ijtima'iyyah*, 5:192.

140. Wardi, *Lamahat Ijtima'iyyah*, 5:193–194.

141. "Abstract of Intelligence," no. 23, June 5, 1920, IOR/L/PS/10/839/7611.

142. "Abstract of Intelligence," no. 24, June 12, 1920, IOR/L/PS/10/839/7611, and no. 23, June 5, 1920, IOR/L/PS/10/839/7611.

143. "Abstract of Intelligence," no. 23, June 5, 1920, IOR/L/PS/10/839/7611.

144. "Abstract of Intelligence," no. 27, July 3, 1920, IOR/L/PS/10/839/6931.

145. "Abstract of Intelligence," no. 23, June 5, 1920, IOR/L/PS/10/839/7611.

146. "Abstract of Intelligence," no. 24, June 12, 1920, IOR/L/PS/10/839/7611.

147. "Abstract of Intelligence," no. 26, June 26, 1920, IOR/L/PS/10/839/6931.

148. "Abstract of Intelligence," no. 26, June 26, 1920, IOR/L/PS/10/839/6931.

149. "Abstract of Intelligence," no. 29, July 17, 1920, IOR/L/PS/10/839/6931.

150. "Abstract of Intelligence," no. 23, June 5, 1920, IOR/L/PS/10/839/7611; "no. 25, June 19, 1920, IOR/L/PS/10/839/7611; no. 28, July 10, 1920, IOR/L/PS/10/839/6931; and "Abstract of Intelligence," no. 29, July 17, 1920, IOR/L/PS/10/839/6931.

151. "Abstract of Intelligence," no. 27, July 3, 1920, IOR/L/PS/10/839/6931; "Abstract of Intelligence," no. 29, July 17, 1920, IOR/L/PS/10/839/6931; and "Abstract of Intelligence," no. 32, August 7, 1920, IOR/L/PS/10/839/6931.

152. "Abstract of Intelligence," no. 27, July 3, 1920, IOR/L/PS/10/839/6931.

153. "Abstract of Intelligence," no. 28, July 10, 1920, IOR/L/PS/10/839/6931.

154. "Abstract of Intelligence," no. 23, June 5, 1920, IOR/L/PS/10/839/7611, and "Abstract of Intelligence," no. 25, June 19, 1920, IOR/L/PS/10/839/7611. See also Wardi, *Lamahat Ijtima'iyya*, 5:189–190.

155. "Abstract of Intelligence," no. 27, July 3, 1920, IOR/L/PS/10/839/6931, and no. 29, July 17, 1920, IOR/L/PS/10/839/6931.

156. "Abstract of Intelligence," no. 30, July 24, 1920, IOR/L/PS/10/839/6931.

157. "Abstract of Intelligence," no. 26, June 26, 1920, IOR/L/PS/10/839/6931.

158. "Abstract of Intelligence," no. 28, July 10, 1920, IOR/L/PS/10/839/6931.

159. "Abstract of Intelligence," no. 27, July 3, 1920, IOR/L/PS/10/839/6931, and no. 29, July 17, 1920, IOR/L/PS/10/839/6931.

160. "Abstract of Intelligence," no. 29, July 17, 1920, IOR/L/PS/10/839/6931;" no. 31, July 31, 1920, IOR/L/PS/10/839/7611; and no. 32, August 7, 1920, IOR/L/PS/10/839/6931. See also Mubarak, *Thawrat 1920*, 85–86.

161. "Abstract of Intelligence," no. 31, July 31, 1920, IOR/L/PS/10/839/6931.

162. "Abstract of Intelligence," no. 32, August 7, 1920, IOR/L/PS/10/839/6931.

163. "Abstract of Intelligence," no. 30, July 24, 1920, IOR/L/PS/10/839/6931.

164. "Abstract of Intelligence, Appendix A" no. 39, September 25, 1920, IOR/L/PS/10/839/8046.

165. Manela, *The Wilsonian Moment*, 3–7.

166. Vinogradov, "The 1920 Revolt in Iraq Reconsidered," 123–139.

167. For example, see "Abstract of Intelligence," no. 13, March 27, 1920; no. 14, April 3, 1920, IOR/L/PS/10/839/7611; and no. 16, April 17, 1920, IOR/L/PS/10/839/7611.

168. Kadhim, *Reclaiming Iraq*, 19–42.

169. "Abstract of Intelligence," no. 28, July 10, 1920, IOR/L/PS/10/839/6931, and Rutledge, *Enemy on the Euphrates*, 180–181.

170. Basir, *al-Majmu'a al-Shi'riyya al-Kamila*, 41.

171. Basir, *al-Majmu'a al-Shi'riyya al-Kamila*.

172. "Abstract of Intelligence," no. 28, July 10, 1920, IOR/L/PS/10/839/6931.

173. Mubarak, *Thawrat 1920*, 87.

174. Wardi, *Lamahat Ijtima'iyya*, 5:190.

175. Ibrahim al-Wa'ili, *Thawrat al-'Ishrin fi al-Shi'r al-Iraqi* (Baghdad: Matba'at al-Iman, 1968), 62.

176. Wardi, *Lamahat Ijtima'iyya*, 5:190–191.

177. 'Abd al-Razzaq al-Hasani, *al-Thawra al-'Iraqiyya al-Kubra* (Sidon: Matba'at al-'Irfan, 1952), 94, and Mubarak, *Thawrat 1920*, 93.

178. Wardi, *Lamahat Ijtima'iyya*, 5:216.

179. Kadhim, *Reclaiming Iraq*, 69–74, and Rutledge, *Enemy on the Euphrates*, 249–253.

180. "Abstract of Intelligence," no. 32, August 7, 1920, IOR/L/PS/10/839/6931.

181. "Abstract of Intelligence," no. 31, July 31, 1920, IOR/L/PS/10/839/6931, and Hanna Batatu, *The Old Social Classes and Revolutionary Movements of Iraq: A Study of Iraq's Old Landed and Commercial Classes and of Its Communists, Ba'thists, and Free Officers* (Princeton: Princeton University Press, 1978), 73–78

182. Wardi, *Lamahat Ijtima'iyya*, 5:323.

183. Fatimah al-Muhsin, *Tamaththulat al-Nahdah fi Thaqafat al-'Iraq al-Hadith* (Beirut: Manshurat al-Jamal, 2010), 23.

184. Hasani, *al-Thawrah al-'Iraqiyyah al-Kubra*, 91.

185. Khaqani, *Shu'ara' al-Ghari*, 6:378.

186. "Abstract of Intelligence," no. 23, June 5, 1920, IOR/L/PS/10/839/7611.

187. Rutledge, *Enemy on the Euphrates*, 341–344.

188. Wardi, *Lamahat Ijtima'iyya*, 5:301–302 and Kadhim, *Reclaiming Iraq*, 86–96.

189. Hasani, *al-Thawrah al-'Iraqiyyah al-Kubra*, 208.

190. Mubarak, *Thawrat 1920*, 89.

191. Rutledge, *Enemy on the Euphrates* 373–379.

192. "Abstract of Intelligence," no. 23, June 5, 1920, IOR/L/PS/10/839/7611, and no. 39, September 25, 1920, IOR/L/PS/10/839/8046.

193. "Abstract of Intelligence," no. 28, July 10, 1920, IOR/L/PS/10/839/6931, and no. 32, August 7, 1920, IOR/L/PS/10/839/6931.

194. "Abstract of Intelligence," no. 23, June 5, 1920, IOR/L/PS/10/839/7611.

195. Basir, *Ta'rikh al-Qadiyya al-'Iraqiyya*, 143–146.

196. Mubarak, *Thawrat 1920*, 107.

## Chapter 3

1. "al-Mawqib al-Fakhim," *al-'Iraq*, October 12, 1920, 1.

2. 'Ali al-Wardi, *Lamahat Ijtima'iyya min Ta'rikh al-'Iraq al-Hadith*, vol. 6 (London: Kufan lil-Nashr, 1991), 15–16.

3. Gertrude Bell to Sir Hugh Bell, October 17, 1920, in Gertrude Bell Archive, http://gertrudebell.ncl.ac.uk.

4. Muhsin J. al-Musawi, *Reading Iraq: Culture and Power in Conflict* (London: I. B. Tauris, 2006), 101.

5. Jamil Sidqi Zahawi, *Diwan al-Zahawi* (Cairo: al-Matba'a al-'Arabiyya, 1924), 176–177, and Muhammad Mahdi al-Basir, *Ta'rikh al-Qadiyya al-'Iraqiyya*, 2$^{nd}$ ed. (London: Dar al-Lam, 1990), 147–148.

6. Muhammad Mahdi al-Basir, *al-Majmu'a al-Shi'riyya al-Kamila: al-Burkan wa Zabad al-Amwaj* (Baghdad: Wizarat al-I'lam, al-Jumhuriyya al- Iraqiyya, 1977), 58–59, and 'Ali Muhammad Hadi Rabi'i, *Muhammad Mahdi al-Basir: Ra'id al-Masrah al-Tahridi fi al-'Iraq* (Cairo: Dar al-Nashr lil-Jami'at, 2013), 34.

7. See Gertrude Bell to Sir Hugh Bell, September 29, 1921, and , July 16, 1924, in Gertrude Bell Archive, http://gertrudebell.ncl.ac.uk.

8. 'Abd al-Husayn al-Azri, *Diwan al-Hajj 'Abd al-Husayn al-Azri* (Beirut: al-Nu'man, 1980) 124.

9. Mahir Hasan Fahmi, *al-Zahawi* (Cairo: al-Mu'assassa al-Misriyya al-'Amma lil-Ta'lif wa al-Anba' wa al-Nashr, 1964), 135–137.

10. Sadok Heskel Masliyah, "The Life and Writings of the Iraqi Poet: Jamil Sidqi al-Zahawi" (PhD diss., UCLA, 1973), 120–121.

11. "Abstract of Intelligence," no. 52, December 31, 1920, CO 730/1/11341.

12. Ali A. Allawi, *Faisal I of Iraq* (New Haven: Yale University Press, 2014), 368–377.

13. 'Abd al-Hamid Rushudi, *al-Rusafi: Hayatuhu, Atharuhu, Shi'ruhu* (Baghdad: Dar al-Shu'un al-Thaqafiyyah al-'Ammah, 1988), 42–43.

14. "Intelligence Report," no. 16, July 1, 1921, CO 730/3/41687.

15. Tony Ballantyne and Antoinette Burton, eds., *Bodies in Contact: Rethinking Colonial Encounters in World History* (Durham: Duke University Press, 2005).

16. Hussein N. Kadhim, *The Poetics of Anti-Colonialism in the Arabic Qasidah* (Leiden: Brill, 2004), 231.

17. "Abstract of Intelligence," no. 1, January 3, 1920, IOR/L/PS/10/839/7611, and no. 9, February 28, 1920, IOR/L/PS/10/839/7611; "Fi Sabil al-Watan," *al-Nafa'is al-'Asriyya*, February 15, 1920, 209–210; and "al-Rusafi," *al-Nafa'is al-'Asriyya* 8:1 (January 1921), 5–8.

18. Safa Khulusi, "Ma'ruf al-Rusafi in Jerusalem," *Jerusalem Quarterly* 22/23 (2005), 63–68.

19. "Arab College for Jerusalem," *Times*, December 29, 1920, 7.

20. "Qasidat al-Rusafi," *al-Nafir*, January 5, 1921, 3.

21. Khulusi, "Ma'ruf al-Rusafi in Jerusalem," 66.

22. "Qasidat al-Rusafi," *al-Nafir*, January 5, 1921, 3.

23. "al-Rusafi," *al-Nafa'is al-'Asriyyah* 8:1 (1921), 5–8.

24. 'Abd al Rahman Yaghi, *Hayat al-Adab al-Filastini al-Hadith* (Beirut: al-Maktab al-Tijari lil-Taba'a wa al-Nashr wa al-Tawzi', 1960), 184–185.

25. Yaghi, *Hayat al-Adab al-Filastini*, 184–185.

26. Khulusi, "Maʿruf al-Rusafi in Jerusalem," 67.

27. Maʿruf al-Rusafi, "Ana wa al-Shiʿr," *al-Nafaʾis al-ʿAsriyya* 8:2 (1921), 1–2, and "Khawatir al-Shiʿr," *al-Nafaʾis al-ʿAsriyya* 8:4 (1921), 1–2.

28. Wardi, *Lamahat Ijtimaʿiyya*, 6:59–60.

29. Peter Sluglett, *Britain in Iraq: Contriving King and Country* (New York: Columbia University Press, 2007), 13–34, and Abbas Kadhim, *Reclaiming Iraq: The 1920 Revolution and the Founding of the Modern State* (Austin: University of Texas Press, 2012), 7–11.

30. Kadhim, *Reclaiming Iraq*, 135–160, and Allawi, *Faisal I*, 229–294.

31. Toby Dodge, *Inventing Iraq: The Failure of Nation Building and a History Denied* (New York: Columbia University Press, 2003), 10–20, and Sluglett, *Britain in Iraq*, 35–41.

32. Allawi, *Faisal I*, 295–313.

33. Allawi, *Faisal I*, 314–336.

34. Elie Kedourie, "The Kingdom of Iraq: A Retrospect," in *The Chatham House Version and other Middle Eastern Studies* (Chicago: Ivan R. Dee, 2004), 239–243.

35. "Fi Shaʾn Malik al-ʿIraq," *al-ʿIraq*, May 7, 1921, 3, and "Daf Iltibas," *al-ʿIraq*, May 10, 1921, 2.

36. Allawi, *Faisal I*, 335–336.

37. "Hawl Qudum Samu al-Amir," *al-ʿIraq*, June 27, 1921, 3.

38. "Abstract of Intelligence," no. 32, August 7, 1920, IOR/L/PS/10/839/6931.

39. "al-Ihtifalat fi al-Basra bi Qudum Samu al-Amir Faysal," *al-ʿIraq*, June 28, 1921, 1.

40. Percy Cox to Winston Churchill, June 28, 1921, CO 730/2/32444; Wardi, *Lamahat Ijtimaʿiyya*, 6:85–88; and Allawi, *Faisal I*, 364.

41. "Samu al-Amir fi al-Samawa," *al-ʿIraq*, June 28, 1921, 2.

42. Wardi, *Lamahat Ijtimaʿiyya*, 6:89

43. "Intelligence Report," no. 16, July 1, 1921, CO 730/3/41687.

44. "Fi Hadhrat Samu al-Amir," *al-ʿIraq*, July 7, 1921, 2; "Intelligence Report," no. 16, July 1, 1921, CO 730/3/41687; and "Intelligence Report," no. 17, July 15, 1921, CO 730/3/44325.

45. "Intelligence Report," no. 17, July 15, 1921, CO 730/3/44325, and no. 19, August 15, 1921, CO 730/4/46069.

46. Percy Cox to Winston Churchill, July 1, 1921, CO 730/3/33043; "Intelligence Report," no. 16, July 1, 1921, CO 730/3/41687; and Wardi, *Lamahat Ijtimaʿiyya*, 6:99–100.

47. "Maʾdubat al-Baladiyya li Sahib al-Samu al-Maliki al-Amir Faysal al-Muʿazzam fi Hadiqat Maude," *al-ʿIraq*, July 2, 1921, 1–2.

48. "Maʾdubat al-Baladiyya," *al-ʿIraq*, July 2, 1921, 2.

49. Percy Cox to Winston Churchill, July 5, 1921, CO 730/3/33043.
50. Wardi, *Lamahat Ijtima'iyya*, 6:96–97.
51. "Ma'dubat Fakhamat Naqib Ashraf Baghdad, Ra'is Majlis al-Wuzara', li Samu al-Amir Faysal al-Mu'azzam," *al-'Iraq*, July 9, 1921, 2–3.
52. Percy Cox to Winston Churchill, July 11, 1921, CO 730/3/34817.
53. "Fi al-Mustansariyya," *al-'Iraq*, July 18, 1921, 3.
54. "Kulliyat al-Mustansariyya," *al-'Iraq*, July 19, 1921, 3.
55. "Fi al-Madrasa al-'Askariyya," *al-'Iraq*, July 22, 1921, 3.
56. "Intelligence Report," no. 18, August 1, 1921, CO 703/4/44326.
57. "Intelligence Report," no. 16, July 1, 1921, CO 730/3/41687.
58. "Intelligence Report," no. 16, July 1, 1921, CO 730/3/41687, and no. 17, July 15, 1921, CO 730/3/44325.
59. "Intelligence Report," no. 18, August 1, 1921, CO 703/4/44326.
60. Orit Bashkin, *The Other Iraq: Pluralism and Culture in Hashemite Iraq* (Stanford: Stanford University Press, 2010), 21.
61. Muhammad al-Hashimi, *Diwan al-Sayyid Muhammad al-Hashimi al-Baghdadi* (Baghdad: Wizarat al-I'lam, 1977), 175–178, and Gertrude Bell to Sir Hugh Bell, August 14, 1921, Gertrude Bell Archive, http://gertrudebell.ncl.ac.uk.
62. Basir, *al-Majmu'a al-Shi'riyya al-Kamila*, 58–59, and Rabi'i, *Muhammad Mahdi al-Basir*, 33–34.
63. "Intelligence Report," no. 4, December 31, 1920, CO 730/1/1152.
64. Basir, *al-Majmu'a al-Shi'riyya al-Kamila*, 45–47.
65. Mesopotamian Police, "Abstract of Intelligence," no. 30, July 24, 1920, IOR/L/PS/10/839/6931.
66. Arab Bureau, "Confidential," no. 5, June 18, 1916, FO 371/2771/125694.
67. Rashid al-Hashimi, "'Arsh al-'Iraq," *al-'Iraq*, May 12, 1921, 2.
68. Rashid al-Hashimi, "Khara'ib Babil," *al-'Iraq*, May 12, 1921, 2.
69. Rashid al-Hashimi, "al-Amir Faysal," *al-'Iraq*, May 24, 1921, 1, and "Intelligence Report," no. 14, June 1, 1921, CO 730/3/36240.
70. "Haflat Madrasat Sharafat Iraniyyan li Takrim Samu al-Amir Faysal al-Mu'azzam," *al-'Iraq*, August 5, 1921, 2; "Intelligence Report," no. 16, July 1, 1921, CO 730/3/41687; and "Intelligence Report," no. 19, August 15, 1921, CO 730/4/46069.
71. "Intelligence Report," no. 19, August 15, 1921.
72. "Haflat Madrasat Sharafat Iraniyyan li Takrim Samu al-Amir Faysal al-Mu'azzam," *al-'Iraq*, August 5, 1921, 2.
73. "Intelligence Report," no. 20, September 1, 1921, CO 730/5/48631.
74. Rashid al-Hashimi, *Diwan Rashid al-Hashimi* (Baghdad: Matba'at al-Ma'arif, 1964), 69–70.
75. Wardi, *Lamahat Ijtima'iyya*, 6:120–121, and Allawi, *Faisal I*, 379–381.
76. Tauber, *The Formation of Modern Iraq and Syria*, 303–305.

77. Hashimi, *Diwan al-Sayyid Muhammad al-Hashimi*, 175.
78. Hashimi, *Diwan al-Sayyid Muhammad al-Hashimi*, 175–178.
79. "Haflat Ta'bin," *al-'Iraq*, September 24, 1921, 2.
80. "Intelligence Report," no. 22, October 1, 1921, CO 730/6/52859.
81. Muhammad al-Hashimi, "al-Yatim al-Baki," *al-'Iraq*, January 1, 1922, 7.
82. "Intelligence Report," no. 28, January 1, 1922, CO 730/19/5810.
83. Muhammad Mahdi al-Jawahiri, *Dhikrayati*, vol. 1 (Damascus: Dar al-Rafidin, 1988), 113. See also Bashkin, *The Other Iraq*, 37–38.
84. "Intelligence Report," no. 22, October 1, 1921, CO 730/6/52859; no. 23, October 15, 1921, CO 730/6/54465; no. 24, November 1, 1921, CO 730/7/60973; no. 25, November 15, 1921, CO 730/7/64310; and no. 26, December 1, 1921, CO 730/8/64133.
85. "Intelligence Report," no. 7, February 14, 1921, CO 730/1/15772, and no. 11, April 15, 1921, CO 730/1/26120.
86. Muhammad Mahdi al-Basir, "Ghayrat al-Nu'man," *al-'Iraq*, December 28, 1921, 3, and Khayri al-Hindawi, "Naza'at al-Nafs," *al-'Iraq*, January 1, 1922, 11. See also Yusuf 'Izz al-Din, *Khayri al-Hindawi: Hayatuhu wa Diwan Shi'rihi* (Baghdad: Matba'at al-Sha'b, 1974), 37–54.
87. Yusuf 'Izz al-Din, *Shu'ara' al-'Iraq fi al-Qarn al-'Ishrin* (Baghdad: Matba'at al-As'ad, 1969), 96–97.
88. Gertrude Bell to Sir Hugh Bell, August 27, 1922, Gertrude Bell Archive, http://gertrudebell.ncl.ac.uk and Allawi, *Faisal I*, 404–406.
89. Bashkin, *The Other Iraq*, 21.
90. 'Izz al-Din, *Shu'ara' al-'Iraq*, 97.
91. "Intelligence Report," no. 15, August 1, 1922, CO 371/23/43335.
92. Muhammad al-Hashimi, "Nakbat Dimashq," *al-Zahra'* 2:10 (1925) 618–620, and "Fatan al-'Arab," *al-Zahra'* 3:1 (1926) 20–21.
93. Jamil Sidqi al-Zahawi, *Ruba'iyat al-Zahawi: Wa Hiya al-Juz' al-Thalith min Mukhtarat Ma Nazamaha al-Ustadh al-Hakim Jamil Sidqi al-Zahawi* (Beirut: Matba'at al-Qamus al-'Amm, 1924), xvi-xvii.
94. Zahawi, *Diwan al-Zahawi*, 145–146, 304, 320.
95. "Proceedings of the Council of Ministers," December 29, 1920, CO 730/1/9566.
96. Jamil Sidqi al-Zahawi, "Afiqi!," *al-Hilal* 29:7 (1921), 641, and *Ruba'iyat al-Zahawi*, xviii
97. *al-'Iraq*, September 17, 1921, and al-Zahawi, *Ruba'iyat al-Zahawi*, xviii.
98. Jamil Sidqi al-Zahawi, "Ruba'iyat al-Khayyam," *al-'Usur* 3:13 (1928), 20–26, 3:14 (1928), 187–190, 3:15 (1928), 353–357, and 3:16 (1928), 561–563.
99. *al-'Iraq*, December 15, 1921, 1.
100. *al-'Iraq*, December 19, 1, 21, 1, 22, 1.
101. *al-'Iraq*, December 20, 1921, 1.
102. *al-'Iraq*, December 21, 1921, 1.

103. al-ʿIraq, December 24, 1921, 1.

104. al-ʿIraq, December 26, 1921, 1, and January 3, 1922, 1.

105. "Intelligence Report," no. 28, January 1, 1922, CO 730/19/5810.

106. al-Zahawi, Rubaʿiyat al-Zahawi, xviii–xix.

107. Jamil Sidqi al-Zahawi, "La Talumini," al-Hilal 30:9 (1922), 842.

108. Jamil Sidqi al-Zahawi, "Nahdat al-Sharq al-ʿArabi," al-Hilal 31:7 (1923), 699–703.

109. Jamil Sidqi al-Zahawi, "Nazarat fi al-Nujum," al-Muqtataf 65:2 (1924), 130–131, and "Nakbat al-Yaban," al-Hilal 32:10 (1924), 1028–1031.

110. Khoury, "Looking for the Modern," 120–121, and Fahmi, al-Zahawi, 157–158.

111. Salma Khadra Jayyusi, *Trends and Movements in Modern Arabic Poetry*, vol. 1 (Leiden: Brill, 1977), 152–175.

112. Khoury, "Looking for the Modern," 121.

113. Jamil Sidqi al-Zahawi, "Baʿd al-Qatiʿa," Lughat al-ʿArab 4:3 (1926), 120–121.

114. Jamil Sidqi al-Zahawi, "al-Qariʿa," Lughat al-ʿArab 4:4 (1926), 183–187.

115. Zahawi, "Baʿd al-Qatiʿa," 120–121.

116. Jamil Sidqi al-Zahawi, "Ila Jahannam," al-Hilal 36:1 (1927), 39–40, and "Minka Ana," al-ʿUsur 3:14 (1928), 301–304.

117. Jamil Sidqi al-Zahawi, "Kalama fi al-Shiʿr," Lughat al-ʿArab 6:2 (1928), 117–120.

118. Jamil Sidqi al-Zahawi, "Baʿd Alf ʿAmm," al-Hilal 35:8 (1927), 913–917.

119. Allawi, *Faisal I*, 511–514.

120. Reuven Snir, "'Religion Is for God, the Fatherland Is for Everyone': Arab-Jewish Writers in Modern Iraq and the Clash of Narratives after Their Immigration to Israel," *Journal of the American Oriental Society* 126:3 (2006), 386.

121. Jamil Sidqi al-Zahawi, "Nakbat al-Fallah," Lughat al-ʿArab 7:7 (1929), 529–533, and "Ayyatuha al-Tabiʿa," Lughat al-ʿArab 9:3 (1931), 171–173.

122. Jamil Sidqi al-Zahawi, al-Awshal (Baghdad: Matbaʿat Baghdad, 1934), 72–75.

123. Rushudi, al-Rusafi, 35.

124. Maʿruf al-Rusafi, "Ila al-Shaʿban," al-ʿIraq, December 23, 1921, 1.

125. Maʿruf al-Rusafi, "Fi al-Maʿhad al-ʿIlmi," al-ʿIraq, January 3, 1922, 1.

126. Maʿruf al-Rusafi, "Unshudat al-Watan," al-ʿIraq, January 1, 1922, 10, and Rachel Beckles Willson, *Orientalism and Musical Mission: Palestine and the West* (Cambridge: Cambridge University Press, 2013), 181–183.

127. Maʿruf al-Rusafi, "Nahnu wa al-Madi," al-Hadiqa 1 (1922), 190–195.

128. "Intelligence Report," no. 5, March 1, 1922, CO 730/20/15491.

129. Bashkin, *The Other Iraq*, 190–193.

130. Rusafi, *Diwan al-Rusafi*, 423–425.

131. Amin al-Rihani, *Qalb al-ʿIraq: Rihlat wa al-Taʿrikh* (Cairo: Muʿassasat Hindawi lil-Taʿlim wa al-Thaqafa, 2012), 175.

132. Rushudi, *al-Rusafi*, 36–37.

133. Rusafi, *Diwan al-Rusafi*, 426–428, and Kadhim, *The Poetics of Anti-Colonialism*, 85–130.

134. Qasim al-Khattat, "Hayat al-Rusafi," in *Ma'ruf al-Rusafi Sha'ir al-'Arab al-Kabir: Hayatuhu wa Shi'ruhu*, ed. Qasim al-Khattat, Mustafa 'Abd al-Latif al-Saharti, and Muhammad 'Abd al-Mun'im Khafaji (Cairo: al-Hayah al-Misriyyah al-'Ammah li al-Ta'lif wa al-Nashr, 1971), 113–114.

135. Rushudi, *al-Rusafi*, 38–39, and Khattat, "Hayat al-Rusafi," 114–116.

136. Rusafi, *Diwan al-Rusafi*, 71–73.

137. Rushudi, *al-Rusafi*, 40–41, and Allawi, *Faisal I*, 495–496.

138. Khattat, "Hayat al-Rusafi," 129–130.

139. "Intelligence Report," no. 24, December 13, 1923, CO 730/44/62283.

140. Rusafi, *Diwan al-Rusafi*, 514; Sati' al-Husri, *Mudhakkirati fi al-'Iraq, 1921–1941*, vol. 1 (Beirut: Dar al-Tali'a, 1967), 51; and Wardi, *Lamahat Ijtima'iyya*, 6:23–27.

141. Rusafi, *Diwan al-Rusafi*, 460.

142. Rusafi, *Diwan al-Rusafi*, 461–464.

143. Ma'ruf al-Rusafi, "Hukumatunah al-Intidabiyya," *al-'Usur* 19 (1929), 270–272.

144. "al-Rusafi Yarthi al-Sa'dun," *Filistin*, January 5, 1930, 1, and "Ma'ruf al-Rusafi Yuhajim al-Mu'ahada," *al-Yarmuk*, November 30, 1930, 3.

145. Rusafi, *Diwan al-Rusafi*, 349–351; Rushdi, *al-Zahawi*, 112–117; and Musawi, *Reading Iraq*, 102.

146. Wiebke Walther, "From Women's Problems to Women as Images in Modern Iraqi Poetry," *Die Welt des Islams* 36:2 (1996), 229.

147. Muhammad Baqir al-Shabibi, "al-Mar'a al-Muslima wa al-Tarbia," *Lughat al-'Arab* 2:10 (1913), 445–451.

148. Samira Haj, *Reconfiguring Islamic Tradition: Reform, Rationality, and Modernity* (Stanford: Stanford University Press, 2009), 153–187.

149. Partha Chatterjee, *The Nation and Its Fragments: Colonial and Postcolonial Histories* (Princeton: Princeton University Press, 1993), 3–13.

150. Noga Efrati, *Women in Iraq: Past Meets Present* (New York: Columbia University Press, 2012), 115–123.

151. *al-'Iraq*, December 19, 1921, 1.

152. "Hadhdhabuha!," *al-'Iraq*, December 15, 1921, 1.

153. Jamil Sidqi al-Zahawi, "Sakat Anti?," *al-Hilal* 29:5 (1921), 457; "al-Mar'a wa al-Rajal," *al-Hilal* 29:9 (1921), 837; and "Indifa'at," *al-'Iraq*, January 1, 1922, 2.

154. Jibran Khalil Jibrah, "Qalb al-Mar'a," *al-'Iraq*, January 1, 1922, 9; Hafiz Ibrahim, "al-Umm," *al-'Iraq*, January 1, 1922, 11; and Ilyas Abu Mahdi, "Ilayha," *al-'Iraq*, January 1, 1922, 12.

155. Ibrahim Munib al-Pachachi, "Ila al-Lu'lu'a al-Bayda'," *al-'Iraq*, January 1, 1922, 12.

156. Efrati, *Women in Iraq*, 121–122.

157. ʿAbd al-Rahman al-Bannaʾ, *Dhikra Istiqlal al-ʿIraq: al-Juzʾ al-Thani min Diwan ʾAbd al-Rahman al-Bannaʾ* (Baghdad: Matbaʿat al-Furat, 1927), 137–142.

158. Gerald De Gaury, *Three Kings in Baghdad, 1921–1958* (London: Hutchinson, 1961), 79–80.

159. Maʿruf al-Rusafi, "al-Marʾa fi al-Sharq," *al-Hilal* 30:8 (1922), 714–715.

160. "Intelligence Report," no. 7, April 1, 1922, CO 730/21/19430, and no. 8, April 15, 1922, CO/730/21/21724; Yousif Izzedien, *Poetry and Iraqi Society, 1900–1945* (Baghdad: Matbaʿat al-ʿAni, 1962), 26.

161. Walther, "From Women's Problems to Women as Images," 219–241, and Bashkin, *The Other Iraq*, 31–35.

162. Leila Ahmed, *Women and Gender in Islam: Historical Roots of a Modern Debate* (New Haven: Yale University Press, 1992), 162–163.

163. ʿAbd al-Husayn al-Azri, "Muqatiʿ Shiʿriyya," *al-Nashiʾa* 3 (1922), 117–118.

164. Azri, *Diwan al-Hajj ʾAbd al-Husayn al-Azri*, 30–31.

165. ʿAli al-Khaqani, *Shuʿaraʾ al-Gharri, aw al-Najafiyyat*, vol. 3 (Qum: Maktabat Ayat Allah al-ʿUzma al-Marʿashi al-Najafi, 1988), 272–275.

166. Rusafi, *Diwan al-Rusafi*, 448–449.

167. Maʿruf al-Rusafi, "al-Marʾa al-ʿIraqiyya," *al-Zahraʾ* 2:9 (1925), 542–543, and Rusafi, *Diwan al-Rusafi*, 347–348.

168. Rusafi, *Diwan al-Rusafi*, 354.

169. ʿIzz al-Din, *Khayri al-Hindawi*, 216.

170. Jamil Sidqi al-Zahawi, "al-Marʾa al-Sharqiyya," *al-Hilal* 33:1 (1924), 49–51.

171. Jamil Sidqi al-Zahawi, *al-Lubab: Wa Huwa Mukhtar mima Qaradahu min al-Shiʿr fi Adwar Hayatihi* (Baghdad: Matbaʿat al-Furat, 1928), 325–326.

172. Zahawi, *al-Awshal*, 293–317.

173. Efrati, *Women in Iraq*, 115–123.

174. Jamil Sidqi al-Zahawi, "Rannat al-Awtar al-Sihriyya," *Layla* 1 (1923), 12; Maʿruf al-Rusafi, "ʿAla Jisr Mawd," *Layla* 1 (1923), 13–14; Kazim al-Dujayli, "Ila Layla," *Layla* 1 (1923), 17–18; Muhammad al-Hashimi, "al-Marʾa al-ʿArabiyya," *Layla* 1 (1923), 20–23; Jamil Sidqi al-Zahawi, "Ya Ibna Yuʿarab, *Layla* 3 (1923), 104–105; Jamil Sidqi al-Zahawi, "Bakat fa-la Tamnaʿuha!," *Layla* 4 (1924), 17; Anwar Shaʾul, "Fatat al-ʿIraq," *Layla* 4 (1924), 191; Maʿruf al-Rusafi, "al-Tarbia," *Layla* 5 (1924), 214–215; Muhammad al-Hashimi, "Ya Fatat al-ʿIraq," *Layla* 7 (1924), 313–314; and Jamil Sidqi al-Zahawi, "Kadhalik Yushji al-ʿAndalib idha Ghani," *Layla* 8 (1924), 363–366.

175. Efrati, *Women in Iraq*, 122–123.

176. Sara Pursley, *Familiar Futures: Time, Selfhood, and Sovereignty in Iraq* (Stanford: Stanford University Press, 2019), 78.

177. "Li Yaqraʾha al-Rajaʿiyyun," *al-ʿIraq*, August 26, 1929, in Muhammad Mahdi al-Jawahiri, *Diwan al-Jawahiri*, vol. 1 (Beirut: Bisan, 2000), 391–394.

178. Sami Zubaida, "Al-Jawahiri: Between Patronage and Revolution," *Revue des mondes musulmans et de la Méditerranée* 117–118 (2007), 81–97.

179. Jawahiri, *Dhikrayati*, 1:211–213, and Allawi, *Faisal I*, 494–495.

180. Sami Zubaida, "The Fragments Imagine the Nation: The Case of Iraq," *International Journal of Middle East Studies* 34:2 (2002), 213.

181. Khaqani, *Shu'ara' al-Gharri*, 10:144.

182. Ja'far al-Khalili, *Hakadha 'Araftuhum: Khawatir 'an Unasin Afdhadhin 'Ashu Ba'd al-Ahyan li-Ghayrihim Akthar Mimma 'Ashu li-Anfusihim* (Baghdad: Matba'at al-Zahra', 1963), 268.

183. Muhammad 'Ali Kamal al-Din, *Sa'd Salih* (Baghdad: Matba'at al-Ma'arif, 1949), 147, and 'Abd al-Husayn al- Mubarak, *Thawrat 1920 fi al-Shi'r al-'Iraqi* (Baghdad: Matba'at Dar al-Basri, 1970), 96.

184. Khaqani, *Shu'ara' al-Gharri*, 10:147–149.

185. Muhammad Mahdi al-Jawahiri, "al-'Azm wa Abna'uhu," *al-Istiqlal*, January 26, 1921, in Jawahiri, *Diwan al-Jawahiri*, 1:53–54.

186. Stephen Sheehi, *Foundations of Modern Arab Identity* (Gainesville: University of Florida Press, 2004), 189–197.

187. Jawahiri, *Dhikrayati*, 1:107–109.

188. Muhammad Mahdi al-Jawahiri, "Thawrat al-'Iraq," *al-'Irfan* 9:7 (1924), 599–601.

189. "Intelligence Report," no. 9, May 1, 1922, CO/730/21/24559.

190. Muhammad Mahdi al-Jawahiri, "Tahiya al-Malik wa al-Intidab," *al-Rafidan*, May 27, 1922, in Jawahiri, *Diwan al-Jawahiri* (Najaf), 55–56.

191. "Intelligence Report," no. 12, June 15, 1922, CO/730/22/32435, and Allawi, *Faisal I*, 398–399.

192. Muhammad Mahdi al-Jawahiri, "Amin al-Rihani," *al-'Irfan* 8:3 (1922), 207–208.

193. "Intelligence Report," no. 5, January 15, 1921, CO/7301/11341; no. 6, January 31, 1921, CO 730/1/14659; and no. 7, February 14, 1921, CO 730/1/15772.

194. "Intelligence Report," no. 8, March 1, 1921, CO 730/1/17770, and no. 24, December 13, 1923, CO 730/44/62283; Percy Cox to Winston Churchill, September 12, 1921, CO 730/5/46048.

195. "Intelligence Report," no. 22, October 1, 1921, CO 730/6/52859; 'Abdullah al-Dulaymi, "Hawl Mas'alat al-Ma'arif," *al-'Iraq*, August 24, 1921, 2; and Husri, *Mudhakkirati*, 1:369–375.

196. Muhammad Rida al-Shabibi, "al-Qaramata wa al-Ikhwan," *al-'Iraq*, January 1, 1922, 4.

197. 'Ali al-Sharqi, *Diwan al-Sharqi* (Baghdad: Dar al-Hurriyya lil-Taba'a, 1979), 153–154, 161.

198. 'Ali al-Sharqi, "Sharar," *al-'Irfan* 13:9 (1926), 1023.

199. Muhammad Baqir al-Shabibi, "Anwabuna," *al-Nahda*, November 30, 1928, in Hilali, *al-Sha'ir al-Tha'ir*, 78.

200. Orit Bashkin, "The Iraqi Afghanis and 'Abduhs: Debate over Reform among Shi'ite and Sunni 'Ulama' in Interwar Iraq," in *Guardians of Faith in Modern Times: 'Ulama' in the Middle East*, ed. Meir Hatina (Leiden: Brill, 2009), 146–164

201. Khaqani, *Shu'ara' al-Gharri*, 10:145.

202. Bashkin, *The Other Iraq*, 47–48.

203. Jawahiri, *Diwan al-Jawahiri* (Najaf), 221–223.

204. Husri, *Mudhakkirati*, 1:588–590.

205. Muhammad Mahdi al-Jawahiri, "Barid al-Ghurba," *al-Fayha'*, March 31, 1927, in Jawahiri, *Diwan al-Jawahiri*, 1: 295–296.

206. 'Ali al-Sharqi, "al-Almas fi al-Fahm," *al-Najaf*, May 8, 1926, in Sharqi, *Diwan al-Sharqi*, 185–186.

207. Husri, *Mudhakkirati*, 1:590.

208. Fanar Haddad, *Sectarianism in Iraq: Antagonistic Vision of Unity* (New York: Columbia University Press, 2011), 43–51.

209. Husri, *Mudhakkirati*, 1:591–602, and al-Jawahiri, *Dhikrayati*, 1:147–152.

210. Jawahiri, *Dhikrayati*, 1:179–185.

211. Allawi, *Faisal I*, 493–495.

212. Jawahiri, *Dhikrayati*, 1:211–214.

213. Muhammad Mahdi al-Jawahiri, "Sababat Sha'ir," *al-'Iraq*, October 23, 1929, in Jawahiri, *Diwan al-Jawahiri*, 1:411–413. See also Jawahiri, *Dhikrayati*, 1:214–216, and Allawi, *Faisal I*, 495.

214. Sharqi, *Diwan al-Sharqi*, 187–189; Allawi, *Faisal I*, 496; and Sugata Bose, *A Hundred Horizons: The Indian Ocean in the Age of Global Empire* (Cambridge, MA: Harvard University Press, 2006), 260–271.

215. Rabindranath Tagore, *Journey to Persia and Iraq: 1932* (Kolkata: Visva-Bharati, 2003), 99.

216. Tagore, *Journey to Persia and Iraq*, 144–146.

217. Jamil Sidqi al-Zahawi, "Rabindranath Tagore," *al-Ma'rifa* 2:2 (1932), 159–160, and Tagore, *Journey to Persia and Iraq*, 103.

218. Muhammad Bahjat al-Athari, *Malahim . . . Wa Azhar* (Cairo: al-Hay'ah al-Misriyyah al-'Ammah li al-Kitab, 1974), 71–72.

219. Bose, *A Hundred Horizons*, 260–271, and Pankaj Mishra, *From the Ruins of Empire: The Intellectuals Who Remade Asia* (New York: Farrar, Straus, and Giroux, 2012), 216–241.

220. Haifa Zangana, *City of Widows: An Iraqi Woman's Account of War and Resistance* (New York: Seven Stories Press, 2007), 31–32.

221. Um Nizar al-Mala'ika, *Anshudat al-Majid* (Baghdad: Matba'at al-Tadamun, 1965).

## Chapter 4

1. Muhammad Bahjat al-Athari, *Malahim . . . wa Azhar* (Cairo: al-Hay'a al-Misriyya al-'Amma lil-Kitab, 1974), 71–72.

2. "Intelligence Reports: Pan-Islamism and Pan-Arabianism, 1931–32," November 5, 1932, AIR 23/405 I/402/5/A, and Ra'uf al-Wa'iz, *al-Ittijahat al-Wataniyya fi al-Shi'r al-'Iraqi al-Hadith, 1914–1941* (Baghdad: Wizarat al-I'lam 1974), 296–301.

3. C. J. Edmonds to Kinahan Cornwallis, July 2, 1941, "Political Situation," FO 624/60; July 14, 1941, "Press," FO 624/24; and July 26, 1941, "Germany: Propaganda," FO 624/24.

4. Muhammad Bahjat al-Athari, *Diwan al-Athari*, vol. 1 (Baghdad: Matba'at al-Majma' al-'Ilmi al-'Iraqi, 1990), 372–390, and al-Wa'iz, *al-Ittijahat al-Wataniyya*, 286–289.

5. Athari, *Diwan al-Athari*, 1:432–436.

6. Yusuf 'Izz al-Din, *Shu'ara' al-'Iraq fi al-Qarn al-'Ishrin* (Baghdad: Matba'at al-As'ad, 1969), 96–97, and Matthew Elliott, *"Independent Iraq": The Monarchy and British Influence, 1941–58* (London: Tauris, 1996), 44–49.

7. Muhammad Bahjat al-Athari, "al-Filastin al-Damiyya," *al-Zahra'* 5:7–8 (1928), 505–506, and "Ya Filastin," *al-Risala*, November 28, 1938, 1953.

8. Muhammad Bahjat al-Athari, "Imara'atan 'Azimatan min Dawlat al-Mughul," *al-Risala*, February 25, 1952, 210–213.

9. Waïl S. Hassan, "Postcolonial Theory and Modern Arabic Literature: Horizons of Application," *Journal of Arabic Literature* 33:1 (2002), 45–64), 55–81, and Atef Alshaer, *Poetry and Politics in the Modern Arab World* (London: Hurst, 2016), 1–11.

10. Anne McClintock, "The Angel of Progress: Pitfalls of the Term 'Post-Colonialism,'" *Social Text* 31/32 (1992), 84–98.

11. Amatzia Baram, "A Case of Imported Identity: The Modernizing Secular Ruling Elites of Iraq and the Conception of Mesopotamian-Inspired Territorial Nationalism, 1922–1992," *Poetics Today* 15 (1994), 273–319; Sami Zubaida, "The Fragments Imagine the Nation: The Case of Iraq," *International Journal of Middle East Studies* 34:2 (2002), 205–215; Eric Davis, *Memories of State: Politics, History, and Collective Identity in Modern Iraq* (Berkeley: University of California Press, 2005); and Orit Bashkin, "Hybrid Nationalisms: Watani and Qawmi Visions in Iraq under 'Abd al-Karim Qasim," *International Journal of Middle East Studies* 43:2 (2011), 293–312.

12. Reeva Spector Simon, *Iraq between the Two World Wars: The Creation and Implementation of a Nationalist Ideology* (New York: Columbia University Press, 1986). For a more nuanced view, see Peter Wien, *Iraqi Arab Nationalism: Authoritarian, Totalitarian, and Pro-Fascist Inclinations, 1932–1941* (London: Routledge, 2006).

13. Toby Dodge, *Inventing Iraq: The Failure of Nation Building and a History Denied* (New York: Columbia University Press, 2003), 30–41; Peter Sluglett, *Britain in Iraq: Contriving King and Country, 1914–1932* (New York: Columbia University Press, 2007),

105–124; and Susan Pederson, "Getting Out of Iraq—in 1932: The League of Nations and the Road to Normative Statehood," *American Historical Review* 115:4 (2010), 975–1000.

14. Waʿiz, *al-Ittijahat al-Wataniyya*, 181–183.

15. Muhammad ʿAli al-Yaʿqubi, *Diwan Muhammad ʿAli al-Yaʿqubi*, vol. 1 (Najaf: Matbaʿat al-Nuʿman, 1957), 198.

16. Mahmud al-Habbubi, *Diwan Mahmud al-Habbubi* (Najaf: Matbaʿat Dar al-Nashr wa al-Taʾlif, 1948), 70.

17. Waʿiz, *al-Ittijahat al-Wataniyya*, 183–185.

18. Habbubi, *Diwan Mahmud al-Habbubi*, 22–23.

19. ʿAli al-Khaqani, *Shuʿaraʾ al-Gharri, aw al-Najafiyyat*, vol. 9 (Qum: Maktabat Ayat Allah al-ʿUzma al-Marʿashi al-Najafi, 1988), 321.

20. Muhammad Salih Bahr al-ʿUlum, *Diwan Bahr al-ʿUlum*, vol. 1 (Baghdad: Matbaʿat Dar al-Tadamun, 1968), 59.

21. Jaʿfar al-Khalili, "al-Muqaddima," in Muhammad Salih Bahr al-ʿUlum, *al-Awatif* (Najaf: Matbaʿat al-Raʿi, 1937), 7, and ʿAbd al-Razzaq al-Hilali, *al-Shaʿir al-Thaʾir: al-Shaykh Muhammad Baqir al-Shabibi 1889–1960* (Baghdad: Maktabat al-Nahda, 1965), 74–75.

22. Bahr al-ʿUlum, *Diwan Bahr al-ʿUlum*, 1:55–56.

23. Bahr al-ʿUlum, *Diwan Bahr al-ʿUlum*, 1:31.

24. Khalili, "al-Muqaddima," 12–13, and Bahr al-ʿUlum, *Diwan Bahr al-ʿUlum*, 1:30, 1:33–134.

25. Zubaida, "The Fragments Imagine the Nation," and Bashkin, "Hybrid Nationalisms."

26. Bahr al-ʿUlum, *Diwan Bahr al-ʿUlum*, 1:31, 1:36.

27. "Memorandum: Anti-Ikhwan Agitation in Najaf," February 5, 1927, AIR 23/429 I/D/23.

28. Bahr al-ʿUlum, *Diwan Bahr al-ʿUlum*, 1:43.

29. Bahr al-ʿUlum, *Diwan Bahr al-ʿUlum*, 1:38, and al-Khaqani, *Shuʿaraʾ al-Gharri*, 9:321–324.

30. Bahr al-ʿUlum, *Diwan Bahr al-ʿUlum*, 1:11, 1:41–42.

31. Bahr al-ʿUlum, *Diwan Bahr al-ʿUlum*, 44–46.

32. Bahr al-ʿUlum, *Diwan Bahr al-ʿUlum*, 1:11.

33. Bahr al-ʿUlum, *Diwan Bahr al-ʿUlum*, 1:57–60.

34. Bahr al-ʿUlum, *Diwan Bahr al-ʿUlum*, 1:65.

35. Khaqani, *Shuʿaraʾ al-Gharri*, 9:324.

36. Bahr al-ʿUlum, *Diwan Bahr al-ʿUlum*, 1:73–75.

37. Bahr al-ʿUlum, *Diwan Bahr al-ʿUlum*, 85–87.

38. Bahr al-ʿUlum, *Diwan Bahr al-ʿUlum*, 12.

39. Muhammad Mahdi al-Jawahiri, *Dhikrayati*, vol. 1 (Damascus: Dar al-Rafidayn, 1988), 219–221.

40. Muhammad Mahdi al-Jawahiri, "al-Awbash aw (Maslakhat) al-Qadha' wa Nizamat," *al-'Iraq*, May 29, 1931, in Muhammad Mahdi al-Jawahiri, *Diwan al-Jawahiri*, vol. 2 (Beirut: Bisan: 2000), 69–73.

41. Samira Haj, *The Making of Iraq, 1900–1963: Capital, Power, and Ideology* (Albany: State University of New York Press, 1997), 33–38.

42. Jawahiri, *Diwan al-Jawahiri*, 2:221.

43. Bahr al-'Ulum, *Diwan Bahr al-'Ulum*, 1:104.

44. Mahmud al-Mallah, "al-'Aqaba," *al-Ikha' al-Watani*, January 6, 1935, in Wa'iz, *al-Ittijahat al-Wataniyya*, 195.

45. *Iraq: Annual Report for 1935*, FO 371/20010 E 851/851/93, and Majid Khadduri, *Independent Iraq, 1932–1958: A Study in Iraqi Politics*, 2nd ed. (London: Oxford University Press, 1960), 49–53.

46. Muhammad Ja'far Abu al-Timman, "al-Baladiyyat wa Wajibatuha," *al-Mabda'*, March 4, 1935, 1, and "Quarterly Report on the Royal Iraqi Air Force," July 1, 1935, AIR 2/1343.

47. Bahr al-'Ulum, *Diwan Bahr al-'Ulum*, 1: 12–13.

48. Bahr al-'Ulum, *Diwan Bahr al-'Ulum*, 1:104–105.

49. Muhammad Salih Bahr al-'Ulum, "al-Falah," *al-Iqtisad*, December 17, 1934, in Bahr al-'Ulum, *al-Awatif*, 119–124.

50. Bahr al-'Ulum, *Diwan Bahr al-'Ulum*, 1:13.

51. *Iraq: Annual Report for 1935*, FO 371/20010 E 851/851/93.

52. Bahr al-'Ulum, *Diwan Bahr al-'Ulum*, 1:109.

53. Basri, *A'lam al-Adab*, 1:180–181.

54. Intelligence Reports on Rumaitha, October 25, 1935, AIR 5/1270.

55. Jawahiri, *Dhikrayati*, 1:310.

56. Muhammad Mahdi al-Jawahiri, "Halluna (fi Sabil al-Hukm)," *al-Islah*, October 12, 1935, in Jawahiri, *Diwan al-Jawahiri*, 2:247–249.

57. Jawahiri, *Dhikrayati*, 1:309–324.

58. Muzaffar 'Abd Allah al-Amin, *Jama'at al-Ahali: Munshu'ha, 'Aqidatuha, wa Dawruha fi al-Siyyasa al-'Iraqiyya, 1932–1946* (Beirut: al-Mu'assasa al-'Arabiyya lil-Dirasat wa al-Nashr, 2001), 104–134, and Orit Bashkin, *The Other Iraq: Pluralism and Culture in Hashemite Iraq* (Stanford: Stanford University Press, 2009), 61–69.

59. Clark Kerr to Foreign Office, November 23, 1936, FO 371/20014 E 7599/1419/93, and Wa'iz, *al-Ittijahat al-Wataniyya*, 249–291.

60. Bahr al-'Ulum, *Diwan Bahr al-'Ulum*, 1:122–123.

61. Ahmad al-Safi al-Najafi, "Dawla 'ala Atlal al-Madhi," *al-Haris*, November 18, 1936, in Wa'iz, *al-Ittijahat al-Wataniyya*, 271–272.

62. Nu'man Mahir al-Kan'ani, "Wahi al-Inqilab," *al-Haras*, November 21, 1936, in Wa'iz, *al-Ittijahat al-Wataniyya*, 266–268.

63. Fu'ad Husayn al-Wakil, *Jama'at al-Ahali fi al-'Iraq, 1932–1937* (Baghdad: Dar al-Rashid li al-Nashr, 1979), 285.

64. Clark Kerr to Foreign Office, November 20, 1936, FO 371/20014 E 7851/1419/93; Bahr al-'Ulum, *Diwan Bahr al-'Ulum*, 1:13; Hanna Batatu, *The Old Social Classes and the Revolutionary Movements of Iraq: A Study of Iraq's Old Landed and Commercial Classes and of Its Communists, Ba'thists and Free Officers* (Princeton: Princeton University Press, 1979), 439–440; and Khalid al-Tamimi, *Muhammad Ja'far Abu al-Timman: Dirasa fi al-Za'ama al-Siyasiyya al'-Iraqiyya* (Damascus: Dar al-Warraq, 1996), 402–415.

65. Bahr al-'Ulum, *Diwan Bahr al-'Ulum*, 1:124.

66. Batatu, *The Old Social Classes*, 440n7

67. Muhsin al-Musawi, "Muhammad Mahdi al-Jawahiri," in *Essays in Arabic Literary Biography, 1850–1950*, ed. Roger Allen (Wiesbaden: Harrassowitz Verlag, 2010), 169.

68. Muhammad Rida al-Khatib, "Dhikra al-Madhi al-Aswad," *al-Inqilab*, January 7, 1937, in al-Wa'iz, *al-Ittijahat al-Wataniyya*, 268–270.

69. Wa'iz, *al-Ittijahat al-Wataniyya*, 255–256.

70. Muhammad Mahdi al-Jawahiri, "Taharrak al-Lahd," *al-Inqilab*, January 19, 1937, in al-Jawahiri, *Diwan al-Jawahiri*, 2:289–290.

71. Wa'iz, *al-Ittijahat al-Wataniyya*, 256–257.

72. Muhammad Salih Bahr al-'Ulum, "Qanun Jabr al-Khawatir," al-*Inqilab*, January 21, 1937, in Bahr al-"Ulum, *al-Awatif*, 141–142.

73. Muhammad Salih Bahr al-'Ulum, "Rab al-Qasr fi al-Nawm," al-*Inqilab*, January 21, 1937, in Bahr al-"Ulum, *al-Awatif*, 142.

74. Muhammad Salih Bahr al-'Ulum, "Fajr al-Aryaf," *al-Inqilab*, January 21, 1937, in Bahr al-"Ulum, *al-Awatif*, 142–143.

75. Husayn Jamil, *al-Haya al-Niyabiyya fi al'-Iraq, 1925–1946: Mawqif Jama'at al-Ahali minha* (Baghdad: Maktabat al-Muthanna, 1983), 294–296, 319–320.

76. *Iraq: Annual Report for 1936*, FO 371/20803 E 1055/1055/93; Kamil al-Chadirchi, *Mudhakkirat Kamil al-Chadirchi wa Ta'rikh al-Hizb al-Watani al-Dimuqrati* (Beirut: Dar al-Tali'a, 1970), 31–45; and Rafa'il Butti, *Dhakira 'Iraqiyya, 1900–1956*, vol. 1 (Damascus: al-Mada, 2000), 259–302.

77. Batatu, *The Old Social Classes*, 442–444; Jamil, *al-Haya al-Niyabiyya*, 272–296, 319–320; and Tamimi, *Muhammad Ja'far Abu al-Timman*, 419–420.

78. 'Abd al-Qadir al-Zahawi, "Ya Nafs," *al-Inqilab*, March 17, 1937, in Wa'iz, *al-Ittijahat al-Wataniyya*, 262–263.

79. Tamimi, *Muhammad Ja'far Abu al-Timman*, 420.

80. Batatu, *The Old Social Classes*, 443.

81. Muhammad Mahdi al-Jawahiri, "Amin al-Rihani," *al-'Irfan* 8:3 (1922), 207–208.

82. Amin al-Rihani, *Qalb al-ʿIraq: Rihlat wa al-Taʾrikh* (Cairo: Muʾassassat Hindawi li al-Taʿlim wa al-Thaqafah, 2012), 152–153.

83. Jawahiri, *Dhikrayati*, 1:327–329.

84. Jawahiri, *Dhikrayati*, 1:330–331.

85. Salim Taha al-Tikriti, *Muhammad Mahdi al-Jawahiri* (London: Riyadh al-Rayyis lil-Kutub wa al-Nashr, 1989), 22–24; Sulayman Jubran, *Majmaʿ al-Addad: Dirasa fi Sirat al-Jawahiri wa Shaʿrihi* (Beirut: al-Muʾassassa al-ʿArabiyya lil-Dirasat wa al-Nashr, 2003), 45–46; and Sasson Somekh, *Baghdad, Yesterday: The Making of an Arab Jew* (Jerusalem: Ibis Editions, 2007), 163–164

86. Taha al-Hashimi, *Mudhakkirat Taha al-Hashimi, 1919–1943* (Beirut: Dar al-Taliʿa, 1967), 201.

87. Jawahiri, *Dhikrayati*, 1:337–338.

88. Jawahiri, *Diwan al-Jawahiri*, 2:294–296.

89. Bahr al-ʿUlum, *Diwan Bahr al-ʿUlum*, 1:126.

90. Bahr al-ʿUlum, *Diwan Bahr al-ʿUlum*, 1:136.

91. Hasani, *Taʾrikh al-Wizarat al-ʿIraqiyyah*, 5:5–20; Jamil, *al-Haya al-Niyabiyya*, 347–353; and Amin, *Jamaʿat al-Ahali*, 232–234.

92. Waʿiz, *al-Ittijahat al-Wataniyya*, 275–278, and Jamil, *al-Haya al-Niyabiyya*, 253–261.

93. ʿAbd al-Husayn al-Azri, *Diwan al-Hajj ʿAbd al-Husayn al-Azri* (Beirut: al-Nuʿman, 1980), 98–99.

94. ʿAli al-Sharqi, *Diwan al-Sharqi* (Baghdad: Dar al-Rashid lil-Nashr, 1979), 232–235.

95. Alshaer, *Poetry and Politics*, 54–55.

96. Maʿruf al-Rusafi, "Khutba fi al-Shuyuʿiyya," in *al-Rusafi Khatiban: Majmuʿ Khutabihi fi Majlis al-Nawwab, 1930–1939*, ed. Mustafa ʿAli and ʿAbd al-Hamid al-Rushudi (Damascus: Dar al-Mada, 2014), 136–137.

97. Maʿruf al-Rusafi, *Diwan al-Rusafi*, vol. 3 (Beirut: Dar al-Muntazar, 1999), 181–184.

98. Michael Provence, *The Last Ottoman Generation and the Making of the Modern Middle East* (Cambridge: Cambridge University Press, 2017), 241–249, and Peter Wien, *Arab Nationalism: The Politics of History and Culture in the Modern Middle East* (London: Routledge, 2017), 121–122.

99. Peter Wien, "The Long and Intricate Funeral of Yasin al-Hashimi: Pan-Arabism, Civil Religion, and Popular Nationalism in Damascus, 1937," *International Journal of Middle East Studies* 43:2 (2011), 271–292.

100. Muhammad Mahdi al-Jawahiri, "Dhikra al-Hashimi," *al-Raʾi al-ʿAmm*, February 12, 1938, in Jawahiri, *Diwan al-Jawahiri*, 2:303–304.

101. Athari, *Malahim*, 73–83.

102. Orit Bashkin, "The Iraqi Afghanis and ʿAbduhs: Debate over Reform among

Shiʿite and Sunni ʿUlamaʾ in Interwar Iraq," in *Guardians of Faith in Modern Times: ʿUlamaʾ in the Middle East*, ed. Meir Hatina (Leiden: Brill, 2009), 165.

103. *Iraq: Annual Report for 1938*, FO 371/23214 E 932/932/93.

104. Waʿiz, *al-Ittijahat al-Wataniyya*, 260–261.

105. Jawahiri, *Dhikrayati*, 1:341–351. See, for example, Muhammad Mahdi al-Jawahiri, "Yawm Filistin," *al-Raʾi al-ʿAmm*, May 5, 1938, in Jawahiri, *Diwan al-Jawahiri*, 2:313.

106. Izzedien, *Poetry and Iraqi Society*, 36.

107. Jawahiri, *Diwan al-Jawahiri*, 2:329–331.

108. Bahr al-ʿUlum, *Diwan Bahr al-ʿUlum*, 1:140.

109. Wien, *Iraqi Arab Nationalism*, and Orit Bashkin, "Iraqi Shadows, Iraqi Lights: Anti-Fascist and Anti-Nazi Voices in Monarchic Iraq, 1932–1941," in *Arab Responses to Fascism and Nazim: Attraction and Repulsion*, ed. Israel Gershoni (Austin: University of Texas Press, 2014), 141–168.

110. Wien, *Iraqi Arab Nationalism*, 78–105.

111. Houstoun Boswell to Foreign Office, October 4, 1938, FO 371/21861 E 6068/6068/93, and April 10, 1939, FO 371/23201 E 2626/72/93.

112. A. H. Marsack, "Enemy and Allied Publicity and Propaganda," May 13, 1940, "Germany: Propaganda," FO 624/18, and C. J. Edmonds to V. Holt, September 23, 1940, "Publicity and Propaganda: Press Bulletin," FO 624/20.

113. Dr. Herbert Melzig, "A Memorandum on German Propaganda in the Near-East," and "Enemy and Allied Publicity and Propaganda" by A. H. Marsack, Air Liaison Officer, Mosul, May 13, 1940, "Germany: Propaganda," FO 624/18.

114. al-Rusafi, *Diwan al-Rusafi* (1999), 3:348–353.

115. Jonathan Derrick, *Africa's "Agitators": Militant Anti-Colonialism in Africa and the West, 1918–1939* (New York: Columbia University Press, 2008); Götz Nordbruch, *Nazism in Syria and Lebanon: The Ambivalence of the German Option, 1933–1945* (London: Routledge, 2009); Israel Gershoni and James Jankowski, *Confronting Fascism in Egypt: Dictatorship versus Democracy in the 1930s* (Stanford: Stanford University Press, 2010); and Sugata Bose, *His Majesty's Opponent: Subhas Chandra Bose and India's Struggle against Empire* (Cambridge, MA: Belknap Press of Harvard University Press, 2011), 203.

116. Bahr al-ʿUlum, *Diwan Bahr al-ʿUlum*, 1:92.

117. Bahr al-ʿUlum, *Diwan Bahr al-ʿUlum*, 1:116.

118. Bahr al-ʿUlum, *Diwan Bahr al-ʿUlum*, 1:146.

119. Basil Newton to Foreign Office, October 9, 1940, "Press," FO 624/18, and Jawahiri, *Dhikrayati*, 1:333.

120. Mahmud al-Durrah, *al-Harb al-ʿIraqiyya al-Britaniyya* (Cairo: Dar al-Maʿrifa, 1982), 122–124.

121. Bahr al-ʿUlum, *Diwan Bahr al-ʿUlum*, 1:177.

122. Kinahan Cornwallis to Foreign Office, April 29, 1941, FO 371/27067; General Wavell to War Office, May 3, 1941, FO 371/27069; and Kinahan Cornwallis to Foreign Office, June 6, 1941, FO 406/79.

123. Muhammad Bahjat al-Athari, "Tashyi' Jinazat Britaniyyah," *al-Bilad*, May 7, 1941, in al-Athari, *Diwan al-Athari*, 1:391–399.

124. 'Abd al-Karim al-'Allaf, "Ba'd 'Ashrin Sana Aqafu bi-Wajh al-Wahsh al-Britani," *al-Istiqlal*, May 22, 1941, in al-Wa'iz, *al-Ittijahat al-Wataniyya*, 302–303.

125. 'Abd al-Sahib al-Dujayli, "Wa Ib'athuha Sarkhat al-Dawiyya," *al-Istiqlal*, May 22, 1941, in Wa'iz, *al-Ittijahat al-Wataniyya*, 303–304.

126. Ahmad al-Safi al-Najafi, "Wathbat al-'Iraq," *al-Bilad*, May 20, 1941, in Wa'iz, *al-Ittijahat al-Wataniyya*, 305.

127. Ahmad al-Safi al-Najafi, "Ana 'Arabi," *Kazima* 1:5 (1948), 180.

128. Kinahan Cornwallis to Foreign Office, June 6, 1941, FO 406/79.

129. Batatu, *The Old Social Classes*, 451–462.

130. Bahr al-'Ulum, *Diwan Bahr al-'Ulum*, 1:178.

131. Bahr al-'Ulum, *Diwan Bahr al-'Ulum*, 1:179–84.

132. Qasim al-Khattat, "Hayat al-Rusafi," in *Ma'ruf al-Rusafi Sha'ir al-'Arab al-Kabir: Hayatuhu wa Shi'ruhu*, ed. Qasim al-Khattat, Mustafa 'Abd al-Latif al-Saharti, and Muhammad 'Abd al-Mun'im Khafaji (Cairo: al-Hayah al-Misriyyah al-'Ammah li al-Ta'lif wa al-Nashr, 1971), 171.

133. John Glubb, "A Report on the Role Played by the Arab Legion in Connection with the Recent Operations in Iraq," June 10, 1941, CAB 106/512.

134. Rusafi, *Diwan al-Rusafi* (1999), 3:343–346.

135. 'Abd al-Hamid Rushudi, *al-Rusafi: Hayatuhu, Atharuhu, Shi'ruhu* (Baghdad: Dar al-Shu'un al-Thaqafiyyah al-'Ammah, 1988), 44–45.

136. Simon, *Iraq between the Two World Wars*, 148–149.

137. Bahr al-'Ulum, *Diwan Bahr al-'Ulum*, 1:185

138. Orit Bashkin, *The New Babylonians: A History of Jews in Modern Iraq* (Stanford: Stanford University Press, 2012), 116–122.

139. Bahr al-'Ulum, *Diwan Bahr al-'Ulum*, 1:187.

140. Bahr al-'Ulum, *Diwan Bahr al-'Ulum*, 1:188.

141. Bahr al-'Ulum, *Diwan Bahr al-'Ulum*, 1:14.

142. Agha Dhahir Bin Agha Tahir to British Embassy, August 7, 1941, "Foreigners: Internment," FO 624/25; Muhammad Taqi Muhammad Husayn to British Embassy, August 15, 1941, "Political Situation," FO 624/60; Sayyid Jabr al-Muntafji to British Embassy, August 20, 1941, "Foreigners: Internment," FO 624/25, and 'Abbas al-'Alwan to British Embassy, August 25, 1941, "Prisoners of War: British," FO 624/25; Kinahan Cornwallis to Foreign Office, December 14, 1941, FO 371/31371 E 258/204/93; and Talib Mushtaq, *Awraq Ayyami, 1900–1958* (Beirut: Dar al-Tali'a, 1968), 418–433.

143. C. J. Edmonds to Kinahan Cornwallis, July 2, 1941, "Political Situation," FO

624/60, and July 14, 1941, "Press," FO 624/24; "Nazi Propaganda in Iraq," enclosed in secret dispatch from C. J. Edmonds to Kinahan Cornwallis, July 26, 1941, "Germany: Propaganda," FO 624/24.

144. ʿAmarah Consulate, Report for Period Ending November 23, 1941, FO 838/1; Kinahan Cornwallis to Foreign Office, March 23, 1943, FO 371/35010 E 1667/489/93; and Mushtaq, *Awraq Ayyami*, 428–459

145. British Embassy to Iraqi Ministry of Foreign Affairs, December 19, 1941, "British Forces: Incidents," FO 624/25; and Bahr al-ʿUlum, *Diwan Bahr al-ʿUlum*, 1:194

146. ʿAli Mahmud al-Shaykh ʿAli, *Muhakimatuna al-Wijahiyya* (Sidon: Dar al-Maktaba al-ʿAsriyya, 1966), 201–204.

147. al-Athari, *Diwan al-Athari*, 1:419–420.

148. al-Athari, *Diwan al-Athari*, 1:406.

149. al-Jawahiri, *Dhikrayati*, 1:367–382.

150. C. J. Edmonds to V. Holt, November 4, 1941 "Press," FO 624/24.

151. al-Athari, *Diwan al-Athari*, 1:432–436.

152. Bahr al-ʿUlum, *Diwan Bahr al-ʿUlum*, 1:14–15.

153. Bahr al-ʿUlum, *Diwan Bahr al-ʿUlum*, 1:199–200.

154. Bahr al-ʿUlum, *Diwan Bahr al-ʿUlum*, 1:201–204

155. Bahr al-ʿUlum, *Diwan Bahr al-ʿUlum*, 1:209.

156. Ahmad al-Safi al-Najafi, *Hasad al-Sijn* (Beirut: Maktabat al-Maʿarif, 1964), 110–111.

157. Ahmad al-Safi al-Najafi, *Mudhakkirat al-Shaʿir Ahmad al-Safi al-Najafi* (Jubayl: Dar wa al-Maktabat Bibliyun, 2011), 228–238.

158. Ahmad Safi al-Najafi, *al-Shallal* (Beirut: Dar al-ʿIlm li al-Malayyin, 1962), 206–207, and Najafi, *Mudhakkirat*, 126.

159. Khattat, "Hayat al-Rusafi," 166–176.

160. Rusafi, *Diwan al-Rusafi* (1999), 3:340–343.

161. C. J. Edmonds to Kinahan Cornwallis, July 2, 1941, "Political Situation," FO 624/60.

162. Rusafi, *Diwan al-Rusafi* (1999), 3:244–247.

163. C. J. Edmonds to Kinahan Cornwallis, June 16, 1941, "Political Situation," FO 624/60.

164. ʿAbd al-Husayn al-Huwayzi, *Diwan al-Huwayzi* (Beirut: Dar Maktabat al-Haya, 1964), 134–136.

165. ʿAbd al-Husayn al-Huwayzi, "Basma Taʿali," *al-Akhbar*, October 4, 1941, in Waʿiz, *al-Ittijahat al-Wataniyya*, 311–312.

166. Yaʿqubi, *Diwan al-Yaʿqubi*, 1:167.

167. Muhammad ʿAli al-Yaʿqubi, "Aʿadta ʿala Baghdad bi-Radd Jamaliha," *al-Akhbar*, September 21, 1941, in Waʿiz, *al-Ittijahat al-Wataniyya*, 315–316.

168. Waʿiz, *al-Ittijahat al-Wataniyya*, 316–332.

169. Muhammad Mahdi al-Jawahiri, "al-Dimuqratiyyah fi al-Jibhat al-Sharqiyyah," *al-Raʾi al-ʿAmm*, December 25, 1941, in Jawahiri, *Diwan al-Jawahiri*, 2:348.

170. al-Tikriti, *Muhammad Mahdi al-Jawahiri*, 25–26.

171. Wilkins to V. Holt, October 20, 1941, "Communism," FO 624/25, and Mosul Consulate to British Embassy, May 13, 1943, "Situation: Mosul," FO 624/33

172. Combined Intelligence Centre, "Communism in Iraq," "Communism," FO 624/25, and C. J. Edmonds to Kinahan Cornwallis, November 29, 1944, "Political Situation," FO 624/67.

173. Muhammad Mahdi al-Jawahiri, "Stalingrad," *al-Raʾi al-ʿAmm*, February 21, 1943, in al-Jawahiri, *Diwan al-Jawahiri*, 2:363–367.

174. British Embassy to Foreign Office, July 17, July 24, and October 16, 1941, "Publicity: Public Opinion on the War," FO 624/22.

175. C.I.C. Report on "Communism in Iraq," C.I.D. Report, January 18, 1942, Wilkins to V. Holt, September 30, October 20, 1941, "Communism," FO 624/25.

176. Chadirchi, *Mudhakkirat Kamil al-Chadirchi*, 55–68, and Muhammad Mahdi Kubba, *Mudhakkirati fi Samim al-Ahdath, 1918–1958* (Beirut: Manshurat Dar al-Taliʿa, 1965).

177. Anwar Shaʾul, *Qissat Hayati fi Wadi al-Rafidayn* (Jerusalem: Manshurat Rabitat al-Jamiʿiyin al-Yahud al-Nazihin min al-ʿIraq, 1980), 251–256.

178. Muhammad Mahdi al-Jawahiri, "Tunis," *al-Raʾi al-ʿAmm*, May 26, 1943, in Jawahiri, *Diwan al-Jawahiri*, 2:397–400. See also Tikriti, *Muhammad Mahdi al-Jawahiri*, 32–39.

179. Jawahiri, *Dhikrayati*, 1:375–376.

180. Muhammad Mahdi al-Jawahiri, "Sawastabul," *al-Raʾi al-ʿAmm*, July 2, 1941, and "Yawm al-Jaysh al-Ahmar," *al-Raʾi al-ʿAmm*, February 26, 1943, in Jawahiri, *Diwan al-Jawahiri*, 2:352–356, 369.

181. Kinahan Cornwallis to Foreign Office, January 16, 1945, FO 371/45302 E 626/195/93.

182. ʿAmarah Consulate, Report for Period Ending December 14, 1941, FO 838/1; C. J. Edmonds to V. Holt, December 23, 1941, "Communism," FO 624/25; Kinahan Cornwallis to Foreign Office, January 22, 1943, FO 371/35010 E 946/489/93, and January 27, 1944, FO 371/40041 E 649/37/93; and Iraqi Criminal Investigation Department Special Report, June 1944, FO 371/40042 E 4037/37/93.

183. Sharqi, *Diwan al-Sharqi*, 232–235.

184. Colonel Lyon to V. Holt, February 12, 1943; Mosul Consulate to British Embassy, February 22, 1943; and V. Holt to J. P. G. Finch, April 26, 1943, "Communism," FO 624/33.

185. Jawahiri, *Dhikrayati*, 1:382.

186. Muhammad Mahdi al-Jawahiri, "Ila al-Rusafi," *al-Raʾi al-ʿAmm*, May 15, 1944, in Jawahiri, *Diwan al-Jawahiri*, 2:413–414.

187. Jawahiri, *Diwan al-Jawahiri*, 2:412.

188. Tikriti, *Muhammad Mahdi al-Jawahiri*, 63–69.

189. Muhammad Mahdi al-Jawahiri, "Ila al-Rusafi," *al-Ra'i al-'Amm*, May 15, 1944, in Jawahiri, *Diwan al-Jawahiri*, 2:413–414.

190. Iraqi Criminal Investigation Department, May 18, 1945, FO 371/45302 E 3819/195/93.

## Chapter 5

1. Hanna Batatu, *The Old Social Classes and the Revolutionary Movements of Iraq: A Study of Iraq's Old Landed and Commercial Classes and of its Communists, Ba'thists and Free Officers* (Princeton: Princeton University Press, 1979), 293–303, and Khalid al-Tamimi, *Muhammad Ja'far Abu al-Timman: Dirasa fi al-Za'ama al-Siyasiyya al'-Iraqiyya* (Damascus: Dar al-Warraq, 1996).

2. Muhammad Salih Bahr al-'Ulum, *Diwan Bahr al-'Ulum*, vol. 2 (Baghdad: Matba'at Dar al-Tadamun, 1968), 73.

3. Bahr al-'Ulum, *Diwan Bahr al-'Ulum*, 2:87–90.

4. Hussein N. Kadhim, *The Poetics of Anti-Colonialism in the Arabic Qasidah* (Leiden: Brill, 2004), vii–xii.

5. Muhammad Mahdi al-Jawahiri, *Dhikrayati*, vol. 1 (Damascus: Dar al-Rafidayn, 1988), 421–426.

6. Muhammad Mahdi al-Jawahiri, "Dhikra Abu al-Timman," *al-Ra'i al-'Amm*, January 6, 1946, in al-Jawahiri, *Diwan al-Jawahiri*, 3:52–57.

7. Bahr al-'Ulum, *Diwan Bahr al-'Ulum*, 2:87.

8. Bahr al-'Ulum, *Diwan Bahr al-'Ulum*, 1:15, and al-Jawahiri, *Dhikrayati*, 1:421–426.

9. Tareq Ismael, *The Rise and Fall of the Communist Party of Iraq* (Cambridge: Cambridge University Press, 2008), 17–39.

10. Batatu, *The Old Social Classes*, 545–566, 666–670.

11. Gha'ib Tu'ama Farman, *al-Hukm al-Aswad fi al-'Iraq* (Cairo: Dar al-Fikr, 1957).

12. Yoav Di-Capua, *No Exit: Arab Existentialism, Jean-Paul Sartre, and Decolonization* (Chicago: University of Chicago Press, 2018), 77–107.

13. Jabra Ibrahim Jabra, "The Palestinian Exile as Writer," *Journal of Palestine Studies* 8:2 (1979), 82, and Di-Capua, *No Exit*, 133–138.

14. Salma Khadra Jayyusi, *Trends and Movements in Modern Arabic Poetry*, vol. 2 (Leiden: Brill, 1977), 530–604.

15. Issa J. Boullata, "Badr Shakir al-Sayyab and the Free Verse Movement," *International Journal of Middle East Studies* 1:3 (1970), 251–252; Salih J. Altoma, "Postwar Iraqi Literature: Agonies of Rebirth," *Books Abroad* 46:2 (1972), 211–217; Jabra I. Jabra, "The Rebels, the Committed and the Others: Transitions in Arabic Poetry Today," in

*Critical Perspectives on Modern Arabic Literature*, ed. Issa J. Boullata (Washington, DC: Three Continents Press, 1980), 190–205; and Terri DeYoung, *Placing the Poet: Badr Shakir al-Sayyab and Postcolonial Iraq* (Albany: State University of New York Press, 1998), 187–220.

16. Muhsin al-Musawi, "Muhammad Mahdi al-Jawahiri (1901–1997)," in *Essays in Arabic Literary Biography*, vol. 3, ed. Roger Allen (Wiesbaden: Harrassowitz Verlag, 2010), 170–171.

17. Alex Lubin, *Geographies of Liberation: The Making of an Afro-Arab Political Imaginary* (Chapel Hill: University of North Carolina Press, 2014), 7–14, and Maha Nassar, *Brothers Apart: Palestinian Citizens of Israel and the Arab World* (Stanford: Stanford University Press, 2017), 78–81.

18. Alain Badiou, *The Age of the Poets: And Other Writings on Twentieth-Century Poetry and Prose*, trans. Emily Apter (London: Verso, 2014), 93–109.

19. Sami Zubaida, "Al-Jawahiri: Between Patronage and Revolution," *Revue des mondes musulmans et de la Méditerranée* 117–118 (2007), 81–97.

20. Foulath Hadid, *Iraq's Democratic Moment* (London: Hurst, 2012), 100–105.

21. Bahr al-'Ulum, *Diwan Bahr al-'Ulum*, 1:15.

22. Bahr al-'Ulum, *Diwan Bahr al-'Ulum*, 2:92.

23. al-Jawahiri, *Dhikrayati*, 1:435–436.

24. Muhammad Mahdi al-Jawahiri, "Tartara," *al-Ra'i al-'Amm*, March 24, 1946, in al-Jawahiri, *Diwan al-Jawahiri*, 3:41–44.

25. al-Jawahiri, *Dhikrayati*, 1:435–436.

26. Charles Tripp, *A History of Iraq*, 2$^{nd}$ ed. (Cambridge: Cambridge University Press, 2000), 117–118.

27. Bahr al-'Ulum, *Diwan Bahr al-'Ulum*, 2:96.

28. "The Iraqi Communist Party's Appeal to the Iraqi Workers and the Iraqi People," March 9, 1946, USDS 890G.5045/4–2545; "Report by Musa al-Shaykh Radi to Political Committee of the National Union Party," *al-Siyasa*, July 17, 1946, USDS 890G.5045/7–2346; "A Declaration by the Communist Party in Iraq," July 26, 1946, USDS 890G.5045/8–1046; and Batatu, *The Old Social Classes*, 532–533, 623–634.

29. Bahr al-'Ulum, *Diwan Bahr al-'Ulum*, 2:99.

30. Bahr al-'Ulum, *Diwan Bahr al-'Ulum*, 2:100–102.

31. Hugh Stonehewer Bird to Foreign Office, August 16, 1946, FO 371/52468 E 8113/8113/93; Douglas Busk to Foreign Office, August 16, 1946, FO 371/52468 E 8334/8113/93; James S. Moose Jr. to Secretary of State, September 16, 1946, USDS 890G.5045/9–1646; and James S. Moose Jr. to Secretary of State, October 7, 1946, USDS 890G.5045/10–74.

32. James S. Moose Jr. to Secretary of State, October 15, 1946, USDS 890G.5045/10–1546, October 28, 1946, USDS 890G.5045/11–2246.

33. Bahr al-'Ulum, *Diwan Bahr al-'Ulum*, 2:103–104.

34. Malcolm Walker to John Richmond, February 13, 1948, FO 371/68446 E 1921/27/93; "Foreign Office Minute," February 26, 1948, FO 371/68447 E 4099/27/93; and "Political Review for the Year 1947," FO 371/58443 E 834/27/93.

35. Bahr al-'Ulum, *Diwan Bahr al-'Ulum*, 2:112–115.

36. al-Jawahiri, *Dhikrayati*, 1:469–472.

37. Douglas Busk to Foreign Office, January 5, 1948, FO 371/68441 E 265/27/93, and Mustafa al-Saharti and Hilal Naji, *Shu'ara' al-Mu'asirun* (Cairo: Dar al-Karnak, 1962), 201–207.

38. G. C. Pelham to Foreign Office, January 7, 1948, FO 371/68441 E 585/27/93, and Jawahiri, *Dhikrayati*, 2:17.

39. Jawahiri, *Dhikrayati*, 1:480–481.

40. Bahr al-'Ulum, *Diwan Bahr al-'Ulum*, 2:129.

41. Bahr al-'Ulum, *Diwan Bahr al-'Ulum*.

42. G. C. Pelham to Foreign Office, January 21, 1948, FO 371/68443 E 880/27/93, January 21, 1948, FO 371/68443 E 892/27/93, January 25, 1948, FO 371/68446 E 2217/27/93; and Douglas Busk to Foreign Office, January 30, 1948, FO 371/68446 E 2254/27/93.

43. G. C. Pelham to Foreign Office, January 22, 1948, FO 371/68443 E 932/27/93, January 22, 1948, FO 371/68443 E 949/27/93, and January 25, 1948, FO 371/68446 E 2217/27/93.

44. Hadid, *Iraq's Democratic Moment*, 130–131.

45. Bahr al-'Ulum, *Diwan Bahr al-'Ulum*, 2:130.

46. al-Jawahiri, *Diwan al-Jawahiri*, 3:149–151.

47. Bahr al-'Ulum, *Diwan Bahr al-'Ulum*, 2:130.

48. Bahr al-'Ulum, *Diwan Bahr al-'Ulum*, 2:131.

49. Bahr al-'Ulum, *Diwan Bahr al-'Ulum*, 2:132–134.

50. G. C. Pelham to Foreign Office, January 25, 1948, FO 371/68446 E 2217/27/93, and Batatu, *The Old Social Classes*, 552–553.

51. "Shahadat Muhammad Salih Bahr al-'Ulum," in *Muhakamat al-Mahkamah al-'Askariyah al-'Ulya al-Khassa: al-Mahadir al-Rasmiyah li al-Jalasat allati Aqadathaha al-Mahkamah li Muhakamat al-Muta'amirin 'ala Salamat al-Watan wa Mufsidi Nizam al-Hukm*, vol. 8 (Baghdad: Wizarat al-Difa', 1960), 131–133.

52. Batatu, *The Old Social Classes*, 555–557.

53. Jawahiri, *Dhikrayati*, 2:22–27.

54. Henry Mack to Foreign Office, February 24, 1948, FO 371/68447 E 3239/27/93.

55. Jawahiri, *Diwan al-Jawahiri*, 3:155–159, and *Dhikrayati*, 2:27–28.

56. Rayyan al-Shawaf, "An Interview with Sargon Boulos," *Parnassus: Poetry in Review* 29:1–2 (2005), 47–48.

57. Abdul-Salaam Yousif, "The Struggle for Cultural Hegemony in Iraq," in *The*

*Iraqi Revolution of 1958: The Old Social Classes Revisited*, ed. Robert A. Fernea and William Roger Louis (London: I. B. Tauris, 1991), 174, and Nadje Sadig Al-Ali, *Iraqi Women: Untold Stories from 1948 to the Present* (London: Zed Books, 2007), 59–60, 72.

58. Arshad al-'Umari to Douglas Busk, February 22, 1948, FO 371/68447 E 3239/27/93; Henry Mack to Foreign Office, April 24, 1948, FO 371/68448 E 5143/27/93; and George Wadsworth, "Baghdad Press Summary, May 2–8, 1948," USDS 890G.9111 RR/5–1048.

59. George Wadsworth, "Baghdad Press Summary, April 11–17, 1948," USDS 890G.9111 RR/4–1948.

60. Jawahiri, *Diwan al-Jawahiri*, 3:163–172.

61. Lami'a 'Abbas 'Amara, *'Awdat al-Rabi' wa al-Zawiyya al-Khaliyya* (La Mesa: Amara Publisher, 2001), 38–39.

62. Hadid, *Iraq's Democratic Moment*, 137–143.

63. Muhammad Mahdi al-Jawahiri, "'Arrat al-Khutub," *al-Hidara*, July 24, 1948, and *al-'Usur*, July 24, 1948, in Jawahiri, *Diwan al-Jawahiri*, 3:189–190. See also Jawahiri, *Dhikrayati*, 2:30

64. Muhammad Mahdi al-Jawahiri, "al-Maqsurah," *al-Ra'i al-'Amm*, August 11, 1948, in al-Jawahiri, *Diwan al-Jawahiri*, 3:309–320.

65. Musawi, "Muhammad Mahdi al-Jawahiri (1901–1997)," 171.

66. Jawahiri, *Dhikrayati*, 2:54–55.

67. Jawahiri, *Dhikrayati*, 2:58–59.

68. Jawahiri, *Diwan al-Jawahiri*, 3:255–259. On the diction, style, and aesthetics of the poem, see M. M. Badawi, *A Critical Introduction of Modern Arabic Poetry* (Cambridge: Cambridge University Press, 1975), 66–67.

69. Jawahiri, *Dhikrayati*, 2:60–66, and *Diwan al-Jawahiri*, 3:247–252.

70. Edward S. Crocker to Department of State, July 7, 1951, USDS 787.001/7–751, and Jawahiri, *Dhikrayati*, 2:33–42.

71. Lawrence S. Wittner, *One World or None: A History of the World Nuclear Disarmament Movement through 1953* (Stanford: Stanford University Press, 1993), 171–243.

72. Tawfiq Munir *Haqiqat Harakat al-Salam* (Cairo: Dar al-Fikr, 1956).

73. Quoted in Batatu, *The Old Social Classes*, 587.

74. Munir, *Haqiqat Harakat al-Salam*, 41–43, and Batatu, *The Old Social Classes*, 666–667, 686–687.

75. Yousif, "The Struggle for Cultural Hegemony in Iraq," 174–177.

76. Bahr al-'Ulum, *Diwan Bahr al-'Ulum*, 2:184.

77. Bahr al-'Ulum, *Diwan Bahr al-'Ulum*, 2:188.

78. Geoffrey Roberts, "Averting Armageddon: The Communist Peace Movement, 1948–1956," in *The Oxford Handbook of the History of Communism*, ed. S. A. Smith (Oxford: Oxford University Press, 2014), 326–332, and Melissa Feinberg, *Curtain of*

*Lies: The Battle over Truth in Stalinist Eastern Europe* (New York: Oxford University Press, 2017), 51–59.

79. Bahr al-ʿUlum, *Diwan Bahr al-ʿUlum*, 2:190.

80. Vijay Prashad, *The Darker Nations: A People's History of the Third World* (New York: New Press, 2007), and Jahan Ramazani, *A Transnational Poetics* (Chicago: University of Chicago Press, 2009), 141–162.

81. Bahr al-ʿUlum, *Diwan Bahr al-ʿUlum*, 2:191.

82. Bahr al-ʿUlum, *Diwan Bahr al-ʿUlum*, 2:204–212.

83. Muhammad Mahdi al-Jawahiri, "Ayyuha al-Wahsh, Ayyuha al-Istiʿmar," *al-Awqat al-Baghdadiyya*, February 23, 1952, in Jawahiri, *Diwan al-Jawahiri*, 3:297–302.

84. Edward S. Crocker to Department of State, July 7, 1951, USDS 787.001/7–751.

85. On socialist realism in literature, see Petre M. Petrov, *Automatic for the Masses: The Death of the Author and the Birth of Socialist Realism* (Toronto: University of Toronto Press, 2015).

86. Badawi, *A Critical Introduction*, 209, and Yousif, "The Struggle for Cultural Hegemony in Iraq," 177.

87. Muhammad Mahdi al-Jawahiri, "Tanwimat al-Jiyaʿ," *al-Awqat al-Baghdadiyya*, March 28, 1951, in Jawahiri, *Diwan al-Jawahiri*, 3:313–317.

88. Jawahiri, *Diwan al-Jawahiri*, 2:329–331.

89. Khalid Kishtainy, *The Prostitute in Progressive Literature* (London: Allison and Busby, 1982), 10.

90. Patrick Iber, *Neither Peace Nor Freedom: The Cultural Cold War in Latin America* (Cambridge, MA: Harvard University Press, 2015), 51.

91. DeYoung, *Placing the Poet*, 222–225.

92. Badr Shakir al-Sayyab, *Diwan Badr Shakir al-Sayyab* (Cairo: Maktabat Jazirat al-Ward, 2009), 252–258.

93. Boullata, "Badr Shakir al-Sayyab" 248–258.

94. Jayyusi, *Trends and Movements*, 2:557–558, and Thomas Levi Thompson, "Speaking Laterally: Transnational Poetics and the Rise of Modern Arabic and Persian Poetry in Iraq and Iran" (PhD diss., University of California Los Angeles, 2017), 32–60.

95. Yusuf ʿIzz al-Din, *Shuʿaraʾ al-ʿIraq fi al-Qarn al-ʿIshrin* (Baghdad: Matbaʿat Asʿad, 1969), 331–341, 353–358, 397–404, and Mir Basri, *Aʿlam al-Adab fi al-ʿIraq al-Hadith*, vol. 2 (London: Dar al-Hikma, 1994), 458–464, 563–568, 569–578, 578–579, 579–585.

96. ʿIzz al-Din, *Shuʿaraʾ al-ʿIraq*, 316–319, 359–372 and Basri, *Aʿlam al-Adab* 2:467–470.

97. Chris Beyers, *A History of Free Verse* (Fayetteville: University of Arkansas Press, 2001), 13–60.

98. DeYoung, *Placing the Poet*, 191–196.

99. Jayyusi, *Trends and Movements*, 2:534–557, 630–640.

100. Nazik al-Mala'ika, *Diwan Nazik al-Mala'ika*, vol. 2 (Beirut: Dar al-'Awdah, 1997), 138–142.

101. Sayyab, *Diwan Badr Shakir al-Sayyab*, 237–238.

102. Musa al-Naqdi, "Hawl Maqal al-Ustadh al-Takarli," *al-Adab* 1:12 (1953), 50–51; Salih Abd al-Ghani Kubba, "Hawl al-Shi'r al-Mutaharrar fi al-'Iraq," *al-Adab* 2:2 (1954), 49–50; Kazim Jawad, "Hawl al-Shi'r al-Hurr," *al-Adab* 2:4 (1954), 69; and Jalal al-Khayat, "al-Shi'r al-Hurr Aydan," *al-Adab* 2:5 (1954), 57.

103. Jayyusi, *Trends and Movements*, 2:558–559, and Badawi, *A Critical Introduction*, 225–226.

104. Verena Klemm, "Different Notions of Commitment (Iltizam) and Committed Literature (al-Adab al-Multazim) in the Literary Circles of the Mashriq," *Arabic and Middle Eastern Literatures* 3:1 (2000), 51–62.

105. Saharti and Naji, *Shu'ara' al-Mu'asirun*, 201–207.

106. 'Abd al-Wahhab al-Bayati, *Tajribati al-Shi'iriyya* (Beirut: Manshurat Nizar Qabbani, 1968), 21–21.

107. Suhayl Idris, "Risalat al-Adab," *al-Adab* 1:1 (1953), 1–2.

108. Buland al-Haydari, *al-A'mal al-Kamila lil-Sha'ir Buland al-Haydari* (Cairo: Dar Su'ad al-Sabah, 1993), 275–278; Shmuel Moreh, "Town and Country in Modern Arabic Poetry from Shawqi to al-Sayyab," *Asian and African Studies* 18:2 (1984), 161–185; and Di-Capua, *No Exit*, 139–145.

109. Bayati, *Tajribati al-Shi'iriyya*, 22–25, and Orit Bashkin, *The Other Iraq: Pluralism and Culture in Hashemite Iraq* (Stanford: Stanford University Press, 2010), 225–226.

110. 'Abd al-Wahhab al-Bayati, *Abariq al-Muhashshamah* (Beirut: Manshurat Dar al-Adab, 1967), 37–39.

111. DeYoung, *Placing the Poet*, 65–96.

112. Badr Shakir al-Sayyab, *Badr Shakir al-Sayyab: Hayatihi wa Shi'rihi* ('Amman: al-Ahliyya li al-Nashr wa al-Tawzi', 2008), 389–392, and DeYoung, *Placing the Poet*, 130.

113. Di-Capua, *No Exit*, 146–147, and Haytham Bahoora, "Baudelaire in Baghdad: Modernism, the Body, and Husayn Mardan's Poetics of the Self," *International Journal of Middle East Studies* 45:2 (2013), 318.

114. Husayn Mardan, *al-A'mal al-Kamila*, vol. 1 (Baghdad: Dar al-Shuun al-Thaqafiyya al-'Amma, 2009), 11.

115. Bahoora, "Baudelaire in Baghdad," 313–315.

116. Jabra Ibrahim Jabra, *Princesses' Street: Baghdad Memories*, trans. Issa J. Boullata (Fayetteville: University of Arkansas Press, 2005), 83–84.

117. Fadhil al-'Azzawi, *al-Ruh al-Hayya: Jil al-Sittinat fi al-'Iraq* (Damascus: Dar al-Thaqafa wa al-Nashr, 2003), 102–104, Bahoora, "Baudelaire in Baghdad," 326–327, and Di-Capua, *No Exit*, 145–147.

118. Husayn Mardan, "al-Hadid," *al-Adab* 2:6 (1954), 41.

119. Hilal Naji and Muhyi al-Din Isma'il, *Jinayyat al-Shuyu'iyin 'ala al-Adab al-'Iraqi* (Cairo: Dar al-Karnak lil-Nashr, 1960), 18.

120. Talib al-Haydari, *Dam al-Shahid* (Baghdad: Matba'at al-Ma'arif, 1950).

121. Talib al-Haydari, *Nidal: Qasa'id Thawriyya min al-'Iraq* (Baghdad: Matba'at al-Ma'arif, 1958), 105–111.

122. Haydari, *Nidal*, 101–104.

123. 'Ali al-Hilli, *Thawrat al-Ba'th* (Beirut: Matabi' Dar al-Andalus, 1963), 76–81, and "Al-Shi'r Ta'bir 'an al-Thawra wa Qadaya al-Insan," *al-Aqdam* 7 (1985), 28–34.

124. Kubba, *Mudhakkirat*, 336, and Batatu, *The Old Social Classes*, 666–667.

125. H. Beeley to Foreign Office, December 3, 1951, FO 371/91634 EQ 109/10, and al-Chadirchi, *Mudhakkirat Kamil al-Chadirchi*, 539–540.

126. Muhammad Mahdi al-Jawahiri, "Yawm al-Shuhada' fi Iran," *al-Jihad*, July 23, 1952, in al-Jawahiri, *Diwan al-Jawahiri*, 3:353. See also Jawahiri, *Dhikrayati*, 2:105.

127. Kubba, *Mudhakkirat*, 343–344; Chadirchi, *Mudhakkirat Kamil al-Chadirchi*, 551–557; and Baha al-Din Nuri, *Mudhakkirat Baha al-Din Nuri: Sikritir al-Lajnah al-Markaziyya lil-Hizb al-Shuyu'i al-'Iraqi* (London: Dar al-Hikmah, 2001), 160.

128. Nuri, *Mudhakkirat Baha al-Din Nuri*, 160–169, and Muhammad Hamdi al-Ja'fari, *Intifadat Tishrin al-Thani 'Amm 1952 wa Inqilab al-Wasi fi al-'Iraq: Dirasa Ta'rikhiyya Tahliliyya Witha'iqiyya* (Cairo: Maktabat Madbuli, 2000), 90–94.

129. Nuri, *Mudhakkirat Baha al-Din Nuri*, 163–169, and al-Ja'fari, *Intifadat Tishrin al-Thani 'Amm 1952*, 93–94.

130. John M. Troutbeck to Foreign Office, November 25, 1952, FO 371/98736 E 1016/64; Kubbah, *Mudhakkirat*, 347; and Nuri, *Mudhakkirat Baha al-Din Nuri*, 170–172.

131. Burton Y. Berry to Department of State, November 25, 1952, USDS 787.00/11–2552, and November 26, 1952, USDS 787.00/11-.2652; John M. Troutbeck to Foreign Office, November 26, 1952, FO 371/98736 E 1016/67, and November 28, 1952, FO 371/98736 E 1016/78; and Jawahiri, *Dhikrayati*, 2:105–106.

132. Bahr al-'Ulum, *Diwan Bahr al-'Ulum*, 1:16–17.

133. Dhu al-Nun Ayyub, "al-Muqaddimah," introduction to *Aqbas al-Thawra: Min A'maq Sha'b 14 Tammuz*, by Muhammad Salih Bahr al-'Ulum (Baghdad: Wizarat al-Ma'arif, 1959), 10–13.

134. Burton Y. Berry to Department of State, December 16, 1952, USDS 787.00/12–1652.

135. Badr Shakir al-Sayyab, "Kuntu Shuyu'iyan," *al-Hurriyya*, October 26, 1959, in Badr Shakir al-Sayyab, *Kuntu Shuyu'iyan* (Cologne: Manshurat al-Jamal, 2007), 204–209. See also Foreign Office Minutes by J. C. Wardrop, November 24, 1952, FO 371/98736 E 1016/69, and Nuri, *Mudhakkirat Baha al-Din Nuri*, 170–171,.

136. Badr Shakir al-Sayyab, "Kuntu Shuyu'iyan," *al-Hurriyya*, October 26, 1959, in al-Sayyab, *Kuntu Shuyu'iyan*, 204–209.

137. "Movements and Plans of Communist Leaders," March 13, 1953, CIA-RDP80–00810A000600310006–5, and Bahr al-'Ulum, *Diwan Bahr al-'Ulum*, 1:17.

138. "Shahadat Muhammad Salih Bahr al-'Ulum," in *Muhakamat al-Mahkamah*, 8:132–133.

139. "Evolution of the Political Situation after the Liberational November Uprising, and the Duties of Our Communist Party to Evolve the Popular Struggle and Realize Its Objectives," *al-Qa'ida*, December 1952, USDS 787.001/3–453.

140. Adeed Dawisha, *Arab Nationalism in the Twentieth Century: From Triumph to Despair* (Princeton: Princeton University Press, 2003), 160–185.

141. Ervand Abrahamian, *The Coup: 1953, the CIA, and the Roots of Modern U.S.-Iranian Relations* (New York: New Press, 2013), 9–80.

142. Haydari, *Nidal*, 112.

143. Jawad, *Min Aghani al-Hurriyyah*, 45–52.

144. John M. Troutbeck to Foreign Office, December 16, 1953, FO 371/104666 EQ 1016/70.

145. Jawad, *Min Aghani al-Hurriyyah*, 39–40.

146. Tissow became a minor character, for example, in Fadhil al-'Azzawi's novel *The Last of the Angels*. See Fadhil al-'Azzawi, *Akhr al-Mala'ika* (Beirut: Manshurat al-Jamal, 2016).

147. Hayat al-Nahr, *Ughniyyat lil-Thawra: Shi'r* (Baghdad: Matba'at al-Rabita, 1960), 21–25. See also Maziar Behrooz, *Rebels with a Cause: The Failure of the Left in Iran* (London: I. B. Tauris, 1999), 3–16.

148. Ervand Abrahamian, *Iran between Two Revolutions* (Princeton: Princeton University Press, 1982), 324–325.

149. Badr Shakir al-Sayyab, "Kuntu Shuyu'iyyan," *al-Hurriyya*, August 16, 1959, in al-Sayyab, *Kuntu Shuyu'iyan*, 12–18.

150. Badr Shakir al-Sayyab, "Kuntu Shuyu'iyyan," *al-Hurriyya*, August 28, September 4, 1959, in al-Sayyab, *Kuntu Shuyu'iyan*, 83–89, 103–108.

151. Badr Shakir al-Sayyab, "al-Mukhbir," *al-Adab* 2:10 (1954), 24–25.

152. Badr Shakir al-Sayyab, "Fi al-Maghrib al-'Arabi," *al-Adab* 4:3 (1956), 6–7, "Garcia Lorca," *al-Adab* 4:6 (June 1956), 24.

153. "Baghdad Press Reviews," February 21, 1951, CIA-RPD83–00415R007500040001–3.

154. 'Adnan al-Rawi, *al-Majmu'a al-Shi'riyya al-Kamila lil-Sha'ir 'Adnan al-Rawi, 1925–1967* (Baghdad: Wizarat al-Thaqafa wa al-Funun, 1978), 9–15, and Michael Doran, *Ike's Gamble: America's Rise to Dominance in the Middle East* (New York: Free Press, 2016), 95–96.

155. 'Adnan al-Rawi, *Diwan al-Sha'ir al-'Arabi wa al-Za'im al-Thawri al-'Iraqi al-Munadil: 'Adnan al-Rawi* (Cairo: Dar al-Hilal, 1974), 650–651.

156. Rawi, *Diwan al-Sha'ir al-'Arabi*, 687–688.

157. Rawi, *al-Majmuʿa al-Shiʿriyya al-Kamila*, 253–254, 266–267.
158. Rawi, *Diwan al-Shaʿir al-ʿArabi*, 671.
159. Hilli, *Thawrat al-Baʿth*, 15–17.
160. ʿAli al-Hilli, "al-Shitaʾ al-Qaris," *al-Adib* 15:3 (1956), 44–46, and "al-Azhar al-Bariyya," *al-Adib* 15:6 (1956), 45–48.
161. Hilli, *Thawrat al-Baʿth*, 25–28 and 32–36.
162. Hilli, "al-Shiʿr Taʿbir," 33.
163. Hilli, *Thawrat al-Baʿth*, 29–31.
164. Hilli, "al-Shiʿr Taʿbir," 33.
165. Hilli, *Thawrat al-Baʿth*, 9–10.
166. Dawisha, *Arab Nationalism in the Twentieth Century*, 157.
167. Jawahiri, *Diwan al-Jawahiri*, 4:33–38.
168. Jawahiri, *Dhikrayati*, 2:133–142.
169. Jawahiri, *Diwan al-Jawahiri*, 4:65–71.
170. al-Saharti and Naji, *Shuʿaraʾ al-Muʿasirun*, 201–207.
171. Kazim Jawad, *Min Aghani al-Hurriyya* (Beirut: Matabiʿ Dar al-ʿIlm li al-Malayyin, 1960), 11–22.
172. Jawad, *Min Aghani al-Hurriya*, 26–30, 79–82.
173. Kazim Jawad, "al-Shams Tashruqu ʿala al-Maghrib," *al-Adab* 3:1 (1955), 78–80.
174. Kazim Jawad, "Did al-Iqlimiyya al-Shufiniyya al-Dayyiqa," *al-Adab* 3:11 (1955), 66–67.
175. Kazim Jawad, "Man Huwa Port Saʿid," *al-Thaqafa* 1:5 (1958), 42.
176. Jawad, *Min Aghani al-Hurriyya*, 120–121.
177. Kazim Jawad, "Abariq Muhashshama: Majmuʿat Shiʿr li-ʿAbd al-Wahhab al-Bayati," *al-Adab* 2:7 (1954), 33–36, and "Kalamati al-Akhira fi ʿAbariq Muhashshama,'" *al-Adab* 2:9 (1954), 60–62.
178. ʿAbd al-Wahhab al-Bayati, "Mau Mau," *al-Adab* 1:7 (1953), 23, and *al-Aʿmal al-Shiʿriyya*, vol. 1 (Beirut: al-Muʾassassa al-ʿArabiyya, 1995), 125–126.
179. Shmuel Moreh, *Modern Arabic Poetry, 1800–1970: The Development of its Forms and Themes under the Influence of Western Literature* (Leiden: E. J. Brill, 1976), 268–269.
180. ʿAbd al-Wahhab al-Bayati, "Ila Nazim Hikmet: li-Howard Fast," *al-Adib* 13:9 (1954), 14.
181. ʿAbd al-Wahhab al-Bayati, "Sha'ir min Asiya," *al-Adib* 13:6 (1954), 42. and *Yanabiʿ al-Shams: al-Sirah al-Shiʿriyya* (Damascus: Dar al-Farqad, 1999), 52–54.
182. Bayati, *al-Aʿmal al-Shiʿriyya*, 1:193–197, 1:234–235.
183. Bayati, *al-Aʿmal al-Shiʿriyya*, 1:191–192.
184. Nahr, *Ughniyyat lil-Thawra*, 29–34, 60–63.
185. Saharti and Naji, *Shuʿaraʾ al-Muʿasirun*, 207–208, and Majid Ahmad al-Samarraʾi, *al-Tayyar al-Qawmi fi al-Shiʿr al-ʿIraqi al-Hadith, Mundhu al-Harb*

*al-'Alamiyya al-Thaniyya 1939 Hatta Naksat Haziran 1967* (Baghdad: Wizarat al-Thaqafa wa al-I'lan, 1983), 335–336.

186. Pierre Rossi, "La Culture Nouvelle: Mouvement Révolutionaire des Intellectuels Irakiens," *Orient* 2:8 (1958), 61–65.

187. Bahr al-'Ulum, *Diwan Bahr al-'Ulum*, 1:17, and Batatu, *The Old Social Classes*, 690–693.

188. Muhammad Salih Bahr al-'Ulum, "Kaffi wa Kaffka Ba'su Kullin Minhuma Mawt al-Tughah," *al-Bayan* 26 (1968), 18–19.

189. Sasson Somekh, *Baghdad, Yesterday: The Making of an Arab Jew* (Jerusalem: Ibis Editions, 2007), 162–167.

190. Orit Bashkin, *Impossible Exodus: Iraqi Jews in Israel* (Stanford: Stanford University Press, 2017), 192–193.

191. Bahr al-'Ulum, "Kaffi wa Kaffka Ba'su Kullin Minhuma Mawt al-Tughah," *al-Bayan* 26 (1968), 18–19.

192. See, for example, the opening lines in Rawi, *Diwan al-Sha'ir al-'Arabi*, 703–704.

193. Haydari, *Nidal*, 13.

194. Salma Khadra Jayyusi, *Trends and Movements in Modern Arabic Poetry*, vol. 1 (Leiden: Brill, 1977), 200.

195. Abdul-Salaam Yacoob Yousif, "Vanguardist Cultural Practices: The Formation of an Alternative Cultural Hegemony in Iraq and Chile, 1930–1970s" (PhD diss, University of Iowa, 1988), 158–159.

196. Muhammad Ali Muhyi al-Din, "Ayna Haqqi . . . al-Ma'thara al-Uzma," *Gilgamesh*, August 18, 2007, http://www.gilgamish.org/2007/08/18/3279.html.

## Chapter 6

1. Elliott Colla, "Badr Shakir al-Sayyab, Cold War Poet," *Middle Eastern Literatures* 18:3 (2015), 258–259.

2. On the Congress for Cultural Freedom, see Peter Coleman, *The Liberal Conspiracy: The Congress for Cultural Freedom and the Struggle for the Mind of Postwar Europe* (New York: New Press, 1989); Giles Scott-Smith, *The Politics of Apolitical Culture: The Congress for Cultural Freedom, the CIA and Post-War American Hegemony* (London: Routledge, 2002); Frances Stoner Saunders, *The Cultural Cold War: The CIA and the World of Arts and Letters* (New York: New Press, 2013); Elizabeth M. Holt, "'Bread or Freedom': The Congress for Cultural Freedom, the CIA, and the Arabic Literary Journal *Hiwar (1962–67)*," *Journal of Arabic Literature* 44:1 (2013), 83–102; Patrick Iber, *Neither Peace Nor Freedom: The Cultural Cold War in Latin America* (Cambridge, MA: Harvard University Press, 2015).

3. Badr Shakir al-Sayyab, "al-Iltizam wa al-La-Iltizam fi al-Adab al-'Arabi al-Hadith," in *al-Adab al-'Arabi al-Mu'asir: A'mal Mu'tamar Ruma al-Mun'aqid fi Tishrin*

*al-Awwal Sanat 1961*, ed. ʿAbd al-Hamid Jidah and Khalil al-Duwayhi (Tripoli: Dar al-Shamal, 1990), 226.

4. Muhammad Salih Bahr al-ʿUlum, *Diwan Bahr al-ʿUlum*, vol. 2 (Baghdad: Matbaʿat Dar al-Tadamun, 1968), 76–82; and Majid Ahmad al-Samarraʾi, *al-Tayyar al-Qawmi fi al-Shiʿr al-ʿIraqi al-Hadith, Mundhu al-Harb al-ʿAlamiyya al-Thaniyya 1939 Hatta Naksat Haziran 1967* (Baghdad: Wizarat al-Thaqafa wa al-Iʿlan, 1983), 62.

5. Sayyab, "al-Iltizam wa al-La-Iltizam," 226.

6. Sayyab, "al-Iltizam wa al-La-Iltizam," 232–233.

7. Hanna Batatu, *The Old Social Classes and the Revolutionary Movements of Iraq: A Study of Iraq's Old Landed and Commercial Classes and of Its Communists, Baʿthists, and Free Officers* (Princeton: Princeton University Press, 1978), 764–925.

8. Marion Farouk-Sluglett and Peter Sluglett, *Iraq since 1958: From Revolution to Dictatorship* (London: I. B. Tauris, 2003), 47–84.

9. Eric Davis, *Memories of State: Politics, History, and Collective Identity in Modern Iraq* (Berkeley: University of California Press, 2005), 109–147, and Tareq Y. Ismael, *The Rise and Fall of the Communist Party of Iraq* (Cambridge: Cambridge University Press, 2008), 79–102.

10. Badr Shakir al-Sayyab, *Kuntu Shuyuʿiyyan* (Cologne: Manshurat al-Jamal, 2007).

11. Marion Farouk-Sluglett and Peter Sluglett, "The Social Classes and the Origins of the Revolution," in *The Iraqi Revolution of 1958: The Old Social Classes Revisited*, ed. Robert A. Fernea and William Roger Louis (London: I. B. Tauris, 1991), 118–141; Roger Owen, "Class and Class Politics in Iraq before 1958: The 'Colonial and Post-Colonial State,'" in Fernea and Louis, eds., *The Iraqi Revolution of 1958*, 154–171; and Sami Zubaida, "Community, Class and Minorities in Iraqi Politics," in Fernea and Louis, eds., *The Iraqi Revolution of 1958*, 197–210.

12. Amatzia Baram, "A Case of Imported Identity: The Modernizing Secular Ruling Elites of Iraq and the Conception of Mesopotamian-Inspired Territorial Nationalism, 1922–1992," *Poetics Today* 15 (1994), 279–319; Sami Zubaida, "The Fragments Imagine the Nation: The Case of Iraq," *International Journal of Middle East Studies* 34:2 (2002), 205–215; and Orit Bashkin, "Hybrid Nationalisms: *Watani* and *Qawmi* Visions in Iraq under ʿAbd al-Karim Qasim, 1958–1961," *International Journal of Middle East Studies* 43:2 (2011), 293–312.

13. Sayyab, "al-Iltizam wa al-La-Iltizam," 227.

14. Badr Shakir al-Sayyab, "Kuntu Shuyuʿiyyan" *al-Hurriyya*, August 16, 1959, in Badr Shakir al-Sayyab, *Kuntu Shuyuʿiyyan* (Cologne: Manshurat al-Jamal, 2007), 12–18. See also Vijay Prashad, *The Darker Nations: A People's History of the Third World* (New York: New Press, 2007), 75–94.

15. Sylvia Naef, "Shiʿi-Shuyuʿi or: How to Become a Communist in a Holy City," in *The Twelver Shia in Modern Times: Religious Culture and Political History*, ed. Rainer

Brunner and Werner Ende (Leiden: Brill, 2001), 255–267; Davis, *Memories of State*, 129–138; Orit Bashkin, *The Other Iraq: Pluralism and Culture in Hashemite Iraq* (Stanford: Stanford University Press, 2009), 157–193; and Fanar Haddad, *Sectarianism in Iraq: Antagonistic Visions of Unity* (London: Hurst, 2011), 31–64.

16. Peter Sluglett, "Dealing with the Past: Methodological Issues," in *Writing the Modern History of Iraq: Historiographical and Political Challenges*, ed. Jordi Tejel, Peter Sluglett, Riccardo Bocco, and Hamit Bozarslan (Hackensack, NJ: World Scientific, 2012), 1–12, and Johan Franzén, "Writing the History of Iraq: The Fallacy of 'Objective' History," in Tejel et al., *Writing the Modern History of Iraq*, 31–46.

17. Eric Davis, "History for the Many or History for the Few? The Historiography of the Iraqi Working Class," in *Workers and Working Classes in the Middle East: Struggles, Histories, Historiographies*, ed. Zackary Lockman (Albany: State University of New York Press, 1994), 271–301, and Zubaida, "Community, Class and Minorities."

18. Wiebke Walther, "From Women's Problems to Women as Images in Modern Iraqi Poetry," *Die Welt des Islams* 36:2 (1996), 219–241, Orit Bashkin, "Representations of Women in the Writings of the Intelligentsia in Hashemite Iraq, 1921–1958," *Journal of Middle East Women's Studies* 4:1 (Winter 2008), 53–82, and Yaseen Noorani, "Iraqi Modernism and the Representation of Femininity: Badr Shakir al-Sayyab and Abd al-Wahhab al-Bayati," *International Journal of Contemporary Iraqi Studies* 4:1–2 (2010), 101–119.

19. Partha Chatterjee, *The Nation and Its Fragments: Colonial and Postcolonial Histories* (Princeton: Princeton University Press, 1993), 116–134, and Laura Bier, *Revolutionary Womanhood: Feminisms, Modernity, and the State in Nasser's Egypt* (Stanford: Stanford University Press, 2011), 13–17.

20. Chandra Talpade Mohanty, *Feminism Without Borders: Decolonizing Theory, Practicing Solidarity* (Durham, NC: Duke University Press, 2003), 57–64.

21. Abdul-Salaam Yousif, "The Struggle for Cultural Hegemony in Iraq," in *The Iraqi Revolution of 1958: The Old Social Classes Revisited*, ed. Robert Fernea and William Roger Louis (London: I. B. Tauris, 1991), 173–196.

22. Zubaida, "Community, Class and Minorities."

23. Al-Ali, *Iraqi Women*, 83.

24. George Mosse, *Nationalism and Sexuality: Middle-Class Morality and Sexual Norms in Modern Europe* (Madison: University of Wisconsin Press, 1985); Ranjoo Seodu Herr, "The Possibility of Nationalist Feminism," *Hypatia* 18:3 (2003), 135–160; Bier, *Revolutionary Womanhood*; and Sikata Banerjee, *Muscular Nationalism: Gender, Violence, and Empire in India and Ireland, 1914–2004* (New York: New York University Press, 2012).

25. Michael Wright, "Observations on and since the Revolution," December 7, 1958, FO 371/133075 EQ 1015/402, and Batatu, *The Old Social Classes*, 764–807.

26. ʿAbd al-Karim al-Dujayli, *Muhadarat ʾan al-Shiʿr al-ʿIraqi* (Cairo: Jamiʿat al-Duwal al-ʿArabiyya, 1959), 160–161.

27. William Roger Louis, "Britain and the Crisis of 1958," in *A Revolutionary Year: The Middle East in 1958*, ed. William Roger Louis and Roger Owen (London: I. B. Tauris, 2002), 57–76.

28. Muhammad Mahdi al-Jawahiri, *Dhikrayati*, vol. 2 (Damascus: Dar al-Rafidayn, 1988), 191–194.

29. Muhammad Mahdi al-Jawahiri, *Diwan al-Jawahiri*, vol. 4 (Beirut: Bisan, 2000), 103–107.

30. Muhammad Mahdi al-Jawahiri, "Bi-Ism al-Sha'b," *al-Ra'i al-'Amm*, November 30, 1958, in al-Jawahiri, *Diwan al-Jawahiri*, 4:111–116.

31. Dhu al-Nun Ayyub, "al-Muqaddimah," introduction to *Aqbas al-Thawra: Min A'maq Sha'b 14 Tammuz*, by Muhammad Salih Bahr al-'Ulum (Baghdad: Wizarat al-Ma'arif, 1959), 10–13.

32. Bahr al-'Ulum, *Aqbas al-Thawra*, 17–21.

33. Bahr al-'Ulum, *Aqbas al-Thawra*, 17.

34. Bahr al-'Ulum, *Aqbas al-Thawra*, 22–27.

35. William Morris to S. J. Whitewell, "State of Iraqi Press," November 21, 1958, FO 371/133120 EQ 1671/8.

36. 'Abd al-Wahhab al-Bayati, "Nahnu al-Ahrar," *al-Adab* 6:9–10 (1958), 28, and *Yanabi' al-Shams: al-Sira al-Shi'riyya* (Damascus: Dar al-Farqad, 1999), 52–63; and Kazim Jawad, "Mudhakkirat Musafir," *al-Adab* 6:12 (1958), 12–13.

37. 'Ali al-Hilli, *Thawrat al-Ba'th* (Beirut: Matabi' Dar al-Andalus, 1963), 53–56.

38. Higher National Committee of the National Unity Front, "To the Noble Iraqi People," November 12, 1958, FO 371/133073 EQ 1015/376, and Chancery Baghdad to Eastern Department, "National Unity Front," November 27, 1958, FO 371/133073 EQ 1015/377.

39. Michael Wright, "Analysis of Reasons for Instability and Factors at Work," December 4, 1958, FO 371/133074 EQ 1015/385, and Sam Falle to William Combs, "Press Interviews with Rikabi and Shanshal," December 24, 1958, FO 371/133706 EQ 1015/430.

40. 'Adnan al-Rawi, *Min al-Qahira ila.. Mu'taqil Qasim!* (Beirut: Dar al-Adab, 1963), 11–33, and "Anti-Communist Elements in Iraq," February 6, 1959, CIA-RDP78-02771R000300520002-7.

41. Michael Wright, "Observations on and since the Revolution," December 7, 1958, FO 371/133075 EQ 1015/402, and Crawford to Foreign Office, December 14, 1959, FO 371/133075 EQ 1015/400.

42. Crawford to Foreign Office, December 9, 1958, FO 371/133705 EQ 1015/391, and December 14, 1958, FO 371/133705 EQ 1015/400; and Chancery Baghdad to Eastern Department, December 18, 1958, FO 371/133705 EQ 1015/409.

43. 'Abd al-Juburi, "Muqaddima," in 'Adnan al-Rawi, *al-Majmu'a al-Shi'riyya al-Kamila lil-Sha'ir 'Adnan al-Rawi, 1925–1967* (Baghdad: Wizarat al-Thaqafa wa al-Funun, 1978), 10–11.

44. 'Adnan al-Rawi, *Diwan al-Sha'ir al-'Arabi wa al-Za'im al-Thawri al-'Iraqi al-Munadil: 'Adnan al-Rawi* (Cairo: Dar al-Hilal, 1974), 731–734.

45. Rawi, *Min al-Qahira*, 36–39.

46. Higher National Committee of the National Unity Front, "To the Noble Iraqi People," November 12, 1958, FO 371/133073 EQ 1015/376; "Iraqi Partisans of Peace," December 31, 1958, FO 371/140900 EQ 1015/6; and Jawahiri, *Dhikrayati*, 2:161–210.

47. "Statement by al-Jawahiri on Return Home from Arab Writers Conference," January 7, 1959, FO 371/140902 EQ 1015/38.

48. Jawahiri, *Dhikrayati*, 2:219–221.

49. Chancery Baghdad to Eastern Department, January 29, 1959, FO 371/140903 EQ 1015/66; and Jawahiri, *Diwan al-Jawahiri*, 3:155–159, and *Dhikrayati*, 2:22–27.

50. Rawi, *Min al-Qahira*, 52–57.

51. Movement of Arab Nationalism in Iraq, "Army Day," January 6, 1959, FO 371/140902 EQ 1015/44.

52. J. Hunter, "Fortnightly Review, September 22–October 7, 1958," October 8, 1958, FO 371/133070 EQ 1015/283, and Chancery Baghdad to Eastern Department, "Trial of Abdul Jalil al-Rawi," October 22, 1958, FO 371/133070 EQ 1015/303.

53. R. S. Crawford, "Colonel Fadhil Abbas al Mahdawi and Colonel Wasfi Taher," November 27, 1958, FO 371/133074 EQ 1015/380.

54. Movement of Arab Nationalism in Iraq, "Army Day," January 6, 1959, FO 371/140902 EQ 1015/44.

55. M.S. Berthoud, "Fortnightly Political Summary, December 4–December 17, 1958," December 22, 1958, FO 371/133706 EQ 1015/425, and Hugh Trevelyan to Foreign Office, "Trial of Major General Abbas Ali Ghalib," December 24, 1958, FO 371/133706 EQ 1015/417.

56. Berthoud, "Fortnightly Political Summary, December 4–December 17, 1958."

57. Muhammad Mahdi al-Jawahiri, "Tahiyya 'ila Rountree," *al-Ra'i al-'Amm*, December 16, 1958, in Jawahiri, *Diwan al-Jawahiri*, 4:117.

58. R. S. Crawford, "Colonel Fadhil Abbas al Mahdawi and Colonel Wasfi Taher," November 27, 1958, FO 371/133074 EQ 1015/380.

59. Chancery Baghdad to Eastern Department, "Trials of Bahjat al-Atiyah and Rafiq Tawfiq," January 15, 1959, FO 371/140902 EQ 1015/46.

60. "Shahadat Muhammad Salih Bahr al-'Ulum," in *Muhakamat al-Mahkama al-'Askariyya al-'Ulya al-Khassa: al-Mahadir al-Rasmiyya lil-Jalasat allati Aqadathaha al-Mahkama li Muhakamat al-Muta'amirin 'ala Salamat al-Watan wa Mufsidi Nizam al-Hukm*, vol. 8 (Baghdad: Wizarat al-Difa', 1960), 128.

61. Crawford to Foreign Office, December 14, 1959, FO 371/133075 EQ 1015/400.

62. Rawi, *Diwan al-Sha'ir al-'Arabi*, 767–769.

63. "Daily Radio Commentary, December 31, 1958, by a Middle East

Correspondent," FO 371/133706 EQ 1015/416(c); British Consulate-General, Basra, "Monthly Summary, January 1959," February 9, 1959, FO 371/140897 EQ 1013/5; and J. M. Hunter, "Fortnightly Political Summary, February 12–February 25, 1959," February 26, 1959, FO 371/140897 EQ 1013/7.

64. Chancery Baghdad to Eastern Department, "Iraqi Partisans of Peace," December 31, 1958, FO 371/140900 EQ 1015/6.

65. Batatu, *The Old Social Classes*, 861–889.

66. J. M. Hunter, "Fortnightly Political Summary, February 26–March 11, 1959," March 12, 1959, FO 371/140897 EQ 1013/8, and British Consulate-General, Basra, "Monthly Summary, March 1959," April 14, 1959, FO 371/140898 EQ 1013/13.

67. Kazim Jawad, *Min Aghani al-Huriyya* (Beirut: Matabi' Dar al-'Ilm lil-Malayyin, 1960), 127–129.

68. Samarra'i, *al-Tayyar al-Qawmi* 139.

69. British Consulate-General, Basra, "Monthly Summary, April 1959," May 11, 1959, FO 371/140898 EQ 1013/15.

70. Rawi, *Diwan al-Sha'ir al-'Arabi*, 770–773.

71. Hilal Naji, *Hatta la Nansa: Fusul min Mujazarat al-Mosul* (Cairo: Dar al-'Alam al-'Arabi, 1962), 19.

72. Naji, *Hatta la Nansa*, 103–104.

73. Badr Shakir al-Sayyab, "Nubu'ah fi 'Amm 1956," *al-Adab* 8:6 (1960), 10–11.

74. Samarra'i, *al-Tayyar al-Qawmi*, 139.

75. 'Abd al-'Aziz al-Duri, *al-Judhur al-Tarikhiyya li al-Shu'ubiyya* (Beirut: Dar al-Tali'a, 1960); 'Abd al-Razzaq al-Hasani, *Ta'rikh al-Wizarat al-'Iraqiyya*, vol. 2 (Sidon: Matba'at al-'Urfan, 1953), 84–85; and Abu Khaldun Sati' al-Husri, *Mudhakkirati fi al-'Iraq*, vol. 1 (Beirut: Dar al-Tali'ah, 1967), 557–569.

76. 'Abd al-Hadi al-Fakiki, *al-Shu'ubiyya wa al-Qawmiyya al-'Arabiyya* (Beirut: Dar al-'Arab, 1962), 97–111.

77. Fakiki, *al-Shu'ubiyya wa al-Qawmiyya al-'Arabiyya*, 13–14.

78. Yunus al-Bahri, *Sab'at Ashhur fi Sujun Baghdad* (Beirut: Maktab al-'Asri lil-Sihafa wa al-Nashr, 1960), 130–132.

79. Sulayman al-'Isa "Qatilat al-Salam al-Ahmar," *al-Adab* 7:5 (1959), 4–5. See also Sulayman al-'Isa, *al-Dam wa al-Nujum al-Khudr* (Beirut: Dar al-'Ilm lil-Malayyin, 1959), 82–98.

80. Salma Khadra Jayyusi, *Trends and Movements in Modern Arabic Poetry*, vol. 2 (Leiden: E. J. Brill, 1977), 592–593.

81. Fa'iz Sayigh, "Mu'arakatuna ma' al-Shiyu'iyya," *al-Adab* 7:6 (1959), 1–3.

82. Sulayman al-'Isa, "al-Najm al-Akhdar.. wa Qatilat al-Mosul," *al-Adab*, 7:6 (1959), 4–5, and *al-Dam wa al-Nujum al-Khudr*, 99–120.

83. Naji, *Hatta la Nansa*, 118.

84. Naji, *Hatta la Nansa*, 119–121.

85. Ali, *Iraqi Women*, 82–83.
86. Bahr al-ʿUlum, *Aqbas al-Thawra*, 137–140.
87. Chancery Baghdad, "Political Summary, April 9–April 20, 1959," April 22, 1959, FO 371/140898 EQ 1013/14.
88. Muhammad Mahdi al-Jawahiri, "Unshudat al-Salam," *al-Raʾi al-ʿAmm*, April 16, 1959, in al-Jawahiri, *Diwan al-Jawahiri*, 4:127–130.
89. Bahr al-ʿUlum, *Aqbas al-Thawra*, 151.
90. Hayyat al-Nahr, *Ughniyyat lil-Thawra: Shiʿr* (Baghdad: Matbaʿat al-Rabita, 1960), 51–53.
91. Batatu, *The Old Social Classes*, 912–921.
92. Samarraʾi, *al-Tayyar al-Qawmi*, 140–143.
93. Walid al-Aʿzami, *Aghani al-Maʿrakah* (al-Kuwait: Maktabat al-Manar 1966), 92–95.
94. Abd al-Jabbar Dawud al-Basri, "Kassab alladhi Yughani bi-Istimrar," *al-Hurriyya*, August 7, 1959, in Samarraʾi, *al-Tayyar al-Qawmi*, 141.
95. ʿAbd al-Qadir al-Rashid al-Nasiri, *Diwan ʿAbd al-Qadir al-Nasiri*, vol. 2 (Baghdad: Maktabat al-ʿAni, 1965), 105.
96. Hilal Naji, *Ughniyat Huzn ila Kirkuk* (Baghdad: al-Matbaʿah al-Misriyya, 1963), 7–9.
97. Naji, *Hatta la Nansa*.
98. Rawi, *Min al-Qahira*, 172–205, and Farouk-Sluglett and Sluglett, *Iraq since 1958*, 72–73.
99. Batatu, *The Old Social Classes*, 931–932.
100. Rawi, *Diwan al-Shaʿir al-ʿArabi*, 774.
101. Nuʿman Mahir al-Kanʿani, *Lahib fi Dijla* (Damascus: Matabiʿ Alif Baʾ, 1960), 100.
102. Muhammad Jamil Shalash, *Diwan Muhammad Jamil Shalash* (Beirut: Dar al-ʿAwda, 1978), 158–159.
103. "Munaqashat al-Multahim Muhammad Jamil Shalash," in *Muhakamat al-Mahkamah*, 22:275–288.
104. "Munaqashat al-Multahim Hashim al-ʿAmir," in *Muhakamat al-Mahkamah*, 22:317–327.
105. ʿAli al-Hilli, "Saq ʿala Danub: Shiʿr Hilal Naji," *al-Adab* 7:10 (1959), 68–69; *Thawrat al-Baʿth*, 18–24.
106. Yousif, "The Struggle for Cultural Hegemony in Iraq," 186–190.
107. Sayyab, *Kuntu Shuyuʿiyyan*, and Colla, "Badr Shakir al-Sayyab," 247–263.
108. M. M. Badawi, *A Critical Introduction to Modern Arabic Poetry* (New York: Cambridge University Press, 1975), 255–256.
109. Badr Shakir al-Sayyab, *Diwan Badr Shakir al-Sayyab: al-Aʿmal al-Shiʿriyya al-Kamila* (Cairo: Maktabat Jazirat al-Ward, 2009), 408–410.
110. Amatzia Baram, *Culture, History and Ideology in the Formation of Baʿthist Iraq, 1968–89* (London: Macmillan, 1991), 87–89.

111. Sayyab, *Diwan Badr Shakir al-Sayyab*, 423–444.

112. Badr Shakir al-Sayyab, "Kuntu Shuyu'iyyan," *al-Hurriyya*, August 17, 1959, in Sayyab, *Kuntu Shuyu'iyyan*, 19–25.

113. Badr Shakir al-Sayyab, "Kuntu Shuyu'iyyan," *al-Hurriyyh*, September 4, 1959, in al-Sayyab, *Kuntu Shuyu'iyyan*, 103–108.

114. Terri DeYoung, *Placing the Poet: Badr Shakir al-Sayyab and Postcolonial Iraq* (Albany: State University of New York Press, 1998), 244–245; Davis, *Memories of State*, 211; and Bashkin, "Representations of Women," 70–71.

115. Ihsan 'Abbas, *Badr Shakir al-Sayyab* (Beirut: Dar al-Thaqafa, 1969), 222–224, and Pieter Smoor, "Modern Poets of Iraq, 1948–79: Cockroach or Martyr in the Inn by the Persian Gulf," *Oriente Moderno* 9:1/6 (1990), 7–38.

116. Badr Shakir al-Sayyab, "Kuntu Shuyu'iyyan" *al-Hurriyya*, August 17, 1959, in Sayyab, *Kuntu Shuyu'iyyan*, 19–25.

117. Badr Shakir al-Sayyab, "Kuntu Shuyu'iyyan" *al-Hurriyya*, August 26, 1959, in al-Sayyab, *Kuntu Shuyu'iyyan*, 70–76.

118. Bashkin, *The Other Iraq*, 136.

119. 'Abd al-Hadi al-Fakiki, Shafiq al-Kamali, Hilal Naji, 'Adnan al-Rawi, and Muhyi al-Din Isma'il, "al-Nashat al-Thaqafi fi al-'Alim al-'Arabi: al-'Iraq," *al-Adab* 8:3 (1960), 69.

120. Issa J. Boullata, "The Poetic Technique of Badr Shakir al-Sayyab (1926–1964)," *Journal of Arabic Literature* 2 (1971), 104–115.

121. Badr Shakir al-Sayyab, "Madinat al-Sindbad," *Shi'r* 4:14 (1960), 7–14.

122. Badr Shakir al-Sayyab, "Nubu'ah fi 'Amm 1956," *al-Adab* 8:6 (1960), 10–11.

123. J. M. Hunter, "Fortnightly Political Summary, March 12–March 25, 1959," March 26, 1959, FO 371/140897 EQ 1013/10; Baha al-Din Nuri, *Mudhakkirat Baha al-Din Nuri* (London: Dar al-Hikmah, 2001), 144; Ali, *Iraqi Women*, 86–87; and Efrati, *Women in Iraq*, 127–136.

124. Efrati, *Women in Iraq*, 160–162.

125. Al-Ali, *Iraqi Women*, 83.

126. Nahr, *Ughniyyat lil-Thawra*, 38–41.

127. Lami'a 'Abbas 'Amara, *'Awdat al-Rabi' wa al-Zawiyya al-Khaliyya*, 97–98.

128. Bahri, *Sab'at Ashhur fi Sujun Baghdad*, 128.

129. Al-Ali, *Iraqi Women*, 82–83.

130. Shakir Mustafa Salim, *Min Mudhakkirat Qawmi Muta'amir* (Beirut: Dar al-Tali'a, 1960), 49–51.

131. J. M. Hunter, "Fortnightly Political Report, October 24–November 5, 1958," FO 371/133702 EQ 1015/341, and Haifa Zangana, *City of Widows: An Iraqi Woman's Account of War and Resistance* (New York: Seven Stories Press, 2007), 48–49.

132. Salim, *Min Mudhakkirat Qawmi Muta'amir*, 52–53.

133. Shadhil Taqa, *al-Majmuʿa al-Shiʿriyya al-Kamila* (Baghdad: Manshurat Wizarat al-Iʿlam, 1977), 235–244.

134. Hasan Tawfiq, *Shiʿr Badr Shakir al-Sayyab: Dirasa Fanniyya wa Fikriyya* (Beirut: al-Muʾassassa al-ʿArabiyya lil-Dirasat wa al-Nashr, 1979), 146–157; Yousif, "The Struggle for Cultural Hegemony in Iraq," 184–185; and Efrati, *Women in Iraq*, 123–126.

135. Yasir Suleiman, "Nationalist Concerns in the Poetry of Nazik al-Malaʾika," *British Journal of Middle Eastern Studies* 22:1/2 (1995), 93–114.

136. Jawahiri, *Dhikrayati*, 2:219–221.

137. Nazik al-Malaʾika, "Thulath Ughniyyat Shuyuʿiyya," *al-Adab* 8:3 (1960), 1–2.

138. Nazik al-Malaʾika, "Fi Dhikra al-Thawratayn," *al-Adab* 7:7 (1959), 1–3.

139. Bashkin, *The Other Iraq*, 136.

140. Nizar Qabbani, "Jamila Buhayrid," *al-Adab* 6:4 (1958), 1–2; Muhammad al-Masri, "Jazaʾiriyya," *al-Adab* 6:4 (1958), 9; Shafiq al-Kamali, "Jamila," *al-Adab* 6:4 (1958), 10; ʿIsa al-Naʿuri, "Jamila al-Jazaʾiriyya," *al-Adab* 6:4 (1958), 11; and Najib Surur, "al-Jumʿa al-Hazina," *al-Adab* 6:4 (1958), 12. On Buhayrid, see also Deniz Kandiyoti, "Identity and Its Discontents: Women and the Nation," *Millennium* 20 (1991), 429–444; Marnia Lazreg, *The Eloquence of Silence: Algerian Women in Question* (New York: Routledge, 1994), 118–141; and Bier, *Revolutionary Womanhood*, 173–174.

141. ʿAli al-Hilli, "Min Jan Dark ila Jamila Buhayrid," *al-Adab* 6:6–8 (1958), 22–23.

142. Lamiʿa ʿAbbas ʿAmara, "Jamila," *al-Adib* 17:5 (1958), 27; Bahr al-ʿUlum, *Aqbas al-Thawra*, 146–150; ʿAbd al-Wahhab al-Bayati, *Kalimat La Tamut* (Beirut: Dar al-ʿIlm li al-Malayin, 1960), 40–44; and Nahr, *Ughniyyat lil-Thawra*, 54–59.

143. Zangana, *City of Widows*, 15.

144. "al-Mahdawi Yuhanaʾ al-Shaʿb al-Jazaʾiri bi-ʿAydihi al-Watani," *Muhakamat al-Mahkama*, 22:xvii–xviii.

145. Nazik al-Malaʾika, "Nahnu wa Jamila," *al-Adab* 7:1 (1959), 18.

146. Zangana, *City of Widows*, 46–48.

147. Taliʿat al-Rifaʿi, "Thawra," *al-Thaqafa* 2:1 (1959), 32–33, and Jayyusi, *Trends and Movements*, 2:592.

148. Taqa, *al-Majmuʿa al-Shiʿriyya al-Kamila*, 219–220.

149. Badr Shakir al-Sayyab, "Jamila Buhayrid," *Aswat* 1:1 (1961), 40–42.

150. "Munaqashat al-Multahim Hashim al-ʿAmir," in *Muhakamat al-Mahkama*, 22:327.

151. Charles Tripp, "'In the Name of the People': The 'People's Court' and the Iraqi Revolution (1958–1960)," in *Staging Politics: Power and Performance in Asia and Africa*, ed. Julia C. Strauss and Donald B. Cruise O'Brien (London: I. B. Tauris, 2007), 31–48.

152. "Shahadat Yusra Saʿid Thabit," in *Muhakamat al-Mahkama*, 22:344–353.

153. Naji, *Hatta La Nansa*, 125–128.

154. Rawi, *Diwan al-Shaʿir al-ʿArabi*, 749–750.

155. Hilli, *Thawrat al-Baʿth*, 89–94.

156. Baghdad Chancery to Eastern Department, December 13, 1961, FO 371/157671 EQ 1015/188.

157. Bayati, *Yanabi' al-Shams*, 72.

158. Lazar Fleishman, *Boris Pasternak: The Poet and His Politics* (Cambridge, MA: Harvard University Press, 1990), 280–297, and Christopher Barnes, *Boris Pasternak: A Literary Biography*, vol. 2 (Cambridge: Cambridge University Press, 1998), 312–351.

159. Bayati, *Kalimat La Tamut*, 85–87.

160. Leon Trotsky, *Literature and Revolution*, trans. Rose Strunsky (Ann Arbor: University of Michigan Press, 1960), 155, and Clare Cavanagh, *Lyric Poetry and Modern Politics: Russia, Poland, and the West* (New Haven: Yale University Press, 2009), 102–103.

161. Bayati, *Yanabi' al-Shams*, 72.

162. Hilal Naji and Muhyi al-Din Isma'il, *Jinayyat al-Shuyu'iyin 'ala al-Adab al-'Iraqi* (Cairo: Dar al-Karnak lil-Nashr, 1960), 5.

163. 'Abd al-Wahhab al-Bayati, *Kalimat La Tamut: Shi'r* (Beirut: Dar al-Adab, 1969).

164. Yousif, "The Struggle for Cultural Hegemony in Iraq," 129–130.

165. Naji and Isma'il, *Jinayyat al-Shuyu'iyin*, 14–20.

166. Jawahiri, *Dhikrayati*, 2:121.

167. Naji and Isma'il, *Jinayyat al-Shuyu'iyin*, 31–32.

168. E. F. Penrose, "Memorandum on Situation in Iraq," January 21, 1959, FO 371/140902 EQ 1015/57.

169. Naji and Isma'il, *Jinayyat al-Shuyu'iyin*, 24–25, 65, 88.

170. 'Abd al-Wahhab al-Bayati, *al-A'mal al-Shi'riyya*, vol. 1 (Beirut: Dar al-Mu'assassa al-'Arabiyya, 1995), 191–192.

171. Muhammad Salih Bahr al-'Ulum, "The People of Iraq Want to Live in Friendship with the Soviet Union," *Culture and Life* 3:1 (1959), 29–30, 67–70; Bahr al-'Ulum, *Aqbas al-Thawra*, 40–43, 71–82, 137–140, 152–155; and Naji and Isma'il, *Jinayyat al-Shuyu'iyin*, 91.

172. 'Amara, *'Awdat al-Rabi' wa al-Zawiyya al-Khaliyya*, 59–60, 97–98, 99–101.

173. Lami'a 'Abbas 'Amara, "al-Adhru' al-Sud," *al-Fikr* 2:2 (1959), 24–25.

174. 'Ali al-Hilli, "Lumumba," *al-Adab* 9:3 (1961), 8.

175. Sayyab, "al-Iltizam wa al-La-Iltizam," 220–234, and Naji and Isma'il, *Jinayyat al-Shuyu'iyin*, 13–33.

176. Baqir Samaka, "Sukran," *al-Adib* 16:1 (1957), 58; Baqir Samaka, "Milak," *al-Adib* 17:4 (1958), 44; and Naji and Isma'il, *Jinayyat al-Shuyu'iyin*, 31.

177. Sa'di Yusuf, *al-A'mal al-Shi'riyya*, vol. 1 (Damascus: Dar al-Mada lil-Thaqafa wa al-Nashr, 1995), 521–522, and Naji and Isma'il, *Jinayyat al-Shuyu'iyin*, 31

178. Kazim Jawad, "Mudhakkirat Musafir," *al-Adab* 6:12 (1958), 12–13, and Naji and Isma'il, *Jinayyat al-Shuyu'iyin*, 63–64.

179. Naji and Isma'il, *Jinayyat al-Shuyu'iyin*, 65.

180. Husayn Mardan, *al-A'mal al-Kamila*, vol. 1 (Baghdad: Dar al-Shu'un, 2009), and Naji and Isma'il, *Jinayyat al-Shuyu'iyin*, 18.

181. Naji and Isma'il, *Jinayyat al-Shuyu'iyin*, 41–50.

182. al-Bayati, *Kalimat La Tamut*, 85–87, and Naji and Isma'il, *Jinayyat al-Shuyu'iyin*, 62.

183. Bahr al-'Ulum, *Aqbas al-Thawra*, 130.

184. Naji and Isma'il, *Jinayyat al-Shuyu'iyin*, 76–77.

185. Yousif, "The Struggle for Cultural Hegemony in Iraq," 186–188.

186. al-Nahr, *Ughniyyat lil-Thawra*, 77–78.

187. Muhammad Mahdi al-Jawahiri, "Kalimat al-Jawahiri," in *al-Mu'tamar al-Thani li Ittihad al-Udaba' al-'Iraqiyyin, 23–26 Haziran, Baghdad, 1960* (Baghdad: Matba'at al-Nujum, 1960), 21–25.

188. Lami'a 'Abbas 'Amara, *al-Zawiyya al-Khaliyya* (Baghdad: Matba'at al-Rabita, 1958); Bahr al-'Ulum, *Aqbas al-Thawra*; 'Abd al-Wahhab al-Bayati, *'Ashrun Qasida min Berlin: Shi'r* (Bahgdad: al-Thaqafa al-Jadida, 1959); Buland al-Haydari, *Ji'tum ma' al-Fajr* (Baghdad: Matba'at al-Rabita, 1960); Baqir Samaka, *Min Hisad al-Thawra* (Baghdad: Matba'at al-Thawra, 1959); and Sa'di Yusuf, *51 Qasida* (Baghdad: Wizarat al-Tarbiyya, 1959).

189. Salah Khalis, "Taqrir al-Sikritariyyah," in *al-Mu'tamar al-Thani*, 26–34.

190. Atef Alshaer, *Poetry and Politics in the Modern Arab World* (London: Hurst, 2016), 54–55.

191. Lami'a 'Abbas 'Amara, "Tahiyyat al-Rusafi," Muhammad Salih Bahr al-'Ulum, "Qasidat Sha'ir al-Sha'b," and Baqir Samaka, "Dhikra al-Rusafi," in *Mihrajan al-Rusafi* (Baghdad: Matba'at al-Ma'arif, 1959), 33–34, 94–95, 117–119.

192. Mirzo Tursunzoda, "Kalimat Wafd al-Ittihad al-Sovieti," in *Mihrajan al-Rusafi*, 47.

193. Muhammad Mahdi al-Jawahiri, "Kalimat al-Ustadh al-Jawahiri" and "Fi Dhikra al-Rusafi," in *Mihrajan al-Rusafi*, 17–27, 128–130.

*194.* Rawi, *Min al-Qahira*, 16.

195. Fa'iq al-Samarra'i, Adnan al-Rawi, and Hilal al-Naji, *Mahkamat al-Mahdawi: Ma'sa wa Malha: Radd Ahrar al-'Iraq* (Cairo: Dar al-Qawmiyya lil-Taba'a wa al-Nashr, 1960), 46–47.

196. Yousif, "The Struggle for Cultural Hegemony in Iraq," 188.

197. Zubaida, "Community, Class and Minorities," 207.

198. Taqa, *al-Majmu'a al-Shi'riyya al-Kamila*, 223–231.

## Conclusion

1. Hanna Batatu, *The Old Social Classes and Revolutionary Movements of Iraq: A Study of Iraq's Old Landed and Commercial Classes and of Its Communists, Ba'thists, and Free Officers* (Princeton: Princeton University Press, 1979), 974–994.

2. Adnan al-Rawi, *Min al-Qahira ila. Mu'taqil Qasim!* (Beirut: Dar al-Adab, 1963), 221.

3. "Baghdad Domestic Service in Arabic 1120 GMT 16 February 1963—M," *Daily Report: Foreign Radio Broadcasts*, no. 35 (February 19, 1963), c3–c4.

4. "Iraq: A Gloomy Prospect," August 1, 1963, CIA-RDP79R00904A001000010008-4.

5. Baghdad Information Office to Eastern Department, March 31, 1961, FO 371/157734 EQ 1671/2.

6. Batatu, *The Old Social Classes*, 942–965.

7. Baghdad Information Office to Eastern Department, April 6, 1961, FO 371/157734 EQ 1671/2, and Abdel-Salaam Yousif, "The Struggle for Cultural Hegemony during the Iraqi Revolution," in *The Iraqi Revolution of 1958: The Old Social Classes Revisited*, ed. Robert A. Fernea and William Roger Louis (London: I. B. Tauris, 1991), 190–191.

8. B.B.C. Monitor Report, "Appeals Against the New Government," March 4, 1963, FO 371/170434 EQ1015/132.

9. C. L. Booth to D. L. N. Goodchild, March 5, 1963, FO 371/170434 EQ 1015/137.

10. "Appeal to the Intellectuals of the World, Men of Letters, Writers and Artists Everywhere, and to World Opinion," March 5, 1963, FO 371/170446 EQ 1018/2.

11. Muhammad Mahdi al-Jawahiri to Harold Macmillan, July 5, 1963, FO 371/170439 EQ 1015/233.

12. "Baghdad Domestic Service in Arabic 1900 GMT 12 August 1963—M," *Daily Report: Foreign Radio Broadcasts*, no. 157 (February 19, 1963), c8.

13. Nazeeha al-Dulaimi to Queen Elizabeth, June 23, 1963, FO 371/170446 EQ 1018/12.

14. Batatu, *The Old Social Classes*, 987–988, and Fouad Ajami, *The Foreigner's Gift: The Americans, the Arabs, and the Iraqis in Iraq* (New York: Free Press, 2006), 340–341.

15. Muhammad Salih Bahr al-'Ulum, *Diwan Bahr al-'Ulum*, vol. 1 (Baghdad: Matba'at Dar al-Tadamun, 1968), 21–22.

16. Fadhil al-'Azzawi, *al-Ruh al-Hayyah: Jil al-Sittinat fi al-'Iraq* (Damascus: Dar al-Thaqafa lil-Nashr, 1997), 30.

17. Abdul-Salaam Yousif, "The Struggle for Cultural Hegemony in Iraq," in *The Iraqi Revolution of 1958*, ed. Robert A. Fernea and William Roger Louis (London: I. B. Tauris, 1991), 190.

18. Muhammad Mahdi al-Jawahiri, *Diwan al-Jawahiri*, vol. 4 (Beirut: Bisan, 2000), 311–314.

19. Muhammad Salih Bahr al-'Ulum, *Diwan Bahr al-'Ulum* (Baghdad: Matba'at Dar al-Tadamun, 1968), 1:21–22.

20. Mahmoud Saeed, "A Legacy of Ruins: Iraqi Letters and Intellectuals under Saddam's Regime," *Aljadid* 9:42–43 (2003), 12–13.

21. ʿAli al-Hilli, *Thawrat al-Baʿth* (Beirut: Matabiʿ Dar al-Andalus, 1963); Hilal Naji, *Ughniyyat Huzn ila Kirkuk* (Baghdad: al-Matbaʿa al-Misriyya, 1963); ʿAdnan al-Rawi, *al-Naft al-Multahib: Qasaʾid min al-ʿIraq* (Beirut: Maktabat al-Maʿarif, 1963); Shadhil Taqa, *Thumma Mata al-Layl: Shiʿr* (Beirut: Dar al-Maktabat al-Hayat, 1963); and Muhammad Jamil Shalash, *al-Hubb wa al-Hurriyya* (Baghdad: Maktabat al-Nahda, 1964).

22. Terri DeYoung, *Placing the Poet: Badr Shakir al-Sayyab and Postcolonial Iraq* (Albany: State University of New York Press, 1998), 255–264.

23. "Shadhil Taqa . . . Awraq ʿanhu," *al-Aqlam* 18:11 (1983), 40.

24. Amatzia Baram, *Culture, History and Ideology in the Formation of Baʿthist Iraq, 1968–89* (New York: St. Martin's Press, 1991), 83–96, and Eric Davis, *Memories of State: Politics, History, and Collective Identity in Modern Iraq* (Berkeley: University of California Press, 2005), 203–226.

25. Abdul-Salaam Yaco Yousif, "Vanguardist Cultural Practice: The Formation of an Alternative Cultural Hegemony in Iraq and Chile, 1930s–1970s" (PhD diss., University of Iowa, 1988), 218.

26. Muzaffar al-Nawwab, *al-Aʿmal al-Shiʿriyya al-Kamila* (London: Dar Qunbur, 1996), 527–532.

27. Yousif, "Vanguardist Cultural Practice," 221–225.

28. Salaam Yousif, "Le Déclin de l'intelligentsia de gauche en Irak/On the Decline of the Leftist Intelligentsia in Iraq," *Revue des mondes musulmans et de la Méditerranée* 117–118 (2007), 51–79.

29. Saeed, "A Legacy of Ruins," 12–13; Yousif, "Le Déclin de l'intelligentsia de gauche en Irak," 51–79; and Elie Chalala, "Youssef al-Sayigh: Poet of Sorrows, Master of Contradictions," *Aljadid* 11:53 (2005), 6–9.

30. Yousif, "Vanguardist Cultural Practice," 159, and Johan Franzén, *Red Star over Iraq: Iraqi Communism before Saddam* (New York: Columbia University Press, 2011), 185–233.

31. Muhammad Salih Bahr al-ʿUlum, *Aqbas al-Thawrah: Min Aʿmaq Saʿb 14 Tammuz* (Baghdad: Matbaʿat al-Irshad, 1959), and Bahr al-ʿUlum, *Diwan Bahr al-ʿUlum*, vols. 1 and 2.

32. Majid Ahmad al-Samarraʾi, *al-Tayyar al-Qawmi fi al-Shiʿr al-ʿIraqi al-Hadith, Mundhu al-Harb al-ʿAlamiyya al-Thaniyya 1939 Hatta Naksat Haziran 1967* (Baghdad: Wizarat al-Thaqafa wa al-Iʿlan, 1983), 62.

33. ʿAbd al-Wahhab al-Bayati, *Yanabiʿ al-Shams: al-Sirah al-Shiʿriyya* (Damascus: Dar al-Farqad, 1999), 73–95, and ʿAbd al-Wahhab al-Bayati, *al-Aʿmal al-Shiʿriyya*, vol. 2 (Beirut: al-Muʾassassa al-ʿArabiyya lil-Dirasat wa al-Nashr, 1995), 7–8.

34. Compare ʿAbd al-Wahhab al-Bayati, *Kalimat La Tamut: Shiʿr* (Beirut: Dar al-ʿIlm lil-Malayyin, 1960), 85–86, with ʿAbd al-Wahhab al-Bayati, *Kalimat La Tamut: Shiʿr* (Beirut: Dar al-Adab, 1969).

35. Buland al-Haydari, *Ji'tum ma' al-Fajr* (Baghdad: Matba'at al-Rabita, 1960). See also Baram, *Culture, History and Ideology*, 87, and Fouad Ajami, *The Dream Palace of the Arabs: A Generation's Odyssey* (New York: Pantheon Books, 1998), 3–9.

36. Buland al-Haydari, *al-A'mal al-Kamila lil-Sha'ir Buland al-Haydari* (Cairo: Dar Su'ad al-Sabah, 1992).

37. Wiebke Walther, "'My Hands Assisted the Hands of Events,'" in *Writing the Self: Autobiographical Writing in Modern Arabic Literature*, ed. Robin Ostle, Ed de Moor, and Stefan Wild (London: Saqi Books, 1998), 258–259.

38. Muhsin al-Musawi, "Muhammad Mahdi al-Jawahiri," in *Essays in Arabic Literary Biography, 1850–1950*, ed. Roger Allen (Wiesbaden: Harrassowitz Verlag, 2010), 173.

39. Saeed, "A Legacy of Ruins," 12–13.

40. Salih J. Altoma, "In Memoriam: Muhammad Mahdi al-Jawahiri (1900?–1997)," Arab Studies *Quarterly* 19:4 (1997), v.

41. Saadi A. Simawi, "The Politics and the Poetics of Sa'di Yusuf," *Arab Studies Quarterly* 19:4 (1997), 173–186.

42. Yousif, "Le Déclin de l'intelligentsia de gauche en Irak," 51–79.

43. Saadi Youssef, "I Have Trained Myself Hard to Be Free," *Banipal: Magazine of Modern Arabic Literature* 20 (2004), 2–14.

44. Youssef, "I Have Trained Myself Hard to Be Free," 13.

45. Muhammad Mahdi al-Jawahiri, *Diwan al-Jawahiri*, vol. 1 (Najaf: Matba'at al-Ghari, 1935), 3.

46. Muhammad Salih Bahr al-'Ulum, *Diwan Bahr al-'Ulum*, vol. 1 (Baghdad: Matba'at Dar al-Tadamun, 1968), 109.

47. Atef Alshaer, *Poetry and Politics in the Modern Arab World* (London: Hurst, 2016), 53.

48. Muhammad Mahdi al-Jawahiri, *Dhikrayati*, vol. 1 (Damascus: Dar al-Rafidin), 1988, 65.

49. 'Abd al-Karim al-Dujayli, *Muhadharat 'an al-Shi'r al-'Iraqi al-Hadith* (Cairo: Jami'at al-Duwal al-'Arabiyya, Ma'had al-Dirasat al-'Arabiyya, 1959), 30.

50. Ayyub, "al-Muqaddimah," 10–13.

51. Abdul-Salaam Yacoob Yousif, "Vanguardist Cultural Practices: The Formation of an Alternative Cultural Hegemony in Iraq and Chile, 1930–1970s" (PhD diss., University of Iowa, 1988), 158–159.

52. Taki al-Husaynawi, "Ayn Haqqi," *YouTube*, March 1, 2019, https://www.youtube.com/watch?v=vbUT-lIx6N8.

53. Ahmad Hadi, "Ba'd Unshuda Ihtijajiyya ... Sahib 'Ayn Haqqi' Sayughani Ash'ar Ahmad Matar Qariban," *Ultra 'Iraq*, March 13, 2019, https://ultrairaq.ultrasawt.com.

54. Turki al-Hamad, *al-Karadib: Atyaf al-Aziqqa al-Muhjura* (Dubai: Dar Madarik lil-Nashr, 2012).

55. Muhammad Ali Muhyi al-Din, "Ayna Haqqi ... al-Ma'thara al-Uzma," *Gilgamesh*, August 18, 2007, http://www.gilgamish.org/2007/08/18/3279.html.

56. Sinan Antoon, "Dead Poets Society," *Nation*, May 26, 2003, 29.

# BIBLIOGRAPHY

## Unpublished Archival Sources

India Office Library, London
IOR/L/PS/10 Letters, Political and Secret
British National Archives, Kew

| | |
|---|---|
| AIR 2 | Air Ministry and Ministry of Defense: Registered Files |
| AIR 5 | Air Ministry: Air Historical Branch: Papers (Series II) |
| AIR 20 | Air Ministry and Ministry of Defense: Unregistered Papers |
| AIR 23 | Air Ministry: Overseas Commands: Reports and Correspondence |
| CAB 106 | War Cabinet and Cabinet Office: Historical Section: Archivist and Library Files |
| CO 730 | Colonial Office: Iraq Original Correspondence |
| FO 371 | Foreign Office: Political Departments: General Correspondence, 1906–1966 |
| FO 406 | Foreign Office: Confidential Print Eastern Affairs |
| FO 624 | Foreign Office: Baghdad Embassy |
| FO 838 | Foreign Office: 'Amara Consulate |

## Published Archival Sources

### US NATIONAL ARCHIVES

*Confidential U.S. State Department Central Files: Iraq, 1945–1949 (Internal Affairs and Foreign Affairs)*. 10 microfilm reels. Frederick, MD: University Publications of America, 1987.

*Confidential U.S. State Department Central Files: Iraq, 1950–1954 (Internal Af-*

*fairs and Foreign Affairs).* 18 microfilm reels. Frederick, MD: University Publications of America, 1987.

*Confidential U.S. State Department Central Files: Iraq, 1955–1959 (Internal Affairs and Foreign Affairs).* 17 microfilm reels. Frederick, MD: University Publications of America, 1991.

*Confidential U.S. State Department Central Files: Iraq, 1960-January 1963 (Internal Affairs and Foreign Affairs).* 13 microfilm reels. Bethesda, MD: University Publications of America, 2002.

*Confidential U.S. State Department Central Files: Iraq, February 1963–1966 (Part 1: Political, Governmental and National Defense Affairs).* 10 microfilm reels. Bethesda, MD: University Publications of America, 2006.

## Electronic Archives

Central Intelligence Agency Freedom of Information Act Electronic Reading Room, https://www.cia.gov/library/readingroom/

Gertrude Bell Archive, http://gertrudebell.ncl.ac.uk

### OFFICIAL GOVERNMENT PUBLICATIONS

Ittihad al-Udaba' al-'Iraqiyyin. *Mihrajan al-Rusafi 1959.* Baghdad: Matba'at al-Ma'arif, 1959.

———. *al-Mu'tamar al-Thani li Ittihad al-Udaba' al-'Iraqiyyin, 23–26 Haziran, Baghdad, 1960.* Baghdad: Matba'at al-Nujum, 1960.

U.S. Foreign Broadcast Information Service. *Daily Report, Foreign Radio Broadcasts.* 1958–1963.

Wizarat al-Difa'. *Muhakamat al-Mahkama al-'Askariyya al-'Ulya al-Khassa: al-Mahadir al-Rasmiyya lil-Jalasat allati Aqadathaha al-Mahkama li Muhakamat al-Muta'amirin 'ala Salamat al-Watan wa Mufsidi Nizam al-Hukm,* 22 vols. Baghdad: Wizarat al-Difa', 1958–1962.

## Arabic Periodicals

*al-Adab*
*al-Adib*
*al-Aqdam*
*al-Aqlam*
*al-'Arab*
*al-Aswat*
*al-Bayan*
*al-Fikr*
*Filastin*

*al-Hadiqa*
*al-Hilal*
*al-'Iraq*
*al-'Irfan*
*Kazima*
*Layla*
*Lughat al-'Arab*
*al-Mabda'*
*al-Muqtabas*
*al-Muqtataf*
*al-Nafa'is al-'Asriyyah*
*al-Nafir*
*al-Nashi'a*
*al-'Usur*
*al-Risala*
*al-Risala al-Jadida*
*Shi'r*
*al-Thaqafa*
*al-Yarmuk*
*al-Zahra'*
*al-Zuhur*

## Published Poetry Collections

Abi al-Muhasin, Muhammad Hasan. *Diwan Abi al-Muhasin al-Karbala'i*. Najaf: Matba'at al-Baqir, 1963.

al-Akhras, 'Abd al-Ghaffar. *al-Tiraz al-Anfas fi Shi'r al-Akhras*. Istanbul: Matba'at al-Sharika al-Martabiyya, 1887.

———. *Diwan al-Akhras*. Beirut: Maktabat al-Nahda al-'Arabiyya, 1986.

'Amara, Lami'a 'Abbas. *al-Zawiyya al-Khaliyya*. Baghdad: Matba'at al-Rabita, 1958.

———. *'Awdat al-Rabi'*. Baghdad: Matba'at Ittihad al-Udaba' al-'Iraqiyyin, 1962.

———. *'Awdat al-Rabi' wa al-Zawiyya al-Khaliyya*. La Mesa, CA: Amara Publisher, 2001.

al-Athari, Muhammad Bahjat. *Malahim . . . Wa Azhar*. Cairo: al-Hay'a al-Misriyya al-'Amma lil-Kitab, 1974.

———. *Diwan al-Athari*. 2 vols. Baghdad: Matba'at al-Majma' al-'Ilmi al-'Iraqi, 1990.

al-A'zami, Walid. *Aghani al-Ma'raka*. al-Kuwait: Maktabat al-Manar 1966.

al-Azri, 'Abd al-Husayn. *Diwan al-Hajj 'Abd al-Husayn al-Azri*. Beirut: al-Nu'man, 1980.

al-Azri, Kazim. *Diwan Shaykh Kazim al-Azri al-Baghdadi*. Bombay: al-Matbaʿa al-Mustafawiyya, 1902.

Bahr al-ʿUlum, Muhammad Salih. *al-Awatif*. Najaf: Matbaʿat al-Raʿi, 1937.

———. *Aqbas al-Thawra: Min Aʿmaq Shaʿb 14 Tammuz*. Baghdad: Wizarat al-Maʿarif, 1959.

———. *Diwan Bahr al-ʿUlum*. 2 vols. Baghdad: Matbaʿat Dar al-Tadamun, 1968.

al-Bannaʾ, ʿAbd al-Rahman. *Dhikra Istiqlal al-ʿIraq: al-Juzʾ al-Thani min Diwan ʿAbd al-Rahman al-Bannaʾ*. Baghdad: Matbaʿat al-Furat, 1927.

al-Basir, Muhammad Mahdi. *al-Majmuʿa al-Shiʿriyya al-Kamila: al-Burkan wa Zabad al-Amwaj*. Baghdad: Wizarat al-Iʿlam, al-Jumhuriyya al-ʿIraqiyya, 1977.

al-Bayati, ʿAbd al-Wahhab. *ʿAshrun Qasida min Berlin: Shiʿr*. Baghdad: al-Thaqafa al-Jadida, 1959.

———. *Kalimat La Tamut*. Beirut: Dar al-ʿIlm li al-Malayin, 1960.

———. *Abariq al-Muhashshama*. Beirut: Manshurat Dar al-Adab, 1967.

———. *Kalimat La Tamut: Shiʿr*. Beirut: Dar al-Adab, 1969.

———. *al-Aʿmal al-Shiʿriyya*. 2 vols. Beirut: al-Muʾassassa al-ʿArabiyya, 1995.

al-Habbubi, Mahmud. *Diwan Mahmud al-Habbubi*. Najaf: Matbaʿat Dar al-Nashr wa al-Taʾlif, 1948.

al-Habbubi, Muhammad Saʿid. *Diwan al-Sayyid Muhammad Saʿid al-Habbubi al-Najafi Ashʿar Shuʿaraʾ al-Sharq Ams wa Akbar ʿUlamaʾihi al-Yawm*. Beirut: al-Matbaʿah al-Ahliyya, 1913.

al-Hashimi, Muhammad. *Diwan al-Sayyid Muhammad al-Hashimi al-Baghdadi*. Baghdad: Wizarat al-Iʿlam, 1977.

al-Hashimi, Rashid. *Diwan Rashid al-Hashimi*. Baghdad: Matbaʿat al-Maʿarif, 1964.

al-Haydari, Buland. *Jiʾtum maʿ al-Fajr*. Baghdad: Matbaʿat al-Rabita, 1960.

———. *al-Aʿmal al-Kamila lil-Shaʿir Buland al-Haydari*. Cairo: Dar Suʿad al-Sabah, 1993.

al-Haydari, Talib. *Nidal: Qasaʾid Thawriyya min al-ʿIraq*. Baghdad: Matbaʿat al-Maʿarif, 1958.

al-Hilli, ʿAli. *Thawrat al-Baʿth*. Beirut: Matabiʿ Dar al-Andalus, 1963.

al-Hilli, Haydar. *Diwan Haydar al-Hilli*. Najaf: Matbaʿat al-Haydariyya, 1950.

al-Hilli, Jaʿfar. *Kitab Sihr Babibl wa Sajaʿ al-Balabil: Aw, Tarajim Al-Aʿyan Wa Al-Afadhil*. Sidon: Matbaʿat al-ʿIrfan, 1912.

al-Huwayzi, ʿAbd al-Husayn. *Diwan al-Huwayzi*. Beirut: Dar Maktabat al-Haya, 1964.

al-ʿIsa, Sulayman. *al-Dam wa al-Nujum al-Khudr*. Beirut: Dar al-ʿIlm lil-Malayyin, 1959.

Jawad, Kazim. *Min Aghani al-Hurriyyah*. Beirut: Matabiʿ Dar al-ʿIlm lil-Malayyin, 1960.

al-Jawahiri, Muhammad Mahdi. *Diwan al-Jawahiri*. Najaf: Matbaʿat al-Ghari, 1935.

———. *Diwan al-Jawahiri.* 5 vols. Beirut: Bisan, 2000.
al-Kaʿbi, Hashim. *Diwan al-Kaʿbi.* Najaf: Matbaʿat al-Haydariyya, 1964.
al-Kanʿani, Nuʿman Mahir. *Lahib fi Dijlah.* Damascus: Matabiʿ Alif Baʾ, 1960.
al-Kazimi, ʿAbd al-Muhsin. *al-Amal al-Shiʿriyya al-Kamila li Shaʿir al-ʿArab ʿAbd al-Muhsin al-Kazimi.* London: Dar al-Hikma, 2002.
al-Kazimi, Rabab. *al-Majmuʿah al-Adabiyya al-Kamilah: Dirasah wa Shiʿr wa Nathr.* London: Dar al-Hikmah, 2000.
Karkhi, ʿAbbud. *Diwan al-Karkhi.* 2 vols. Baghdad: Matbaʿat al-Karkh, 1933.
al-Malaʾika, Nazik. *Diwan Nazik al-Malaʾika.* 2 vols. Beirut: Dar al-ʿAwda, 1997.
al-Malaʾika, Um Nizar. *Anshudat al-Majid.* Baghdad: Matba'at al-Tadamun, 1965.
Mardan, Husayn. *al-Aʿmal al-Kamila.* 2 vols. Baghdad: Dar al-Shuun al-Thaqafiyya al-ʿAmma, 2009.
Nahr, Hayyat. *Ughniyyat lil-Thawra: Shiʿr.* Baghdad: Matbaʿat al-Rabita, 1960.
al-Najafi, Ahmad al-Safi. *al-Amwaj.* Beirut: Dar al-ʿIlm lil-Malayyin, 1961.
———. *al-Shallal.* Beirut: Dar al-ʿIlm lil-Malayyin, 1962.
———. *Hasad al-Sijn.* Beirut: Maktabat al-Maʿarif, 1964.
Naji, Hilal. *Ughniyyat Huzn ila Kirkuk.* Beirut: Dar al-Aʿlam lil-Malayyin, 1959.
———. *Ughniyyat Huzn ila Kirkuk.* Baghdad: al-Matbaʿa al-Misriyya, 1963.
al-Nasiri, ʿAbd al-Qadir al-Rashid. *Diwan ʿAbd al-Qadir al-Nasiri.* 2 vols. Baghdad: Maktabat al-ʿAni, 1965.
al-Nawwab, Muzaffar. *al-Aʿmal al-Shiʿriyya al-Kamila.* London: Dar Qunbur, 1996.
al-Rawi, ʿAdnan. *Min al-Iraq: Shiʿr.* Beirut: Matabiʿ Dar al-Kashshaf, 1949.
———. *Ayyam al-Nidal.* Cairo: Ittihad Baʿathat al-Kuwayt, 1961.
———. *al-Mashaniq . . . wa al-Salam!* Beirut: Dar al-Adab, 1962.
———. *al-Naft al-Multahib: Qasaʾid min al-ʿIraq.* Beirut: Maktabat al-Maʿarif, 1963.
———. *Diwan al-Shaʿir al-ʿArabi wa al-Zaʿim al-Thawri al-ʿIraqi al-Munadil: ʿAdnan al-Rawi.* Cairo: Dar al-Hilal, 1974.
———. *al-Majmuʿa al-Shiʿriyya al-Kamila lil-Shaʿir ʿAdnan al-Rawi, 1925–1967.* Baghdad: Wizarat al-Thaqafa wa al-Funun, 1978.
Rida, Ahmad, Sulayman Zahir, and Ahmad ʿArif al-Zayn, eds. *al-ʿIraqiyyat, al-Juzʾ al-Awwal: Wa Huwa Mukhtar min Shiʿr ʿAsharat Shuʿaraʾ min Mashahir Shuʿaraʾ al-ʿIraq.* Sidon: Matbaʿat al-ʿIrfan, 1912.
al-Rusafi, Maʿruf. *Diwan al-Rusafi.* Beirut: al-Maktaba al-Ahliyya, 1910.
———. *Diwan al-Rusafi.* Cairo: Dar al-Kitab al-ʿArabi, 1949.
———. *Diwan al-Rusafi.* 5 vols. Beirut: Dar al-Muntazar, 1999.
Samaka, Baqir. *Min Hisad al-Thawra.* Baghdad: Matbaʿat al-Thawra, 1959.
al-Sayyab, Badr Shakir. *Badr Shakir al-Sayyab: Hayatihi wa Shiʿrihi.* ʿAmman: al-Ahliyya lil-Nashr wa al-Tawziʿ, 2008.
———. *Diwan Badr Shakir al-Sayyab: al-Aʿmal al-Shiʿriyyah al-Kamilah.* Cairo: Maktabat Jazirat al-Ward, 2009.

al-Shabibi, Muhammad Rida. *Diwan al-Shabibi*. Cairo: Matba'ah Lajnat al-Ta'lif wa al-Tarjama wa al-Nashr, 1940.

Shalash, Muhammad Jamil. *al-Hubb wa al-Hurriyya*. Baghdad: Maktabat al-Nahda, 1964.

———. *Diwan Muhammad Jamil Shalash*. Beirut: Dar al-'Awda, 1978.

al-Sharqi, 'Ali. *Diwan al-Sharqi*. Baghdad: Dar al-Hurriyya lil-Taba'a, 1979.

al-Tabataba'i, Ibrahim. *Diwan al-Tabataba'i: Wa Huwa Diwan al-Sayyid Ibrahim al-Tabataba'i Sha'ir al-Iraq al-Shahir al-Mutawaffin Sinat 1319 Hijri*. Sidon: Matba'at al-'Irfan, 1914.

al-Tamimi, Salih. *Diwan al-Tamimi*. Najaf: Majallat al-Bayan, 1947.

Taqa, Shadhil. *Thumma Mata al-Layl: Shi'r*. Beirut: Dar al-Maktabat al-Haya, 1963.

———. *al-Majmu'a al-Shi'riyya al-Kamila*. Baghdad: Manshurat Wizarat al-I'lam, 1977.

al-Ya'qubi, Muhammad 'Ali. *Diwan Muhammad 'Ali al-Ya'qubi*. 2 vols. Najaf: Matba'at al-Nu'man, 1957.

Yusuf, Sa'di. *51 Qasida*. Baghdad: Wizarat al-Tarbiyya, 1959.

———. *al-A'mal al-Shi'riyya*. 2 vols. Damascus: Dar al-Mada lil-Thaqafa wa al-Nashr, 1995.

al-Zahawi, Jamil Sidqi. *al-Kalim al-Manzum*. Beirut: al-Matba'a a-Ahliyya, 1909.

———. *Diwan al-Zahawi*. Cairo: al-Matba'a al-'Arabiyya, 1924.

———. *Ruba'iyat al-Zahawi: Wa Hiya al-Juz' al-Thalith min Mukhtarat Ma Nazamaha al-Ustadh al-Hakim Jamil Sidqi al-Zahawi*. Beirut: Matba'at al-Qamus al-'Amm, 1924.

———. *al-Lubab: Wa Huwa al-Mukhtar mima Qaradhuha min al-Shi'r fi Awakhir Hayatihi*. Baghdad: Matba'at al-Furat, 1928.

———. *al-Awshal*. Baghdad: Matba'at Baghdad, 1934.

## Published Diaries, Memoirs, Novels, Speeches, and Treatises

Abu Tabikh, Muhsin. *Mudhakkirat al-Sayyid Muhsin Abu Tabikh, 1910–1960: Khamsun 'Amman min Ta'rikh al-'Iraq al-Siyasi al-Hadith*. Beirut: al-Mu'assassah al-'Arabiyya lil-Dirasat wa al-Nashr, 2001.

Antoon, Sinan. "Dead Poets Society." *Nation*, May 26, 2003, 25–29.

al-Athari, Muhammad Bahjat. "al-Muqaddama." Introduction to *Diwan Rashid al-Hashimi*, by Rashid al-Hashimi, 11–12. Baghdad: Matba'at al-Ma'arif, 1964.

Ayyub, Dhu al-Nun. "al-Muqaddimah." Introduction to *Aqbas al-Thawra: Min A'maq Sha'b 14 Tammuz*, by Muhammad Salih Bahr al-'Ulum, 10–13. Baghdad: Wizarat al-Ma'arif, 1959.

al-'Azzawi, Fadhil. *al-Ruh al-Haya: Jil al-Sittinat fi al-'Iraq*. Damascus: Dar al-Thaqafa wa al-Nashr, 2003.

———. *Akhr al-Mala'ika*. Beirut: Manshurat al-Jamal, 2016.

Bahr al-ʿUlum, Muhammad Salih. "The People of Iraq Want to Live in Friendship with the Soviet Union." *Culture and Life* 3:1 (1959), 29–30.

al-Bahri, Yunus. *Sabʿat Ashhur fi Sujun Baghdad*. Beirut: al-Maktab al-ʿAsri lil-Sihafa wa al-Nashr, 1960.

al-Basir, Muhammad Mahdi. *Taʾrikh al-Qadiyya al-ʿIraqiyya*. Baghdad: Matbaʿat al-Falah, 1923.

al-Bayati, ʿAbd al-Wahhab. *Tajribati al-Shiʿiriyya*. Beirut: Manshurat Nizar Qabbani, 1968.

———. *Yanabiʿ al-Shams: al-Sirah al-Shiʿriyya*. Damascus: Dar al-Farqad, 1999.

al-Bazirkan, ʿAli. *al-Waqaʾiʿ al-Haqiqiyya fi al-Thawra al-ʿIraqiyya: Risala Tatadamman Munaqasha wa Tahlilan li Hawadith Thawrat al-ʿIraq Sanat 1920 Warada Ma Ulsiqa bihi min Muftarayat wa Tashih Ma Dara Hawlaha min Akhtaʾ*. Baghdad: Matbaʿat Asʿad, 1954.

Butti, Rafaʾil. *Dhakira ʿIraqiyya, 1900–1956*. Damascus: al-Mada, 2000.

al-Chadirchi, Kamil. *Mudhakkirat Kamil al-Chadirchi wa Taʾrikh al-Hizb al-Watani al-Dimuqrati*. Beirut: Dar al-Taliʿa, 1970.

De Gaury, Gerald. *Three Kings in Baghdad, 1921–1958*. London: Hutchinson, 1961.

al-Duri, ʿAbd al-ʿAziz. *al-Judhur al-Tarikhiyya li al-Shuʿubiyya*. Beirut: Dar al-Taliʿa, 1960.

al-Fakiki, ʿAbd al-Hadi. *al-Shuʿubiyya wa al-Qawmiyya al-ʿArabiyya*. Beirut: Dar al-ʿArab, 1962.

Farman, Ghaʾib Tuʿamah. *al-Hukm al-Aswad fi al-ʿIraq*. Cairo: Dar al-Fikr, 1957.

al-Hamad, Turki. *al-Karadib: Atyaf al-Aziqqa al-Muhjura*. Dubai: Dar Madarik lil-Nashr, 2012.

al-Hashimi, Taha. *Mudhakkirat Taha al-Hashimi, 1919–1943*. Beirut: Dar al-Taliʿa, 1967.

al-Haydari, Talib. *Dam al-Shahid*. Baghdad: Matbaʿat al-Maʿarif, 1950.

al-Husri, Abu Khaldun Satiʿ. *Mudhakkirati fi al-ʿIraq, 1921–1941*. 2 vols. Beirut: Dar al-Taliʿa, 1967.

al-Isfahani, Abu al-Majid Muhammad Rida. *Kitab Naqd Falsafat Darwin*. 2 vols. Baghdad: Matbaʿat al-Wilaya al-ʿAmira, 1912.

Ittihad al-Udabaʾ al-ʿIraqiyyin. *Mihrajan al-Rusafi 1959*. Baghdad: Matbaʿat al-Maʿarif, 1959.

Jabra, Jabra Ibrahim. *Princesses' Street: Baghdad Memories*. Translated by Issa J. Boullata. Fayetteville: University of Arkansas Press, 2005.

al-Jabburi, ʿAbdullah. "Muqaddamat al-Diwan." Introduction to *Diwan al-Sayyid Muhammad al-Hashimi al-Baghdadi*, by Muhammad al-Hashimi, 16–17. Baghdad: Wizarat al-Iʿlam, 1977.

Jamil, Husayn. *al-Haya al-Niyabiyya fi alʿ-Iraq, 1925–1946: Mawqif Jamaʿat al-Ahali minha*. Baghdad: Maktabat al-Muthanna, 1983.

al-Jawahiri, ʿAbd al- ʿAziz. Introduction to *Diwan al-Sayyid Muhammad Saʿid al-Habubi al-Najafi Ashʿar Shuʿaraʾ al-Sharq Ams wa Akbar ʿUlamaʾihi al-Yawm*, by Muhammad Saʿid al-Habubi, 5–16. Beirut: al-Matbaʿa al-Ahliyya, 1913.

al-Jawahiri, Muhammad Mahdi. *Dhikrayati*. 2 vols. Damascus: Dar al-Rafidin, 1988.

Jidah, ʿAbd al-Hamid and Khalil al-Duwayhi, eds. *al-Adab al-ʿArabi al-Muʿasir: Aʿmal Muʿtamar Ruma al-Munʿaqid fi Tishrin al-Awwal Sanat 1961*. Tripoli: Dar al-Shamal, 1990.

Kemal, Orhan. *In Jail with Nazim Hikmet*. Translated by Bengisa Rona. London: Saqi, 2010.

al-Khalili, Jaʿfar. *Hakadha ʿAraftuhum: Khawatir ʿan Unasin Afdhadhin ʿAshu Baʿd al-Ahyan li-Ghayrihim Akthar Mimma ʿAshu li-Anfusihim*. Baghdad: Matbaʿat al-Zahraʾ, 1963.

Kubba, Muhammad Mahdi. *Mudhakkirati fi Samim al-Ahdath, 1918–1958*. Beirut: Manshurat Dar al-Taliʿa, 1965.

Mushtaq, Talib. *Awraq Ayyami, 1900–1958*. Beirut: Dar al-Taliʿa, 1968.

al-Najafi, Ahmad al-Safi. *Mudhakkirat al-Shaʿir Ahmad al-Safi al-Najafi*. Jubayl: Dar wa al-Maktabat Bibliyun, 2011.

Naji, Hilal. *The Bloody Hands in Iraq*. Cairo: al-Karnak Publishing House, 1961.

———. *Hatta la Nansa: Fusul min Mujazarat al-Mosul*. Cairo: Dar al-ʿAlam al-ʿArabi, 1962.

Naji, Hilal and Muhyi al-Din Ismaʿil. *Jinayyat al-Shuyuʿiyin ʿala al-Adab al-ʿIraqi*. Cairo: Dar al-Karnak lil-Nashr, 1960.

Nuri, Baha al-Din. *Mudhakkirat Baha al-Din Nuri: Sikritir al-Lajna al-Markaziyya li al-Hizb al-Shuyuʿi al-ʿIraqi*. London: Dar al-Hikmah, 2001.

al-Rawi, ʿAdnan. *Min al-Qahira ila.. Muʿtaqil Qasim!* Beirut: Dar al-Adab, 1963.

Rejwan, Nissim. *The Last Jews in Baghdad: Remembering a Lost Homeland*. Austin: University of Texas Press, 2004.

al-Rihani, Amin. *Qalb al-Iraq: Siyaha wa Siyasa wa Adab wa Taʾrikh, Muzayyan bi al-Rusum*. 2nd ed. Beirut: Dar al-Rihani, 1957.

———. *Qalb al-ʿIraq: Rihlat wa al-Taʾrikh*. Cairo: Muʾassasat Hindawi lil-Taʿlim wa al-Thaqafa, 2012.

al-Rusafi, Maʿruf. *al-Risala al-ʿIraqiyya fi al-Siyasa wa al-Din wa al-Ijtimaʿ: Yalihi Kamil al-Jadirji fi Hiwar maʿ al-Rusafi*. Cologne: Manshurat al-Jamal, 2007.

———. *al-Rusafi Khatiban: Majmuʿ Khutabihi fi Majlis al-Nawwab, 1930–1939*, edited by Mustafa ʿAli and ʿAbd al-Hamid al-Rushudi. Damascus: Dar al-Mada, 2014.

Salim, Shakir Mustafa. *Min Mudhakkirat Qawmi Mutaʾamir*. Beirut: Dar al-Taliʿa, 1960.

al-Samarraʾi, Faʾiq, Adnan al-Rawi, and Hilal al-Naji. *Mahkamat al-Mahdawi: Maʾsa wa Malha: Radd Ahrar al-ʿIraq*. Cairo: Dar al-Qawmiyya lil-Tabaʿa wa al-Nashr, 1960.

al-Sayyab, Badr Shakir. *Kuntu Shuyuʿiyyan.* Cologne: Manshurat al-Jamal, 2007.
al-Shabibi, Muhammad Rida. *Mudhakkirat al-Shaykh Muhammad Rida al-Shabibi wa Rihlatuhu.* Beirut: Dar al-Rafidayn lil-Tabaʿa wa al-Nashr wa al-Tawziʿ, 2011.
al-Sharqi, ʿAli. Introduction to *Diwan al-Tabatabaʾi: Wa Huwa Diwan al-Sayyid Ibrahim al-Tabatabaʾi Shaʿir al-Iraq al-Shahir al-Mutawaffin Sinat 1319 Hijri*, by Ibrahim al-Tabatabaʾi, 2–7. Sidon: Matbaʿat al-ʿIrfan, 1914.
———. *al-Ahlam.* Baghdad: Shirkat al-Tabaʿ wa al-Nashr al-Ahliyya, 1963.
Shaʾul, Anwar. *Qissat Hayati fi Wadi al-Rafidayn.* Jerusalem: Manshurat Rabitat al-Jamiʿiyin al-Yahud al-Nazihin min al-ʿIraq, 1980.
al-Shaykh ʿAli, ʿAli Mahmud. *Muhakimatuna al-Wijahiya.* Sidon: Dar al-Maktaba al-ʿAsriyya, 1966.
Shumayyil, Shibli. *Falsafat al-Nushuʾ wa al-Irtiqaʾ.* Cairo: Matbaʿat al-Muqtataf, 1910.
Somekh, Sasson. *Baghdad, Yesterday: The Making of an Arab Jew.* Jerusalem: Ibis Editions, 2007.
al-Suwaydi, Tawfiq. *Mudhakkirati: Nisf Qarn min Taʾrikh al-ʿIraq wa al-Qadiyah al-ʿArabiyya.* London: Dar al-Hikmah, 1999.
Tagore, Rabindranath. *Journey to Persia and Iraq: 1932.* Kolkata: Visva-Bharati, 2003.
al-Tikriti, Salim Taha. *Muhammad Mahdi al-Jawahiri.* London: Riyadh al-Rayyis lil-Kutub wa al-Nashr, 1989.
Twena, Abraham. "The Diary of Abraham Twena." *The Scribe: Journal of Babylonian Journal* 11:2 (1973), 3–7.
Wilson, Arnold. *Mesopotamia, 1917–1920: A Clash of Loyalties.* London: H. Milford, 1931.
Youssef, Saadi. "I Have Trained Myself Hard to Be Free." *Banipal: Magazine of Modern Arabic Literature* 20 (2004), 2–14.
al-Zahawi, Jamil Sidqi. "al-Marʾa wa al-Difaʿ ʿanha," In *al-Zahawi: Dirasat wa Nusus*, edited by ʿAbd al-Hamid Rushdi, 112–117. Beirut: Dar Maktabat al-Hayat, 1966.
———. "Risala al-Zahawi ilaʾ al-Ustadh Ahmad Muhammad al-ʿAysh." In *al-Zahawi: Dirasat wa Nusus*, edited by ʿAbd al-Hamid Rushdi, 25–28. Beirut: Dar Maktabat al-Hayat, 1966.
———. "Risaʾil al-Zahawi." In *al-Zahawi: Dirasat wa Nusus*, edited by ʿAbd al-Hamid Rushdi, 25–45. Beirut: Dar Maktabat al-Hayat, 1966.
———. "Tarjamat Hayati Mulakhkh." In *al-Zahawi: Dirasat wa Nusus*, edited by ʿAbd al-Hamid Rushdi, 46–67. Beirut: Dar Maktabat al-Hayat, 1966.
Zangana, Haifa. *City of Widows: An Iraqi Womanʾs Account of War and Resistance.* New York: Seven Stories Press, 2007.

## Secondary Sources
*Arabic*

'Abbas, Ihsan. *Badr Shakir al-Sayyab*. Beirut: Dar al-Thaqafa, 1969.
al-Amin, Muzaffar 'Abd Allah. *Jama'at al-Ahali: Mansha'uha, 'Aqidatuha, wa Dawruha fi al-Siyasa al-Iraqiyya, 1932–1946*. Beirut: al-Mu'assassa al-'Arabiyya lil-Dirasat wa al-Nashr, 2001.
Asdi, Hassan. *Thawrat al-Najaf: aw al-Shirara al-Awla li Thawrat al-'Ishrin*. Baghdad: Manshurat Wizarat al-I'lam, 1975.
Basri, Mir. *A'lam al-Adab fi al-'Iraq al-Hadith*. 2 vols. London: Dar al-Hikmah, 1994.
Butti, Rafa'il. *al-Adab al-'Asri fi al-'Iraq al-'Arabi: Kitab Ta'rikhi Adabi Intiqadi, Yahwa Tarajim Udaba' al-'Iraq wa Rusumihim wa Nukhbah min Atharihim bayna Manshur wa Manzum*. 2 vols. Baghdad: al-Maktaba al-'Arabiyya, 1923.
Dhaif, Shawqi "Jamil Sidqi al-Zahawi." In *al-Zahawi: Dirasat wa Nusus*, edited by 'Abd al-Hamid Rushdi, 330–345. Beirut: Dar Maktabat al-Hayat, 1966
al-Dujayli, 'Abd al-Karim. *Muhadharat 'an al-Shi'r al-'Iraqi al-Hadith*. Cairo: Jami'at al-Duwal al-'Arabiyya, Ma'had al-Dirasat al-'Arabiyya, 1959.
al-Durrah, Mahmud. *al-Harb al-'Iraqiyya al-Britaniyya*. Cairo: Dar al-Ma'rifa, 1982.
Fahmi, Mahir Hasan. *al-Zahawi*. Cairo: al-Mu'assassa al-Misriyya al-'Amma lil-Ta'lif wa al-Anba' wa al-Nashr, 1964.
Hasan, Nuri Kamal Muhammad. *Muhammad Hasan Abi al-Mahasin: Dirasa fi Hayatihi wa Ittijah Shi'rihi wa Siyasi*. Beirut: Mu'assassat al-'Arif li al-Matbu'at, 2000.
al-Hasani, 'Abd al-Razzaq. *al-Thawra al-'Iraqiyya al-Kubra*. Sidon: Matba'at al-'Irfan, 1952.
———. *Ta'rikh al-Wizarat al-'Iraqiyya*. 10 vols. Sidon: Matba'at al-'Irfan, 1953–1961.
al-Hilali, 'Abd al-Razzaq. *al-Sha'ir al-Tha'ir: al-Shaykh Muhammad Baqir al-Shabibi 1889–1960*. Baghdad: Maktabat al-Nahda, 1965.
'Izz al-Din, Yusuf. "Jamil Sidqi al-Zahawi." In *al-Zahawi: Dirasat wa Nusus*, edited by 'Abd al-Hamid Rushdi, 403–407. Beirut: Dar Maktabat al-Hayat, 1966)
———. "Tasdir al-Kitab." In *al-Zahawi: Dirasat wa Nusus*, edited by 'Abd al-Hamid Rushdi, 7–13. Beirut: Dar Maktabat al-Hayat, 1966.
———. *al-Ishtirakiyya wa al-Qawmiyya wa Atharahuma fi al-Adab al-Hadith*. Cairo: Jami'at al-Duwal al-'Arabiyya, 1968.
———. *Shu'ara' al-'Iraq fi al-Qarn al-'Ishrin*. Baghdad: Matba'at As'ad, 1969.
———. *Khayri al-Hindawi: Hayatuhu wa Diwan Shi'rihi*. Baghdad: Matba'at al-Sha'b, 1974.
Jabra, Jabra Ibrahim. "al-Sha'ir wa al-Hakim wa al-Madina." In *Muhammad Mahdi al-Jawahiri: Dirasat Naqdiyya*, edited by Hadi al-'Alawi, 41–80. Baghdad: Matba'at al-Nu'man, 1969.
al-Ja'fari, Muhammad Hamdi. *Intifadat Tishrin al-Thani 'Amm 1952 wa Inqilab*

*al-Wasi fi al-ʿIraq: Dirasa Taʾrikhiyya Tahliliyya Withaʾiqiyya*. Cairo: Maktabat Madbuli, 2000.

Jubran, Sulayman. *Majmaʿ al-Addad: Dirasah fi Sirat al-Jawahiri wa Shaʿrihi*. Beirut: al- Muʾassassa al-ʿArabiyya lil-Dirasat wa al-Nashr, 2003.

Kamal al-Din, Muhammad ʿAli. *Saʿd Salih*. Baghdad: Matbaʿat al-Maʿarif, 1949.

al-Khaqani, ʿAli. *Shuʿaraʾ al-Gharri, aw al-Najafiyyat*. 12 vols. Qum: Maktabat Ayat Allah al-ʿUzma al-Marʿashi al-Najafi, 1988.

al-Khattat, Qasim. "Hayat al-Rusafi." In *Maʿruf al-Rusafi Shaʿir al-ʿArab al-Kabir: Hayatuhu wa Shiʿruhu*, edited by Qasim al-Khattat, Mustafa ʿAbd al-Latif al-Saharti, and Muhammad ʿAbd al-Munʿim Khafaji, 11–203. Cairo: al-Haya al-Misriyya al-ʿAmma lil-Taʾlif wa al-Nashr, 1971.

Mubarak, ʿAbd al-Husayn. *Thawrat Alf wa Tisaʿ Miʾa wa ʿIsrhin fi al-Shiʿr al-ʿIraqi*. Baghdad: Dar al-Basri, 1970.

al-Muhsin, Fatima. *Tamaththulat al-Nahda fi Thaqafat al-ʿIraq al-Hadith*. Beirut: Manshurat al-Jamal, 2010.

Munir, Tawfiq. *Haqiqat Harakat al-Salam*. Cairo: Dar al-Fikr, 1956.

Rabiʿi, ʿAli Muhammad Hadi. *Muhammad Mahdi al-Basir: Raʾid al-Masrah al-Tahridi fi al-ʿIraq*. Cairo: Dar al-Nashr lil-Jamiʿat, 2013.

Rushdi, ʿAbd al-Hamid, ed. *al-Zahawi: Dirasat wa Nusus*. Beirut: Dar Maktabat al-Hayat, 1966/

Rushudi, ʿAbd al-Hamid. *al-Rusafi: Hayatuhu, Atharuhu, Shiʿruhu*. Baghdad: Dar al-Shuʾun al-Thaqafiyya al-ʿAmma, 1988.

al-Saharti, Mustafa, and Hilal Naji. *Shuʿaraʾ al-Muʿasirun*. Cairo: Dar al-Karnak, 1962.

al-Samarraʾi, Majid Ahmad. *al-Tayyar al-Qawmi fi al-Shiʿr al-ʿIraqi al-Hadith, Mundhu al-Harb al-ʿAlamiyya al-Thaniyya 1939 Hatta Naksat Haziran 1967*. Baghdad: Wizarat al-Thaqafa wa al-Iʿlan, 1983.

al-Tamimi, Khalid. *Muhammad Jaʿfar Abu al-Timman: Dirasa fi al-Zaʿama al-Siyasiyya alʿ-Iraqiyya*. Damascus: Dar al-Warraq, 1996.

Tawfiq, Hasan. *Shiʿr Badr Shakir al-Sayyab: Dirasa Fanniyya wa Fikriyya*. Beirut: al-Muʾassassa al-ʿArabiyya lil-Dirasat wa al-Nashr, 1979.

al-Waʾili, Ibrahim. *al-Shiʿr al-Siyasi al-ʿIraqi fi al-Qarn al-Tasiʿ ʿAshar*. Baghdad: Matbaʿat al-ʿAni, 1961.

———. *Thawrat al-ʿIshrin fi al-Shiʿr al-ʿIraqi*. Baghdad: Matbaʿat al-Iman, 1968.

al-Waʿiz, ʿAbd al-Ilah Najm al-Din. *ʿAdnan al-Rawi: Hayatuhu wa Adabuhu*. Baghdad: Wizarat al-Thaqafa wa al-Iʿlam, 1981.

al-Waʿiz, Raʾuf. *al-Ittijahat al-Wataniyya fi al-Shiʿr al-ʿIraqi al-Hadith, 1914–1941*. Baghdad: Wizarat al-Iʿlam al-Jumhuriyya al-ʿIraqiyya, 1974.

al-Wardi, ʿAli. *Lamahat Ijtimaʿiyya min Taʾrikh al-ʿIraq al-Hadith*. 6 vols. London: Kufan lil-Nashr, 1991.

Yaghi, ʿAbd al Rahman. *Hayat al-Adab al-Filastini al-Hadith*. Beirut: al-Maktab al-Tijari lil-Tabaʿa wa al-Nashr wa al-Tawziʿ, 1960.

al-Zayyat, Ahmad Hasan. "al-Zahawi bi-Munasabat Dhikrahu al-Awla." In *al-Zahawi: Dirasat wa Nusus*, edited by ʿAbd al-Hamid Rushdi, 205–213. Beirut: Dar Maktabat al-Hayat, 1966.

*English and French*

Abdel Nasser, Tahia. "Revolutionary Poetics and Translation." In *Translating Dissent: Voices From and With the Egyptian Revolution*, edited by Mona Baker, 107–122. New York: Routledge, 2016.

Abisaab, Rula Jurdi, and Malik Abisaab. *The Shiʿites of Lebanon: Modernism, Communism, and Hizbullah's Islamists*. Syracuse: Syracuse University Press, 2014.

Abrahamian, Ervand. *Iran between Two Revolutions*. Princeton: Princeton University Press, 1982.

———. *The Coup: 1953, the CIA, and the Roots of Modern U.S.-Iranian Relations*. New York: New Press, 2013.

Abu-Lughod, Ibrahim. *The Arab Rediscovery of Europe: A Study in Cultural Encounters*. London: Saqi Books, 2011.

Adorno, Theodor. "On Lyric Poetry and Society." In *Poetry in Theory: An Anthology, 1900–2000*, edited by Jon Cook, 342–349. Malden, MA: Blackwell, 2004.

Ahmed, Leila. *Women and Gender in Islam: Historical Roots of a Modern Debate*. New Haven: Yale University Press, 1992.

Ajami, Fouad. *The Dream Palace of the Arabs: A Generation's Odyssey*. New York: Pantheon Books, 1998.

———. *The Foreigner's Gift: The Americans, the Arabs, and the Iraqis in Iraq*. New York: Free Press, 2006.

al-Ali, Nadje Sadig. *Iraqi Women: Untold Stories from 1948 to the Present*. London: Zed Books, 2007.

Ali, Nosheen. "Poetry, Power, Protest: Reimagining the Muslim Brotherhood in Pakistan." *Comparative Studies of South Asia, Africa, and the Middle East* 32:1 (2012), 13–23.

Allawi, Ali A. *Faisal I of Iraq*. New Haven: Yale University Press, 2014.

Allen, Roger. *The Arabic Literary Heritage: The Development of Its Genres and Criticism*. Cambridge: Cambridge University Press, 1998.

Alshaer, Atef. *Poetry and Politics in the Modern Arab World*. London: Hurst, 2016.

Altoma, Salih J. "Postwar Iraqi Literature: Agonies of Rebirth." *Books Abroad* 46:2 (1972), 211–17.

———. "In Memoriam: Muhammad Mahdi al-Jawahiri (1900?–1997)." *Arab Studies Quarterly* 19:4 (1997), v–viii.

Anderson, Benedict. *Under Three Flags: Anarchism and the Anti-Colonial Imagination*. London: Verso, 2007.

———. *Imagined Communities: Reflection on the Origin and Spread of Nationalism.* London: Verso, 2016.

Antliff, Mark. *Avant-Garde Fascism: The Mobilization of Myth, Art, and Culture in France, 1909–1939.* Durham, NC: Duke University Press, 2007.

Antoon, Sinan. "Abu 'l-'Ala' al-Ma'ari (973–1058)." In *Essays in Arabic Literary Biography, 925–1350,* edited by Terri DeYoung and Mary St. Germain, 228–234. Weisbaden: Harrasowitz Verlag, 2011.

Antonius, George. *The Arab Awakening: The Story of the Arab National Movement.* New York: Paragon Books, 1979.

Armbrust, Walter. *Mass Culture and Modernism in Egypt.* Cambridge: Cambridge University Press, 1996.

Ashcroft, Bill, Gareth Griffiths, and Helen Tiffin. *The Empire Writes Back.* London: Routledge, 2002.

Ayalon, Ami. *The Press in the Arab Middle East: A History.* New York: Oxford University Press, 1995.

———. *The Arabic Print Revolution: Cultural Production and Mass Readership.* Cambridge: Cambridge University Press, 2016.

Aydin, Cemil. *The Politics of Anti-Westernism in Asia: Visions of World Order in Pan-Islamic and Pan-Asian Thought.* New York: Columbia University Press, 2007.

Badawi, M. M. *A Critical Introduction to Modern Arabic Poetry.* Cambridge: Cambridge University Press, 1975.

———. "Introduction." In *Modern Arabic Literature,* edited by M. M. Badawi, 1–23. Cambridge: Cambridge University Press, 1992.

Badiou, Alain. *The Age of the Poets: And Other Writings on Twentieth-Century Poetry and Prose.* Translated by Emily Apter. London: Verso, 2014.

Bahoora, Haytham. "Baudelaire in Baghdad: Modernism, the Body, and Husayn Mardan's Poetics of the Self." *International Journal of Middle East Studies* 45:2 (2013), 313–329.

Ballantyne, Tony, and Antoinette Burton, eds. *Bodies in Contact: Rethinking Colonial Encounters in World History.* Durham, NC: Duke University Press, 2005.

Banerjee, Sikata. *Muscular Nationalism: Gender, Violence, and Empire in India and Ireland, 1914–2004.* New York: New York University Press, 2012.

Baram, Amatzia. *Culture, History and Ideology in the Formation of Ba'thist Iraq, 1968–89.* London: Macmillan, 1991.

———. "A Case of Imported Identity: The Modernizing Secular Ruling Elites of Iraq and the Conception of Mesopotamian-Inspired Territorial Nationalism, 1922–1992." *Poetics Today* 15 (1994), 279–319.

Barnes, Christopher. *Boris Pasternak: A Literary Biography.* 2 vols. Cambridge: Cambridge University Press, 1998.

Bashkin, Orit. "Representations of Women in the Writings of the Intelligentsia in

Hashemite Iraq, 1921–1958." *Journal of Middle East Women's Studies* 4:1 (2008), 53–82.

———. "The Iraqi Afghanis and ʿAbduhs: Debate over Reform among Shiʿite and Sunni ʿUlamaʾ in Interwar Iraq." In *Guardians of Faith in Modern Times: ʿUlamaʾ in the Middle East*, edited by Meir Hatina, 141–169. Leiden: Brill, 2009.

———. *The Other Iraq: Pluralism and Culture in Hashemite Iraq*. Stanford: Stanford University Press, 2009.

———. "Hybrid Nationalisms: Watani and Qawmi Visions in Iraq under ʿAbd al-Karim Qasim." *International Journal of Middle East Studies* 43:2 (2011), 293–312.

———. *The New Babylonians: A History of Jews in Modern Iraq*. Stanford: Stanford University Press, 2012.

———. "Iraqi Shadows, Iraqi Lights: Anti-Fascist and Anti-Nazi Voices in Monarchic Iraq, 1932–1941." In *Arab Responses to Fascism and Nazism: Attraction and Repulsion*, edited by Israel Gershoni, 141–168. Austin: University of Texas Press, 2014.

———. *Impossible Exodus: Iraqi Jews in Israel*. Stanford: Stanford University Press, 2017.

Batatu, Hanna. *The Old Social Classes and Revolutionary Movements of Iraq: A Study of Iraq's Old Landed and Commercial Classes and of Its Communists, Baʿthists, and Free Officers*. Princeton: Princeton University Press, 1978.

Beevor, Antony. *The Battle for Spain: The Spanish Civil War, 1936–1939*. New York: Penguin Books, 2006.

Behrooz, Maziar. *Rebels with a Cause: The Failure of the Left in Iran*. London: I. B. Tauris, 1999.

Beinin, Joel. "Writing Class: Workers and Modern Egyptian Colloquial Poetry (Zajal)." *Poetics Today* 15:2 (1994), 191–215.

Benjamin, Walter. "The Work of Art in the Age of Mechanical Reproduction." In *Illuminations: Essays and Reflections*, edited by Hannah Arendt and translated by Harry Zohn, 217–251. New York: Schocken Books, 2007.

Berman, Marshall. *All That Is Solid Melts into Air: The Experience of Modernity*. London: Verso, 1983.

Beyers, Chris. *A History of Free Verse*. Fayetteville: University of Arkansas Press, 2001.

Bhabha, Homi K. *The Location of Culture*. London: Routledge, 1994.

Bier, Laura. *Revolutionary Womanhood: Feminisms, Modernity, and the State in Nasser's Egypt*. Stanford: Stanford University Press, 2011.

Blasing, Mutlu Konuk. *Nazim Hikmet: The Life and Times of Turkey's World Poet*. New York: Persea, 2013.

Bleiker, Roland. *Aesthetics and World Politics*. New York: Palgrave Macmillan, 2009.

Bose, Sugata. *A Hundred Horizons: The Indian Ocean in the Age of Global Empire*. Cambridge, MA: Harvard University Press, 2006.

———. *His Majesty's Opponent: Subhas Chandra Bose and India's Struggle against Empire.* Cambridge, MA: Belknap Press of Harvard University Press, 2011.

Boullata, Issa J. "Badr Shakir al-Sayyab and the Free Verse Movement." *International Journal of Middle East Studies* 1:3 (1970), 248–258.

———. "The Poetic Technique of Badr Shakir al-Sayyab (1926–1964)." *Journal of Arabic Literature* 2 (1971), 104–115.

Bourdieu, Pierre. "Structures, Habitus, Power: Basis for a Theory of Symbolic Power." In *Culture/Power/History: A Reader in Contemporary Social Theory*, edited by Nicholas B. Dirks, Geoff Eley, and Sherry B. Ortner, 155–199. Princeton: Princeton University Press, 1994.

Brecht, Bertolt. *Brecht on Art and Politics.* Edited by Tom Kuhn and Steve Giles. London: Methuen, 2003.

Brown, Edward J. *Mayakovsky: A Poet in the Revolution.* Princeton: Princeton University Press, 1973.

Buelens, Geert. *Everything to Nothing: The Poetry of the Great War, Revolution and the Transformation of Europe.* Translated by David McKay. London: Verso, 2015.

Burke, Peter. *Popular Culture in Early Modern Europe.* London: T. Smith, 1978.

Campos, Michelle U. *Ottoman Brothers: Muslims, Christians, and Jews in Early Twentieth-Century Palestine.* Stanford: Stanford University Press, 2011.

Caton, Steve C. *"Peaks of Yemen I Summon": Poetry as Cultural Practice in a North Yemeni Tribe.* Berkeley: University of California Press, 1990.

Caudwell, Christopher. *Illusion and Reality: A Study of the Sources of Poetry.* New York: International Publishers, 1973.

Cavanagh, Clare. *Lyric Poetry and Modern Politics: Russia, Poland, and the West.* New Haven: Yale University Press, 2009.

Chalala, Elie. "Youssef al-Sayigh: Poet of Sorrows, Master of Contradictions." *Aljadid* 11:53 (2005), 6–9.

Chatterjee, Partha. *The Nation and Its Fragments: Colonial and Postcolonial Histories.* Princeton: Princeton University Press, 1993.

Chávez, Joaquín M. *Poets and Prophets of the Resistance: Intellectuals and the Origins of El Salvador's Civil War.* Oxford: Oxford University Press, 2017.

Chejne, Anwar G. *The Arabic Language: Its Role in History.* Minneapolis: University of Minnesota Press, 1969.

Cleveland, William L. *The Making of an Arab Nationalist: Ottomanism and Arabism in the Life and Thought of Sati' al-Husri.* Princeton: Princeton University Press, 1971.

Cole, Juan R. I. *Colonialism and Revolution in the Middle East: Social and Cultural Origins of Egypt's 'Urabi Movement.* Cairo: American University in Cairo Press, 1999.

Coleman, Peter. *The Liberal Conspiracy: The Congress for Cultural Freedom and the Struggle for the Mind of Postwar Europe.* New York: New Press, 1989.

Colla, Elliott. "The Poetry of Revolt." In *Dawn of the Arab Uprisings: End of an Old Order?*, edited by Bassam Haddad, Rosie Bsheer, and Ziad Abu-Rish, 77–82. London: Pluto Press, 2012.

———. "Badr Shakir al-Sayyab, Cold War Poet," *Middle Eastern Literatures* 18:3 (2015), 258–259.

Craib, Raymond B. *The Cry of the Renegade: Politics and Poetry in Interwar Chile*. New York: Oxford University Press, 2016.

Dabashi, Hamid. *Islamic Liberation Theology: Resisting the Empire*. London: Routledge, 2008.

Daniel, Norman. "Contemporary Perceptions of the Revolution in Iraq on 14 July 1958." In *The Iraqi Revolution of 1958: The Old Social Classes Revisited*, edited by Robert A. Fernea and William Roger Louis, 1–30. London: I. B. Tauris, 1991.

Danton, Robert. *Poetry and the Police: Communication Networks in Eighteenth-Century Paris*. Cambridge, MA: Belknap Press of Harvard University Press, 2010.

Davis, Eric. "History for the Many or History for the Few? The Historiography of the Iraqi Working Class." In *Workers and Working Classes in the Middle East: Struggles, Histories, Historiographies*, edited by Zackary Lockman, 271–301. Albany: State University of New York Press, 1994.

———. *Memories of State: Politics, History, and Collective Identity in Modern Iraq*. Berkeley: University of California Press, 2005.

Davis, Natalie Zemon. *Society and Culture in Early Modern France: Eight Essays*. Stanford: Stanford University Press, 1975.

Denning, Michael. *Culture in the Age of Three Worlds*. London: Verso, 2004.

Deringil, Selim, "The Struggle against Shiism in Hamidian Iraq: A Study in Ottoman Counter-Propaganda," *Die Welt des Islams* 30:1/4 (1990), 45–62.

Derrick, Jonathan. *Africa's 'Agitators': Militant Anti-Colonialism in Africa and the West, 1918–1939*. New York: Columbia University Press, 2008.

DeYoung, Terri. *Placing the Poet: Badr Shakir al-Sayyab and Postcolonial Iraq*. Albany: State University of New York Press, 1998.

———. "Ma'ruf al-Rusafi." In *Essays in Arabic Literary Biography 1850–1950*, edited by Roger Allen, 274–284. Weisbaden: Harrassowitz Verlag, 2010.

———. *Mahmud Sami al-Barudi: Reconfiguring Society and the Self*. Syracuse, NY: Syracuse University Press, 2015.

Di-Capua, Yoav. *Nahda*: The Arab Project of Enlightenment." *The Cambridge Companion to Modern Arab Culture*, edited by Dwight F. Reynolds, 54–74. Cambridge: Cambridge University Press, 2015.

———. *No Exit: Arab Existentialism, Jean-Paul Sartre, and Decolonization*. Chicago: University of Chicago Press, 2018.

Dodge, Toby. *Inventing Iraq: The Failure of Nation Building and a History Denied*. New York: Columbia University Press, 2003.

Doran, Michael. *Ike's Gamble: America's Rise to Dominance in the Middle East*. New York: Free Press, 2016.

Dryland, Estelle. "Faiz Ahmad Faiz and the Rawalpindi Conspiracy Case." *Journal of South Asian Literature* 27:2 (1992), 175–185.

Dumluji, Mona, Arbella Bet-Shlimon, Alda Benjamen, Saleem Al-Bahloly, Haytham Bahoora, Caecilia Pieri, Bridge L. Guarasci, Zainab Saleh, and Peter Sluglett. "Roundtable: Perspectives on Researching Iraq Today." *Arab Studies Journal* 23:1 (2015), 236–265.

Efrati, Noga. *Women in Iraq: Past Meets Present*. New York: Columbia University Press, 2012.

Eisner, Mark. *Neruda: The Poet's Calling*. New York: Ecco, 2018.

Eley, Geoff. "Nations, Public, and Political Cultures: Placing Habermas in the Nineteenth Century." In *Habermas and the Public Sphere*, edited by Craig Calhoun, 289–339. Cambridge, MA: MIT Press, 1997.

———. *A Crooked Line: From Cultural History to the History of Society*. Ann Arbor: University of Michigan Press, 2005.

Elliot, Matthew. *"Independent Iraq": The Monarchy and British Influence, 1941–58*. London: Tauris Academic Studies, 1996.

Fahmy, Ziad. *Ordinary Egyptians: Creating the Modern Nation through Popular Culture*. Stanford: Stanford University Press, 2011.

Fanon, Frantz. *The Wretched of the Earth*. Translated by Constance Farrington. New York: Grove Press, 1963.

Farouk-Sluglett, Marion, and Peter Sluglett. "The Social Classes and the Origins of the Revolution." In *The Iraqi Revolution of 1958: The Old Social Classes Revisited*, edited by Robert A. Fernea and William Roger Louis, 118–141. London: I. B. Tauris, 1991.

———. *Iraq since 1958: From Revolution to Dictatorship*. London: I. B. Tauris, 2003.

Fast, Howard. "To Nazim Hikmet." *Masses and Mainstream* 3:10 (1950), 8–9.

Fattah, Hala. *The Politics of Regional Trade in Iraq, Arabia, and the Gulf, 1745–1900*. Albany: State University of New York Press, 1997.

Fawaz, Leila Tarazi. *A Land of Aching Hearts: The Middle East in the Great War*. Cambridge, MA: Harvard University Press, 2014.

Feinberg, Melissa. *Curtain of Lies: The Battle over Truth in Stalinist Eastern Europe*. New York: Oxford University Press, 2017.

Fleishman, Lazar. *Boris Pasternak: The Poet and His Politics*. Cambridge, MA: Harvard University Press, 1990.

Frankel, Edith Rogovin. *Novy Mir: A Case Study in the Politics of Literature, 1952–1958*. Cambridge: Cambridge University Press, 1981.

Franzén, Johan. *Red Star over Iraq: Iraqi Communism before Saddam*. New York: Columbia University Press, 2011.

———. "Writing the History of Iraq: The Fallacy of 'Objective' History." In *Writing the Modern History of Iraq: Historiographical and Political Challenges*, edited by Jordi Tejel, Peter Sluglett, Riccardo Bocco, and Hamit Bozarslan, 31–46. Hackensack, NJ: World Scientific, 2012.

Fraser, Nancy. "Rethinking the Public Sphere: A Contribution to the Critique of Actually Existing Democracy." In *Habermas and the Public Sphere*, edited by Craig Calhoun, 109–142. Cambridge, MA: MIT Press, 1997.

Fromkin, David. *A Peace to End All Peace: The Fall of the Ottoman Empire and the Creation of the Modern Middle East*. New York: Owl Books, 1995.

Furani, Khaled. *Silencing the Sea: Secular Rhythms in Palestinian Poetry*. Stanford: Stanford University Press, 2012.

Gandhi, Leela. *Affective Communities: Anticolonial Thought, Fin-de-Siècle Radicalism, and the Politics of Friendship*. Durham, NC: Duke University Press, 2006.

Gaonkar, Dilip Parameshwar. "On Alternative Modernities." In *Alternative Modernities*, edited by Dilip Parameshwar Gaonkar, 1–23. Durham, NC: Duke University Press, 2001.

Gelvin, James L. *Divided Loyalties: Nationalism and Mass Politics in Syria at the Close of Empire*. Berkeley: University of California Press, 1998.

Gershoni, Israel, and James Jankowski. *Confronting Fascism in Egypt: Dictatorship versus Democracy in the 1930s*. Stanford: Stanford University Press, 2010.

Ghazal, Amal. "'Illiberal' Thought in the Liberal Age: Yusuf al-Nabhani (1849–1932), Dream Stories and Sufi Polemics against the Modern Era." In *Arabic Thought beyond the Liberal Age: Towards an Intellectual History of the Nahda*, edited by Jens Hanssen and Max Weiss, 214–233. Cambridge: Cambridge University Press, 2016.

Goebel, Michael. *Anti-Imperial Metropolis: Interwar Paris and the Seeds of Third World Nationalism*. Cambridge: Cambridge University Press, 2015.

Gramsci, Antonio. *Selections from the Prison Notebooks*. Edited and translated by Quintin Hoare and Geoffrey Nowell Smith. New York: International Publishers, 1971.

Gregory, James. *The Poetry and the Politics: Radical Reform in Victorian England*. London: I. B. Tauris, 2014.

Haddad, Fanar. *Sectarianism in Iraq: Antagonistic Vision of Unity*. New York: Columbia University Press, 2011.

Hadid, Foulath. *Iraq's Democratic Moment*. London: Hurst, 2012.

Haj, Samira. *The Making of Iraq, 1900–1963: Capital, Power, and Ideology*. Albany: State University of New York Press, 1997.

———. *Reconfiguring Islamic Tradition: Reform, Rationality, and Modernity*. Stanford: Stanford University Press, 2009.

Hammond, Marlé. "'If Only al-Barraq Could See . . .': Violence and Voyeurism in an Early Modern Reformulation of the Pre-Islamic Call to Arms." In *Warfare and Poetry in the Middle East*, edited by Hugh Kennedy, 215–240. London: I. B. Tauris, 2013.

Hamzah, Dyala. *The Making of the Arab Intellectual (1880–1960): Empire, Public Sphere and the Colonial Coordinates of Selfhood.* London: Routledge, 2013.

Hanioğlu, M. Şükrü. *A Brief History of the Late Ottoman Empire.* Princeton: Princeton University Press, 2008.

Hanoosh, Yasmeen. "Contempt: State Literati vs. Street Literati in Modern Iraq." *Journal of Arabic Literature* 43:2/3 (2012), 372–408.

Hariri, Alua. "The Iraqi Independence Movement: A Case of Transgressive Contention (1918–1920)." In *Contentious Politics in the Middle East: Popular Resistance and Marginalized Activism beyond the Arab Uprisings*, edited by Fawaz A. Gerges, 97–124. New York: Palgrave Macmillan, 2015.

Harlow, Barbara. *Resistance Literature.* New York: Methuen, 1987.

Hassan, Waïl S. "Postcolonial Theory and Modern Arabic Literature: Horizons of Application." *Journal of Arabic Literature* 33:1 (2002), 45–64.

Haywood, John A. *Modern Arabic Literary, 1800–1970: An Introduction, with Extracts in Translation.* London: Lund Humphries, 1971.

Herr, Ranjoo Seodu. "The Possibility of Nationalist Feminism." *Hypatia* 18:3 (2003), 135–160.

Hingley, Ronald. *Nightingale Fever: Russian Poets in Revolution.* New York: Knopf, 1981.

Holt, Elizabeth M. "'Bread or Freedom': The Congress for Cultural Freedom, the CIA, and the Arabic Literary Journal *Hiwar* (1962–67)." *Journal of Arabic Literature* 44:1 (2013), 83–102.

Hourani, Albert. *Arabic Thought in the Liberal Age, 1798–1939.* Cambridge: Cambridge University Press, 1983.

Hudson, Leila. *Transforming Damascus: Space and Modernity in an Islamic City.* London: Tauris Academic Studies, 2008.

Husni, R. "al-Jawahiri, Muhammad Mahdi," In *Encyclopedia of Arabic Literature*, vol. 1, edited by Julie Scott Meisami and Paul Starkey, 413. London: Routledge, 1998.

Iber, Patrick. *Neither Peace Nor Freedom: The Cultural Cold War in Latin America.* Cambridge, MA: Harvard University Press, 2015.

Ismael, Tareq. *The Rise and Fall of the Communist Party of Iraq.* Cambridge: Cambridge University Press, 2008.

Izzedien, Yousif. *Poetry and Iraqi Society, 1900–1945.* Baghdad: Matbaʿat al-ʿAni, 1962.

Jabr, Fadel K. "The Children of Gilgamesh: A Half Century of Modern Iraqi Poetry." *Metamorphoses* 19:1–2 (2011), 341–376.

Jabra, Jabra Ibrahim. "The Palestinian Exile as Writer." *Journal of Palestine Studies* 8:2 (1979), 77–87.

———. "The Rebels, the Committed and the Others: Transitions in Arabic Poetry Today." In *Critical Perspectives on Modern Arabic Literature*, edited by Issa J. Boullata, 190–205. Washington, DC: Three Continents Press, 1980.

Jacobi, Renate. "The Origins of the Qasida Form." in *Qasida Poetry in Islamic Asia and Africa, Volume 1: Classical Traditions and Modern Meanings*, edited by Stefan Sperl and Christopher Shackle, 21–34. Leiden: E. J. Brill, 1996.

Jameson, Frederic. *Marxism and Form: Twentieth-Century Dialectical Theories of Literature*. Princeton: Princeton University Press, 1974.

Jayyusi, Salma Khadra. *Trends and Movements in Modern Arabic Poetry*. 2 vols. Leiden: Brill, 1977.

Kadhem, Fouad J. "Communism in Najaf: The Rise and Fall of a Secular Movement between 1918 and 1963." In *Najaf: Portrait of a Holy City*, edited by Sabrina Mervin, Robert Gleave, and Géraldine Chatelard, 295–331. Paris: UNESCO, 2017.

Kadhim, Abbas. *Reclaiming Iraq: The 1920 Revolution and the Founding of the Modern State*. Austin: University of Texas Press, 2012.

———. "The Najaf Revolt of 1918: Its Importance and Potential, and the Cause of Its Collapse." In *Najaf: Portrait of a Holy City*, edited by Sabrina Mervin, Robert Gleave, and Géraldine Chatelard, 277–294. Paris: UNESCO, 2017.

Kadhim, Hussein N. *The Poetics of Anti-Colonialism in the Arabic Qasidah*. Leiden: Brill, 2004.

Kandiyoti, Deniz. "Identity and Its Discontents: Women and the Nation." *Millennium* 20 (1991), 429–444.

Kane, Patrick. *The Politics of Art in Modern Egypt: Aesthetics, Ideology, and Nation-Building*. London: I. B. Tauris, 2012.

Kayali, Hasan. *Ottomanism, Arabism, and Islamism in the Ottoman Empire, 1908–1918*. Berkeley: University of California Press, 1997.

Keddie, Nikki R. *Sayyid Jamal al-Din "al-Afghani": A Political Biography*. Berkeley: University of California Press, 1972.

Kedourie, Elie. "Reflexions sur l'histoire du Royaume d'Irak (1921–1958)." *Orient* 11:3 (1959), 55–79.

———. *The Chatham House Version and Other Middle Eastern Studies*. Chicago: Ivan R. Dee, 2004.

Kendall, Elizabeth. *Literature, Journalism, and the Avant-Garde: Intersection in Egypt*. London: Routledge, 2006.

Kennedy, Hugh. "Pity and Defiance in the Poetry of the Siege of Baghdad (197/813)." In *Warfare and Poetry in the Middle East*, edited by Hugh Kennedy, 149–166. London: I. B. Tauris, 2013.

Khadduri, Majid. *Independent Iraq, 1932–1958: A Study in Iraqi Politics*, 2nd ed. London: Oxford University Press, 1960.

Khaleel, Ahmed Faisal. "The Poetics of Human Rights: Auden and al-Jawahiri in the 1930s." PhD diss., University of York, 2015.

Khalidi, Tarif. "Shaykh Ahmad ʿArif az-Zayn and *al-ʿIrfan*." In *Intellectual Life in the Arab East, 1890–1939*, edited by M. R. Buheiry, 285–397. Beirut: AUB Press, 1981.

Khouri, Mounah A. *Poetry and the Making of Modern Egypt (1882–1922)*. Leiden: E. J. Brill, 1971.

Khoury, Dina Rizk. "Looking for the Modern: A Biography of an Iraqi Modernist." In *Auto/Biography and the Construction of Identity and Community in the Middle East*, edited by Mary Ann Fay, 109–124. London: Palgrave, 2001.

———. "Ambiguities of the Modern: The Great War in the Memoirs and Poetry of the Iraqis." In *The World in World Wars: Experiences, Perceptions and Perspectives from Africa and Asia*, edited by Heike Liebau, Katrin Bromber, Katharina Lange, Dyala Hamzah, and Ravi Ahuja, 313–340. Leiden: Brill, 2010.

Khulusi, Safa. "Maʿruf al-Rusafi in Jerusalem." *Jerusalem Quarterly* 22/23 (2005), 63–68.

Khuri-Makdisi, Ilham. *The Eastern Mediterranean and the Making of Global Radicalism, 1860–1914*. Berkeley: University of California Press, 2010.

Kishtainy, Khalid. *The Prostitute in Progressive Literature*. London: Allison and Busby, 1982.

Klemm, Verena. "Different Notions of Commitment (Iltizam) and Committed Literature (al-Adab al-Multazim) in the Literary Circles of the Mashriq." *Arabic and Middle Eastern Literatures* 3:1 (2000), 51–62.

Koselleck, Reinhart. *Futures Past: On the Semantics of Historical Time*. Translated by Keith Tribe. New York: Columbia University Press, 2004.

LaCapra, Dominick. *History and Criticism*. Ithaca, NY: Cornell University Press, 1985.

Latiff, Osman. *The Cutting Edge of the Poet's Sword: Muslim Poetic Responses to the Crusades*. Leiden: Brill, 2018.

Lazreg, Marnia. *The Eloquence of Silence: Algerian Women in Question*. New York: Routledge, 1994.

Litvak, Meir. *Shiʿi Scholars of Nineteenth-Century Iraq: The ʿUlamaʾ of Najaf and Karbalaʾ*. Cambridge: Cambridge University Press, 1998.

Lockman Zachary. *Comrades and Enemies: Arab and Jewish Workers in Palestine, 1906–1948*. Berkeley: University of California Press, 1996.

Louis, William Roger. "Britain and the Crisis of 1958." In *A Revolutionary Year: The Middle East in 1958*, edited by William Roger Louis and Roger Owen, 15–76. London: I. B. Tauris, 2002.

Lubin, Alex. *Geographies of Liberation: The Making of an Afro-Arab Political Imaginary*. Chapel Hill: University of North Carolina Press, 2014.

Luizard, Pierre-Jean. *La formation de l'Irak contemporain: Le rôle politique des ulémas chiites à la fin de la domination ottomane et au moment de la creation de l'État irakien.* Paris: CRNIS Editions, 1991.

Manela, Erez. *The Wilsonian Moment: Self-Determination and the International Origins of Anticolonial Nationalism.* Oxford: Oxford University Press, 2007.

Marozzi, Justin. *Baghdad: City of Peace, City of Blood—A History in Thirteen Centuries.* Boston: Da Capo Press, 2014.

Marr, Phebe. *The Modern History of Iraq*, 4th ed. Boulder, CO: Westview Press, 2016.

Masliyah, Sadok Heskel. "The Life and Writings of the Iraqi Poet: Jamil Sidqi al-Zahawi." PhD diss., UCLA, 1973.

Mattawa, Khaled. *Mahmoud Darwish: The Poet's Art and His Nation.* Syracuse, NY: Syracuse University Press, 2014.

McClintock, Ann. "The Angel of Progress: Pitfalls of the Term 'Post-Colonialism.'" *Social Text* 31/32 (1992), 84–98.

McGuinness, Patrick. *Poetry and Radical Politics in fin de siècle France: From Anarchism to Action française.* Oxford: Oxford University Press, 2015.

Mishra, Pankaj. *From the Ruins of Empire: The Intellectuals Who Remade Asia.* New York: Farrar, Straus and Giroux, 2012.

Mohaghegh, Jason Bahbak. *Insurgent, Poet, Mystic, Sectarian: The Four Masks of Eastern Postmodernism.* Albany: State University of New York Press, 2015.

Mohanty, Chandra Talpade. *Feminism without Borders: Decolonizing Theory, Practicing Solidarity.* Durham, NC: Duke University Press, 2003.

Moreh, Shmuel. *Modern Arabic Poetry, 1800–1970: The Development of its Forms and Themes under the Influence of Western Literature.* Leiden: E. J. Brill, 1976.

———. "Town and Country in Modern Arabic Poetry from Shawqi to al-Sayyab." *Asian and African Studies* 18:2 (1984), 161–185.

———. *Studies in Modern Arabic Prose and Poetry.* Leiden: E. J. Brill, 1988.

Mosse, George. *Nationalism and Sexuality: Middle-Class Morality and Sexual Norms in Modern Europe.* Madison: University of Wisconsin Press, 1985.

Munro, Martin. "Exile, Deterritorialization, and Exoticism in René Depestre's 'Hadriana dans tous mes rêves." *Journal of Haitian Studies* 9:1 (2003), 23–38

al-Musawi, Muhsin. *Arabic Poetry: Trajectories of Modernity and Tradition.* London: Routledge, 2006.

———. *Reading Iraq: Culture and Power in Conflict.* London: I. B. Tauris, 2006.

———. "Muhammad Mahdi al-Jawahiri (1901–1997)." In *Essays in Arabic Literary Bibliography*, vol. 3, edited by Roger Allen, 166–175. Wiesbaden: Harrassowitz Verlag, 2010.

Naef, Sylvia. "La presse en tant que moteur du renouveau culturel et littéraire: La revue chiite libanaise al-'Irfan." *Asiatische Studien/Études Asiatiques* 50:2 (1996), 385–397.

———. "Shi'i-Shuyu'i or: How to Become a Communist in a Holy City." In *The Twelver Shia in Modern Times: Religious Culture and Political History*, eds. Rainer Brunner and Werner Ende, 255–267. Leiden: Brill, 2001.

Nakash, Yitzhak. "The Conversion of Iraq's Tribes to Shi'ism." *International Journal of Middle East Studies* 26:3 (1994), 443–463.

———. *The Shi'is of Iraq*. Princeton: Princeton University Press, 1994.

———. *Reaching for Power: The Shi'a in the Modern Arab World*. Princeton: Princeton University Press, 2006.

Nassar, Maha. *Brothers Apart: Palestinian Citizens of Israel and the Arab World*. Stanford: Stanford University Press, 2017.

Nicholson, Reynold A. *A Literary History of the Arabs*. New York: Charles Scribner's Sons, 1907.

Noorani, Yaseen. *Culture and Hegemony in the Colonial Middle East*. New York: Palgrave Macmillan, 2010.

———. "Iraqi Modernism and the Representation of Femininity: Badr Shakir al-Sayyab and Abd al-Wahhab al-Bayati." *International Journal of Contemporary Iraqi Studies* 4:1–2 (2010), 101–119.

Nordbruch, Götz. *Nazism in Syria and Lebanon: The Ambivalence of the German Option, 1933–1945*. London: Routledge, 2009.

Owen, Roger. "Class and Class Politics in Iraq before 1958: The 'Colonial and Post-Colonial State.'" In *The Iraqi Revolution of 1958: The Old Social Classes Revisited*, edited by Robert A. Fernea and William Roger Louis, 154–171. London: I. B. Tauris, 1991.

Palmier, Jean-Michel. *Weimar in Exile: The Antifascist Emigration in Europe and America*. Translated by David Fernbach. London: Verso, 2006.

Park, Sunyoung. *The Proletarian Wave: Literature and Leftist Culture in Colonial Korea, 1910–1945*. Cambridge, MA: Harvard University Asia Center, 2015.

Parthé, Kahtleen F. *Russia's Dangerous Texts: Politics Between the Lines*. New Haven: Yale University Press, 2004.

Patel, Abdulrazzak. *The Arab Nahdah: The Making of the Intellectual and Humanist Movement*. Edinburgh: Edinburgh University Press, 2013.

Pavone, Claudio. *A Civil War: A History of the Italian Resistance*. Translated by Peter Levy. London: Verso, 2013.

Pedersen, Susan. "Getting Out of Iraq—in 1932: The League of Nations and the Road to Normative Statehood." *American Historical Review* 115:4 (2010), 975–1000.

Peled-Shapira, Hilla. *The Prose Works of Gha'ib Tu'ma Farman: The City and the Beast*. Lanham, MD: Lexington Books, 2018.

Peppis, Paul. *Literature, Politics, and the English Avant-Garde: Nation and Empire, 1901–1918*. Cambridge: Cambridge University Press, 2000.

Petrov, Petre M. *Automatic for the Masses: The Death of the Author and the Birth of Socialist Realism.* Toronto: University of Toronto Press, 2015.

Prashad, Vijay. *The Darker Nations: A People's History of the Third World.* New York: New Press, 2007.

Provence, Michael. *The Last Ottoman Generation and the Making of the Modern Middle East.* Cambridge: Cambridge University Press, 2017.

Ramazani, Jahan. *A Transnational Poetics.* Chicago: University of Chicago Press, 2009.

Roberts, Geoffrey. "Averting Armageddon: The Communist Peace Movement, 1948–1956." In *The Oxford Handbook of the History of Communism*, edited by. S. A. Smith, 326–332. Oxford: Oxford University Press, 2014.

Rogan, Eugene. *The Fall of the Ottomans: The Great War in the Middle East.* New York: Basic Books, 2015.

Rogers, Gayle. *Modernism and the New Spain: Britain, Cosmopolitan Europe, and Literary History.* Oxford: Oxford University Press, 2012.

Romero, Juan. *The Iraqi Revolution of 1958: A Revolutionary Quest for Unity and Security.* Lanham, MD: University Press of America, 2011.

Ross, Kristin. *The Emergence of Social Space: Rimbaud and the Paris Commune.* London: Verso, 2008.

Rossi, Pierre. "La Culture Nouvelle: Mouvement Révolutionaire des Intellectuels Irakiens." *Orient* 2:8 (1958), 61–65.

el-Rouayeb, Khaled. "Opening the Gate of Verification: The Forgotten Arab-Islamic Florescence of the 17th Century." *International Journal of Middle East Studies* 38:2 (2006), 263–281.

Rutledge, Ian. *Enemy on the Euphrates: The Battle for Iraq, 1914–1921.* London: Saqi Books, 2015.

Ryzova, Lucie. *The Age of the Efendiyya: Passages to Modernity in National-Colonial Egypt.* Oxford: Oxford University Press, 2014.

Saeed, Mahmoud. "A Legacy of Ruins: Iraqi Letters and Intellectuals under Saddam's Regime." *Aljadid* 9:42–43 (2003), 12–13.

Said, Edward. *The World, the Text, and the Critic.* Cambridge, MA: Harvard University Press, 1983.

Samata, Said S. *Oral Poetry and Somali Nationalism: The Case of Sayyid Mahammad 'Abdille Hasan.* Cambridge: Cambridge University Press, 1982.

Sanders, Mike. *The Poetry of Chartism: Aesthetics, Politics, History.* Cambridge: Cambridge University Press, 2009.

Satia, Priya. *Spies in Arabia: The Great War and the Cultural Foundations of Britain's Covert Empire in the Middle East.* New York: Oxford University Press, 2008.

Saunders, Frances Stoner. *The Cultural Cold War: The CIA and the World of Arts and Letters.* New York: New Press, 2013.

Scott, David. *Conscripts of Modernity: The Tragedy of Colonial Enlightenment*. Durham, NC: Duke University Press, 2004.
Scott-Smith, Giles. *The Politics of Apolitical Culture: The Congress for Cultural Freedom, the CIA and Post-War American Hegemony*. London: Routledge, 2002.
Senghor, Léopold Sédar. "L'esprit de la civilisation ou les lois de la culture négro-africaine." *Présence Africaine* 8/10 (1956), 51–65.
al-Shawaf, Rayyan. "An Interview with Sargon Boulos." *Parnassus: Poetry in Review* 29:1–2 (2005), 31–63.
Shirabi, Hisham. *Arab Intellectuals and the West: The Formative Years, 1875–1914*. Baltimore: Johns Hopkins University Press, 1970.
Sheehi, Stephen. *Foundations of Modern Arab Identity*. Gainesville: University of Florida Press, 2004.
Shore, Marci. *Caviar and Ashes: A Warsaw Generation's Life and Death in Marxism, 1918–1968*. New Haven: Yale University Press, 2006.
Shryock, Andrew. *Nationalism and the Genealogical Imagination: Oral History and Textual Authority in Tribal Jordan*. Berkeley: University of California Press, 1997.
Simawi, Saadi A. "The Politics and the Poetics of Saʿdi Yusuf." *Arab Studies Quarterly* 19:4 (1997), 173–186.
Simon, Reeva Spector. *Iraq between the Two World Wars: The Creation and Implementation of a Nationalist Ideology*. New York: Columbia University Press, 1986.1
Sluglett, Peter. *Britain in Iraq: Contriving King and Country, 1914–1932*. New York: Columbia University Press, 2007.
———. "Dealing with the Past: Methodological Issues." In *Writing the Modern History of Iraq: Historiographical and Political Challenge*s, edited by Jordi Tejel, Peter Sluglett, Riccardo Bocco, and Hamit Bozarslan, 1–12. Hackensack, NJ: World Scientific, 2012.
Smoor, Pieter. "Modern Poets of Iraq, 1948–79: Cockroach or Martyr in the Inn by the Persian Gulf." *Oriente Moderno* 9:1 (1990), 7–38.
Snir, Reuven. "'Religion Is for God, the Fatherland Is for Everyone': Arab-Jewish Writers in Modern Iraq and the Clash of Narratives after Their Immigration to Israel." *Journal of the American Oriental Society* 126:3 (2006), 379–399.
Somekh, Sasson. *Genre and Language in Modern Arabic Literature*. Weisbaden: Otto Harrassowitz, 1991.
———. "The Neo-Classical Arabic Poets." In *Modern Arabic Literature*, edited by M. M. Badawi, 26–81. Cambridge: Cambridge University Press, 1992.
Spivak, Gayatri Chakravorty. "The Politics of Translation." In *Outside in the Teaching Machine*, 179–200. New York: Routledge, 1993.
Starkey, Paul. *Modern Arabic Literature*. Edinburgh: Edinburgh University Press, 2006.

Sturrock, John. *The Word from Paris: Essays on Modern French Thinkers and Writers.* London: Verso, 1998.

Suleiman, Yasir. "Nationalist Concerns in the Poetry of Nazik al-Malaʾika." *British Journal of Middle Eastern Studies* 22:1/2 (1995), 93–114.

———. *Arabic in the Fray: Language, Ideology, and Cultural Politics.* Edinburgh: Edinburgh University Press, 2013.

Tauber, Eliezer. *The Formation of Modern Iraq and Syria.* London: Frank Cass, 1995.

———. *The Arab Movements in World War I.* London: Routledge, 2013.

Thompson, Edward P. "Patrician Society, Plebian Culture." *Journal of Social History* 7 (1974), 384–205.

Thompson, Thomas Levi. "Speaking Laterally: Transnational Poetics and the Rise of Modern Arabic and Persian Poetry in Iraq and Iran." PhD diss., University of California Los Angeles, 2017.

al-Tikriti, Nabil. "'Stuff Happens': A Brief Overview of the 2003 Destruction of Iraqi Manuscript Collections, Archives, and Libraries." *Library Trends* 55:3 (2007), 730–745.

Toor, Saadia. *The State of Islam: Culture and Cold War Politics in Pakistan.* London: Pluto Press, 2011.

Toorawa, Shakwat M. "Poetry." *The Cambridge Companion to Modern Arab Culture*, edited by Dwight F. Reynolds, 96–111. Cambridge: Cambridge University Press, 2015.

Townshend, Charles. *Desert Hell: The British Invasion of Mesopotamia.* Cambridge, MA: Belknap Press of Harvard University Press, 2011.

Tramontini, Leslie. "Fatherland, If Ever I Betrayed You . . . : Reflections on Nationalist Iraqi Poetry of Thawrat al-ʿIshrin." *al-Abhath* 50–51 (2002–2003), 161–186.

———. "Poetry in the Service of Nation Building? Political Commitment and Self-Assertion." In *Writing the Modern History of Iraq: Historiographical and Political Challenges*, edited by Jordi Tejel, Peter Sluglett, Riccardo Bocco, and Hamit Bozarslan, 459–474. Hackensack, NJ: World Scientific, 2013.

Tripp, Charles. *A History of Iraq*, 2nd ed. Cambridge: Cambridge University Press, 2000.

———. "'In the Name of the People': The 'People's Court' and the Iraqi Revolution (1958–1960)." In *Staging Politics: Power and Performance in Asia and Africa*, edited by Julia C. Strauss and Donald B. Cruise O'Brien, 31–48. London: I. B. Tauris, 2007.

Vinogradov, Amal. "The 1920 Revolt in Iraq Reconsidered: The Role of Tribes in National Politics." *International Journal of Middle East Studies* 3:2 (1972), 123–139.

Visser, Reidar. *Basra, the Failed Gulf State: Separatism and Nationalism in Southern Iraq.* Münster: Lit, 2005.

———. "Sectarian Coexistence in Iraq: The Experiences of the Shiʿa in Areas North of Baghdad." In *The Shi'a of Samarra: The Politics and Heritage of a Community in Iraq*, edited by Imranli Panjwani, 163–176. London: I. B. Tauris, 2012.

Walther, Wiebke. "From Women's Problems to Women as Images in Modern Iraqi Poetry." *Die Welt des Islams* 36:2 (1996), 219–241.

———. "My Hands Assisted the Hands of Events." In *Writing the Self: Autobiographical Writing in Modern Arabic Literature*, edited by Robin Ostle, Ed de Moor, and Stefan Wild, 249–259. London: Saqi, 1998.

Watenpaugh, Keith David. *Being Modern in the Middle East: Revolution, Nationalism, Colonialism, and the Arab Middle Class.* Princeton: Princeton University Press, 2006.

Wells, Colin. *Poetry Wars: Verse and Politics in the American Revolution and Early Republic.* Philadelphia: University of Pennsylvania Press, 2018.

Wien, Peter. *Iraqi Arab Nationalism: Authoritarian, Totalitarian, and Pro-Fascist Inclinations, 1932–1941.* London: Routledge, 2006.

———. "The Long and Intricate Funeral of Yasin al-Hashimi: Pan-Arabism, Civil Religion, and Popular Nationalism in Damascus, 1937." *International Journal of Middle East Studies* 43:2 (2011), 271–292.

———. *Arab Nationalism: The Politics of History and Culture in the Modern Middle East.* London: Routledge, 2017.

Wilder, Gary. *Freedom Time: Negritude: Decolonization, and the Future of the World.* Durham, NC: Duke University Press, 2015.

Williams, Raymond. *Marxism and Literature.* Oxford: Oxford University Press, 1977.

———. *Culture and Materialism: Selected Essays.* London: Verso, 1980.

———. *The Long Revolution.* Orchard Park, NY: Broadview Press, 2001.

Willson, Rachel Beckles. *Orientalism and Musical Mission: Palestine and the West.* Cambridge: Cambridge University Press, 2013.

Winter, Jay. *War Beyond Words: Languages of Remembrance from the Great War to the Present.* Cambridge: Cambridge University Press, 2017.

Wittner, Lawrence S. *One World or None: A History of the World Nuclear Disarmament Movement through 1953.* Stanford: Stanford University Press, 1993.

al-Yousfi, Muhammad Lutfi. "Poetic Creativity in the Sixteenth to Eighteenth Centuries." In *The Cambridge History of Arabic Literature*, vol. 6: *Arabic Literature in the Post-Classical Period*, edited by Roger Allen and D. S. Richards, 60–73. Cambridge, MA: Cambridge University Press, 2006.

Yousif, Abdul-Salaam. "Vanguardist Cultural Practice: The Formation of an Alternative Cultural Hegemony in Iraq and Chile, 1930s–1970s." PhD diss., University of Iowa, 1988.

———. "The Struggle for Cultural Hegemony in Iraq." In *The Iraqi Revolution of 1958: The Old Social Classes Revisited*, edited by Robert A. Fernea and William Roger Louis, 173–196. London: I. B. Tauris, 1991.

———. "Le Déclin de l'intelligentsia de gauche en Irak/On the Decline of the Leftist Intelligentsia in Iraq," *Revue des mondes musulmans et de la Méditerranée* 117–118 (2007), 51–79.

Zubaida, Sami. "Community, Class and Minorities in Iraqi Politics." In *The Iraqi Revolution of 1958: The Old Social Classes Revisited*, edited by Robert A. Fernea and William Roger Louis, 197–210. London: I. B. Tauris, 1991.

———. "The Fragments Imagine the Nation: The Case of Iraq." *International Journal of Middle East Studies* 34:2 (2002), 205–215.

———. "Al-Jawahiri: Between Patronage and Revolution." *Revue des mondes musulmans et de la Méditerranée* 117–118 (2007), 81–97.

# INDEX

'Abduh, Muhammad, 23, 30
'Abbasid poets, 22, 24
'Abd al-Mahdi, Sayyid, 98
Abdülhamid II, Ottoman Sultan, 32, 34–35, 40
Abu al-Muhasin, Muhammad Hasan, 51, 52–53
Abu Tabikh, Sayyid Muhsin, 71
*al-Adab* (periodical), 145, 172, 176
aesthetics of Iraqi poetry: inextricable from social context, 11; intellectual content and, 194–95
al-Afghani, Jamal al-Din, 29, 41, 42
*al-Akhbar* (periodical), 125
Akhmatova, Anna, 10
al-Akhras, 'Abd al-Ghaffar, 27, 36, 43
Algerian Revolution, 176, 177
al-'Allaf, 'Abd al-Karim, 68, 72, 119
Altoma, Salih J., 190
al-Alusi, Mahmud Shukri, 32, 60, 93
'Alwan, Shamran, 136–37
'Amara, Lami'a 'Abbas, 139, 144, 145, 174, 175, 176, 179, 181, 182, 185, 186, 190
Amin, Khalil, 81
'Ammash, Salih Mahdi, 189–90

Anderson, Benedict, 37
Anglo-Iraqi alliance, 6, 59, 88, 91, 108, 118, 136
Anglo-Iraqi War of May 1941, 103, 193
anti-Americanism, 13, 142, 148, 165, 180
anticolonial discourse: anti-British sentiment, 60–61; globalizing of, 6; Hashemites and, 62; nationalist poets and Rashid 'Ali movement, 7; radicalizing of, 6
anticolonialism: Arab poets' role, 6, 7, 10, 15, 16, 19; of Bahr al-'Ulum, 107–9; al-Barudi and, 26; cultural politics of, 4–8, 104, 105; globalization of radical ideas by contribution of communist poets and national liberation struggles for, 10; Hashimi's, 59; Iraqi cultural history links to global history of, 19; meaning transformation during Qasim era, 18; nationalism and, 10, 122; of neoclassical poets during/after WWI, 17; partisan politics and, 193; resistance strategies, 18
anticolonial poetry: dissident nature of, 18; neoclassical modernity presaging of, 17; public readings at cafes, 8

anticommunist poetry: hidden social history of cultural concepts and, 19; during Qasim years, 178, 188; al-Sayyab, Badr Shakir, 151
anti-Ottomanism, 54
anti-Stalinist politics, 9–10
anti-Turkish rhetoric, 54–56, 55
anti-Zionism, 135, 136, 139, 156, 173
Antonius, George, 25
Antoon, Sinan, 197
al-'Aqqad, 'Abbas Mahmud, 30
*al-'Arab* (periodical), 54, 55, 56, 61
Arab Cold War, 149
Arabic poetry, popular resonance of, 10
Arabism, 41, 50, 51, 60, 73–74; Arab cultural revival, 17; Arab modernity, 17, 22; Arab Nahda, 22, 24, 25, 26; divided loyalties of Iraqi poets, 56–63; reimagining history of, 24; evolution from Ottomanism, 56–57, 74. See also al-Banna, 'Abd al-Rahman; Abu al-Muhasin, Muhammad Hasan; al-Hashimi, Muhammad; al-Hashimi, Rashid; al-Hindawi Khayri; al-Kazimi, 'Abd al-Muhsin; al-Shabibi, Muhammad Baqir; al-Shabibi, Muhammad Rida
Arab nationalism: Arab resistance, 7; ethnic chauvinism of, 59, 172–73; evolution from Ottomanism to, 56–57, 74; executions of nationalists, 55, 57; female nationalists, 175–76; tensions of, 61
Arab Revolt of June 1916, 82
Arab Writers' Conference, 152, 164
'Arif, 'Abd al-Rahman, 188
'Arif, 'Abd al-Salam, 164, 188
al-'Askari, Sulyman, 52
*Aswat* (periodical), 172
al-Athari, Muhammad Bahjat, 93, 100, 103–4, 116, 119, 123, 129
Atiyya, Bahjat, 137–38, 165
al-'Awwadi, Sayyid Qati', 70

Ayyub, Dhu al-Nun, 163, 186, 195
al-A'zami, Walid, 170
'Azmi, Khalil, 72
al-Azri, 'Abd al-Husayn, 54, 57–58, 76, 93, 93–94, 115
al-Azri, Kazim, 43
al-'Azzawi, Fadhil, 186–87

*al-Baghdad* (periodical), 39
Baghdad poetry scene, 6, 26, 49; Baghdadi poets, 12–13; cultural revival, 17; focus on, 12–13; Haydarkhana Mosque and, 63–68; links with, 29
Bahr al-'Ulum, Muhammad Salih, 3–4, 104, 107–10, 113, 114, 117–23, 118, 140–43, 148–49, 151, 155–57, 159, 160; Ba'thist regime and, 187, 189, 190; critiques of, 193, 195; on female Algerian rebels, 176; imprisonment of, 186–87; Jawahiri and, 187; Khalis on, 181; legacy of, 195, 196, 197; in Moscow, 180; nationalism of, 130–38; nationalist themes of, 129; Peace Partisans and, 169–70; on political violence, 181; rebel poetry and, 163–64; research or overview, 15; revolutionary spirit of, 192; Rusafi Festival, 182; state repression of, 185; testifying against Atiyya, 165–66
Bahri, Yunis, 122, 168
al-Bakr, Ahmad Hasan, 189
Bakr Sidqi, 7, 111, 113, 114, 115, 116, 171
Bakr Sidqi coup: cultural politics of nationalism (1932-1945), 111–14; leftist poets backing, 7; support for, 171
Balfour Declaration, 61
al-Banna', 'Abd al-Rahman, 51, 54, 56, 62–63, 66, 67, 68, 84–85, 91, 92
Baqir, Muhammad, 60
*al-Barq* (periodical), 41
al-Barudi, Mahmud Sami, 26, 27, 30
Bashkin, Orit, 5, 7, 23

al-Basir, Muhammad Mahdi, 40, 48–49, 55, 56, 58, 61, 63, 64, 65, 66–67, 69, 72–73, 74, 75–76, 82, 83, 84–85
Basra Petroleum Company strike, 150
al-Basri, ʿAbd al-Jabbar Daʾud, 170
*al-Baʿth* (periodical), 152
Baʿthist regimes, 19, 190, 194
Baʿthists, 152, 154, 160–61, 163–64, 166, 173, 177, 184, 185, 188, 189
al-Bayati, ʿAbd al-Wahhab, 144, 145, 148, 151, 154, 163, 176, 178, 178–79, 180, 181, 186, 190
al-Bazirgan, ʿAli, 65, 71
Beimler, Hans, 10
Beirut Reform Committee, 36
Bell, Gertrude, 8, 10, 61, 75–76, 83, 86, 90, 97, 170
Berman, Marshall, 22
*al-Bilad* (periodical), 119, 122, 129
blank verse, 37, 144
Bolsheviks, 103–4, 117
Boupacha, Jamila, 177
bourgeoise class, 10
Boxer Rebellion, 42
British Arabists, 8. *See also* Bell, Gertrude
British Mandate, 6, 18; anticolonial nationalism and, 73; anticolonial spirit of poetry during, 18; Churchill's defense of, 97; commissioners of, 72, 75; declaration of, 63; end of, 104, 106, 107; Iraqi poetry during, 76–77; poetry, role of in, 13; pro-British perspective, 6, 56–57, 61, 62; public space regulations during, 17; rise of, 50
British National Archives, 13
British rule resistance, motives for, 7
Buhayrid, Jamila, 176–77, 184
Bustani, Wadiʿ, 78
Butti, Rafaʾil, 91–92, 163

Caldwell, Erskine, 152
Caudwell, Christopher, 10
censorship, 5, 8, 24, 36–37

al-Chadirchi, Kamil, 21
Chiang Kai-shek, 141
Churchill, Winston, 119, 126
classical aesthetics, 10, 17, 28
Coalition Provisional Authority, archive destruction, 13
colonialism: overview, 48–50, 73–74; alienation in, 16; divided loyalties of Iraqi poets, 56–63; interventions, 17; poetics of collaboration, 53–56; poetry and tribal uprising in Middle Euphrates, 69–73; radical critique of social structure of, 18; rebel poetry and Haydarkhana Mosque, 63–68; surveillance, 8, 10; WWI and poetry of jihad, 50–53
commitment (*iltizam*), ethos of, 11, 16, 160, 178–82, 191–92
Committee of Union and Progress (CUP), 33, 35, 36, 51, 57
communist poets, 151, 153; aftermath of intifada, 149; cultural hegemony of, 161; exile and imprisonment of, 10; female, 174, 175; female Algerian rebels and, 176; feminism and, 161, 175–76; gender issues and, 161, 162, 175–76; global communist poets, 182; globalization of radical ideas, 10; Hashemite monarchy and, 159; internationalism and, 149–55, 156; internationalism of, 179–80; hidden social history of cultural concepts, 19; Iraqi Writers Union and, 181–82; Mosul revolt and, 166, 171; modernist poets and, 9; popular opinion and, 162; Popular Reform League, 111–116, 127, 129; praise for, 151; Rusafi and, 182–83; sexual liberation and, 161; Soviet ideology, 125–27; traditional social/religious mores and, 183; transnational commitments of, 10; violence of Kirkuk and, 169–71. *See also* ʿAmara, Lamiʿa ʿAbbas; al-Bayati,

'Abd al-Wahhab; al-Nahr, Hayyat; Samaka, Baqir; Iraqi Communist Party (ICP)
Congress of Cultural Freedom (CCF), 159
constitutionalism, 24, 33–36
Cornford, John, struggles against fascism, 10
couplet (*mathnawi*) genre, 24
Cox, Percy, 72, 75–76, 81, 85
cultural issues: authenticity, 17, 22, 23, 25–26; cultural hegemony, 7, 171–74; cultural historians, 8; cultural loyalty, 22–23; cultural production, 8–9, 15; poetry wars in Qasim era, 18; revivals, 23, 41; social status, 27; traditions, 16; values, 7
cultural politics of anticolonialism: dangers of poetry in, 11; of class, 7; of gender, 7; shaping by colonial surveillance, 8; rebel poet rebellion, 4–8; as unique in time and space, 7–8
cultural politics of nationalism (1932-1945): overview, 103–6, 127–29; Bakr Sidqi coup, 111–14; dangers of poetry in, 11; dissident poetry and tribal rebellion of 1935, 109–10; independence and disillusionment, 106–9; prison poetry and public apologies, 121–25; Rashid 'Ali movement 117–21; regret, recrimination, and retaliation, 114–17; Stalingrad and triumph of Iraqi left, 125–27

Dalton, Roque, 10
Damascus, 55; Arab poetry festival in, 168, 177; Basir and, 63; Bayati in, 154; cultural revival in, 42; executions in, 55, 57; Faisal in, 57–63; Hashimi brothers in, 58–59, 61–62; Hilli in, 152; Jawahiri in, 153, 190, 197; Najafi in, 96, 111, 119; Rusafi in, 61, 74, 78; Salih in, 96; Shabibi brothers and, 59, 60; Yasin in, 116
dangers of poetry: colonial anxiety about, 17; in cultural politics of anticolonialism, 11; in cultural politics of nationalism, 11; poets' confrontations with the state and, 10–11; in poets' persecution by rivals and enemies, 15; poets who suffered in prison and exile, 19, 29, 30, 57, 79, 108, 189; state persecution of radical poets as prima facie evidence of, 10; in transformative impact on society and politics, 15; we are what flows through every soul and spirit, 191–95
Danton, Robert, 14
*Dar al-Salam* (periodical), 39, 54, 55, 61
Darwin, Charles, 37, 40
Da'ud, Ahmad al-Shaykh, 63, 65
Davis, Eric, 5, 7
decentralization movement, 36, 39, 57
decolonization, 11, 141–42
Depestre, René, 10
*al-Dijla* (periodical), 81, 82, 85, 93, 97
al-Din, Nazira Zayn, 94
al-Din, Sa'id Kamal, 96
dissident poetry: Bahr al-'Ulum and, 108–10; Basir and, 49; as challenge, 129; of Nawwab, 188; psychological disposition toward rebellion and, 191–92; recitation of, 193; Rusafi and, 129
diwans: of Akhras and Tamimi, 36; of Rusafi, 42; of Zahawi, 37, 42
al-Dujayli, Kazim, 39, 41, 57, 68, 80, 92, 94, 119
al-Dulaymi, Naziha, 175

Edmonds, C. J., 124, 125
Egypt: British Egypt, 23; conceptions of Iraqi poetry in, 31; cosmopolitanism of, 24; cultural revivals, 23; Egyptian Revolution of 1919, 59; periodical

contributions, 57; presses in, 23, 26, 31
Egyptian poets, 6, 8, 12, 26. *See also* al-Barudi, Mahmud Sami; Shawqi, Ahmad; Ibrahim, Hafiz
elegy (*marthiyya*) genre, 10, 26
evolution of public poetry, 23, 140–43

Fahmy, Ziad, 8–9
Faiz, Faiz Ahmad, 10
*fakhr* (self-glorifcation), 2–3, 30
al-Fakiki, ʿAbd al-Hadi, 166, 168
*al-Fallah* (periodical), 82
Farid, Muhammad, 30
Farman, Ghaʾib Tuʿama, 186
al-Faruqi, ʿAbd al-Baqi, 43
fascism: in Europe, 9; struggles against, 10, 120, 186; leftist poets and, 10, 117, 126
Faysal I, King of Iraq: Arab Kingdom collapse, 78; Bazi on, 71; coronation of, 80, 85; expulsion of, 78; Hashimi and, 59, 62; Hashimi brothers and, 84; Jawahiri and, 95–96, 97, 99; panegyrics and, 101; poets' competing to praise, 106; rebel poets and, 82; Rusafi and, 82, 83–84, 88–90; Shabibi and, 60, 80–81; Sharqi and, 98; support of court poets, 77; Tagore and, 100; visit to Najaf, 108, 193; Zahawi and, 81–82, 85–86
Faysal II, King of Iraq, 179
free verse poetry: aesthetics, conveying of, 14, 149; eclipsing of neoclassical style, 18; high culture/mass culture distinctions and, 12; Iraqi poets and, 145; as metrical and rhymed, 144; political/social force convergence and, 18; revolutionized modern concepts of, 143; stylistic innovations of, 16; triumph of, 132–33
Fučík, Julius, 153
*al-Furat* (periodical), 71

García Lorca, Federico, 10
Gawurpaghi strike, 135
gender issues: anticolonial poetry and, 18; communist poets and, 161, 162; during Qasim era, 19; nationalist poets and, 161, 162
Ghannam, Razzuq Daʾud, 54
al-Ghasibah, Hasan, 82–83
Gibran, Khalil, 144
globalization, 10, 19

al-Habbubi, Mahmud, 125
al-Habbubi, Muhammad Saʿid, 17, 28, 29, 43, 46–47, 52, 60, 106–7, 190, 192
Hached, Farhat, 152
al-Haddad, Muhammad Hasan, 67
al-Hajj, ʿAziz, 165
al-Hajj Hashim al-Kaʿbi, 26
al-Hamad, Turki, 197
Hamidian despotism, 55
Hanoosh, Yasmeen, 5
Haras al-Istiqlal, 69, 72, 84
*al-Haris* (periodical), 111
Hashemite Arab Revolt, 50, 58, 59, 60, 62–63
Hashemites: Anglo-Hashemite relations, 101; anticolonial rhetoric supporting, 62; evolution of nationalism under, 122; Hilli and, 70; Iraqi poets and, 79–82; military coup of July 14, 1958, 162; monarchy of, 82–85, 159, 192–93; panegyrics and, 77; pro-Hashemite perspective, 56–57. *See also* Faysal I; Faysal II
al-Hashimi, ʿAbd al-Muhsin, 125
al-Hashimi, ʿAbd al-Razzaq, 67
al-Hashimi, Muhammad, 51, 59, 60, 62, 83, 83–84, 94, 96, 97, 116
al-Hashimi, Rashid, 62, 83–84, 85, 97
al-Hashimi, Yasin, 61–62, 109–11, 112, 115–16
al-Hassu, Sabriyya, 175
Haydar, Muhammad Hasan, 39, 41

al-Haydari, Buland, 144, 145, 181–82, 186, 189
al-Haydari, Jamal, 186
al-Haydari, Talib, 144, 146–47, 150, 156
Haydarkhana Mosque, 48, 49, 63–68, 83
Higher Committee for the Defense of the Iraqi People's Movement Abroad, 186
hijab wars, 91–96
Hikmet, Nazim, 10
*al-Hilal* (periodical), 17, 22, 26, 34, 39, 40, 41, 57, 85
al-Hilli, ʿAbd al-Mutallib, 34, 51, 52, 57, 163, 188
al-Hilli, ʿAli, 11, 26, 144, 147, 152, 153, 154, 157, 171, 176, 177, 179, 184, 188
al-Hilli, Maqbula, 175
al-Hilli, Sayyid Haydar, 43
al-Hilli, Sayyid Jaʿfar, 43
al-Hilli, Sayyid Muhammad Baqir, 70
al-Hindawi, Khayri, 51, 57
historical agency of poetry, 9–10
historical context of poems, 13–14
Ho Chi Minh, 15
*al-Hurriyya* (periodical), 171–72, 173
al-Husaynawi, Taqi, 195–96
Husayn ibn Ali, Sharif of Mecca, 57, 58, 59–60, 63, 71, 80, 129
al-Husri, Satiʿ, 95, 98, 99, 113
Hussein, Saddam, 189, 190
al-Huwayzi, ʿAbd al-Husayn, 124

Ibn al-Furatayn (pseudonym), 54, 55
Ibn al-Saliqa (pseudonym), 56
Ibn al-Sayyara (pseudonym), 56
Ibn Babil (pseudonym), 61, 63, 83. *See also* al-Basir, Muhammad Mahdi
Ibn Maʿ al-Sama (pseudonym), 56, 62. *See also* al-Bannaʾ, ʿAbd al-Rahman
Ibrahim, Hafiz, 26, 30
Idris, Suhayl, 145
al-Ihah, ʿAbd, 125
India Office Library, 13

*al-Inqilab* (periodical), 111, 112, 113, 114
insularity, 8, 9
intellectual content, aesthetics of Iraqi poetry and, 194–95; controversies, 11–12; discourse of cultural representation, 12; intellectual restrictions, 8; poets as intelligentsia, 16, 22
internationalism of nationalist/leftist poets, 149–55
Iran, Operation AJAX (CIA), 149–50
Iranian constitutional revolution, 17, 24
*al-Iraq* (periodical), 82, 85, 92, 101
Iraqi Baʿth Party, 190. *See also* Baʿthist regimes; Baʿthists
Iraqi Communist Party (ICP), 111, 119, 141, 149, 160, 174, 190, 194
Iraqi intifada of November 1948, 147–49, 153
Iraqi modernists, 23, 31–33
Iraqi poets/poetry, 12; collective national consciousness, articulations of, 16; divided loyalties of, 56–63; engagement with concepts of modernity and nationalism, 16–17; Hashemites and, 79–82; loyalty of, 56–63; Nahda discourse and, 22; in 19th century, 29; poetry revival, 31; *qasida* (ode) genre, 10, 22, 24–26, 45; revival of, 31; story of, 15–19; supporting national liberation, 18
Iraqi Revolution of 1920, 17, 50, 65, 69–73, 77, 79, 80, 82, 101, 108, 122, 125, 131
Iraqi Women's League, 174
Iraqi Writers Union, 164, 175, 181, 182, 190
*al-ʿIrfan* (periodical), 17, 22, 39, 40, 41, 44
*al-Irshad* (periodical), 39
al-ʿIsa, Sulayman, 168
al-Isfahani, Muhammad Rida, 40
Ismaʿil, Muhyi al-Din, 178–81
Israeli Communist Party, 186
*al-Istiqlal* (periodical), 72, 76, 82, 83, 85, 93, 96, 119, 122

INDEX 299

Italo-Ottoman War, 30
al-Ittihad (periodical), 190

Jabr, Salih, 122, 134
Jabra, Jabra Ibrahim, 132
Jalib, Habib, 10
Jamil, Hafiz, 179
Jawad, Kazim, 136, 144, 145, 150, 151, 153–54, 157, 163, 166, 180
al-Jawahiri, ʿAbd al-ʿAziz, 39, 40, 42–43, 96
al-Jawahiri, Muhammad Mahdi: overview, 1–3, 15; ʿAmmash and, 189–90; anti-Americanism of, 142–43, 148, 165; arrests of, 114, 149; in Baghdad, 96–97, 197; Bahr al-ʿUlum and, 163, 187, 195; Bakr Sidqi coup and, 111–13; Bayati and, 154; commitment of, 192; communist politics of, 140–43, 181; in Damascus, 153, 190, 197; death of, 190, 197; denunciation of WWI, 118; denouncing of, 114–16; elegy for Abu al-Timman, 131; exile of, 185–86; Faysal I and, 95–96; "Feudalism," 117; Husri and, 96; intifada of November 1952 and, 147–48; "Lust of a Poet" ("Try Me"), 97–99; al-Malaʾika and, 181; Mardan and, 146; Mosul Rebellion and, 166, 169; "My Brother Jaʿfar," 2–3, 139, 152, 157, 165, 179, 197; Naji on, 179, 180; National Unity Party and, 133, 164; panegyrics of, 97, 162, 193; patronage issues, 96–100, 101; on poetry in Najaf, 27, 40; postwar dissidence of, 132–34, 133, 156–57, 193; Qasim, ʿAbd al-Karim and, 162–65; Qasim and, 162, 186; Rashid ʿAli movement and, 118, 164; Rawi on, 151; Rihani and, 113–14; Rusafi and, 97, 99, 128, 129; Rusafi and, 182; sectarianism and, 97–99; sectarianism and, 98; socialist vision of, 109; war poems of, 125–27, 129; Wathba demonstrations of 1948 and, 135–40, 187; on Yasin, 110, 112, 116; Yusuf and, 190–91
al-Jazaʾiri, ʿAbd al-Karim, 70
jihad, 50–53, 57, 60, 62, 106
July Revolution of 1958, 155

al-Kalim al-Manzum (collection), 55
al-Kamali, Shafiq, 179
Kamil, Husayn, 58
Kamil, Mustafa, 30
al-Kanʿani, Nuʿman Mahir, 111, 179
Karim, Fawzi, 189
al-Karkhi, Mullah ʿAbbud, 28
al-Karmali, Anastas Mari, 39
al-Kaylani, ʿAbd al Rahman, 66, 79, 81, 88, 112, 118, 164
al-Kaylani, Rashid ʿAli, 112, 118–20, 124–25, 164
al-Kazimi, ʿAbd al-Muhsin, 193; anti-British sentiment, 61; appearance of, 30; dangers of poetry and, 193; early life, 29–30; in Egypt, 30, 31, 36–37, 43; fakhr (self-glorification), 28; inclusion in al-ʿIraqiyyat (Rida), 43–44; influence of, 39, 41; jihad and, 51; movement of, 46; patrons of, 30; Rusafi and, 32; Sharqi on, 43; Tabatabaʾi and, 43; transnational links and, 17
al-Kazimi, Rabab, 30
Kemal, Orhan, 10
al-Khalili, ʿAbbas, 40, 41
Khalis, Salah, 181, 182
al-Khatib, ʿAta Effendi, 67, 68
al-Khatib, Muhammad Ridha, 111–12
al-Khayyam, ʿUmar, 86
al-Khazraji, ʿAtika Wahbi, 144
Khunda, Sami, 82–83
al-Khurasani, Kazim, 28
al-Kirmili, Anatas Mari, 54, 56
Kubba, Muhammad Hasan, 27, 29, 81
Kubba, Muhammad Mahdi, 140

Kurd 'Ali, Muhammad, 32–33, 38
Kurds, 12, 160, 161, 168, 170, 173, 186
Kut, siege of, 50, 53

Labaki, Na'um, 33
Latin America, 10
*Layla* (periodical), 39
Lebanon, 37, 46, 83, 98
leftist poets, 125; aftermath of intifada, 149; Athari and, 104; repression and censorship of, 188; shared fate of, 10; shu'ubiyya accusations, 99, 103, 106, 115–17, 119, 128; shu'ubiyya rhetoric, 160, 161, 168, 170; socialization in internment camps of WWII of, 18; Soviet ideology, 125–27; Wathba demonstrations of 1948, 135–40. *See also* Bahr al-'Ulum, Muhammad Salih; al-Haydari, Talib; Jawad, Kazim; al-Jawahiri, Muhammad Mahdi; al-Nahr, Hayyat
legacy of rebel poetry, 195–97
Levi, Calro, 10
*al*-Lisan (periodical), 63, 82
Litvinov, Maxim, 118
*Lughat al-'Arab* (periodical), 39, 54
Lumumba, Patrice, 180

al-Ma'arri, Abu al-'Ala', 32, 33, 40
al-Mala'ika, Nazik, 102, 144, 145, 173, 175, 176, 179, 181
al-Maliki, 'Adnan, 153
al-Mallah, Mahmud, 109
Mandelstam, Osip, 10
Mao Zedong, 141, 153, 174
Mardan, Husayn, 144, 145, 146, 181
martyrdom: 'Alwan, Shamran, 136–37; of Husayn ibn Ali, 59–60, 63, 146; al-Maliki, 'Adnan, 153; Misri and, 59; Nahr's poem honoring, 150; nationalism and, 48, 84, 150; poetry dedicated to martyrs, 147; 'Ulum and, 137; Um al-Tabul Mosque martyrs, 171;
Wathba martyrs, 2, 138–39; Zahawi's elegy for Rumaytha martyrs, 75
Marxism, 117, 142–43
mass politics era (1946-1958): communists, nationalists and national front poetry, 149–55; evolution of public poetry, 140–43; free verse revolution in Iraqi poetry, 143–47; overview, 130–33, 155–58; poetry and cultural politics of Wathba, 135–40; poetry and intifada of November 1952, 147–49; poetry and mass politics in Iraq (1946-1948), 133–35
Maude, Stanley, 53, 56, 90
mawlids (Sunni rites) recitations, 48–50, 63–68, 70, 72, 73, 83, 101
Mayakovski, Vladimir, 178
al-Mazandarani, Sayyid Muhammad, 29–30
al-Mazini, Ibrahim, 87
Mikunis, Shmuel, 156, 157
Miłosz, Czesław, 10
Mir, Madeleine, 173
al-Misri, 'Abd al-'Aziz 'Ali, 59
modernist poets: al-Barudi, 26; classical aesthetics and, 10; defending modernity, 24; social capital of, 22–23; social realism and, 145, 149; social responsibility of, 16; transnational links, 9; 19
modernity: conceptions of, 5; cosmopolitan visions and, 19; expressions of ambivalence about, 57; as long revolution (Williams quote), 15; modernity in Iraqi poetry revival, 36–39. *See also* neoclassical modernity
al-Mosuli, Sayyid Habib al-'Ubadyi, 66
al-Mosuli, 'Uthman, 64, 65–66, 68
Mosul poetry scene, 12, 29, 43
Mosul Rebellion, 134–35, 166–69, 170–71, 173, 176–77, 181, 182
*al-Mu'ayyad* (periodical), 30, 32, 40
*al-Mufid* (periodical), 85
Muhammad, Zahid, 182

Mühsam, Erich, struggles against fascism, 10
*mujtahids* (religious scholars), 33, 34, 41
al-Mukhtar, Tawfiq, 67
*al-Munazir* (periodical), 33
Munif, 'Abd al-Rahman, 190
*al-Muqtabas* (periodical), 32, 33, 38, 39
*al-Muqtataf* (periodical), 17, 21, 22, 26, 32, 34, 39, 40, 41, 57, 59, 60
Muruwawa, Karim and Husayn, 3
Musaddaq, Muhammad, 149–50
muscular nationalism, 175
Muslim reformers, 22
*al-Mustaqbal* (periodical), 39
al-Mutanabbi, 32
"My Brother Ja'far" (al-Jawahiri), 2–3, 139, 152, 157, 165, 179, 197

*Nahda* (periodical), 5, 23, 26
al-Nahr, Hayyat, 150, 155, 170, 174, 175, 176
al-Najafi, 'Ali, 43
al-Najafi, Ahmad al-Safi, 40, 96, 119, 123
Najafi poetry scene, 6, 12–13, 17, 24, 26, 29, 39–45
Najafi poets, 12–13, 24; Najafi modernists, 22; Nahda periodicals and, 39–45; on neoclassical pioneers, 28–29; tribal uprisings of 1920 and, 69–73. *See also* al-Basir, Muhammad Mahdi; al-Habbubi, Muhammad Sa'id; Haydar, Muhammad Hasan; al-Jawahiri, 'Abd al-'Aziz; al-Jawahiri, Muhammad Mahdi; al-Khalili, 'Abbas; al-Najaf, Ahmad al-Safi; Salih, Sa'd; al-Shabibi, Muhammad Baqir; al-Shabibi, Muhammad Rida; al-Sharqi, 'Ali; al-Tabataba'i, Ibrahim; al-Ya'qubi, Muhammad 'Ali
Najafi uprising of March 1918, 60
Naji, Hilal, 136, 144, 167, 170–71, 171, 177, 178–81, 179, 180, 184, 188
al-Naqib, Sayyid Talib, 72, 78

al-Nasiri, 'Abd al-Qadir, 179
Nassar, Maha, 5
al-Nasser, Gamal 'Abd, 154, 155, 164, 180, 189
National Brotherhood Party (Hizb al-Ikha' al-Watani), 108, 109
National Front Party, 149
nationalism, 6; anticolonialism and, 122; al-Barudi and, 26; in Europe, 9; meaning transformation during Qasim era, 18; modern terminology of, 17; *qasida* (ode) genre and, 26; secular language of, 49; social responsibility of poets and, 15, 16
nationalist feminism, 175–76
nationalist poetry, 69, 71, 119, 69–73
nationalist poets, 6, 7, 68, 82–85, 93, 105, 116; after Ramadan Revolution, 188; anti-Zionism of, 156; communism and, 151, 153; condemnation of communist internationalism, 18, 179–80; critiques of communist poets, 179–81; cultural backlash of, 17; gender issues and, 161, 162, 166, 175–76, 183; Hashemite monarchy and, 82–85, 159; intifada aftermath and, 149; internationalism and, 179; against Iraqi communists, 168; Iraqi Writers Union and, 181–82; Jawahiri and, 164; leftist rhetoric of, 149; Mosul revolt and, 166, 171; poetic dissidence of, 17; popular opinion and, 162; Rusafi and, 182–83; sectarian solidarity, 168; socialism and, 132, 152; socialization in internment camps of WWII of, 18; traditional social/religious mores and, 183–84. *See also* al-Hilli, 'Ali; Jamil, Hafiz; al-Kamali, Shafiq; al-Kan'ani, Nu'man Mahir; Nazik al-Mala'ika; Naji, Hilal; al-Nasiri, 'Abd al-Qadir; al-Rawi, 'Adnan;

Sa'id, Hazim; al-Sayyab, Badr Shakir; Shalash, Muhammad Jamil; Taqa, Shadhil
Nationalist Union Alliance, 164
National Unity Party, 133, 135
al-Nawwab, Muzaffar, 188, 197
Nazif, Sulayman, 53
Nazim, Pasha of Baghdad, 35–36
Nazism, 103, 117–18, 119, 121, 122, 123, 126
neoclassical genres, 10. *See also* elegy (*marthiyya*) genre; ode (*qasida*) genre
neoclassical modernity (1876-1914): overview, 17, 21–24, 45–47; awakening of Iraqi Modernists, 31–33; borders, crossings, and networks of Arabic Poetry, 29–30; constitutionalism and Iraqi public sphere, 33–36; conveying aesthetics of, 14–15; innovation in content, 16; modernity in Iraqi poetry revival, 36–39; neoclassical *qasida* (ode) genre, 24–26; poetry and Najafi Nahda, 39–45; poetry and society in late Ottoman Iraq, 26–29; presaging of anticolonial poetry, 17; rejection of innovation in form, 16
neoclassical poetry, 6; cadence and rhyme as mnemonic devices for oral transmission, 8; free verse poetry eclipsing of, 18; as poetry of collaboration, 17; roles monopolized by in first half of 20th century in Iraq, 10
neoclassical poets, 17; contributions to bourgeoise class consciousness, 10; contributions to collective nationalist identity, 10; revisionist reconstruction, 17. *See also* al-Habbubi, Muhammad Sa'id; al-Kazimi, 'Abd al-Muhsin; al-Tabataba'i, Ibrahim
Neruda, Pablo, 10
Nuh, Kazim Al, 125
Nuri, Baha al-Din, 149, 173
al-Nusuli, Anis, 98

ode (*qasida*) genre, 10, 22, 24–26, 45
Operation AJAX (CIA), 149–50
oral culture, 8, 9, 23
Ottoman Constitutional Revolution of 1908, 17, 24, 33–34, 39
Ottoman era: attitudes toward, 40, 50; collapse of, 50; corruption and stagnation of, 25; defense of, 58; Ottoman jihad of WWI, 6; pan-Ottomanism, 54; poetry in, 23, 26; pro-Ottoman perspective, 56–57, 62; secularism and, 23; free expression limits during, 23; society in, 26
Ottomanism, 41, 50, 51, 56–57, 73–74. *See also* al-Hilli, 'Abd al-Mutallib; al-Rusafi, Ma'ruf; al-Zahawi, Jamil Sidqi

al-Pachachi, Ibrahim Munib, 92
Palestinian Nakba, 143
pan-Arabists, 103; chauvinism of, 161; communism and, 153–54; critiques of, 153–54; ethnic nationalism (*qawmiyya*) of, 7, 105; Husri, 98; Muthanna Club, 117; national secularism of, 62; as privileged minority, 160–61; qawmi-watani divide, 160; al-Sayyab, 151; sectarianism of, 161. *See also* al-Athari, Muhammad Bahjat
panegyrics: after recantation, 188–89; in Baghdad, 26–27; for British military/political authorities, 50; dangers and, 192; decline of, 101; Hashemite approval and, 59, 80; iconic poets and, 193; Jawahiri and, 97; patronage prologue and, 77–78; for Rashid 'Ali, 125; reputations from, 43; revival of, 76–77; Sharqi and, 98; Zahawi and, 113
pan-Islamism, 54; agenda of, 40–41, 58; pan-Islamic poets, 23, 29; 56–58; during WWI, 50

Pasternak, Boris, 10, 178, 181
patronage (1920-1932): overview, 75–77, 100–102; dangers and, 192; hijab wars in Iraqi Poetry, 91–96; Iraqi poets and Hashemites, 79–82; Jawahiri and the Lure of Bagdad, 96–100; nationalist poets and Hashemite monarchy, 82–85; new ideas about, 27; with Ottoman elites, 53; Political Odyssey of Maʿruf al-Rusafi, 88–91; prologue to patronage wars, 77–79; Rubaʿiyat of Jamil Sidqi al-Zahawi, 85–88; shifting relationship with poetry, 101
Pavese, Cesare, 10
Peace Partisans, 141–42, 147, 165, 166, 169–70
Personal Status Law, 174
political prisoners, 121–25
politics of class, gender, and nation (1958-1963): Badr Shakir al-Sayyab and the struggle for cultural hegemony, 171–74; commitment, debauchery, and cold war politics in Iraqi poetry, 178–82; communists, nationalists and violence of Kirkuk, 169–71; Mosul revolt in nationalist imagination, 166–69; nationalist struggle for feminist legitimacy, 174–78; overview, 159–62, 182–84; revolutionary poetics and political conspiracies, 162–66
Popular Reform League, 111, 112, 113, 114, 115, 116, 127, 129
Popular Resistance Forces, 164, 174
Portsmouth Treaty, 2, 136, 137
print culture: evolution of public poetry, 23; regional disparities of markets, 31; print capitalism, 29;
prison poetry, 121–25, 188
pseudonyms, 54
public protests: dissident poem recitations as acts of, 8, 133–35; national front politics and, 18; neoclassical poets and, 157; public recitations as, 17;

social role of poetry, 11; revolutionized modern concepts of, 17
public scandals, 11–12, 13
public spaces, poetry of: geographic scope, 133; Haydarkhana Mosque, 63–68, 82, 83; legacy of, 195–96; Mustansariyya University ruins, 82; politics of literary commitment and, 18; as public acts of dissidence, 193–94; recession of rebel poetry from, 190; regulations of during British Mandate, 17; revolution and, 73; social context of mass politics and, 18; social role of poetry in postwar era and, 156–57; Zubaida on, 11

Qabbani, Nizar, 197
al-Qadi, Munir, 58, 66
al-Qadir, ʿIsa ʿAbd, 64–65, 66, 68–69
al-Qaftan, Hamzan, 94
Qalam, Wafiyya Abu, 175
al-Qashtini, Naji, 168
*qasida* (ode) genre, 10, 22, 24–26, 45
Qasim, ʿAbd al-Karim: amnesty for nationalist prisoners, 171; assassination attempt, 173, 177; Jawahiri and, 162–65; Popular Resistance Forces support for, 174; rallies in support of, 166; Ramadan Revolution, 185. *See also* Qasim era (1958-1963)
Qasim era (1958-1963), 160; cultural wars of, 193; gender culture war during, 184; poetry wars of cultural politics in, 18
qawmi nationalists, 7, 105–7, 160–61
Qazanchi, Kamil, 165, 166
al-Qazini, Muhammad Mahdi, 52
al-Qazzaz, Muhammad Salik, 111
quatrain (*rubaʿi*), 24
Qutban, Sayyid Jamil, 72

al-Raʿi al-ʿAmm (periodical), 126, 127, 128, 134, 140

al-Rafaʿi, Talʿat, 176–77
*al-Rafidan* (periodical), 82, 83, 84, 97
al-Rafiʿi, Mustafa Sadiq, 30
Ramadan Revolution, 185, 186
Rashid ʿAli movement: Athari and, 103; Huwayzi and, 124–25; Jawahiri on, 164; poetics of nationalism and, 7, 117–21; prosecution of partisans of, 121–22. *See also* al-Kaylani, Rashid ʿAli
al-Rawi, ʿAdnan, 136, 144, 151, 151–52, 152, 153, 156, 164, 165, 167, 171, 177, 179, 182, 184, 188; Ramadan Revolution, 185
al-Razzaq, Salma ʿAbd, 102
rebel poet: overview, 1–4, 19; cultural politics of anticolonialism and, 4–8; idealized prototype of, 17–18; in politics and history, 8–11; Iraqi poetry and, 15–19; texts, acts, and reception, 11–15
rebel poetry: commitment to danger, 191–92; Haydarkhana Mosque and, 63–68; innovations of, 49; legacy of, 195–97; popular resonance and, 191; public spaces and, 73; recitations as public protest, 8; rebellion as political and cultural process, 15, 16
Renan, Ernest, 37
revolution: activist role, 6; poetics of, 18, 162–66; as political and cultural process, 16; Ramadan Revolution, 185, 186; revolutionary culture, 19; Revolution of July 14, 1958, 18. *See also* Iraqi Revolution of 1920
Rida, Ahmad, *al-ʿIraqiyyat* (compilation), 43–44
al-Rihani, Amin, 89, 97, 113–14, 144
Rountree, William, 165
*Rubaʿiyat* of Jamil Sidqi al-Zahawi, 85–88
al-Rusafi, Maʿruf: Athari and, 104; Azri and, 115; commemoration festival, 182–83; communism and, 115; comparison to, 47; diwan of, 38; "The English in Their Colonial Policies," 124; exclusion from *al-ʿIraqiyyat* (Rida), 43–44; in Falluja, 120; on Faysal, 80, 81–82; final years, 128, 129; hijab wars in Iraqi Poetry, 91–95; homoeroticism in poems of, 28; influence of, 39, 41, 42; Jawahiri and, 97, 99, 128, 129; jihad and, 51; modernism of, 34–36; nationalism and, 115–16, 124, 129; neoclassical *qasida* genre and, 22; as Ottoman patriot, 53, 58; patronage and, 101; political odyssey of, 88–91; Rashid ʿAli movement and, 118, 120; Rashid's rebuke of, 83; Rawi on, 151; rebel poetry of, 193; reception of, 31; recitation in Damascus, 61–62, 74; revolution and, 72; Saʿdun and, 87; scandal in Jerusalem, 77–79; support for women's reform, 92; ʿUlum and, 107; Yusuf and, 190, 191; Zahawi and, 21, 32–33
Rushdi, Husayn, 58
Russo-Japanese War of 1905, 34, 42

al-Sabʿawi, Yunis, 117, 165
al-Sadr, Sayyid Muhammad, 2, 68, 80, 82, 83, 99
al-Saʿdun, ʿAbd al-Muhsin, 87–88, 90, 91
Saʿid, Hazim, 179
al-Saʿid, Nuri, 80, 108, 118, 120, 126, 130–31, 135, 136, 152, 162, 164, 185, 193
Salafiyya movement, 32
Salih, Saʿd, 40, 96, 131, 133, 134
Salim, Shakir Mustafa, 174–75
Samaka, Baqir, 179, 180, 182
al-Samarraʾi, Faʾiq, 182
Samuel, Herbert, 78–79
Sayigh, Faʾiz, 168–69
al-Sayigh, Yusuf, 189

al-Sayyab, Badr Shakir, 11, 143, 144, 145–46, 148–49, 150–51, 159–60, 171–74, 175, 180, 188, 195
al-Sayyigh, Daʾud, 165
sectarianism: anticolonial resistance strategies and, 18; determinism, 16; fanaticism, 22; Jawahiri and, 98; al-Kazimi's critique of, 29; Najafi-Baghdadi poetry axis and, 13; opposition to, 34; of pan-Arabists, 161; poetry of period infused with, 13; secularism/sectarianism relationship, 13
secularism, 22; in neoclassical poetry, 23; poets and intellectuals defending, 24; political implications of, 73; *qasida* (ode) genre and, 26, 62; secularism/sectarianism relationship, 13; secular nationalism, 5, 50, 57; secular poetry, 27
al-Shabibi, Jawad, 27–28, 43
al-Shabibi, Muhammad Baqir, 39, 41–42, 45, 51, 52, 60–61, 71, 80–81
al-Shabibi, Muhammad Rida, 39, 43, 44, 45, 51, 52, 59, 60–61, 71, 147
Shadi, Ahmad Zaki Abu, 144
Shalash, Muhammad Jamil, 171, 179, 184, 188
al-Sharif, ʿAziz, 141
al-Sharqi, ʿAli, 24, 39, 41, 42, 44, 47, 49, 52, 72, 96, 98, 99, 115, 127, 129
Shaʾul, Anwar, 94, 126
Shawqi, Ahmad, 26, 30
al-Shawwaf, ʿAbd al-Wahhab, 166
al-Shawwaf, Khalid, 144
Sheehi, Stephen, 22
Shiʿism, 98; activists, 63, 68; authority, 71, 95; mujtahids, 27, 58, 95, 99; Shiʿi poets, 26, 34, 39, 40, 43, 65–66, 97–98. *See also* al-Dujayli, Kazim; al-Hilli, ʿAbd al-Mutallib
*Shiʿr* (periodical), 172, 173
al-Shirazi, Muhammad Taqi, 71

al-Shukra, Fadhil, 171
Shukri, ʿAbd al-Rahman, 144
Shumayyil, Shibli, 40
shuʿubi sympathies, 179–80
shuʿubiyya accusations, 99, 103, 106, 115–17, 119, 128
shuʿubiyya rhetoric, 160, 161, 168, 170
Sibaʾi, Yusuf, 178–79
social issues: cultural politics, 16, 19; of poetry, 7, 12, 16, 19, 24; social capital, 22–23; social class; 9, socialism, 126; Arab Socialist Baʿth Party, 152; in Europe, 9; nationalism and, 18; social relevance of poetry, 7, 8, 16
Steed, William Thomas, 44
*al-Subh* (periodical), 102
Sulayman, Hikmat, 34–35, 111–14, 115
Sulayman, Khalid, 34–35
Sunnis: activists, 63–64, 68, 98, 160; poets, 43, 66; Sunni-Shiʿi cooperation, 49, 59, 64; Sunni-Shiʿi unity, 107–8; ʿulama, 5, 27. *See also* mawlids (Sunni rites) recitations
al-Suwaydi, Tawfiq, 133
al-Suwaydi, Yusuf, 68, 71, 80, 82
Syria/Syrians, 12, 31, 60, 62, 63, 83, 106, 153, 166, 168, 176–77

al-Tabatabaʾi, Ibrahim, 17, 27, 28, 29, 42–43, 43, 46–47, 107, 192
Tagore, Rabindranath, 41, 100, 103
al-Tahtawi, Rifaʿa Rafiʿ, 40
Talib, Sayyid, 68
al-Tamimi, Salih, 27, 36
Taqa, Shadhil, 144, 175, 184, 188
Thabit, Yusra Saʾid, 175, 177–78
Third Worldism, 143, 145
al-Timman, Jaʿfar Abu, 65, 72, 109–10, 113, 130–31, 193
Toorawa, Shawkat, 10
translation, ethics of, 14–15
tribal uprisings of 1920, 6, 69–73
Tsvetayeva, Marina, 10

*al-Turath al-Sha'bi* (periodical), 190
Tursunzoda, Mirzo, 182

Um al-Tabul Mosque martyrs, 171
al-'Umari, 'Abd al-Baqi, 27
al-'Umari, 'Arshad, 134–35
al-'Umari, Hafsa, 167–68, 173–74
al-'Umari, 'Mustafa, 124
Um Nizar (pseudonym), 102. *See also* al-Razzaq, Salma 'Abd
United Arab Republic, 166
*al-'Usur* (periodical), 40

Wahhabi incursions, 26, 32
al-Wahid, 'Abd al-Razzaq 'Abd, 189, 190
al-Wa'iz, Ra'uf, 125
al-Wardi, 'Ali, 9, 162
Wat, Aleksander, 10
watani nationalists, 7, 105–7, 160
Wathba demonstrations of 1948, 2–3, 132, 135–40, 143, 147, 152, 153, 187
Wien, Peter, 7
Williams, Raymond, 15
Wilson, A. T., 65, 72–73
al-Witri, Hashim, 1, 2, 140
women's rights: dissident poetry and, 101; feminism and, 161; hijab wars, 91–96; nationalist struggle for feminist legitimacy, 174–78; portrayal in nationalist discourse, 169; qawmi nationalists and, 161; Rusafi and, 128, 183; Sati' al-Husri's education agenda, 95, 96
World War I: anticolonialism of neoclassical poets during/after, 17; Iraqi as theater of war, 50; poetry, role of in, 13; poetry of collaboration, 53–56; poetry of jihad and, 50–53

al-Ya'qubi, Muhammad 'Ali, 40, 58, 106, 125
al-Yasiri, Sayyid 'Alwan, 70
Yat-Sen, Sun, 41
al-Yaziji, Ibrahim, 25, 168
Yehuda, Abraham Shlomo, 78
Yusuf, 'Ali, 30
Yusuf, Sa'di, 182, 190–91, 197

al-Zahawi, 'Abd al-Qadir, 113
al-Zahawi, Asma,' 94
al-Zahawi, Jamil Sidqi, 144; *al-Kalim al-Manzum*, 37; anti-Ottomanism of, 32, 55; Azri and, 115; blank verse of, 38, 144; comparison to, 47; early life, 31; exclusion from *al-'Iraqiyyat* (Rida), 43; exiles of, 32; Faysal and, 81–82; Hashimi brothers and, 58; influence of, 39, 41, 42; jihad and, 51; during mandatory period, 75–76; memorialization of, 102; modernism of, 34–36, 76; neoclassical *qasida* genre and, 22; patronage and, 77, 100–101; rebel poetry of, 193; reception of, 31; revolution and, 72; Ruba'iyat of, 85–88; Rusafi and, 38; Rusafi on, 21; Rusafi rivalry, 32–33, 88; Sa'dun and, 91; state surveillance of, 32; support for women's reform, 91–96, 102; Tagore and, 100
*al-Zaman* (periodical), 119, 122
Zangana, Haifa, 176
Zarif, Zahra, 176
Zola, Émile, 109
Zubaida, Sami, 7, 11
*al-Zuhur* (periodical), 39, 41–42
Zwain, Sayyid Hadi, 69

CPSIA information can be obtained
at www.ICGtesting.com
Printed in the USA
LVHW021542131220
674069LV00004B/170